IRAQ AND IRAN

Contemporary Issues in the Middle East

IRAQ
AND
IRAN
Roots of Conflict

TAREQ Y. ISMAEL

Syracuse University Press   1982

Copyright © 1982 by SYRACUSE UNIVERSITY PRESS
Syracuse, New York 13210

All Rights Reserved
First Edition

Library of Congress Cataloging in Publication Data
Ismael, Tareq Y.
Iraq and Iran.

(Contemporary issues in the Middle East)
Bibliography: p.
1. Iran — Foreign relations — Iraq.   2. Iraq — Foreign
relations — Iran.   I. Title.   II. Series.
DS274.2.I57I85 1982   327.550567   82-10562
ISBN 0-8156-2279-1
ISBN 0-8156-2280-5 (pbk.)

Manufactured in the United States of America

وَقُل رَبِّ ارْحَمْهُمَا كَمَا رَبَّيَانِي صَغِيرًا

To my father
YOUSIF ISMAEL (AGHA) AL-HUSSAINI
(1911–1981)
In fondest memory

TAREQ Y. ISMAEL is Professor of Political Science at the University of Calgary, Calgary, Alberta, Canada. He is the author or editor of many books on the Middle East, including *Canada and the Third World, The Middle East in World Politics, The Arab Left, The UAR in Africa,* and *Governments and Politics of the Contemporary Middle East.*

Contents

MAPS AND CHART

Preface

*T*HE WAR between Iran and Iraq erupted in early September 1980, adding new dimensions to the already turbulent affairs of the Middle East. This violent confrontation has disrupted the economies of both countries and has inflamed international tensions, precipitating both covert and overt threats by the major powers of military intervention in the region. The intricacies of the conflict between Iraq and Iran transcend the manifestation of current events, however. The conflict has historical, legal and ideological dimensions that are deep-rooted and complex. It is the purpose of this study to place in perspective each of these dimensions.

Because the names of places in the region have been changed frequently over the centuries, there exists confusion and disagreement in designation. This is reflected in the text, where variations are often used in different documents or historical periods, or by different individuals. To alleviate any confusion in reference, following is a list of names commonly used for the same geographical entity:

Arab(ian) Gulf, Persian Gulf, the Gulf
Constantinople, Istanbul
Persia, Iran
Arabistan, Khuzistan, Ahwaz region
Abadan, Khidr, Khizr
Muhammara, Khorramshahr

The Library of Congress system of transliteration was utilized, although it was adopted with a major modification: the diacritical marks were dropped. However, where a particular transliteration is widely used, this has been adopted.

The documents in the appendices have all been translated from Arabic or verified against the original document where a translation was already available. Official translations of documents have been utilized in those cases where I have been able to obtain them. Such government translations are usually made for official use and are not readily available. In using official translations, minor alterations in style and usage have been made where clarity required. All treaties, protocols, and amendments are official translations.

I would like to acknowledge the support of the University of Calgary, which facilitated the completion of this manuscript with a Killam Resident Fellowship for the winter term, 1982, and with a research grant for the preparation of the chart and maps. The Department of Political Science and the Strategic Studies Program of the University of Calgary provided some support for the initiation of the project. I also wish to express my appreciation to the members of the Graphics Unit, Communications Media, the University of Calgary, particularly Bill Matheson, for their fine cartography and patience.

Calgary, Alberta   TYI
Summer 1982

IRAQ AND IRAN

Introduction

HISTORICAL ROOTS OF THE CONFLICT

ISPUTE OVER the Shatt al-Arab has a long history and has been a theme of power struggles in the region for many centuries. In fact, the historical dimension of this issue reflects, on the one hand, the way the issue of boundaries has changed with the changing powers, and on the other, the interests of these powers with respect to boundary issues. In this framework, three successive periods can be identified in the history of the Shatt al-Arab dispute: the rivalry between regional empires, where the conflict over boundaries was manifested in efforts to demarcate them through fluid tribal allegiances; imperialist penetration, where the conflict over boundaries was manifested in efforts to demarcate them through fixed geographic points; and nationalist rivalry, where the conflict over boundaries has been manifested in efforts to demarcate them through variable cultural characteristics of populations.

The first period, rivalry between regional empires, may be traced from the early Islamic period. The rise of Islam in the seventh century led to the fall of Persia and its absorption into the emerging Islamic Empire. However, this absorption was incomplete, for with the weakening of the Abbasid Caliphate a distinctly Persian power reemerged. The emergence of the Shi'i-Sunni schism in the late seventh century was the first manifest sign of the fragmentation of the empire. The conquest and consequent incorporation of the Middle East into the Ottoman Empire in the fourteenth century, and the rise of the Safawid Dynasty in Persia in the sixteenth century placed two empires at loggerheads in the Middle East, each seeking expansion at the expense of the other. (The Safawid Dynasty presented itself as the protector of the Shi'is, while the Ottoman Empire claimed the role of protector of the Sunnis.)

1

The Mesopotamian region (Iraq) became a target of the rivalry between the two empires. Under Shah Ismail, the Safawid ruler of Persia, Iraq fell under Persian occupation in 1508. The Ottoman Sultan Selim I regained control of Iraq in 1514, after the battle of Jaldiran. In 1529, Iraq was occupied by Persia, but was retaken by the Ottoman Sultan Sulaiman the Magnificent in 1543.

This tug-of-war over Mesopotamia reflected, in effect, the precarious military balance between the two empires on the one hand, and on the other, the administrative weaknesses of each of them. Neither could decisively defeat the other and achieve permanent military control over Iraq; nor could either establish effective administrative control when in possession of it. Since the issue could not be resolved through military means, a political solution was attempted in the first treaty between the two empires, the Amassia Treaty of 1555. Although the treaty endured for only twenty years, the region remained an Ottoman province until 1623, when it was again occupied by Persia. However, in 1638, the Ottoman Sultan Murad IV drove the Persians out of Iraq by capturing Baghdad. In 1639, the Treaty of Zuhab was signed establishing a peace and defining the border between the two empires.

As was customary of border treaties in the region prior to European penetration of the area, this treaty defined the boundaries in accordance with the loyalties of the tribes inhabiting the frontier between the two empires. In essence, control of Iraq was defined by the limits of effective Ottoman administrative control emanating from Baghdad. While the core of the Ottoman province was clearly defined by the strength of the Ottoman hold on Baghdad, it became progressively weaker, and hence more contentious, with geographic and administrative distance. In the peripheral areas, then, the tribes exercised a form of self-determination and considerable autonomy, while the two empires variously tried to coerce and coax their allegiance.

In this way, conflict between the two empires was contained in a frontier zone and was manifested in shifting tribal allegiances, inter-tribal conflicts and raiding. In the 1639 treaty, the frontier zone was over one hundred miles wide, between the Zagros Mountains in the east and the Tigris and Shatt al-Arab rivers in the west.

While the containment of conflict was short-lived, the 1639 treaty is significant because it became the basis of future treaties and, in effect, established the framework of future contentions over borders. By 1730, the two empires were again in full-scale war with possession of Iraq a focus of conflict. A treaty in 1746 between the two empires reestablished the 1639 boundary, affirming this as the point of reference of future negotiations and the focus of future conflicts.

The two frontier areas of particular concern were Kurdish areas in the north and Arabistan in the south. Both areas were inhabited by tribes who maintained a precarious autonomy by intriguing between Persia and the Ottoman Empire. Kurdish tribes inhabited the Zagros Mountains in the north, which constituted a strategic buffer zone between the two hostile empires. In efforts to establish suzerainty in the region occurring about 1806 and again in 1811, the Ottoman and Persian empires were at war in the area. In both cases, the results were indecisive, and the empires were, for the most part, each content to allow the region to maintain a semi-independent status, functioning as a check to the expansive ambitions of the other.

However, the issue of suzerainty over Arabistan was a much more volatile one. Bounded by the Kerkhah and Shatt al-Arab rivers on the west, the Arab Gulf on the south, and the Zagros Mountains on the north and east, the region was strategically situated in relation to major navigational arteries feeding into the Gulf, as well as the important Shatt al-Arab port of Basra. While the region was vital to the interests and security of Iraq, its remoteness and inaccessibility due to rivers and marshes rendered its subjugation to Ottoman authority problematic. Furthermore, the Arab tribes that inhabited the area gave nominal allegiance to the Persian Empire in order to maintain their independence from Ottoman encroachment, while the topography and distance protected them from unwanted Persian interference. The treaties of 1639 and 1746 simply gave recognition to the effective autonomy of the Arab tribes of the region, which the Ottomans could not change, and to their nominal Persian allegiance, which the Persians could not enforce. Thus, the region enjoyed virtual independence from its two powerful and antagonistic neighbors. Map 1 delineates this nominal frontier line between the two empires.

The intractability of the area to either Ottoman or Persian subjugation and its strategic location vis-à-vis Iraqi and Gulf commerce is highlighted by the rise of the Ka'ab tribe in the eighteenth century. The Ka'ab tribe migrated to Arabistan from the Arab regions sometime in the early seventeenth century and by mid-century had established themselves as the dominant tribe in the region. In efforts to subjugate the tribe to Persian authority, the Persian ruler Karim Khan led an unsuccessful expedition against them in 1757. In 1761, the Ottoman government in Baghdad ordered an expedition against the Ka'ab, and engaged British assistance. But this too ended indecisively, and in 1762 the Ka'ab blockaded Basra by closing the Shatt al-Arab to all vessels. Emboldened by their successes, the Ka'ab began encroaching upon the western side of the Shatt al-Arab and harassing commerce in the river. As a result, in 1763 and 1768 the Ottoman government, with British assistance, undertook military expeditions against the tribe, but these ended inconclusively. Because of Ka'ab harassment of British shipping, the British, in alliance with the Ottoman government, led a vigorous campaign against the tribe in 1766–68, and suffered a humiliating defeat.

Throughout the eighteenth century, hostilities between the Persian and Turkish empires continued to wax and wane. One of the most significant events was the Persian occupation of Basra in 1776. They held it until 1779, when an internal disorganization of the empire, which was precipitated by Karim Khan's death, resulted in their evacuation. Hence, the city peacefully reverted to Ottoman suzerainty. In 1821, the two empires again went to war.

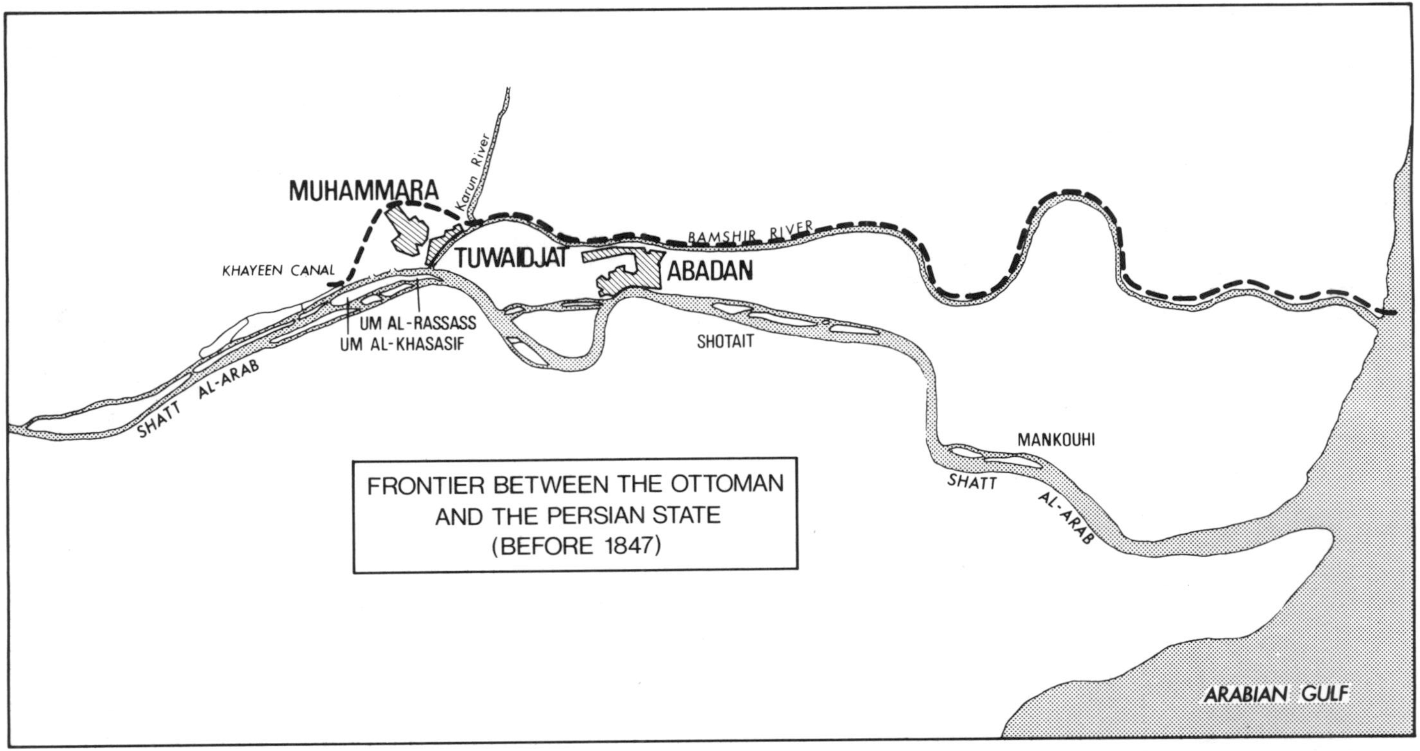

FRONTIER BETWEEN THE OTTOMAN
AND THE PERSIAN STATE
(BEFORE 1847)

ARABIAN GULF

MANKOUHI

SHATT AL-ARAB

SHOTAIT

BAMSHIR RIVER

ABADAN

TUWAIDJAT

MUHAMMARA

Karun River

UM AL-RASSASS
UM AL-KHASASIF

KHAYEEN CANAL

SHATT AL-ARAB

Map 1

This conflict was resolved by the first Treaty of Erzerum in 1823. The treaty reaffirmed the indeterminate boundaries between the two empires of earlier treaties. It was to be the last boundary convention of this kind, for new powers with different interests had entered the arena.

By the nineteenth century, the growth of British imperialist power in the region had transformed the power balance and changed the nature of the conflict. During the seventeenth and eighteenth centuries, British imperialist interests had eliminated in succession Portuguese, Dutch and French commercial and political penetration of the Middle East. By 1820, Britain had, in effect, turned the Gulf into a British lake and turned its attention to Ottoman Iraq and Persia in its efforts to protect British interests in India against European imperialist rivalries, develop a secure line of commerce between India and Britain via the Middle East, and expand commercial markets in the region.

In this framework the instability maintained in the area by Ottoman-Persian rivalries, the political autonomy of many tribes in the frontier zones between the two empires, and the general instability of the two empires themselves posed problems for the progress of British imperialism. Centralized governments strong enough to enforce observance of British treaty rights and privileges among unruly tribes (but not strong enough to oppose British penetration effectively) were required for the progress of British trade and commerce within and through the area.

By the nineteenth century, Russia was Britain's only serious imperialist rival in the Middle East. Russia's expansive ambitions vis-à-vis Persia were manifested in the Russo-Persian wars of 1804–13 and 1826–28, which resulted in Russia's absorption of Persian territories along their common border. The Treaty of Turkmanchai of 1828 gave Russia not only Persian territory but also a commanding influence in Persian affairs previously enjoyed only by Britain. In the same period, the Russo-Turkish wars of 1806–12 and 1828–29 increased Russian influence in Ottoman affairs at the expense of Britain. As a result, British imperialist policy became obsessed with Russophobia — fear of Russian designs on the British Empire.

Stability of the Ottoman and Persian empires as buffers against further rival imperialist expansion became important strategies of both Russian and British policies in the Middle East. This common interest in stabilizing the region as a buffer zone brought them into cooperation and collusion in settling Ottoman-Persian disputes, even while they competed and conspired against each other. Hence, both supported the ascension of Muhammad Mirza to the throne of Persia in 1834 to forestall the disorganization of the empire in fractious rivalry for the throne. Furthermore, in the same year, they established an understanding to maintain the integrity and independence of Persia; this was renewed in 1838. In effect, Britain and Russia had control of Persian affairs and were cooperating to share power between themselves.

This common interest in stabilizing the region resulted in British and Russian cooperation in intervening in the frontier disputes between Ottoman Iraq and Persia. In 1843, they set up a joint Turko-Persian Commission to settle the boundary dispute. Both Russia and Britain were represented on the commission and had mediating powers. This commission resulted in the signing of the second Treaty of Erzerum in 1847.

The second Treaty of Erzerum (see Appendix) did not reflect the settlement of regional issues with respect to territorial claims. Rather, it reflected the commonality of imperialist interests with respect to stabilizing zones of influence. In effect, the treaty imposed upon the Ottoman and Persian empires a settlement that served the imperalist interests of Britain and Russia by disposing of disputed claims in principle (Article 2) and leaving the settlement of detail to a Delimitation Commission on which Britain and Russia were also to have mediation powers (Article 3). Utilizing the 1823 Treaty of Erzerum as the point of reference (Article 9), the treaty established who had sovereignty over contested regions along the frontier (Article 2). Reflecting the commonality of British and Russian interests in Persia, the settlement of issues of sovereignty was generally more favorable to the interests of Persia than to the interests of Ottoman Iraq. This is reflected in Map 2, which shows that the treaty extended Persian sovereignty to include the island of Khizr (Abadan), Muhammara (including its Karun River anchorage), and the eastern banks of the Shatt al-Arab.

Another factor in the inequitable settlement was that the interests of the Ottoman Empire in the matter were themselves not commensurate with the interests of its unruly, remote province of Iraq. Mounting imperialist pressures on its European and North African borders were of more immediate concern to the Istanbul government. The interminable and destructive conflicts with Persia in Iraq were an increasing burden to the beleaguered empire. Indeed, Iraq's particular interests were not to be represented until it became an independent state. Nonetheless, the Istanbul government did not want to compromise its established interests in Iraq, especially in respect to the strategically vital Shatt al-Arab. At the last moment, it refused to sign the agreement without assurances that the stipulations regarding the anchorage of Muhammara (Article 2) would not compromise Ottoman sovereignty over the Shatt al-Arab. The British and Russian ambassadors gave this assurance in an Explanatory Note (Appendix) attached to the treaty.

A Delimitation Commission was first formed in 1848. Successive commissions worked intermittently and largely unsuccessfully at demarcating the border, being interrupted by the Crimean War (1854–56) and the Anglo-Persian War (1856–57). The Russo-Turkish War of 1876 finally brought these efforts to a close.

The Explanatory Note attached to the 1847 treaty proved to be one of the principle points of contention forestalling the progress of the commissions. The Ottoman government had indeed anticipated Persia's ambitions vis-à-vis the Shatt al-Arab when it insisted upon the Explanatory Note. The Note presented an effective limitation to these ambitions and itself became the focus of dispute. The Persian government claimed that their representative to the 1847 negotiations was not authorized to sign the government's approval of the Explanatory Note. In reflecting on the issue more than a century later, the Iranian Ministry of Foreign Affairs summarized Persia's argument accordingly:

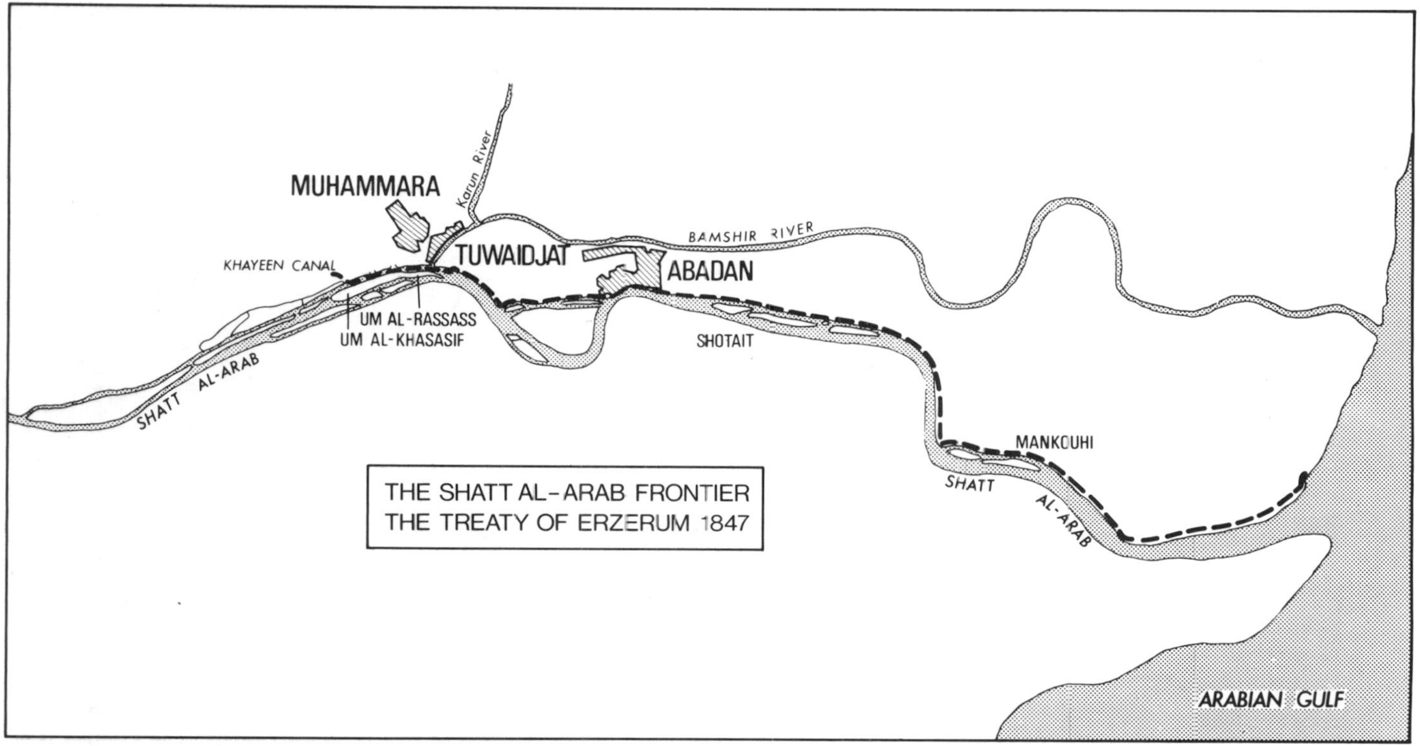

THE SHATT AL-ARAB FRONTIER
THE TREATY OF ERZERUM 1847

ARABIAN GULF

MANKCUHI

SHATT AL-ARAB

BAMSHIR RIVER

ABADAN

SHOTAIT

TUWAIDJAT

Karun River

MUHAMMARA

UM AL-RASSASS

UM AL-KHASASIF

KHAYEEN CANAL

SHATT AL-ARAB

Map 2

When he arrived at Istanbul the Russian and British representatives requested him to sign, over and above the exchange of instruments of approval,
a note containing an interpretation of the articles of the Treaty which were in
favor of the Ottoman government. The Government of Iran had not the
slightest information on the text of the interpretation, and the said Mirza
Mohammad Ali Khan, trusting in the influence of the Russians and the
British upon the Iranian Court of that time, signed it on his own initiative and
without any authority to do so.[1]

The second Treaty of Erzerum was no more effective in resolving
Persian-Ottoman conflict in the frontier than earlier treaties had been.
Throughout the rest of the century, each continued to encroach upon the
other's territory whenever the opportunity arose. Generally, the Ottomans
made successful encroachments in the north, while the Persians advanced
upon Ottoman territories in the south.

Nevertheless, from the point of view of the imperialist powers, particularly Britain, the treaty achieved its purpose. In effect, the treaty placed
control of the conflict into the hands of the mediating powers. This allowed
them to stabilize the conflict and keep it from interfering with their pursuits in
the area. In particular, it gave Britain the stability necessary to consolidate its
penetration of Mesopotamia.

During the half century following the treaty, Britain acquired interests, privileges and priorities in Mesopotamia that effectively made it a British
sphere of influence. The strategic importance Britain placed on Mesopotamia
as a line of communications and defense of its eastern empire is reflected in
the efforts and costs it expended in completely surveying the country and its
river systems. By the end of the century, Britain had acquired a dominant
commercial and strategic position in Mesopotamia, to which the 1847 treaty
had contributed.

In Persia, too, Britain assiduously expanded its influence as it
mediated between Ottoman and Persian conflicts. Unlike Mesopotamia,
where the growth of British influence was unimpeded by imperialist rivalries,
in Persia Britain had to contend with Russian competition. With Russia pant-
ing on its northern frontier, and the British firmly in command of the Gulf to
the south, Persia played the two powers off against each other in an effort to
maintain its autonomy. The two powers competed in a race for vast concessions to exploit Persia's natural resources. Each undertook to build communications and transportation infrastructures that would facilitate the exploitation
of these resources. As Lord Curzon, a main architect of British policy in the
Middle East in the period, observed, Persia was regarded as one of the key
pieces "on a chessboard upon which is being played out a game for the dominion of the world."[2]

[1] *The Iranian Green Booklet: Some Facts Concerning the Dispute between Iran and Iraq
Over Shatt al-Arab* (Teheran: Ministry of Foreign Affairs, May 1969), p. 6.
[2] George N. Curzon, *Persia and the Persian Question,* 2 vols. (New York: Barnes and
Noble, 1966), I:4.

Russian and British competition in Persia gave the Persians extra leverage on the Delimitation Commission in its frontier disputes with the Ottoman Empire. Over its history, indeed, the commission was generally more sensitive to Persia's complaints over Ottoman violations than vice versa. Furthermore, it was with British assistance that Arabistan's effective independence was ended and Persian military and administrative control of the region increasingly consolidated. The 1847 treaty had essentially awarded the province to Persia in recognizing Persian sovereignty over Muhammara. Thereafter, the British began commercial penetration of the region. In the last quarter of the century, the British opened up the Karun River to commercial navigation and considered the development of rail and road systems to further its commercial and strategic penetration. At the same time, effective Persian control of the region was increasing, due largely to the administrative and technical assistance of Britain. By the end of the century, Lord Curzon observed that Arabistan's independence "is fast vanishing before a power that is in command of the electric telegraph, and possesses breech-loading guns."[3]

By the turn of the century, two new factors affecting the border issue between Ottoman Iraq and Persia were added to the imperialist chess game being played out in the Middle East. The first was the emergence of Germany's *drang nach osten* ("drive to the East"). As a result of Germany's vigorous efforts to penetrate the region commercially, Britain became preoccupied with German rivalry to its hegemony of the Middle East. Having acquired considerable influence in the Turkish court at Britain's expense, Germany by 1899 had secured a concession for the construction of a railway from Konia to the Gulf via Baghdad. This concession was formalized in 1903. In addition, in 1906 Germany initiated steamer service between Europe and the Gulf. Alarmed by the vitality of German nationalism and the increasing possibility of a German-Turkish alliance, Britain responded to German expansionism in the Middle East by attempting to consolidate its own position.

In Ottoman Iraq, Britain at first sought to obstruct the Berlin-to-Baghdad railway project by raising obstacles to its completion. This strategy was only partially successful. It did prevent Germany from acquiring a Gulf terminus at Kuwait. Nevertheless, by 1910 major sections of the line were already completed or under construction, and completion of the line to Basra appeared inevitable. The advantages of the line to European commerce with the East via the Gulf were clear enough. Hence, Britain pragmatically changed its strategy to negotiate with Germany for maximum effective participation in the line.

At the same time, Britain was also attempting to consolidate its position in Ottoman Iraq. The Anglo-Ottoman Agreement of July 29, 1913 gave Britain an effective monopoly on river commerce in Iraq. This agreement prepared the way for a definitive agreement with Germany on British participa-

[3] Ibid., 2:328.

tion in the rail line. This was formalized in the Anglo-German Convention of June 15, 1914, on the eve of the First World War.

In this same period, Britain was also attempting to counterbalance increasing German influence in the Ottoman court and the resulting competition to British hegemony in Iraq by strengthening its position in Persia. By the Anglo-Russian agreement of 1907, Persia was divided into spheres of Russian and British influence. This was an effort to end Anglo-Russian competition in Persia and forestall German penetration. Persia, politically destabilized by foreign interference and corrupt government, was in political ferment. Ironically, Persia's reaction to the Anglo-Russian agreement opened the door to German penetration.

Nevertheless, the Anglo-Russian agreement of 1907 stabilized British and Russian cooperation in Persia by delimiting competition to a neutral zone in the southwest which included the region of Arabistan. In its effect on the border issue, this gave both Russia and Britain a vested interest in improving the Persian position vis-à-vis Ottoman Iraq. This interest was both a reflection of their common opposition to and fear of increasing German-Ottoman ties and of their particular interests in Persia.

The second factor that affected the border issue was directly related to British interests in Persia. In 1901, British interests had acquired a vast oil concession that included the whole of Persia except the five northern provinces (the sphere of influence subsequently allotted to Russia in the 1907 Anglo-Russian agreement). The conversion of British industry to oil was already underway by the turn of the century, and the search for oil became a new dimension of British imperialism in the Middle East. Furthermore, the British Navy was converting to oil-fueled ships, making secure oil sources a strategic necessity as well as an industrial advantage. By 1908, commercial quantities of oil were found in Arabistan. A refinery was built on the island of Abadan and connected to the fields by a pipeline.

These factors were reflected in the Iraqi-Persian border negotiations. The Delimitation Commission created by the 1847 treaty was not revived following the Russo-Turkish War of 1876. From the point of view of the imperialist powers, the issues involving the border were satisfactorily held in abeyance. However, Teheran and Istanbul, both experiencing internal political turmoil and foreign interference, were interested in resolving the border issue. They initiated bipartite negotiations and in 1911 signed the Teheran Protocol (see Appendix I). This agreement established a Joint Delimitation Commission with arbitration powers to settle outstanding issues on the basis of the 1847 Treaty of Erzerum. Article IV of the agreement provided that:

> Should the delegates of the two Parties fail to agree on the interpretation and application of certain clauses of that treaty, it is agreed that, at the end of a period of six months of negotiation, in order completely to settle the question of the delimitation of the frontiers, all the points on which any divergence exists shall be submitted together to the Hague Court of Arbitration, in order that the entire question may thus be definitely settled.

The thorny issue of the Explanatory Note came up again. Persia refused to accept the legality of the note, as previously mentioned. Turkey, on the other hand, insisted on referring the issue to the Hague Court of Arbitration in accordance with Article IV of the Teheran Protocol. However, in the closing session of August 15, 1912, the Persian representative announced his government's acceptance of the Explanatory Note accordingly:

> An examination of the documents dispatched from Teheran confirms the point of view consistently upheld by the Persian representative, namely, that Mirza Mohammad Ali Khan ... did not possess full powers for the signature of additional stipulations which were not embodied in the authentic text of the Treaty. ... While maintaining this observation of principle, the Persian Delegation, actuated by a sincere desire to arrive at a settlement of the frontier question and in view of the acts of mediation of Great Britain and Russia exercised for the past seventy years, ... recognizes the explanations contained therein as forming an integral part of the Treaty of Erzerum.[4]

British and Russian interest in the Shatt al-Arab had changed significantly since the 1847 negotiations, however. The development of the British oil industry in Arabistan resulted in increased shipping on the Shatt al-Arab. The drilling equipment and other heavy material required larger ships than the Karun anchorage at Muhammara could accommodate. These ships had to unload their cargoes in the Shatt al-Arab off Muhammara. On the basis of the earlier conventions, this was in Ottoman territorial waters. Neither Russia nor Britain was anxious to back the Explanatory Note, as both were fearful of German influence at Istanbul and more secure in their stranglehold on Persia. Britain, in particular, was anxious to extend Persian sovereignty in the Shatt al-Arab, at least to the extent required by its own interests.

Thus, in the face of a potential bipartite settlement of the border issue along lines that were no longer commensurate with their particular interests, Britain and Russia intervened to reestablish their mediating powers. This intervention resulted in the signing, on November 4, 1913, of another protocol (in Appendix) which was affirmed in the *proces verbaux* of 1914. This agreement described the boundary in detail along the lines established in the 1847 treaty and subsequent conventions, but with some expansion of Persian territorial control. The most notable from the present perspective was the inclusion of the Shatt al-Arab anchorage off Muhammara in the demarcation of the Persian border along the river (Article I). This is reflected in Map 3. Furthermore, the protocol established a Delimitation Commission on which Britain and Russia were vested with arbitral powers to decide all disputes (Articles II and III). About 227 boundary pillars were erected by the Delimitation Commission, before World War I brought this effort to a close.

In the interwar period, the border issue between Persia and Iraq changed dramatically as a result of changing power configurations of the

[4]*The League of Nations Official Journal,* February 1935, p. 219.

Middle East. The collapse of Czarist Russia and the new Soviet government's repudiation of past imperialist policies in Persia left Britain as the sole imperialist power there. However, Britain's efforts to turn Persia into a virtual protectorate, through the Anglo-Persian Treaty of August 9, 1919, met with strong opposition from the emerging nationalist forces in Persia. In addition, the United States and France both opposed the treaty.

While Britain was forced to abandon the treaty, it nevertheless found another avenue through which to maintain its influence in Persia. The rise to power of Reza Khan through a coup on February 21, 1921, culminating in his inauguration as Shah in 1926, provided that avenue. In exchange for cooperation with British policy, Reza Khan used British power to consolidate his control over Persia and centralize all powers in his hands.

The alliance between Britain and Reza Khan was amply demonstrated vis-à-vis Arabistan. The British had given tacit support to the Sheikh of Muhammara since the turn of the century to sustain Arabistan's autonomy against Teheran, in exchange for an agreement with the Anglo-Persian Oil Company. According to Sir Arnold Wilson, who participated in British negotiations with the Sheikh of Muhammara in May 1909:

> The negotiations were prolonged for three or four days: for the Shaikh it was a momentous occasion. He was called upon actively to assist in the establishment within his bailiwick of a company which, as he foresaw, would eventually overshadow all other commercial and other interests and would inevitably cause the Persian Government to seek to extend their administration (hitherto delegated to him) to every part of Arabstan—a country as different from Persia as is Spain from Germany. As an Arab he hated and feared such a prospect as did his people. Could he rely upon us to protect him? Without a guarantee that we would assist him to the utmost of our power in maintaining his hereditary and customary rights and his property in Persia it would be suicidal for him to meet our wishes. The Home Government authorized Cox to give such assurances, and to extend them to his heirs and successors. The Shaikh thereupon gave the Company full way-leave for the pipe-line and sold them the land they required, on the understanding that it would revert to him when the concession expired.[5]

However, by the interwar period, this policy had become dysfunctional to British interests in Arabistan. Oil had made this a most strategic location to the British and a most valuable possession for Teheran, at the same time as Arab nationalism among Arabistan's tribes was developing. This emerging national consciousness augured ill for both Persian and British interests in Arabistan. Hence, the British withdrew their support of Arabistan's autonomy, and Reza Khan occupied the region with a military force in 1925.

In the aftermath of the First World War and the subsequent dismantling of the Ottoman Empire, the Fertile Crescent was divided between the

[5] *SW Persia: A Political Officer's Diary, 1907–1914* (London: Oxford, 1941), p. 93.

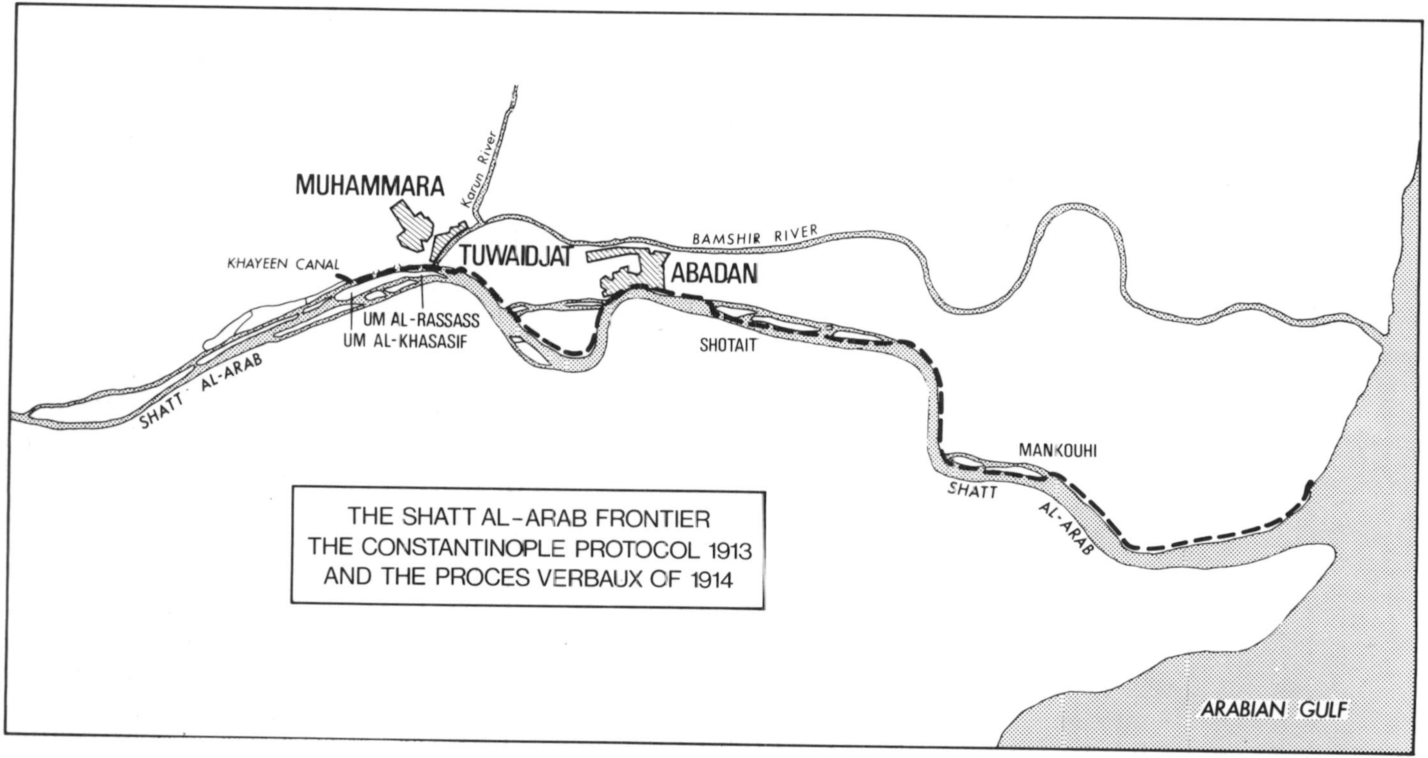

THE SHATT AL-ARAB FRONTIER
THE CONSTANTINOPLE PROTOCOL 1913
AND THE PROCES VERBAUX OF 1914

ARABIAN GULF

MANKOUHI

SHATT AL-ARAB

BAMSHIR RIVER

ABADAN

SHOTAIT

Karun River

TUWAIDJAT

MUHAMMARA

UM AL-RASSASS
UM AL-KHASASIF

KHAYEEN CANAL

SHATT AL-ARAB

Map 3

French and the British in accordance with the Sykes Picot Treaty, which had been surreptitiously concluded between France and Britain. Iraq fell under British dominance, to emerge as a semi-independent state on August 23, 1921. Iran, hoping to gain more concessions from the newly independent state, withheld its recognition of Iraq unless the Iraqi government accorded privileges to Persian nationals in Iraq similar to ones given to British nationals in the Judicial Treaty of March 25, 1924 between Britain and Iraq.

Relations between Iraq and Iran remained tense. Iraq convinced the British to renounce the Judicial Treaty. Britain consented and the treaty was abrogated on April 1, 1929. Finally, Iran recognized Iraq on April 20, 1929. Hopes of a stable and cordial relationship were high.

Tawfiq al-Suwaidi, first Iraqi representative in Iran, identified three basic issues in Iraq-Iran relations during the period of his tenure, 1931–34:

> The Iraqi legation had the worst relations with the Iranian Government, although it appeared on the surface cordial and friendly. The reason for the problems was the centralization of all powers—large and small—in the hands of the Shah. . . . One of the most complicated issues exhausting both sides, Iraq and Iran, was the Kurdish borders problem which included the return of criminals and related problems. . . .
>
> There were other issues which were no less problematic. The condition of the Arabs in Khuzistan [Arabistan] caused complaints and communications between the two governments. The Iranian government believed that the Arabs of Khuzistan were encouraged by the Iraqi government to rebel. At the same time, the Iraqi government believed that a harsh oppression was exercised by Iran against the Arabs of Khuzistan. This policy resulted in a number of uprisings which forced the Arabs of Arabistan to seek refuge in Iraq. The Iraqi government between the years 1932–34 thought of asking Iran to allow those people [of Arabistan] to move into Iraq if they wished, where they would be given land in Iraq to utilize and would be able to enjoy their language and traditions. This appeared to be impossible for no member of the Iranian government was willing to even broach the topic with the Shah. . . .
>
> The third issue which required debate between the two governments was the position of Iraq in regard to Shatt al-Arab and its right to complete sovereignty over the whole river.[6]

King Faisal I visited Iran on April 22, 1932, to be confronted by an Iranian request to adjust the border according to the thalweg principle, i.e., following the midpoint of the river's narrow and deep main channel of navigation. This request was rejected by Iraq. Tension began to mount. Charges and countercharges of border violations, trespassing, hazardous navigation, and

---

[6] Tawfiq al-Suwaidi, *Mudhakkarati: -Nisf Qarn Min tarikh al-'Iraq wa-al-Qadiyah al-'Arabiyah* [My Memories: Half a Century of the History of Iraq and the Arab Question] (Beirut: Dar al-Katib al-Arabi, 1969) pp. 216–21.

misconduct were raised by both sides. Iraq appealed its case to the League of Nations on November 29, 1934.

Iran's argument centered on the following: (1) a revival of the old argument about the illegality of the second Erzerum Treaty because of the already mentioned Explanatory Note; (2) a rejection of the Teheran and Constantinople Protocols since they were based on that treaty; (3) the same rejection based on the fact that the Protocol of 1913 was neither ratified by the Ottoman Chamber of Deputies nor by the Sultan; and (4) a political argument based on the fact that Britain and Russia, as the dominant imperialist powers in the area at the time, forced their will and interests on the Persian and Ottoman empires and set the procedure for negotiation and border settlement in a way to serve their own designs in the Middle East.

Iraq's position was stated by its foreign minister before the League of Nations on January 14, 1935:

> On the general question of equity, the Iraqi Government feels that it is Iraq and not Persia that has grounds for complaint. Persia has a coastline of almost two thousand kilometers, with many ports and anchorages. In the Khor Musa, only fifty kilometers away to the east of the Shatt al-Arab, Persia possesses a deep-water harbor penetrating far into Persian territory, where she has already constructed the terminus of the Trans-Persian Railway. Iraq is essentially the land of the two rivers, Euphrates and Tigris. The Shatt al-Arab, formed by their junction, constitutes Iraq's only access to the sea; it requires constant attention if it is to be kept fit for navigation by modern shipping, and Basra, 100 kilometers from the mouth, is Iraq's only port. It is highly undesirable, from Iraq's point of view, that another Power should command this channel from one bank. Iraq is not asking that the frontier should be altered, but I make these remarks to show that this is not because the existing line is unduly to its advantage. . . .
>
> This document [the Constantinople Protocol of 1913] defines the boundary in some detail, mainly by reference to geographical features, and provides for a Delimitation Commission consisting of representatives of each of the signatory Powers, with power to the two mediating Commissioners to decide finally on disputed questions. . . . The Delimitation Commission was duly constituted, as provided by the Protocol of Constantinople, and proceeded in due course to the Persian Gulf. For nine months—from January to October 1914—the Commission proceeded with the most painstaking care to delimit and mark the frontier on the spot. The records of the Commission show the thoroughness and impartiality with which they considered every question raised, and, incidentally, they show the constant appeals that were made, particularly by the Persian delegate, to the Treaty of Erzerum as the basis of the boundary. The Commission completed the whole of its work, except for one small sector north of Mount Dalampar and therefore outside the area with which we are concerned. I desire to emphasize that the task of the Commission was an extremely difficult and arduous one, performed with the greatest care and ability, and that as a result of its labors the whole of the boundary between Persia and Iraq was marked out by frontier-posts and precise indications on large-scale maps. It is this clear and well-considered boundary which

my Government wishes to see respected as the frontier between the two countries.[7]

No solution was obtained at the League of Nations. Both Iraq and Iran resumed direct negotiations after they had respectively agreed to withdraw the case on April 27 and May 4, 1936. Five months later, on October 29, 1936, a coup d'etat by General Bakr Sidky overthrew the government in Baghdad. The newly appointed government of Hekmat Suleiman succumbed to Iranian pressures and agreed to make the border between Iraq and Iran follow the thalweg for only four miles opposite Abadan. This agreement was consecrated in the Iraqi-Iranian Frontier Treaty of 1937 (see Appendix I).

After affirming the validity of the Constantinople Protocol of 1913 and hence affirming the validity (for the second time) of the Erzerum Treaty of 1847 and the Teheran Protocol of 1911, which had been continuously questioned by Iran, the new treaty of 1937 affirmed the following:

> Article 2: At the extreme point of the island of Shotait ... the frontier shall run perpendicularly from low water mark to the thalweg of the Shatt al-Arab, and shall follow the same as far as a point opposite the present Jetty No. 1 at Abadan. ... From this point it shall return to low water mark, and follow the frontier line indicated in the 1914 minutes.

Map 4 illustrates the frontiers between Iraq and Iran according to the 1937 treaty. As it reflects, Iran secured a territorial gain in the Shatt al-Arab. This gain was opposite the port of Abadan — the site of the Anglo-Persian oil refinery. Again, the change served British interests by consolidating administration of the oil tanker anchorage and refinery.

The 1937 treaty stabilized the boundary conflict, although it hardly settled it. While this treaty represented the first accord where Iraq, as a national entity, represented its own interests on the border issue, Iraq at the time was nevertheless under indirect British tutelage. Thus, border frictions continued to plague relations between Iraq and Iran, but these were superceded by the regional manifestations of international events that were the primary concern of the British.

Imperial rivalries still dominated Middle East politics; but the nature of the competition for world dominion was undergoing transformation as the Second World War approached. The already weakened colonial empires were facing a rival of a different kind in the emerging Soviet challenge. Treaties and alliances were replacing colonies and dependencies as symbols of spheres of influence. Between 1926 and 1928, the Soviet Union had signed mutual friendship treaties with Iran, Turkey and Afghanistan. Ten years later, immediately after the conclusion of the 1937 border treaty between Iraq and Iran,

---

[7] *The League of Nations Official Journal,* February 1935, pp. 113–14.

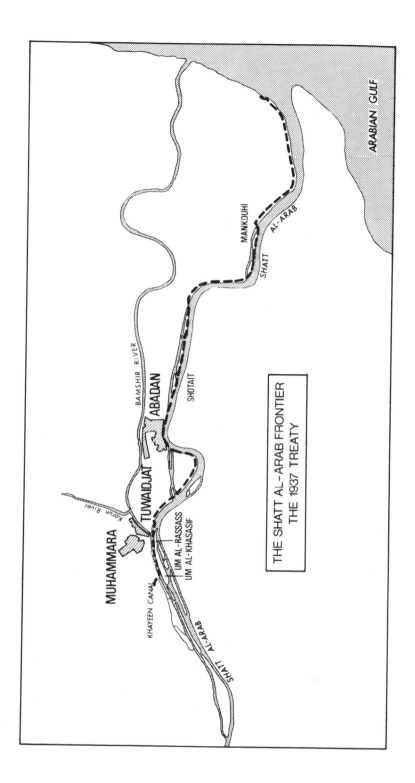

THE SHATT AL-ARAB FRONTIER
THE 1937 TREATY

MUHAMMARA

TUWAIDJAT

ABADAN

BAMSHIR RIVER

Karun River

KHAYEEN CANAL

UM AL-RASSASS

UM AL-KHASASIF

SHATT AL-ARAB

SHOTAIT

MANKOUHI

SHATT AL-ARAB

ARABIAN GULF

Map 4

the Saadabad Entente, directed against Soviet infiltration of the area, was engineered by Britain and signed by Iran, Turkey, Afghanistan and Iraq.

The Second World War brought the colonial empires to an end and the Cold War to the forefront of world politics. Through the Baghdad Pact of 1955, the Middle East became the West's front-line tier against Soviet expansion. Iraq, Iran, Turkey and Pakistan joined with Britain in forming the Middle East Treaty Organization. Thus, Iraq and Iran became allies in a Western military alliance formed to forestall Soviet penetration of the region.

In the aftermath of the Second World War, however, nationalist unrest (focused particularly against corrupt governments and neo-imperialist domination) swept across the Middle East. Nationalist forces challenged autocratic regimes in one country after another: in 1952, the Egyptian monarchy was toppled by Col. Gamal Abdul Nasser's nationalist revolution, and the powers of the Iranian monarchy were significantly curtailed by Dr. Mohammed Mossadegh's nationalist government; in 1956, Suleiman Pasha al-Nabulsi's nationalist government challenged the power of the Jordanian monarchy; in 1958, Syria joined with Nasser's Egypt to form the United Arab Republic, and a civil war broke out in Lebanon. In July 1958, the staunchest pro-British ally in the region fell when the Iraqi monarchy was toppled by General Abdul Karim Kasim in a military coup.

Within less than a year (1953), Mossadegh's nationalist government in Iran had been toppled by a military coup which the Central Intelligence Agency of the United States engineered. The event signaled the emergence of the United States as the main external actor in the Middle East, in effect taking Britain's traditional role in the area. Furthermore, the Shah was now indebted to the U.S. for regaining his autocratic powers. The growing relationship between American military strategy in the region and the Shah following the coup d'etat was made explicit in 1957 by the Eisenhower Doctrine, which the Shah welcomed.

The Iraqi nationalist revolution of 1958 sent shock waves through Iran's ruling class and the West. In effect, the revolution shifted the balance of power in the Arab world to nationalist forces. Furthermore, it tore an irreparable hole in the Baghdad Pact alliance. With the power balance in the region so disturbed, Iran responded by inflaming the border issue with Iraq. In November 1959, the Shah himself revived the dispute by demanding the adjustment of the frontier to the thalweg along the length of the whole Shatt al-Arab River. Iranian newspapers claimed Iran's rights to sovereignty over the Kurdish-inhabited territories of Iraq. The newspaper *Tolu,* published in Teheran (December 20, 1959), claimed that the Kurds were "Iranians," and "Aryans racially." Even the port of Basra was claimed as Iranian territory. The rhetoric was buttressed by military measures. Iran moved units of its army and air force close to the Iraqi border. Iranian vessels ceased the payment of fees to Iraqi authorities. Iran began using her own pilots to navigate the Shatt al-Arab, in violation of the agreed practice of using Iraqi Port Authority pilots.

While no serious confrontation took place, the border issue became the central issue in Iraq-Iran relations. Republican Iraq, for the first time a fully independent actor in world affairs, not only resisted Iranian pressures for further adjustments in the border but also asserted nationalist interests vis-à-vis its frontiers. These interests had never really been represented before in frontier negotiations and agreements. The emergence of Republican Iraq, then, represented the beginning of the third phase of the dispute, when the border issue began to focus on nationalist issues — sovereignty, unity and self-determination.

However, Iraq's internal politics in the 1960s passed through political turmoil. In less than ten years, Iraq experienced five different regimes and three coups d'etat. The ascendance to power of the Arab Ba'ath Socialist Party in July 1968 ended this period of political turmoil. The Ba'ath, however, inherited a rebellion of Kurdish forces in northern Iraq.

With the emergence of a pan-Arab socialist regime in Iraq and growing Arab nationalist unrest in Khuzistan (Arabistan, renamed by the Shah of Iran in 1925), Iran sought to thwart any potential alliance between these forces and at the same time to increase its leverage on border adjustments through substantial aid to the Kurdish rebels in northern Iraq. While the new Ba'ath government was attempting to negotiate a settlement with the Kurds, rebel forces were in effect rendered more intransigent by substantial increases in military aid from Iran. Iraq resisted this with a determined military campaign, thus transforming the rebellion into civil war.

In April 1969, Iran unilaterally abrogated the Frontier Treaty of 1937. Announcing this in the Iranian Parliament, Iran's deputy minister of foreign affairs declared:

> On the basis of established international principles, the 1937 Frontier Treaty is considered null and void and worthless by the Imperial Government ... the Imperial Government does not recognize, along the entire length of Shatt al-Arab any principle except the established principle of international law, i.e., the median of base line. Hence, it will use all that is in its power to prevent any violation of its sovereign rights in the Shatt al-Arab and will not allow anyone to violate them.[8]

Following Iran's unilateral abrogation of the 1937 treaty, relations between Iraq and Iran took a sharp decline. Iran continued to supply arms and offer a haven to the Kurdish rebels in northern Iraq. Iraq accused the Shah of engineering an attempted coup d'etat against the Ba'ath government in 1970. Propaganda warfare escalated between the two countries. Military units were concentrated along the borders.

Iran's abrogation of the treaty marked the initiation of an aggressive

---

[8] Ministry of Foreign Affairs, Teheran, *Some Facts Concerning the Dispute between Iran and Iraq over Shatt al-Arab* (May 1969), p. 6.

military and territorial policy in the region. By this time, the Shah of Iran had become the pillar of American policy and strategy in the Middle East. Consequently, the country's military might had been built up to the most powerful arsenal in the region through American aid. With the impending British military withdrawal from the Gulf in 1971, Iran asserted its intention not only to police the entire Gulf region, but also to extend its sovereignty to the limits of its national interests. In an interview with *Le Figaro* (Paris), on September 28, 1971, the Shah justified Iran's occupation of three Gulf islands this way:

> They are Iranian lands which we do not have the right to put up for auction. Already before World War II, my father wanted to call attention to our sovereignty over those islands, but the English had sent warships and he had to yield. Things have changed now. I have a war fleet, Phantom planes, parachute troops. I could challenge England and have the islands occupied militarily. That would win me great popularity and headlines in newspapers all over the world. But that would not be fitting. I prefer to talk with the British. When they have left, if necessary, I shall send a royal navy detachment.

A military clash between Iraq and Iran erupted on April 14, 1971, in the Khanaqin region of northern Iraq. On November 30, 1971, Iran occupied the three Gulf islands of Abu Musa, Greater Tunb and Lesser Tunb. (The location of the islands is shown on Map 5.)

In reaction to this, the national leadership of the Arab Socialist Party issued a statement in which it condemned imperialism and Arab reactionary countries for their "collusion in this conspiracy." The statement went on to state: "The landing of Iranian military forces in the island of Abu Musa and the occupation of Greater and Smaller Tunbs is a preliminary step to the creation of a new Palestine in the Arab Gulf."[9]

Iraq severed its diplomatic relations with Iran and Britain in protest against the occupation. Protest notes were sent to the Security Council, the Arab League, and to members of the diplomatic corps in Iraq. No military action, however, was taken by Iraq or any other Arab country against Iran.

While border clashes between Iraq and Iran recurred throughout the period 1971 to 1974, the Iraqi army, locked in internecine war with the Kurds, was hardly in a position to resist Iranian pressures. The Kurdish rebellion was a serious drain on Iraqi military and economic capabilities, especially in the face of Iran's military aid to the rebels and continuous pressures on Iraq's borders. In February 1974, Iraq took the border dispute to the United Nations Security Council. Negotiations to settle all pending issues were initiated. It was another year, however, before a settlement was reached.

Saddam Hussein, the present President of Iraq, and the Shah of Iran met in Algiers on March 6, 1975. In the treaty that resulted from this meeting

[9] *Al-Thawra* (Baghdad), December 1, 1971.

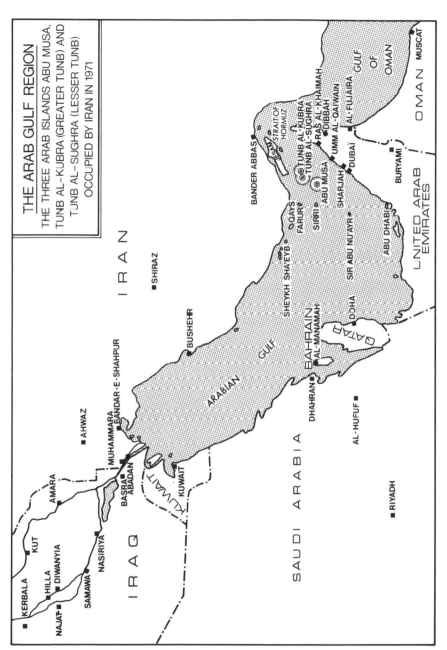

THE ARAB GULF REGION

THE THREE ARAB ISLANDS ABU MUSA, TUNB AL-KUBRA (GREATER TUNB) AND TJNB AL-SUGHRA (LESSER TUNB) OCCUPIED BY IRAN IN 1971

IRAN

SHIRAZ

BANDER ABBAS

STRAIT OF HORMUZ

TUNB AL-KUBRA
TUNB AL-SUGHRA
RAS AL-KHAIMAH
DIBBAH
UMM AL-QAIWAIN
ABU MUSA
SHARJAH
DUBAI
AL-FUJAIRA

GULF OF OMAN

MUSCAT

OMAN

BURYAMI

UNITED ARAB EMIRATES

QAYS
FARUR
SIRRI
SHEYKH SHA'EYB
SIR ABU NU'AYR
ABU DHABI

BUSHEHR

ARABIAN GULF

DOHA

QATAR

BAHRAIN
AL-MANAMAH

DHAHRAN

AL-HUFUF

SAUDI ARABIA

RIYADH

BANDAR-E-SHAHPUR

AHWAZ

MUHAMMARA

BASRA
ABADAN

KUWAIT

KUWAIT

IRAQ

AMARA

KUT

NASIRIYA

DIWANYIA

SAMAWA

HILLA

NAJAF

KERBALA

Map 5

(in Appendix), the following terms were reached: first, Iran would cease its support for the Kurdish rebellion; second, the frontier between Iraq and Iran would be adjusted, including the following of the thalweg along the entire length of the Shatt al-Arab; third, the propaganda war between the two countries would cease, along with Iraq's active opposition to Iran's occupation of the three islands and any interference in each other's internal affairs. Map 6 reflects the frontier adjustment between Iraq and Iran according to the Algiers Agreement of March 6, 1975.

In 1979, the Shah of Iran was toppled by a revolution led by Islamic revivalists under Ayatollah Khomeini. The revolution in Iran considerably destabilized the country. In particular, the new government purged the military of pro-Shah officers, effectively decimating its leadership. Although the new government initiated fundamental changes in Iran's foreign policy, relations with its neighbors, particularly Iraq, deteriorated with the regime's efforts to export its Islamic revolution. Friction between Iraq and Iran continued to escalate, erupting to full-scale war in early September. On September 17, 1980, Iraq abrogated the 1975 treaty. The question of who did what on any particular day in the cycle of provocations and counter provocations that led to open warfare is irrelevant in the historical context of the conflict. Both Iraq and Iran point to their adversary as the aggressor, and depending upon the perspective of the observer, the evidence of each may be more or less compelling.

Within weeks of Iran's revolution, a war of words had erupted between Iraq and Iran. On the surface, this appeared to be a personality conflict between Iraq's president Saddam Hussein and Iran's leader, Ayatollah Khomeini. But underlying this was a deep-seated ideological conflict. The inherent contradictions between the secular, nationalist ideology of Iraq's Arab Ba'ath socialism and the religious, universalist ideology of Khomeini's Islamic revolution, which are examined in a subsequent section, in effect made the two nations incompatible neighbors.[1]

From Iraq's perspective, Khomeini's Islamic revolution was merely Persian expansionism garbed in new symbols. Iran's efforts to export its revolution, particularly among the Shi'is of Iraq, were merely extensions of Persia's traditional efforts to expand eastward into Iraq under the guise of protecting their coreligionists.

This interpretation is reflected in the following statement issued by Iraq's Foreign Ministry:

> These quoted statements [of Bani-Sadr] are nothing but a repetition of previous Iranian positions and Iran's expansionist ambitions at the expense of the adjacent regions and an attempt at enforcing her hegemony on the area. She also belittles the independence of the states in the area, and thus interferes blatantly in their internal affairs in violation of the principles of the Charter of the United Nations and the principles of good neighborliness.[10]

[10]*Al-Thawra* (Baghdad), March 26, 1980.

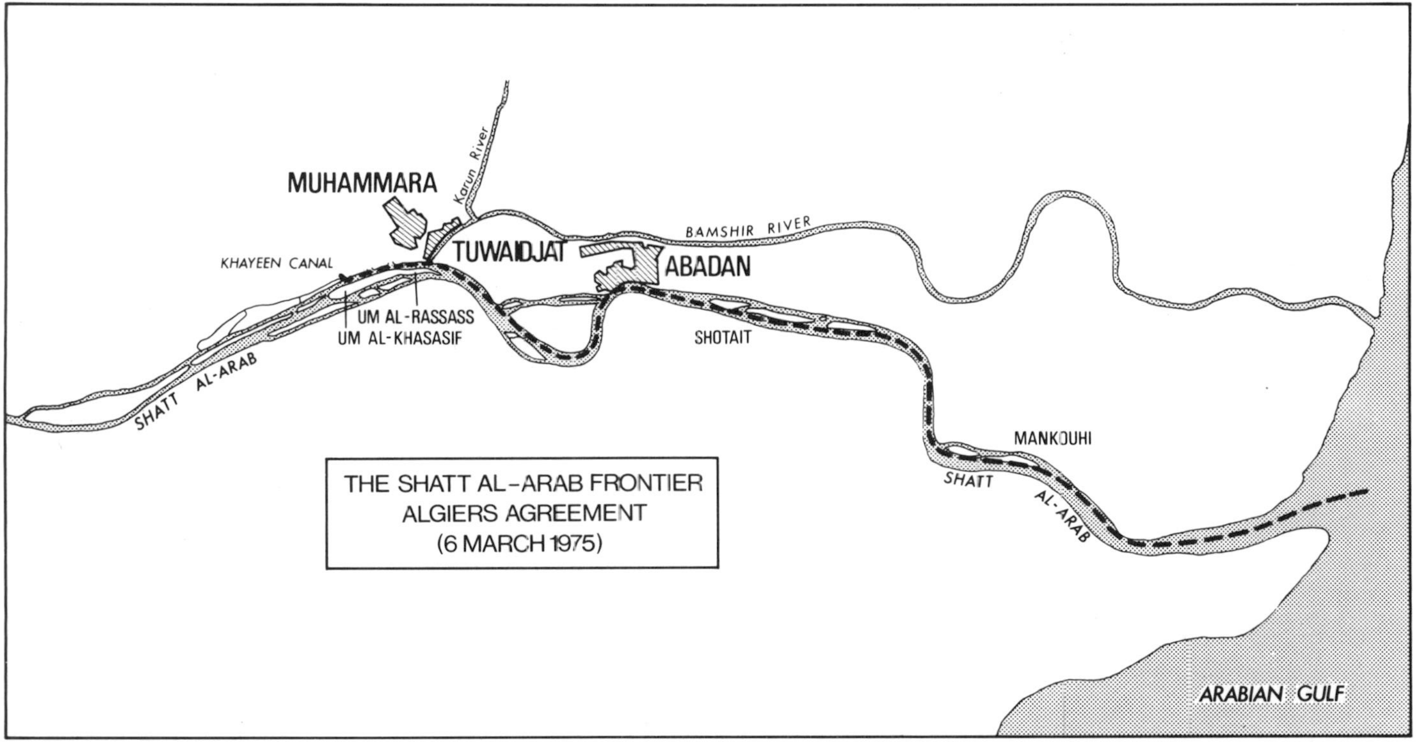

THE SHATT AL-ARAB FRONTIER
ALGIERS AGREEMENT
(6 MARCH 1975)

ARABIAN GULF

MANKOUHI

SHATT AL-ARAB

BAMSHIR RIVER

ABADAN

SHOTAIT

TUWADJAT

Karun River

MUHAMMARA

UM AL-RASSASS
UM AL-KHASASIF

KHAYEEN CANAL

SHATT AL-ARAB

Map 6

From Iran's perspective, Arab nationalism in general, and Ba'ath Arab socialism in particular, represented a particularist barrier to Islamic universalism and a nemesis inflicted on the Arab people for their deviations from the true path. This was a recurring theme of Ayatollah Khomeini's attacks on Saddam Hussein and is reflected in his following statement: "This deviated person [Saddam Hussein] is completely uninformed about Islam, and, among other things, is an Arab. God, the Most High, said, the Arabs are very hard in infidelity and hypocrisy and more inclined not to know the limits that God has sent down unto His Messenger."[11]

LEGAL DIMENSION OF THE CONFLICT

The first legal argument raised by Iran concerns the second Erzerum Treaty of 1847. Iran claimed that the treaty was forced upon it by Britain and Russia. Such a treaty, Iran argued, was a relic of the colonial era and therefore could no longer be accepted by a free and independent Iran. Iraq, for its part, argued that this treaty was unjust to Iraq because when the treaty was signed by the Ottoman Empire, it was the Empire, and not Iraq, that agreed to Persian sovereignty over Arab territory in Muhammara (Khorramshahr), Abadan, and the left bank of the Shatt al-Arab. Moreover, from 1849 to 1852, Iran participated in the Delimitation Commission, stipulated by the agreement, thereby implicitly recognizing the treaty. Even assuming that Iranian claims about Russian and British pressures were true, Iraq argued, the treaty still remained a valid one.

The second Iranian argument related to the unauthorized signing of the 1847 treaty by its representative. According to the Iranian government, Mirza Mohammad Ali Khan's action was unauthorized and therefore the treaty, and in particular the Explanatory Note which gave the Ottomans sovereignty over the Shatt al-Arab, were both null and void. Iraq, on the other hand, argued that Iranian protestations did not prevent Iran from signing the Teheran Protocol of 1911 and the Protocol of Constantinople in 1913, which affirmed the validity of the 1847 Treaty. However, Iran argued that neither the Constantinople Protocol of 1913 nor the proceedings of the Turco-Persian Delimitation Commission of 1914 were ratified by the Persian Parliament. Iraq attempted to refute this Iranian claim by citing the principles of the Vienna Convention on the Law of Treaties, which states that "a party may not invoke the provisions of its internal law as justification for its failure to perform a treaty."

The third argument used by Iran to justify its unilateral abrogation of

---

[11] Ministry of Islamic Guidance, Teheran, "Selected Messages of Imam Khomeini Concerning Iraq and the War Iraq Imposed upon Iran," p. 125.

the 1937 treaty claimed that the abrogation was justified on the basis of Iraq's failure to abide by the terms of that treaty. Iraq argued that even if this was true, Iran would have been on more solid legal ground had it referred the matter to the International Court of Justice or attempted to resolve it through bilateral negotiations. On the basis of Article 57 of the Draft Convention on the Law of Treaties, which was unanimously approved by the United Nations Conferences on the Law of Treaties of 1968 and 1969, Iraq maintained that the unilateral abrogation represented a direct violation of international law. Article 57 stipulates that "the operation of a treaty in regard to all the parties or to a particular party may be suspended: (a) in conformity with the provisions of the treaty; or (b) at any time by consent of all the parties after consideration with the other contracting states."

The fourth Iranian argument centered on the understanding of *rebus sic stantibus,* or a fundamental change in circumstances. Iran's legal representative put the case as follows:

> It is a recognized principle of international law that vital changes of circumstances may be of such a kind as to justify a party to a treaty in demanding to be released from its obligations. It is further held that all treaties are concluded under the tacit condition *rebus sic stantibus*. This doctrine embodies a principle of law similar to those expressed in the doctrine of frustration, supervening impossibility of performance or the like.[12]

The Iranian sentiments on this legal doctrine were echoed in the Iranian Senate by the deputy minister of foreign affairs on April 19, 1969:

> The Frontier Treaty of 1937 between Iraq and Iran was concluded at a time when the British colonial system was at the height of its power, and was keeping Iraq under its protective wings, using force and bringing pressure upon Iran to sign that Treaty which ceded all Shatt al-Arab, except two sections of it, to Iraq.... At the present time, now that the period of colonialism has ended, the effects and the results emanating from colonialism must also vanish with it.[13]

The principle of *rebus sic stantibus* challenges the principle of *pacta sunt servanda,* which protects the legal sanctity of treaties and was endorsed both by the League of Nations and in the Charter of the United Nations. However, *rebus sic stantibus* continues to plague both jurists and politicians. The Vienna Conference on the Law of Treaties attempted a definition of the principle. Article 62 of the Draft Convention of the Law of Treaties claimed

[12] Ramesh Sanghvi, *Shatt al-Arab: The Facts behind the Issue* (London: Trans Orient Books, 1969), p. 21.

[13] Ministry of Foreign Affairs, Teheran, *Dispute ... over Shatt al-Arab,* p. 81.

that a fundamental change of circumstances may not be invoked as grounds for terminating a treaty unless "the existence of those circumstances constituted an essential basis of the consent of the parties to be bound by the treaty; and the effect of the change is radically to transform the extent of obligations still to be performed under the treaty." Article 62 also stated that a fundamental change of circumstances could not be used if the treaty establishes a boundary.

On these grounds, therefore, Iraq argued that Iran's abrogation of the Treaty of 1937 was in violation of international law: the 1937 treaty was a boundary treaty and therefore could not be abrogated unilaterally without the approval of the other party. International law, Iraq added, requires that treaties must be observed by the contracting parties in good faith and that disputes concerning them, like other international disputes, must be settled by peaceful means and in conformity with the principles of justice and international law.

It must be noted at this stage that Iran invoked the principle of *rebus sic stantibus* in order to justify its claims for changing its boundary with Iraq in accordance with the principle of the thalweg. Iran maintained that the Shatt al-Arab is a boundary river and therefore must be held under joint sovereignty with Iraq. The Iraqi government rejected this logic on the grounds that historically and in accordance with all the treaties between Iraq and Iran, the Shatt al-Arab has always been considered an Iraqi national river.

Iraq agreed to sign a treaty with Iran — the Algiers Treaty of 1975 — under which the boundaries between the two states were determined on the basis of the thalweg. But six years later, in September 1980, the Treaty of Algiers was abrogated by Iraq.

The first argument advanced by Iraq in defending its abrogation of the 1975 Algiers Treaty was that the Shatt al-Arab River, along with the province of Ahwaz in Arabistan, are Iraqi territories. Iraq pointed out that in the Treaty of Erzerum of 1847, the Ottoman Empire relinquished its sovereignty on the area and ceded it to Persia. Moreover, Iraq argued that the region of Ahwaz has always been inhabited by an Arab majority who are descendents of tribes which inhabited the area since Islam dominated that part of the world. Ahwaz maintained its status as an independent princedom under the rule of an Arab tribal chief until 1925, when Ahwaz was forcibly annexed by Iran.[14]

Iraq also rejected the Iranian allegation that the treaty was terminated unilaterally. Iraq argued that Iran itself had already terminated the agreement by word and deed. Iraq maintained that since the elements of the 1975 agreement constituted an indivisible whole, a violation of one aspect rendered the entire treaty null and void.[15] This argument was used by Saadoun Hamadi, the Iraqi foreign minister, in his speech to the General Assembly on

[14] Embassy of Iraq, Beirut, *Arabistan Qutrun Aribiyn Asil* [Arabistan: An Authentic Arab Region], September 1980, pp. 22–36.

[15] Ministry of Foreign Affairs, Baghdad, "The Iraqi-Iranian Dispute: Facts vs. Allegations" (October 1980), p. 4.

October 3, 1980. He maintained that Iran had invited the sons of Mustafa Barzani (leader of the Kurdish rebellion) to

> use Iranian territory as a base of operations for threatening Iraq and interfering with its internal security and national integrity. Moreover, the Iranian government has never ceased harming the good neighborly relations between the two countries. It facilitated acts of infiltration of a subversive nature. In many Iraqi towns, acts of murder, sabotage and poisoning of water and fishery resources were committed with the support of the Iranian government.... The Iranian acts went further to instigate trouble, sectarian and religious dissension and the commission of acts of plunder in the border areas by groups of so-called "revolutionary guards."[16]

These acts of "terrorism" were also emphasized by Tareq Aziz, member of the Revolutionary Command Council and deputy prime minister of Iraq, in a series of articles on Arab-Iranian relations published by *al-Watan al-Araby*, a weekly magazine published in Paris (see selections in Appendix). Aziz claimed that the Iranian President, Bani-Sadr, threatened to "export the Iranian revolution."[17] Iraq also maintained that between June and September 1980, there were 187 Iranian "violations and military actions" across the Iraqi border. Since Iraqi protests to the Iranian government went unheeded, Baghdad maintained that the responsibility for the termination of the treaty fell on the shoulders of the Iranian government.[18]

IDEOLOGICAL ASPECTS

The present conflict between Iraq and Iran also represents a conflict of two diametrically opposed ideologies. On the one hand, Iraq adheres to an ideology that is basically secularist and nationalist; on the other hand, Iran's is a religiously oriented ideology with a messianic, universalist doctrine. This section examines the main ideological features of Iraq's Arab Ba'ath Socialist Party (ABSP), and Ayatollah Khomeini's ideology in Iran. (See the selected ideological documents in the Appendix.)

The basic motto of the ABSP is "One Arab nation with an eternal mission." The ideology of the Ba'ath is based on the idea that Arabs have always constituted a single nation despite the divisions that have characterized their modern history, coupled with a nostalgic notion of reviving the glory of

[16] Ibid., p. 60.

[17] Tareq Aziz, *On Arab-Iranian Relations* (Baghdad: Ministry of Culture and Information, 1980), pp. 25, 40.

[18] Ministry of Foreign Affairs, Baghdad, *Iraqi-Iranian Dispute,* pp. 45–50, 60–61.

the Umayyad and Abbasid empires. The founder of the party, Michel Aflaq, has stated that

> the eternal mission of the Arab people is to launch themselves totally, audaciously, into changing their destiny and their present condition. ... This mission resides in their determination to reveal to the world the calamities of their society and the degrading nature of their lives, with the same candor they reveal in examining their own defects. They will need fierce, bold determination; they must rely on their own resources, without counting on any help from the outside world. ... It [the mission] is intimately bound up with the [Arab] nation's sons, their lives and experiences.[19]

To realize this eternal mission of the Arab nation requires, by definition, certain prerequisites which, according to the theoreticians of the Ba'ath, are indivisible and dialectically linked. These prerequisites are unity, freedom and socialism. Unity of the Arabs is a means rather than an end in itself. Aflaq claims that "the unification of the Arab homeland is not the final aim, but a means for the Arab nation to accomplish its mission in life."[20] To Shibli al-Aysami, the deputy secretary general of the party, the concept of unity acquires some mystical qualities reminiscent of Hegel's "Idea," a constant, unconscious motive: "The idea of unity is synonymous with the existence of the Arab nation and has been in its consciousness ever since it was subjected to partitions and divisions as a result of complicated historical circumstances."[21] Although unity, freedom, and socialism are indivisible and fundamentally equal in importance and although their achievement cannot be postponed or delayed, "unity has a moral priority and superiority which should not be overlooked by the Ba'athists lest they follow ideological and political currents that are most remote from the idea of Arab renaissance."[22]

Unity, according to Aflaq, is also a means for achieving greater cultural and spiritual rejuvenation. It is a "revolution coming to eradicate distortion and change the actual situation, discover the depths, release imprisoned forces and put an end to negative thinking, as well as regional characteristics whether genuine or fake and negative, the latter being nothing but the consequences of the absence of unity."

However, according to Aflaq, unity is not a goal that can be fully achieved in a single move. Development in stages is acceptable, provided that each stage prepares the grounds for a higher stage of unity. For example,

---

[19] Quoted in Elyas Farah, *Evolution of Arab Revolutionary Ideology* (Madrid: Arab Ba'ath Socialist Party, 1978), p. 94.

[20] Ibid., p. 135.

[21] Shibli al-'Aysami, *Unity, Freedom, Socialism* (Madrid: ABSP, 1977), p. 35.

[22] Michel Aflaq, *Choice of Texts from the Ba'ath Party Founder's Thoughts* (Rome: ABSP, 1977), p. 10.

"federation between two or three regions is a stage on which all our efforts should concentrate until they come to fruition; this stage, in turn, will facilitate reaching a higher stage, on the path towards a larger and greater unification." Nor can unity be expected to happen automatically as a result of regional progress or some unseen circumstances. "Every progress remains superficial, distorted, and disfigured unless unity gives it the natural soil for its growth." Unity is "efficiency creation" in a "race with time."[23]

Because of this deep and unwavering conception of Arab unity, the Ba'ath believes that "the fight of the Arab people in every region is one and the same. This fight must be unified: in other words, it must have the same all-over vision, common aims and a single practical project."[24] Thus the struggle for unity implies "unity of the struggle." The Arab cause is one, the "Arab fate is one."[25] Consequently, the frontiers of the Arab nation become sacrosanct and inviolable. Since "the frontiers of every Arab region are the frontiers of the whole Arab nation, its boundaries are the boundaries of the entire Arab homeland, the boundaries of the whole Arab existence."[26] Arab land must remain Arab. It is the duty of members of the Arab nation to liberate territory under alien or foreign rule.

Consequently, the Ba'ath preoccupation with Palestine and the Arabian Gulf becomes understandable. Indeed, the political report of the 1974 Eighth Congress of the ABSP drew a parallel between Palestine and the Gulf: it saw the center of the conflict as a struggle between Arab nationalism on the one hand, and Zionism and Persian nationalism on the other. Iranian immigration to the Gulf region and Iran's occupation of the three Arab islands were seen as an imperialist plot whose objective was to "circumscribe centers of revolution, primarily Iraq, and to work for their enfeeblement and fall."[27]

The fear of encirclement and the firm belief in Arab unity puts Iraq in direct conflict with what it sees as Western imperialism, which created one problem in Palestine and is planning to create another in the Gulf. Therefore, "the interest of the Arab homeland can never be to side with the Western Bloc or with [any] of its members. ... It is imperative that we should relieve ourselves of any bond with them."[28] The conflict with imperialism has created a strong fear of changes in the Gulf; the Iranian revolution was thus viewed as another imperialist attempt to destabilize Iraq and bring about the downfall of the regime there. This is best illustrated by President Saddam Hussein in his speech in the National Assembly on November 4, 1980:

[23] Ibid., pp. 10–21.
[24] Quoted by Farah, *Arab Revolutionary Ideology*, p. 130.
[25] Aflaq, *Choice of Texts*, pp. 12, 21.
[26] Ibid., p. 29.
[27] *The 1968 Revolution in Iraq — Experience and Prospects*. The Political Report of the Eighth Congress of the Arab Ba'ath Socialist Party in Iraq in January 1974 (London: Ithaca Press, 1979), pp. 130, 131.
[28] Aflaq, *Choice of Texts*, p. 100.

> They took turns on Iraq; [Ottoman] Turkey goes, Iran comes. This is all done in the name of Islam. It is enough; no more Turkey, no more Iran, no more any human being in this universe.... We are Iraqis and we are a part of the Arab homeland and the Arab nation.... We will not accept anybody coming with a new path every day which aims at dividing Iraq and dividing the Arab nation.[29]

The battle with Iran was viewed as an act of national defense to keep the area free from foreign interference and encirclement. As Saddam Hussein stated, "Whenever we act nationally, we do not discount the interests of the Arab nation and the interest and security of humanity.... Therefore, we want this area to be stable and we have tried every means to keep it free from military conflicts, especially the Arab Gulf area which is sensitive to the interests of the world."[30]

The war with Iran was also viewed by President Hussein as a measure to rectify injustices and to assert the right of Iraq to practice full sovereignty over its lands and waterways in accordance with the Algiers Agreement of 1975. It was not a war of expansion: the Iranians could recover this territory once they recognized Iraqi legitimate rights. The war was viewed by Iraq as an Arab war and as an acid test of Arabism.

Iraq sees its conflict with Iran as Arab nationalism locked in a struggle with Persian nationalism; it is not a religious war in which Sunnis are fighting Shi'is. As a secular party, the Ba'ath has always separated state and religion. This does not mean, however, an antagonistic attitude towards religion. On the contrary, Islam is viewed as the cultural and spiritual source for Arab nationalism.

The reason for the Ba'ath's demand for a secular state, in the words of the founder, Aflaq, is "to avoid religion being weighted down by the burden of politics, to avoid its implication in political ambiguities. Only if it is free in this way can religion find its true place in the lives of individuals and of society."[31] Nationalism constitutes the social basis of the state, while freedom constitutes its moral basis: "The state's secular character will only confirm freedom in its spiritual and moral aspect." Elyas Farah, a leading Ba'ath theoretician, suggests that the Ba'ath ideology

> is marked by an attitude to religion based on the unity of the dialectical links between the social and the spiritual and their indissoluble bond. In the beginning, religion is itself a revolution.... Revolution assembles and coordinates the initial impetus of religion and the contemporary revolutionary movement; the latter in turn invigorates society's urge to shake itself free from the fetters which neutralize the historical energies of the masses.[32]

[29] *Al-Thawra* (Baghdad), November 5, 1980.
[30] Ibid., November 12, 1980.
[31] Quoted in Farah, *Arab Revolutionary Ideology,* p. 124.
[32] Ibid., p. 126.

Rather than acting as a unifying force religion can play a divisive role, especially in a multireligious society. "Arabs have no desire to see their nationalism identified with religion, because this is a specific problem, and one which cannot be of help in the unification of the nation and can, on the contrary, divide an otherwise united group." As a result, the emphasis on Arab nationalism helps to avoid the "distortions and errors of both abstract and religious nationalism."[33]

Such arguments, from the point of view of Ayatollah Khomeini and the Iranian Islamic revolution, are heresies.[34] To Khomeini, religion cannot be separated from the state. The fusion of the two is the basis of true Islamic government. Unlike the Ba'ath, which emphasizes Arab unity, Khomeini asserts the necessity of Islamic unity. To achieve that unity, Islamic government becomes a prerequisite for defeating imperialism — "smashing the heads of traitors, demolishing human idols and dictators who spread injustice and corruption on earth."[35]

It is the duty of the *ulema* or religious leaders, and all Muslims, to bring to an end injustice and corruption, and to achieve happiness for the people by "destroying corrupt governments and establishing an active and sincere Islamic government."[36] The Islamic government is one that is run according to the laws of God, and therefore, the real ruler is God alone!

> It is not an absolutist government, rather a constitutional one... in the sense that the holders of power follow all the conditions and norms established in the Koran and the Suna [Traditions, the life and sayings of the Prophet].... Thus the Islamic government is the government of divine law. The difference between an Islamic government and constitutional governments (republican and royal) resides in the fact that the representatives of the people or the king are the ones who devise laws and legislation, while the power to legislate resides with God Almighty; no one has the power to legislate, and no one has the power to pass judgment on something contrary to God's will.[37]

The Islamic ruler must be knowledgeable about Islamic law, and must also be a just person. Only the ulema fit such a characterization and therefore, only they have the right to rulership.[38]

---

[33] Ibid., pp. 147, 99.

[34] The following discussion is based on Ayatollah Khomeini, *al-Hukumah al-Islamiyah* [The Islamic Government] (Beirut: Dar al-Tali'ah lil taba'ah wa-al-Nashr, 1979), and an "Interview on the Islamic Revolutionary Movement" with Khomeini in *Al-Safir* (Beirut), January 18 and 19, 1979.

[35] Khomeini, *al-Hukumah al-Islamiyah,* p. 35.

[36] Ibid., p. 37.

[37] Ibid., pp. 41–42.

[38] Ibid., pp. 45–54.

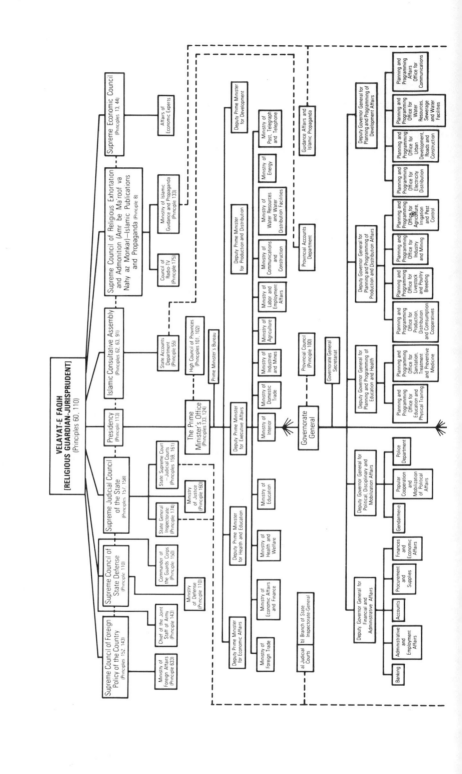

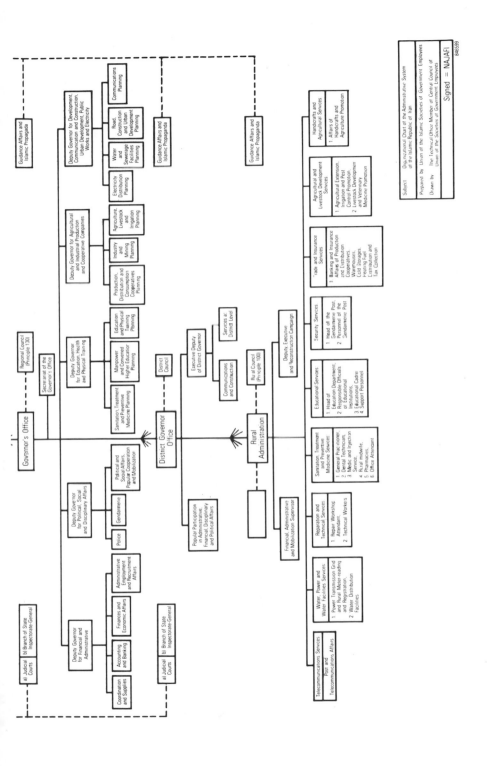

> If we [the ulema] want to immortalize the rules of the shari'a [Islamic juris-
> prudence] in practice, to prevent violation of the rights of weak people, to
> prevent corruption on earth, to apply the shari'a laws justly, to fight the
> heresies and the deviations decided upon by the sham parliaments and to
> prevent the influence and intervention of the enemies in the affairs of the
> Muslims, we must form the government because all this is carried out by a
> government led by a trustworthy and pious ruler who commits no injustice,
> deviation or corruption.[39]

The structure of Khomeini's concept of Islamic government (see Appendix for
selections of Khomeini's writings on this) is embodied in Iran's constitution
(see Appendix), ratified on December 2–3, 1979 and implemented in Iran's
governmental organization. The accompanying chart on the structure of Iran's
Islamic government reflects the relationship between religious roles and political positions on the one hand and the special position of guardianship
(*velayat-e faqih*) on the other hand.

Ayatollah Khomeini has argued that nationalism is un-Islamic. Instead, he believes in Islamic internationalism:

> There are no nationalities in Islam. It supercedes and abolishes all of them. In
> a sense, nationalism is a pre-Islamic legacy. Islam came to eliminate [national]
> fanaticism. The subject of Islam is man and not his nationalism. Islam is a
> message addressed to all mankind, without distinction between one color and
> another or one race and another. There is no difference between an Arab and a
> non-Arab, even though the prophet is Arab and the Koran was revealed in
> Arabic.... All Muslims are brothers in the view of Islam and all Muslims must
> shed whatever divides them, be its source nationalism, race or color.[40]

By advocating an active Islamic ideology, and by declaring his open
hostility to secular nationalism — including Arab nationalism — Khomeini put
himself on a collision course with the countries of the region, primarily Iraq.
As a country with long common borders with Iran, the exponents of the ideas
of Arab nationalism were bound to clash with the exponents of Islam and
Islamic government. A confrontation between an ideology which aspires to
dominate the Arab world and an ideology which aspires to dominate the Muslim world, the Arab world included, was inevitable. Highlighting this, on the
anniversary of the Iraq-Iran war, Khomeini stated: "Those who bring separation and division among the Muslims by resorting to phrases such as

---

[39] Ibid., p. 39.

[40] See Ayatollah Khomeini, "Interview on the Islamic Revolutionary Movement." For an
Iraqi reaction to such views, see Mowaffak Khidr, "Waqa'ei' Ajiba Min Dajal al-
Khumayni" [Strange Facts from the Fraud Khomeini], *al-Thawra* (Baghdad), Nov. 10,
1981.

nationalism or nationality and the like are the army of Satan, contributing to the superpowers and the enemies of the Koran."[41]

The advent of the Iranian revolution on the Middle Eastern political scene changed the power configuration in the area. The subsequent Iraq-Iran war caused realignments within the Arab world. Jordan and Morocco were the most vociferous in support of Iraq. Jordan's support took a number of forms. First, Jordan offered the port of Aqaba for unloading ships destined for Iraq. In addition, a propaganda campaign in favor of Iraq and condemning Ayatollah Khomeini and the Iranian revolution was initiated. Iraqi transport planes were permitted to be stationed in eastern Jordan to avoid Iranian air strikes. Finally, Jordan sent food, non-military goods, and volunteers to Iraq. Some news reports indicated Jordan's intention to commit its troops in the battlefield, a step which was thwarted by American and British diplomatic pressure on King Hussein not to expand the scope of the war. Similar pressures were allegedly exerted on Oman not to allow an "Iraqi move, to be mounted from Oman, to seize the three disputed islands in the strait held by Iran."[42] King Hussein's support for Iraq was seen as a way of balancing Jordan's dependency on Saudi Arabia, and as a way of showing gratitude for Iraqi financial assistance to Jordan which had amounted to $200 to $300 million annually.

Jordan's enthusiastic support for Iraq was countered by Syria's vehement condemnation of Iraq's war against Iran. The motives behind Syria's support for Iran were seen as another manifestation of the rivalry between the two Ba'ath regimes in Damascus and Baghdad over the leadership of the Ba'ath and the Arab world. It was also attributed to Syria's increased isolation in the Arab world, and Assad's unstable regime (particularly the internal resistance to his regime which is allegedly led by the Muslim Brotherhood, an extremist fundamentalist political organization, with Jordanian backing). In addition, the ruling elite of Syria are from the Alawi, a minority sect in Syria which is an offshoot of Shi'ism. Syria's sympathy for Iran's Islamic revolution is also attributed to this factor. As a result the Gulf war almost sparked a military confrontation between Jordan and Syria.[43]

The reaction of other Arab countries to the Iraqi-Iranian war fell between the positions of Jordan and Syria. The United Arab Emirates declared

[41] *Ettela'at International* (Teheran), "Statements of Imam Khomeini Concerning the War Imposed on Iran by Iraq," September 23, 1981.

[42] Daniel Southerland, "Washington publicly calm, privately concerned over Jordan's aid to Iraq," *Christian Science Monitor,* October 8, 1980; also Geoffrey Godsell, "Keeping Gulf War from Spreading: An Analysis," ibid.

[43] See *Christian Science Monitor:* "Keeping Gulf War from Spreading," and "Iran-Iraq War May Jolt Arab Power Equation," October 8, 1980; "Gulf War Only One Cause of Syria-Jordan Confrontation," December 1, 1980; and "Behind Syria's Troop Buildup," December 3, 1980; and "Israel Gains and Loses by Latest Split in Arab World," December 10, 1980.

an official neutral position: Shaikh Saqr ibn Muhammad al-Qasimi, ruler of Ras al-Khaymah, indicated that the issue of the three islands was a question which fell under UAE jurisdiction. He claimed that contacts had already been made with Ayatollah Khomeini over the islands, and an understanding had been reached on the matter. He neither supported nor condemned Iraq, but indicated his preference for peace and non-interference as the basis for Gulf security.

The Dubai newspaper, *al-Bayan*, called upon Iraq and Iran to cease fighting and to accept the decision of an Islamic Mediation Committee. "The two sides' acceptance of the principle of Islamic mediation will be clear evidence of their concern for the feelings of the Islamic world, which is now sending its mediators to the battlefield, and a true test of their respect for these feelings, which have almost been slaughtered by this fratricide." *Al-Bayan* accused the United States of planning to escalate tension in the Gulf as an excuse to intervene: "There is no doubt that anyone who tries to expand the circle of war is aiming, even unconsciously, at serving the interests of those who are intending to repress the peoples of the area and plunder their wealth."[44]

Kuwaiti newspapers supported the Iraqi war effort and called upon the Arab countries to back Iraq against Iran. The Kuwaiti News Agency accused Iran of attempting to export its revolution by calling upon Iranian pilgrims to agitate among the Muslims gathered during the pilgrimage to Mecca. (Indeed, several arson attempts and bomb explosions led the Kuwaiti government to deport an Iranian religious leader). One Kuwaiti paper viewed the war as an "asset for all the Arabs [which] will lift them from their humiliating position and will put them in their appropriate place among peoples and nations." By claiming that only Israel fears an Iraqi victory in the war, *al-Watan* argued that "the battle Iraq is fighting now is an Arab battle in the full sense of the word. Victory in it means victory for the Arabs and defeat ... means defeat for all the Arabs. Therefore, all the Arabs without exception are called upon to stand with all their capabilities and resources on the side of Saddam Hussein who is fighting the battle of freedom, dignity, and defense of Arab rights."[45]

The formation of the Gulf Cooperation Council in May 1981 was catalyzed by the perceived Iranian threat to the region. Saudi Arabia, Kuwait, Qatar, the United Arab Emirates, Oman, and Bahrain formed the council as a mutual security and defense arrangement. The council's fears of Iran and support for Iraq were subsequently consolidated by an abortive coup attempt in mid-December 1981 in Bahrain organized by the pro-Iranian Islamic Front for the Liberation of Bahrain. In reaction, there was a decisive increase in regional diplomatic and financial support for Iraq. Reflecting this, the Saudi minister of

[44] *Al-Bayan* (Dubai), September 28 and 30, 1980.
[45] "Diversification of Kuwait's Investments," *Neue Zuercher Zeitung* (Zurich), September 17, 1980; *Al-Watan* (Kuwait), September 26, 1980; and *KUNA* (Kuwaiti News Agency), October 11, 1980.

the interior, Prince Nayaf Ibn Abdul Aziz, declared that Saudi Arabia "stands with Iraq in one position based on the dictates of our beliefs and nationalism... we appreciate the heroic stand of Iraq. The war that Iraq is engaged in is not only a defense of its land and sovereignty; it is also a defense of all the Arab nation."[46] The Kuwaiti minister of the interior, Sheikh Nawaf al-Ahmad, called for the creation of an inter-Gulf security plan to "face any subversive plan plotted against the security and stability of the region."[47]

The Palestine Liberation Organization (PLO) took a neutral stand and branded the war as a fratricide that would only strengthen Israel and serve American interests. The PLO played an active role in seeking a ceasefire and a negotiated settlement. It also helped form a mediation committee of non-aligned nations. Zehdi Tarazi, the PLO representative at the United Nations, succeeded in arranging a meeting between the Iraqi and Iranian representatives. The PLO's formula, which was submitted to the non-aligned nations' peace mission, included a ceasefire, Iraqi withdrawal to the 1975 frontiers, and a negotiated settlement of all claims.[48]

While the conflict appeared unrelated to the Arab-Israeli conflict, in fact it was later revealed by President Bani-Sadr, in a television interview in Paris and quoted in the *New York Times* (August 22, 1981), that Israel was supplying spare parts and armaments to Iran. Irrespective of Khomeini's inflammatory rhetoric against Israel, according to the *New York Times* (same date), Menachem Begin viewed Iraq as Israel's major adversary in the Middle East and had "an overwhelming desire not to see Iraq win the war." This position was apparently shared by both the U.S. and France, which helped arrange the spare parts deal between Israel and Iran. On June 7, 1981, Israel destroyed Iraq's nuclear reactor and Iraq accused Iran of collusion in this. According to Bani-Sadr, his opposition to dealing with Israel was overruled by the religious leaders close to Khomeini.

Revelations of the Khomeini regime's covert arms dealings with Israel significantly dampened whatever revolutionary and/or religious appeal the movement had in the Arab world. In October 1981, the leader of the Lebanese National Movement, Walid Jumblatt, strongly denounced Khomeini's interference in Lebanese and Palestinian affairs.[49] In addition, PLO leaders abruptly stopped visiting Iran and many factions of the Palestinian movement began openly condemning Khomeini and supporting Iraq.[50] The PLO representative in Saudi Arabia noted in late December the deteriorating relations between the PLO and Iran.[51]

[46] *Al-Nahar* (Beirut), December 26, 1981.

[47] *Al-Nahar* (Beirut), December 25, 1981. See also *Christian Science Monitor,* February 5, 1982.

[48] "New Bids to Halt Gulf War Spurred by U.N. and P.L.O.," *Christian Science Monitor,* November 4, 1980.

[49] *Iran Press Service* (London), October 1, 1981.

[50] *8 Days* (London), October 10, 1981.

[51] *Al-Nahar* (Beirut), December 27, 1981.

The Gulf's increasing support for Iraq is in contrast to the position taken by the so-called Steadfastness Front, composed of Syria, Algeria, Libya, Southern Yemen, and the PLO.[52] While this group officially declared support for Iran, the level of support varied from Syria's outright condemnation of Iraq to the more neutral and mediative efforts of the PLO and Algeria. Thus, the ideological conflict between Arab nationalism and Islamic universalism, as well as that between state legitimacy and revolutionary transformation, have created diametric pressures on the governments of the region. These tensions were manifest in the dilemma which Iraq's invasion of Iran posed.

Iraq, cast in the role of an invading army, was placed on the ideological defensive. This is reflected in President Saddam Hussein's continuous denial of territorial ambitions vis-à-vis Iran and his encouragement of PLO, Algerian, and Islamic mediation efforts. Indeed, Iraq was very anxious to extricate itself from Iranian territory.

Iran, cast in the role of a transgressed state defending its territorial integrity, took the ideological offensive and rejected all mediation efforts. The military invasion of Iran was in fact advantageous to the ruling ulema in several respects: it kept the army out of Teheran, bogged down in a sanguinary military campaign in Khūzistan, and served to consolidate power in their own hands; it inflamed nationalist sentiment in Iran; and it dampened internal opposition to an increasingly repressive and reactionary government.

The two superpowers took a declared neutral position on the war. Soviet-Iraqi relations have been cooling since the late 1970s. The invasion of Afghanistan, Soviet support for Ethiopia and South Yemen, together with Iraq's increased shift towards West European nations for armaments and trade have all contributed to the chill in their relations. Thus, the Soviet Union warned both Iran and Iraq that such a war would only benefit "Western imperialists." Moscow's neutral position might have been dictated by a fear of American military action in the Gulf and particularly increased military aid to Saudi Arabia. Soviet uneasiness about the increasing international stature of President Zia al-Haq of Pakistan as a mediator; and fear of a military coup in Iran that would bring a regime similar to that of the Shah to play a subserviant role for the United States no doubt also were factors considered by the Soviet Union. This does not mean that Moscow is not worried about Ayatollah Khomeini's possible future influence on Soviet Muslims who number close to 50 million. It is estimated that by the year 2000, there will be 100 million Muslims in the USSR, compared with 150 million Russians.[53]

For its part, the United States pursued a policy of official neutrality primarily because of Washington's fear that the war would spread to the rest of the Gulf region. The consequences, in the eyes of the United States, of a widening of the war raised the specter of a further interruption in the supply of oil from the Gulf region, which represents more than 60 percent of the world's

[52] *Asharg Al-Awsat* (London, Arabic), May 26, 1982.
[53] See "The World of Islam," *Time,* April 16, 1979.

oil supplies. There was also a fear that the Soviet Union would intervene directly if Iran began to disintegrate because of the war. Finally, in the early months of the conflict, Washington remained concerned over the safety of the American hostages still being held by Teheran.[54]

In May 1982, Iran launched a major offensive and recaptured Khorramshahr. With this event, concern spread throughout the Gulf that Iran would overrun the Iraqi army and invade Iraq. Egypt, a dormant actor in Middle East politics since the Camp David accord, warned Iran that an invasion of Iraq would not be tolerated and would precipitate the commitment of Egyptian troops to the defense of Iraq.

However, these developments were overshadowed by Israel's invasion of Lebanon in early June 1982. Within days, Iraq announced its withdrawal from all Iranian territory, in effect resolving the dilemma of its own invasion. Assuming the ideological offensive, Iraq offered Iran a complete cease fire, so that troops could be committed to the support of Lebanon and the PLO. Iran rejected this offer.

The Iraq-Iran conflict has deep-seated historical, legal and ideological dimensions. These dimensions reflect tensions that have, over the centuries, resisted military, negotiated and imposed solutions. While temporarily subdued from time to time, the tensions have merely been rekindled with shifts in the balance of power. Thus, Iran's 1969 abrogation of the 1937 treaty and imposition of the 1975 treaty reflected a power equation favorable to Teheran; Iraq's abrogation of the 1975 treaty and the eruption of hostilities between the two countries reflected the dramatic changes in that power equation resulting from Iran's destabilization.

The contemporary conflict, then, is the latest manifestation of a centuries-old drama. What kind of climax will this latest chapter have? The present stalemate appears stable and entrenched. With the war safely circumscribed to Iraq and Iran — doing no more damage (from the superpower perspective) than dissipating the energies and resources of these two countries — there are no powerful external pressures to bring the war to an end.

However, the internal pressures resulting from this dissipation of energies, resources and lives do generate a rationale for compromise and negotiation. Indeed, the Iraqi foreign minister, Dr. Saadoun Hamadi has articulated Iraq's position accordingly:

> ... we envisage an agreement to be a formal recognition of our sovereignty over Shatt al-Arab on our land frontier formalized in a clear-cut agreement which

[54]*Christian Science Monitor,* "Iran-Iraq Conflict Threatens Gulf's Oil-Producing Areas" and "U.S. Speaks Softly on Iran-Iraq Conflict with Hostages in Mind," September 24, 1980; and "U.S. Studies Options on Spare Parts for Iran," November 4, 1980.

includes guarantees that no side will trespass on the other side, signed by the two countries, deposited with the United Nations, maybe under the auspices of international groups so that no country would try again to reopen the issue. Those would be the guarantees which we are thinking of. We are not thinking of holding land, Iranian land, forever as an insurance.[55]

On the other hand, Ayatollah Khomeini's sense of religious mission and righteousness may be fueled by sacrifice. Responding to Iraqi overtures for negotation, Ayatollah Khomeini, for example, declared:

> Saddam Hussein is asking for a compromise. We cannot compromise with him. He is a pagan. He is corrupt. He is an infidel. We can not compromise with such a person. We will fight to the end and will come out triumphant with the help of God. We do not care if other countries extend their assistance to the Iraqi regime because we have to implement our religious duties. We are religiously bound to protect and preserve Islam.
>
> If we are killed, we have fulfilled our duties. This was the same logic which we pursued in our fighting against the corrupt Pahlavi regime. Our logic was not to become victorious in any case. Our logic was based on this fact that Islam had confronted problems. Islamic teachings were going to be eradicated and the Islamic principles were going to be erased, therefore, we were bound by our religion to resist it as much as we could. If we are martyred, we will go to paradise and if we kill, we are victorious.[56]

Similarly, on the first anniversary of the war, Khomeini declared: "I have good tidings that if you kill the enemy you will be rewarded by going to paradise and if you are killed you will go to paradise."[57]

In this situation, decisive victory or defeat can be the only outcome. But whether this zeal for battle on the part of Iran's leaders is shared by the population is another matter. The turmoil within Iran may alter the situation. Indeed, the Israeli invasion of Lebanon will create turmoil throughout the region that will no doubt affect the Iraq-Iran conflict. However, it is too early to assess the impact.

[55] Embassy of Iraq, London, Statement for a press conference, March 1, 1981, p. 14.
[56] Selected Messages of Imam Khomeini, p. 68.
[57] *Ettela'at International* (Teheran), September 23, 1981.

Appendix 1

LEGAL AND HISTORICAL DOCUMENTS

1. TREATY OF ERZERUM OF MAY 31st, 1847

ARTICLE 1

*T*HE TWO MUSSULMAN POWERS waive the totality of their existing pecuniary claims on one another, provided always that nothing in this arrangement shall affect the provisions made for the settlement of the claims to which Article 4 relates.

ARTICLE 2

The Persian Government undertakes to cede to the Ottoman Government all the lowlands — that is to say, the land in the western part of the province of Zohab; and the Ottoman Government undertakes to cede to the Persian Government the eastern — that is to say, all the mountains — part of the said province, including the Kirind Valley.

The Persian Government abandons all claim to the city and province of Suleimani, and formally undertakes not to interfere with or infringe the sovereign rights of the Ottoman Government over the said province.

The Ottoman Government formally recognizes the unrestricted sovereignty of the Persian Government over the city and port of Muhammara, the island of Khizr, the anchorage, and the land on the eastern bank — that is to say, the left bank — of the Shatt-al-Arab, which are in the possession of the tribes, recognized as belonging to Persia. Further, Persian vessels shall have the right to navigate freely without let or hindrance on the Shatt-al-Arab from the mouth of the same to the point of contact of the frontiers of the two Parties.

ARTICLE 3

The two Contracting Parties, having by the present Treaty waived their other territorial claims, undertake forthwith to appoint commisioners and engineers as their respective representatives for the purpose of determining the frontiers between the two States in conformity with the preceding article.

ARTICLE 4

Both Parties are agreed as to the appointment forthwith, by both Parties, of commissioners for the purpose of adjudicating and making a fair settlement in all cases of damage suffered by either Party since the acceptance of the friendly proposals drawn up and communicated by the two Mediating Great Powers in the month of Jemaziyyu-'l-evvel, 1261, together with all questions of pasturage dues since the year in which the arrears in the payment of the latter began.

ARTICLE 5

The Ottoman Government undertakes that the fugitive Persian princes shall reside at Brussa, and shall not be permitted to leave that place or maintain secret relations with Persia. The two High Contracting Powers further undertake that all the other refugees shall be handed over in conformity with the earlier Treaty of Erzerum.

ARTICLE 6

Persian merchants shall pay the customs dues on their goods, in kind or in cash, according to the current present value of such goods, in the manner specified in the article relating to trade in the Treaty of Erzerum concluded in 1238*. No additional charge whatsoever shall be levied over and above the amounts fixed in the said Treaty.

*A.H. 1238 = A.D. 1823.

ARTICLE 7

The Ottoman Government undertakes to accord the requisite privileges to enable Persian pilgrims, in accordance with the former treaties, to visit the Holy Places in the Ottoman dominions in complete safety and without vexatious treatment of any kind. Further, the Ottoman Government, being desirous of strengthening and consolidating the bonds of friendship and concord which should subsist between the two Mussulman Powers and between their respective subjects, undertakes to adopt such measures as may be most appropriate to ensure the participation, not only of Persian pilgrims, but of all other Persian subjects, in all the said privileges in the Ottoman dominions, in such manner as to protect them from any sort of injustice, molestation, or incivility, whether in respect of their commercial activities or in any other respect.

Furthermore, the Ottoman Government undertakes to recognize Consuls to be appointed by the Persian Government in places in the Ottoman dominions where their presence may be required on account of commercial interests, or for the protection of Persian merchants and other Persian subjects, save only in Mecca the Revered and Medina the Resplendent, and to respect in the case of the said Consuls all the privileges due in virtue of their official character and accorded to Consuls of other friendly Powers.

The Persian Government, for its part, undertakes to accord reciprocity of treatment in every respect to Consuls to be appointed by the Ottoman Government in places in Persia in which the latter may consider the appointment of Consuls to be necessary, as also to Ottoman merchants and other Ottoman subjects visiting Persia.

ARTICLE 8

The two High Contracting Mussulman Powers undertake to adopt and enforce the measures necessary to prevent and punish theft and brigandage on the part of the tribes and peoples settled on the frontier, to which end they will quarter troops in suitable localities. They further undertake to do their duty in respect of all forms of aggressive acts, such as pillage, robbery, or murder, which may occur in their respective territories.

Contested tribes over which the suzerainty is not known shall be left free by the two High Contracting Powers to choose once and for all and specify the localities which they will henceforward always inhabit. Tribes over which the suzerainty is known shall be compelled to come within the territory of the State to which they belong.

ARTICLE 9

All points or articles of previous treaties, and especially of the Treaty concluded at Erzerum in 1238, which are not specifically amended or annulled by the present Treaty, are hereby reaffirmed in respect of any and all of their provisions, as if they were reproduced in their entirety in the present Treaty.

The two High Contracting Powers agree that, when the texts of this Treaty have been exchanged, they will accept and sign the same, and that the ratifications thereof shall be exchanged within the space of two months, or earlier.

2. EXPLANATORY NOTE RELATIVE TO CERTAIN STIPULATIONS IN THE PROPOSED TREATY OF ERZERUM, ADDRESSED BY THE BRITISH AND RUSSIAN AMBASSADORS AT CONSTANTINOPLE TO THE OTTOMAN GOVERNMENT ON APRIL 26th, 1847

The undersigned, representing the Mediating Courts of Great Britain and Russia, have had the honor to receive the identic note, with annex, which His Excellency Ali Effendi, Minister for Foreign Affairs, was pleased to address to them on the 11th instant, relating to the Turco-Persian negotiations.

The undersigned are highly gratified to note from the communication in question His Excellency's statement, on behalf of the Sublime Porte, of the decision to issue instructions forthwith to the Ottoman Plenipotentiary at Erzerum to sign the articles of the Treaty with the Court of Persia unamended, according to the text drawn up by the Commissioners of the two Mediating Courts, as submitted for the acceptance of the Governments concerned by their plenipotentiaries at Erzerum, subject to explanations by the representatives of the said Courts at Constantinople to the Sublime Porte on certain points which the latter does not consider sufficiently clear.

The points on which the Sublime Porte requires explanations are as follows:

1. The Sublime Porte presumes that the clause of Article 2 of the draft Treaty ceding the city, port, and anchorage of Muhammara, and the island of Khizr, to Persia, cannot include either the territory of the Sublime Porte comprised* outside the city or the other ports of the Sublime Porte situate in these parts.

The Sublime Porte is also concerned to know whether, under the terms of another part of the same article relating to tribes which, while actually belonging to Persia, may happen to be divided, one half being settled in Ottoman territory and the other half in Persian territory, it follows that those parts of the tribes which are in Turkey will also become subject to Persia, and the territory in their possession will accordingly also be ceded to Persia; and

---

*The word "situate" (*situees*) is used instead of "comprised" (*comprises*) in the extract communicated to the Persian Envoy in January 1848.

whether Persia will ever be entitled at some future date to dispute with the Porte the right to the possession of such territory.

2. The Sublime Porte is concerned to know whether, under the existing terms of Article 1 and 4, the Persian Government is entitled to include the pecuniary compensations as between the two Governments which it had entirely renounced, in the category of individual claims. The Porte understands these claims to apply solely to certain pasturage dues and to losses incurred by the respective subjects of the two Governments as a result of the activities of brigands and the like.

The Sublime Porte further asks whether the Persian Government's assent will be obtained on the question of fortifications added to Article 2, as also in respect of the passages regarding reciprocity which were omitted in Article 7 of the Commissioner's draft.

The undersigned Representatives, being anxious and bound to dispel the uncertainties of the Sublime Porte on all the above questions, hereby declare as follows:

Ad 1. The anchorage of Muhammara is the part situated opposite the city of Muhammara in the Haffar Canal, and this definition is not susceptible of any other interpretation.

The undersigned Representatives are further in agreement with the Ottoman Minister in the view, that, in ceding to Persia in the region in question the city, port and anchorage of Muhammara and the island of Khizr, the Sublime Porte is not ceding any other territory or any other ports there may be in this region.

The undersigned Representatives further declare that Persia will not be entitled on any pretext whatsoever to put forward claims in regard to the regions situate on the right bank of the Shatt-al-Arab, or to the territory on the left bank belonging to Turkey, even where Persian tribes or parts of such tribes are established on the said bank or in the said territory.

Ad 2. As regards the Sublime Porte's apprehension that Articles 1 and 4 of the draft Treaty may be irregularly interpreted in such a way as to give rise to the revival by the Persian Government of the Pecuniary claims as between the two Governments, the undersigned Representatives hereby declare that, inasmuch as it is explicitly stipulated in Articles 1 and 4 of the draft Treaty that all claims of this kind from whatever source are, and are to continue to be, waived, there can be no resumption of the discussions on the matter in any case, and that only the claims of individuals will be entitled to satisfaction by the two Parties respectively; and, further, that the examination and validity of such individual claims will be subject, as agreed, to a special commission to be appointed ad hoc and that the decision as to what claims are to be regarded as individual claims will also have to be referred to this commission.

In reply to the two subsidiary questions raised at the conclusion of His Excellency Ali Effendi's note, the undersigned Representatives believe that they are justified in stating that the Persian Government will readily agree to the insertion in Article 7 of the clauses with regard to reciprocity of treatment to be observed by both Governments in the mutual interest of their respective subjects, pilgrims and Consular Agents. As regards the question of fortifications, they can only express their personal opinion that a reciprocal undertaking on the part of the two Mussulman Governments not to fortify the banks of the Shatt-al-Arab would constitute one more guarantee of the maintenance of peaceful relations between the two countries, well calculated powerfully to cement the bonds of good will which it is the object of the Treaty in question to establish.

The undersigned Representatives are accordingly entirely prepared to support the fulfillment of the wishes of the Sublime Porte on this point through the intermediary of their colleagues in Teheran; and they have reason to hope that their representations in this connection will not be without effect.

At the same time, the undersigned Representatives are of [the] opinion that the signature of the Treaty might without inconvenience take place without waiting for the issue of the negotiations on the special point in question, as to which there would be no difficulty in appending subsequently an additional clause to the Treaty.

The undersigned, etc.
Oustinof
H. Wellesley

Pera, April 14th (26th), 1847

3. REPLY OF THE OTTOMAN GOVERNMENT TO THE BRITISH AND RUSSIAN AMBASSADORS AT CONSTANTINOPLE

I am in receipt of Your Excellencies' collective official note of April 14th (26th) last in reply to my official note to Your Excellencies asking for certain explanations on the subject of the Persian Treaty.

Your Excellencies' note states in regard to the territories and tribes to which Article 2 of the draft Treaty relates that, although the Sublime Porte agrees in this article to the retention by Persia of the city and port of Muhammara, the anchorage opposite the city in the Haffar Canal and the island of Khizr, the Sublime Porte does not thereby cede any other port or territory in this region; and, further, that the Persian Government will not be entitled to put forward any claim to proprietary rights either in respect of the regions situate on the right bank of the Shatt-al-Arab or in respect of the regions belonging to the Sublime Porte on the left bank, even where a Persian tribe or part of such tribe is established in such regions; further, that the claims as between the two Governments which are waived in their totality by both Governments under Article 1 will not be included in the category of individual claims to which Article 4 relates; and, further, that you have good grounds for hoping that the Court of Persia will readily agree to the insertion of the clause embodying the principle of reciprocity which was omitted in Article 7.

The Sublime Porte is satisfied with the above official explanations and assurances; and His Majesty the Sultan, having complete confidence in the two Mediating Courts and in their Representatives, has ordered in the exercise of His Sovereign Will that instructions should be issued to His Excellency Enver Effendi, Plenipotentiary of the Sublime Porte at Erzerum, to sign the draft Treaty submitted by the Commissioners of the two mediating Courts without amendment, on the understanding that the Court of Persia will accept the assurances which have been given by the Representatives of the two Mediating Courts to the effect that it will raise no claim going counter to those assurances, and on the further understanding that, in the event of any such claim being raised, the Treaty will be deemed to be null and void.

It is for the purpose of bringing all the above considerations to Your Excellencies' notice that this official note has been drawn up and is communicated to you.

(L.S.) Es-Said Mehmed Emin 'Ali

Jemaziyyu-'l-evvel 29th, 1263.

4. NOTE FROM MIRZA MOHAMMAD ALI KHAN TO THE RUSSIAN AND BRITISH AMBASSADORS, DATED JANUARY 14th (31st), 1848

I hereby declare to Your Excellency that, in virtue of the mission with which I am entrusted by my Government for the exchange of ratifications of the Treaty of Erzerum, I concur entirely with the explanations given to the Porte by the representatives of the two Mediating Powers with reference to the three first points of Your Excellency's communication. I further declare with reference to the fourth point of the same communication that I have no objection to the insertion in Article 7 of the passages in regard to reciprocity of treatment to be observed by the two Governments in relation to their respective subjects, pilgrims, and Consular Agents, and further that, in the matter of the fortifications, His Majesty the Shah agrees, that so long as Turkey refrains from the construction of fortifications on the right bank of the Shatt-al-Arab opposite Persian territory, Persia will for her part refrain from such constructions of the left bank, possession of which is assured to her under the provisions of the Treaty.

In faith whereof I have signed these presents and sealed them with my seal.

(Signed) Mohammad Ali

Pera, Sefer 23rd, 1264, corresponding
to January 19th (31st), 1848.

5. TEHERAN PROTOCOL OF DECEMBER 21st, 1911

The Persian and Ottoman Governments, inspired by a common desire to avoid henceforward any subjects of controversy in respect of their common frontiers, having instructed the Persian Minister for Foreign Affairs and the Turkish Ambassador at Teheran, respectively, to establish the bases of negotiations and the procedure to be followed for the delimitation of the said frontiers, the undersigned, after discussion, have agreed on the following points:

I. A Commission consisting of an equal number of delegates of either Party shall meet as early as possible at Constantinople.

II. The delegates of the two Governments, furnished with all the documents and evidence in support of their claims, shall be instructed to establish the boundary line separating the two countries in a spirit of sincere impartiality; after which, a technical commission shall have merely to apply the definite delimitation on the spot, on the basis laid down by the former commission.

III. The work of the Joint Commission, which will meet at Constantinople, shall be based on the clauses of the treaty known as the Treaty of Erzerum, concluded in 1847.

IV. Should the delegates of the two Parties fail to agree on the interpretation and application of certain clauses of that treaty, it is agreed that, at the end of a period of six months of negotiation, in order completely to settle the question of the delimitation of the frontiers, all the points on which any divergence exists shall be submitted together to the Hague Court of Arbitration, in order that the entire question may thus be definitely settled.

V. It is understood that neither of the two Parties may adduce the military occupation of the territories in dispute as a legal argument.

Done in duplicate and exchange in original between the undersigned, acting on behalf of their Governments.

The Imperial Ottoman Embassy, Teheran, December 21, 1911.

(signed) Wossughed-Dowleh
(signed) H. Hassib

6. PROTOCOL SIGNED AT CONSTANTINOPLE ON NOVEMBER 4th (17th), 1913

The undersigned: His Excellency Sir Louis Mallet, Ambassador Extraordinary and Plenipotentiary of His Britannic Majesty to His Majesty the Sultan; His Excellency Mirza Mahmud Khan Kajar 'Ahd-i-Shamus Saltaneh, Ambassador

Extraordinary and Plenipotentiary of His Majesty the Shah of Persia to His Majesty the Sultan; His Excellency M. Michel de Giers, Ambassador Extraordinary and Plenipotentiary of His Majesty the Emperor of Russia to His Majesty the Sultan; His Highness Prince Said Halim Pasha, Grand Vizier and Minister for Foreign Affairs of the Ottoman Empire; have met for the purpose of recording in the present Protocol the Agreement concluded between their respective Governments with regard to the Turco-Persian boundary.

They began by recapitulating the progress, up to date, of the negotiations recently instituted among them.

The Joint Commission provided for in Article 1 of the Protocol signed at Teheran between the Imperial Ottoman Embassy and the Persian Minister for Foreign Affairs with a view to determining the bases for the negotiations relating to the delimitation of the Turco-Persian boundary held eighteen meetings, the first on May 12th (25th) and the last on August 9th (22nd), 1912.

On August 9th (22nd), 1912, the Imperial Russian Embassy at Constantinople addressed to the Sublime Porte, under No. 264, a note stating that "the Imperial Government considers that too much emphasis cannot be laid on the necessity of putting into effect without delay the explicit stipulations of the Treaty of Erzerum, which are tantamount to the restoration of the status quo of 1848."

The Imperial Embassy at the same time forwarded to the Imperial Ottoman Government a memorandum showing in detail the frontier-line in conformity with the stipulations of the treaties in force.

The Imperial Ottoman Government replied to this communication by a note dated March 18th(31st), 1913, No. 30469/47. It stated that "the Sublime Porte, being anxious to comply with the desire expressed by the Imperial Russian Government by eliminating any cause of difference in its cordial relations with the latter, and wishing, further, to demonstrate to the Persian Government its entire good faith in regard to the dispute existing on the subject between the two countries, has decided to accept the line mentioned in the aforesaid note and memorandum of the Ambassador of His Majesty the Emperor of Russia for the delimitation of the northern part of the Turco-Persian frontier from Serdar Bulak to Bane — that is to say, down to the 36th parallel of latitude."

Nevertheless, the Imperial Ottoman Government suggested a number of modifications in the line proposed in the memorandum annexed to the note of the Imperial Russian Embassy dated August 9th (22nd), 1912, No. 264.

The Imperial Ottoman Government also appended to its note "an explanatory note on the situation of the Zohab boundaries and the arrangement that it would be able to accept in order to reach a final and equitable understanding with the Persian Government on that part of the frontier."

The Imperial Russian Embassy replied by a note dated March 28th (April 10th), 1913, No. 78. It noted the statement "by which the Imperial Ottoman Government recognizes as a principle for the delimitation of the

Ararat-Bane section the exact sense of Article 3 of the Treaty of 1848 , known as the Treaty of Erzerum, as set forth in the note of August 9th (22nd), 1912, No. 264." As regards the modifications proposed by the Sublime Porte, the Imperial Embassy stated (with a reservation on the question of Egri-chai) that it could not sufficiently emphasize the necessity of making no change in the line established in its note of August 9th (22nd), 1912.

As regards the question of Zohab, the Imperial Russian Embassy, while reserving the right to submit its detailed observations concerning that frontier, expressed "its opinion on the whole of the Ottoman draft, which does not seem to it to guarantee sufficiently, for the future, the maintenance of order and peace on the frontiers."

On April 20th (May 3rd), 1913, the Russian and British Embassies addressed an identic note to His Highness Prince Said Halim Pasha, accompanied by a memorandum summarizing their point of view regarding the delimitation of Zohab and the regions situate south of that district.

This exchange of notes was followed by conversations between Their Excellencies M. de Giers and Sir Gerard Lowther, of the one part, and His Late Highness Mahmud Shefket Pasha, of the other part. The result of these conversations was recorded in an *aide-mémoire* presented by His Excellency the Russian Ambassador to His Highness the Grand Vizier on June 6th, 1913, and in a note from the Sublime Porte addressed on June 26th (July 9th), 1913, No. 34553/95, to the Russian Embassy, and on July 12th, 1913, to the British Embassy.

On July 29th, 1913, a "declaration" was signed in London by Sir Edward Grey and His Highness Ibrahim Hakky Pasha concerning the demarcation of the southern boundary between Persia and Turkey.

The Imperial Russian Embassy then proceeded to recapitulate the principles of delimitation established in the correspondence concerning the Turco-Persian boundary. It addressed to the Sublime Porte a note dated August 5th (18th), 1913, No. 166. An identic note was addressed to the Sublime Porte by the British Embassy on the same date.

The Sublime Porte replied to these communications by identic notes dated September 23rd, 1913, No. 37063/113.

As a result of the subsequent negotiations, the four plenipotentiaries of Great Britain, Persia, Russia and Turkey, agreed on the following provisions:

I

It is agreed that the boundary between Persia and Turkey shall be defined as follows:

The boundary in the north shall start from boundary-mark No. XXXVII on the Turco-Russian frontier, situate close to Serdar Bulak, on the crest between Little and Great Ararat. It shall then drop southwards by way of the ridges, leaving on the Persian side the valley of Dambat, Sarnvitch, and the water system of Yarym-Kaya, which rises to the south of mount Ayubeg. The boundary shall then leave Bulakbashi, in Persia, and shall continue to follow the highest ridge, the southern extremity of which is situate at about 44°22' longitude and 30°28' latitude. Then, skirting the west side of the marsh which extends to the west of Yarym-Kaya, the boundary shall cross the Sary-Su stream, pass between the villages of Girde-baran (Turkish) and Bazyrgan (Persian), and, ascending to the ridge to the west of Bazyrgan, follow the watershed formed by the Saranli, Zenduli, Gir-Kelime, Kanly-baba, Geduki-Khasineh, and Deveji ridges.

After Deveji, the line shall cross the valley of Egri-chai at the place to be designated by the Delimitation Commission in conformity with the status quo, leaving the villages of Nado and Nifto in Persia.

The ownership of the village of Kyzyl-Kaya (Bellasor) shall be established after an examination of the geographical situation of the village, the western side of the watershed in that region being allocated to Turkey, and the eastern side to Persia.

Should the final boundary line leave outside Ottoman territory a section of the road which passes close to Kyzyl-Kaya and connects the district of Bayazid with the province of Van, it is understood that the Persian Government shall give free passage over this section of the road to the Imperial Ottoman Posts and to travelers and goods, other than military troops and convoys.

The frontier shall then ascend to the ridges forming the watershed: Kyzyl-Ziaret Sarychimene, Dumanlu, Kara-burga, the hill between the reservoirs of Ayry-chai (Persian) and of Jelli-gol (Turkish), Avdal-dashi, Reshkan, the hill between Akhurek and Tavin Bevra-begzadan, Gevri-Mahine, Khydyr-baba, Avristan.

As regards Kotur, the Protocol of July 15th (28th), 1880, known as the Protocol of Sary-Kamiche, shall be applied in such a way that the village of Kevlik shall remain in Turkey, and the villages of Bilejik, Razi, Gharatil (Haratil), the two Jelliks, and Panamerik shall remain in Persia.

The frontier following the Mir-Omar ridge shall ascend the mountain of Surava, and leaving Khanyga on the Turkish side, shall pass by way of the watershed formed by the pass of Borush-Khuran, the mountain of Haravil, Beleko, Shinetal, Sardul, Gulamli, Kepper, Bergabend, Peri-Khan, Iskander, Avene, and Kotul. The valley of Bajirga shall remain in Turkey, and the villages of Sartyk and Sero in Persia, and the frontier shall pass from the southern extremity of Kotur over the ridge rising to the west of the Persian village of Behik, and, following the peaks of Seri-Baydost, shall join the crest of Mount Zont.

From Mount Zont the frontier shall follow continuously the watershed between the Persian districts of Tergever, Desht, and Mergever, and the Turkish sanjak [district] of Hakkiari — that is to say, the crests of Shiveh-Shishali, Chil-Chovri, Chel-Berdir, Kuna-Koter, Kazi-beg, Avukh, Mai-Helaneh, the mountains to the west of Binar and Delamper; then, leaving on the Persian side the basin emptying by way of Ushnu into the lake of Urumiya, including the sources of the Gadyr river known as Abiserigadyr (the valley of which is situated to the south of Delamper and to the east of Mount Girdeh), it shall reach the pass of Keleh-Shin.

To the south of Keleh-Shin the frontier shall leave on the Persian side the reservoir of Lavene, including the valley of Chumi-Geli (situate to the east of Zerdegel and to the south-west of Spi-rez), and on the Turkish side the waters of Revnaduz, and shall pass by the following peaks and passes: Siah-Kuh, Zerdeh-Gel, Boz, Barzin, Ser-shiva, Kevi-Khoja-Ibrahim. Thence the frontier shall continue to follow towards the south the main chain of Kandil, leaving on the Persian side the basin of the affluents of Kialu on the right side: the streams Purdanan Khydyrava and Talkhatan.

It is understood that the Turkish tribes which are in the habit of spending the summer in the said valleys at the Gadyr and Lavene springs shall still have the use of their pastures under the same conditions as in the past.

Having reached the summit of Seri-Kele-Kelin, the line shall pass over Zinvi-Jasusan and the pass of Bamin, and shall cross the Vezne river near the Purde-Berdan bridge. The Delimitation Commission will have to decide as to the future of the village of Shenieh, on the basis of the general principle of the status quo.

After Purde-Berdan, the frontier shall ascend over the chains of Foka-baba-kyr, Berde-spian, Berde-Abul-Fath and the pass of Kaniresh. It shall then follow the watershed formed by Lagav-Ghird, Donleri, the pass of Khan-Ahmed, and the southern extremity of Tepe-Salos. The frontier will thus pass between the villages of Kandol (Turkish) and Kesh-keshiva and Mazynava (Persian), and reach the course of the Kialu river (the Little Zab).

After joining the course of the Kialu river, the frontier shall follow it upstream, leaving on the Persian side the right bank (the Alani-ajem) and on the Turkish side the left bank of that river. On reaching the mouth of the Khileh-resh river (an affluent of the Kialu on the left side), the frontier shall follow the course of that river upstream, leaving on the Persian side the villages of Alot, Kovero, etc., and on the Turkish side the district of Alani-Mavont. At the south-western extremity of Mount Balu, the frontier shall leave the course of the Hileh-resh river, and, ascending over the north-west extremity of the Surkew chain, extending to the south of the Hileh-resh river, shall pass over the Surkew ridge, leaving the districts of Siwel and Shive-Kel on the Turkish side.

On reaching the astronomical point of Surkew almost at latitude 35°49′, the frontier shall pass in the direction of the village of Champar-aw, the future of which shall be decided by the Delimitation Commission on the basis of the accepted principle of the status quo. The line shall then ascend over the chain of mountains which form the frontier between the Persian district of Baneh and the Turkish district of Kyzyieja; Galash, Berdi-Kechel, Pusht-Hangajal, Du-bera, Parajal, and Spi-Kana, after which it shall reach the pass of Now-Khuvan. Thence, still following the watershed, the frontier shall turn southwards and then westwards, passing by way of the summits of Vul-Guza, Pushti-Shehidan, Hazar-Mal, Bali-Keder, Keleh-Melaik, and Kuhi-Koce-resha, separating the Turkish district of Teretul from the Persian district of Merivan.

From there, the frontier shall follow the course of the Khalil-Abad brook downstream as far as its confluence with the Chami-Kyzylja, and then this last-named river upstream as far as the mouth of its left affluent flowing from the village of Bnava-Suta; it shall follow this Bnava-Suta brook upstream and, by way of the passes of Keli-Naveh-Sar and Keli-Piran, shall reach the pass of Surene, known, it appears, by the name of Chigan (or Chakan).

The main chain of Avroman, extending in the direction north-west–south-east, shall then form the frontier between Persia and the Ottoman district of Shehrisor. On reaching the peak of Kemadjar (south-east of Kala-Selm and north-west of Sheri-Avroman), the frontier shall continue to follow the main ridge as far as its ramification on the western side, rising to the north of the valley of Dere-Vuli, leaving the villages of Khan-Germela and Nowsud on the Persian side. For the remainder of the frontier as far as Sirvan, the Commission shall — by way of exception — delimit the ground, taking into consideration such changes as may have occurred there between the year 1848 and the year 1905.

South of Sirvan, the frontier shall begin close to the mouth of the Chami-Zimkan, shall pass by way of the Beyzel (Bezel) mountain, and shall descend to the Chemi-Zerishk watercourse. Next, following the watershed between this last-named watercourse and the river which, rising in the Bend-Bemo, bears, according to the identic map, the name of Pushti-Gherav (Arkhevendu), it shall ascend to the summit of Bend-Bemo.

After following the ridge of Bamu (Bemo), the frontier, on reaching the defile of Derbendi-Dehul (Derbendi-Hur), shall follow the course of the Zengeneh (Abbasan) river as far as the point nearest to the summit of the Shevaldir (astronomical point) and situate below the village of Mamyshan. It shall ascend this summit and shall next pass by way of the crests of the hills forming a watershed between the plans of Tileku and Serkaleh, then by way of the chains of Khuli-Baghan, Jebel-Ali-Beg, Bender-Chok-Chermik, Sengler, and Asengueran, as far as the point in the Tengi-Hammam defile situate opposite the northern extremity of the Karawiz mountains.

Thence the frontier shall follow the course of the river Kuretu as far as the village of that name. The future of the village of Kuretu shall be decided by the Delimitation Commission on the basis of the nationality of its inhabitants. Thence the frontier shall pass by way of the road between the villages of Kuretu and Kush-Kurrek, then along the crests of Mounts Kishka and Ak-Dag, and then, leaving Kala-Sebzi in Persia, it shall turn southwards as far as the Ottoman post of Kanibez. Thence it shall follow the course of the Elvend river upstream as far as the point a quarter of an hour's distance downstream from its confluence with the Gilan watercourse; from that point it shall continue as far as the Naft-Su, skirting the Ab-Bakhshan in accordance with the line agreed upon with the late Mahmud Shefket Pasha and shown roughly on the map annexed to the note of the Imperial Russian Embassy dated August 5th (18th), 1913, and leaving Naft-Mukataasy to Turkey. Thence, the frontier-line, following the Naft-Deressi, on reaching the point where the Kassri Shirin road cuts that waterway, shall continue along the mountains of Varbulend,

Koherigh-Keleshuvan, and Jebel-Gerebi (the extension of the Jebeli-Hamrinach in).

The Delimitation Commission shall draw up a special agreement for the distribution of the Gengir (Sumar) waters between the parties concerned.

The part of the frontier between Mendeli and the northern point of the line indicated in the declaration made in London on July 29th (Shuaib) between Hakky Pasha and Sir E. Grey not having yet been discussed in detail, the undersigned leave the establishment of that part of the frontier to the Delimitation Commission.

As regards delimitation from the region of Hawizeh as far as the sea, the frontier-line shall start from the place called Umm-Shir, where the Khor-el-Duvel divides from the Khor-el-Azem. Umm-Shir is situate east of the junction of the Khor-el-Muhaisin with the Khor-el-Azem, nine miles north-west of Bisaitin, a place situated at latitude 31°43′29″. From Umm-Shirr, the line shall turn south-westwards as far as longitude 45° at the southern extremity of a small lake known also by the name of Azem and situate in the Khor-el-Azem some distance north-west of Shuaib. From this point the line shall continue to the south along the marsh as far as latitude 31°, which it shall follow directly eastwards as far as a point northeast of Kushk-i-Basra, so as to leave this place in Ottoman territory. From this point the line shall go southwards as far as the Khayeen canal at a point between the Nahr-Diaiji and the Nahr-Abu'l-Arabid; it shall follow the *medium filum aquae* of the Khayeen canal as far as the point where the latter joins the Shatt-al-Arab, at the mouth of the Nahr-Nazaileh. From this point the frontier shall follow the course of the Shatt-al-Arab as far as the sea, leaving under Ottoman sovereignty the river and all the islands therein, subject to the following conditions and exceptions:

(a) The following shall belong to Persia: (1) the island of Muhalla and the two islands situate between the latter and the left bank of the Shatt-al-Arab (Persian bank of Abadan); (2) the four islands between Shetait and Maawiyeh and the two islands opposite Mankuhi which are both dependencies of the island of Abadan; (3) any small islands now existing or that may be formed which are connected at low water with the island of Abadan or with Persian *terra firma* below Nahr-Nazaileh.

(b) The modern port and anchorage of Muhammara, above and below the junction of the river Karun with the Shatt-al-Arab, shall remain within Persian jurisdiction in conformity with the Treaty of Erzerum; the Ottoman right of usage of this part of the river shall not, however, be affected thereby, nor shall Persian jurisdiction extend to the parts of the river outside the anchorage.

(c) No change shall be made in the existing rights, usages and customs as regards fishing on the Persian bank of the Shatt-al-Arab, the word "bank" including also the lands connected with the coast at low water.

(d) Ottoman jurisdiction shall not extend over the parts of the Persian coast that may be temporarily covered by water at high tide or by other accidental causes. Persian jurisdiction, on its side, shall not be exercised over lands that may be temporarily or accidentally uncovered when the water is below the normal low-water level.

(e) The Sheik of Muhammara shall continue to enjoy in conformity with the Ottoman laws his rights of ownership in Ottoman territory.

The frontier-line established in the declaration is shown in red on the map annexed hereto.*

The parts of the frontier not detailed in the above-mentioned frontier-line shall be established on the basis of the principle of the status quo, in conformity with the stipulations of Article 3 of the Treaty of Erzerum.

II

The frontier-line shall be delimited on the spot by a Delimitation Commission, consisting of commissioners of the four Governments.

Each Government shall be represented on this Commission by a commissioner and a deputy commissioner. The latter shall take the commissioner's place on the Commission in case of need.

III

The Delimitation Commission, in the performance of the task devolving upon it, shall comply:

(1) With the provisions of the present Protocol;
(2) With the Rules of Procedure of the Delimitation Commission annexed (Annex [A]) to the present Protocol.

IV

In the event of a divergence of opinion in the Commission as to the boundary-line of any part of the frontier, the Ottoman and Persian commissioners shall submit a written statement of their respective points of view within forty-eight hours to the Russian and British commissioners, who shall hold a private meeting and shall give a decision on the questions in dispute and communicate their decision to their Ottoman and Persian colleagues. This

*Note by the Secretariat: This map was not annexed to the memorandum from the Persian Government.

decision shall be inserted in the Minutes of the plenary meeting and shall be recognized as binding on all four Governments.

V

As soon as part of the frontier has been delimited, such part shall be regarded as finally fixed and shall not be liable to subsequent examination or revision.

VI

As the work of delimitation proceeds, the Ottoman and Persian Governments shall have the right to establish posts on the frontier.

VII

It is understood that the concession granted by the Convention of May 28th, 1901 (9 sefer, 1319, of the Hegira), by the Government of His Imperial Majesty the Shah of Persia to William Knox D'Arcy and now being worked, in conformity with the provisions of Article 9 of the said Convention, by the Anglo-Persian Oil Company (Limited), having its registered office at Winchester House, London (the said Convention being referred to hereunder as "the Convention" in the Annex [B] to the present Protocol), shall remain in full and unrestricted force throughout the territories transferred by Persia to Turkey in virtue of the provisions of the present Protocol and of Annex [B] thereto.

VIII

The Ottoman and Persian Governments will distribute among the officials on the frontier a sufficient number of copies of the delimitation map drawn up by the Commission, together with copies of translations of the statement provided for in Article XV of the Commission's Rules of Procedure. It is understood, however, that the French text alone shall be regarded as authentic.

(signed) Louis Mallet
Ehtechamos-Saltaneh Mahmud
Michel de Giers
Said Halim

7. FRONTIER TREATY BETWEEN THE KINGDOM OF IRAQ AND THE EMPIRE OF IRAN WITH THE ANNEXED PROTOCOL SIGNED ON JULY 4th, 1937 IN TEHERAN

His Majesty the King of Iraq, of the one part
His Imperial Majesty the Shahinshah of Iran of the other part,
Sincerely desirous of consolidating the bonds of brotherly friendship and good understanding between the two States, and in order to settle definitely the frontier question between their two countries, have decided to conclude the present Treaty and for this purpose have appointed as their Plenipotentiaries:
His Majesty the King of Iraq:
His Excellency Dr. Naji al-Asil
Minister for Foreign Affairs
His Imperial Majesty the Shahinshah of Iran:
His Excellency Enayatollah Samiy
Minister for Foreign Affairs
who, having exchanged their full powers, found in good and due form, have agreed on the following:

ARTICLE 1

The High Contracting Parties agree that the following documents, with the exception of the modification specified in Article 2 of the present Treaty, are considered valid and that They are bound to observe them:
(a) The Protocol relating to the Turko-Persian Delimitation signed at Constantinople on November 4, 1913;
(b) The Proceedings of the Commission of Delimitation of the Frontier of 1914.

Having regard to the provisions of this Article and with the exception of the provisions made in the next following Article, the boundary line between the two States is that defined and traced by the above-mentioned Commission.

ARTICLE 2

The boundary line on reaching the furthest point of Shoteit Island (approximately latitude 30°17'25" North, longitude 48°19'28" East) rejoins, in a line drawn perpendicularly to the low-water mark, the thalweg of Shatt-al-Arab and follows it as far as a point situated opposite the existing jetty No. 1 of Abadan (approximately latitude 30°20'8.4" North, longitude 48°16'13" East). From this point the boundary line rejoins the line of low-water and follows the tracing of the frontier as described in the Proceedings of 1914.

ARTICLE 3

Immediately after the signature of the present treaty the High Contracting Parties shall appoint a Commission for the purpose of erecting frontier pillars, the location of which has been fixed by the Commission mentioned in paragraph (b) of Article 1 of the present treaty and of fixing additional pillars, which it considers useful to erect.

The composition of the Commission and the program of its work shall be fixed by a special arrangement between the two High Contracting Parties.

ARTICLE 4

The following provisions shall apply to the Shatt-al-Arab from the point where the land frontier of the two States descends into the said river as far as the open sea:

(a) The Shatt-al-Arab shall remain open to merchant ships of all countries equally. All dues levied shall be in the nature of payment for services rendered and intended solely to cover, in an equitable manner, the expenses of maintaining the navigability and improving the navigable channel and the approach of the Shatt-al-Arab from the seaward side, or to meet expenditures incurred in the interest of navigation. The said dues shall be calculated on the basis of the official tonnage of ships or their draught, or both together.

(b) The Shatt-al-Arab shall remain open to the passage of war ships and other vessels belonging to the two High Contracting Parties used for non-commercial purposes.

(c) The fact that in the Shatt-al-Arab the boundary line sometimes follows the low-water mark and sometimes the thalweg or the *medium filum aquae* does not prejudice in any way the two High Contracting Parties' right of user in the whole course of the river.

ARTICLE 5

The two High Contracting Parties, having a common interest in the navigation of the Shatt-al-Arab as defined in Article 4 of the present Treaty, undertake to conclude a convention concerning the maintenance and improvement of the navigable channel, dredging, pilotage, dues to be levied, sanitary measures, measures to be taken for the prevention of smuggling, and all other matters relating to navigation in the Shatt-al-Arab as defined in Article 4 of the present Treaty.

ARTICLE 6

The present treaty shall be ratified and the instruments of ratification shall be exchanged at Baghdad as soon as possible. It shall come into force as from the day when this exchange takes place.

In witness whereof the Plenipotentiaries of the two High Contracting Parties have signed the present Treaty.

DONE at Teheran, in Arabic, Persian and French, of which, in case of difference, the French text shall prevail, the fourth day of July, one thousand nine hundred and thirty-seven.

(Signed) Naji Al-Asil
(Signed) Samiy

PROTOCOL

At the time of proceeding to the signing of the Treaty concerning the delimitation of the boundaries between Iraq and Iran, the two High Contracting Parties have agreed as follows:

I

The geographical coordinates shown approximately in Article 2 of the above-mentioned Treaty shall be definitely fixed by a Commission of experts composed of an equal number of members nominated by each of the High Contracting Parties.

The geographical coordinates so determined definitely within the limits fixed in the above-mentioned Article shall be recorded in a *proces-verbaux* which, after having been signed by the members of the above-mentioned Commission, shall be an integral part of the Boundary Treaty.

II

The High Contracting Parties undertake to conclude the convention mentioned in Article 5 of the Treaty in the course of one year from the entry into force of the Treaty.

If, notwithstanding the efforts exerted by Them, this convention is not concluded in the course of the year, this period may be extended by common agreement of the High Contracting Parties.

The Imperial Government of Iran agrees that during the period of one year mentioned in the first paragraph of this article and during the extension of this period, if this extension takes place, the Royal Government of Iraq shall undertake on the bases now in force all matters which are to be dealt with by this Convention. The Royal Government of Iraq shall, by means of biannual communications, keep the Imperial Government of Iran informed of the works carried out, the dues levied, the expenses incurred and of all other measures taken.

III

The authorization given by one of the High Contracting Parties to a war ship or other public vessel used for non-commercial purposes belonging to a third State to enter ports belonging to the said High Contracting Party and situated on the Shatt-al-Arab shall be regarded as having been given by the other High Contracting Party in order that such vessel may make use of its waters when passing through the Shatt-al-Arab.

Nevertheless, that High Contracting Party who has given such an authorization must inform the other Party thereof immediately.

IV

It is understood that subject to the rights of Iran in Shatt-al-Arab, nothing in this Treaty prejudices the rights of Iraq and its obligations undertaken towards the British Government regarding the Shatt-al-Arab in accordance with Article 4 of the Treaty dated June 30, 1930, and paragraph 7 of its Annexure, signed on the same day.

V

The present Protocol shall be ratified at the same time as the Treaty concerning the delimitation of the frontiers of which it shall form, as an Annexure, an integral part. It shall come into force at the same time as this Treaty.

The present Protocol is made in Arabic, Persian and French. In case of difference the French text shall prevail.

DONE at Teheran in duplicate, on the fourth day of July, one thousand nine hundred and thirty-seven.

(Signed) Naji Al-Asil
(Signed) Samiy

8. ALGIERS DECLARATION OF MARCH 6th, 1975. JOINT COMMUNIQUÉ BETWEEN IRAQ AND IRAN

During the meeting in Algiers of the Summit Conference of the Member Countries of OPEC and on the initiative of President BOUMEDIENNE, His Majesty the SHAHINSHAH of Iran and H. E. SADDAM HUSSEIN, Vice President of the Revolutionary Command Council of Iraq, held two meetings and had lengthy discussions on the subject of relations between the two countries.

These meetings, which took place in the presence of President BOUMEDIENNE, were marked by great frankness and a sincere wish on both sides to reach a final and permanent solution to all the problems existing between the two countries.

In application of the principles of territorial integrity, the inviolability of borders and non-interference in internal affairs, the two contractual parties have decided:

1. To effect a definitive demarcation of their land frontiers on the basis of the Protocol of Constantinople, 1913, and the *proces-verbaux* of the Delimitation of Frontiers Commission of 1914.
2. To delimit their fluvial frontiers according to the thalweg line.
3. Accordingly, the two parties will restore security and mutual trust along their common boundaries, and hence will commit themselves to exercising a strict and effective control over their common boundaries with a view to putting a definitive end to all acts of infiltration of a subversive character no matter where they originate from.
4. The two parties also agreed to consider the arrangements referred to above as integral elements of a comprehensive solution. Hence any impairment of any of their components shall naturally be contrary to the spirit of the Algiers agreement.

The two parties will remain in permanent touch with President BOUMEDIENNE who will offer, in case of need, the fraternal assistance of Algeria to implement the decisions which have been taken.

The parties have decided to reestablish traditional ties of good neighborliness and friendship, particularly by the elimination of all negative factors in their relations, the continuous exchange of views on questions of mutual interest and the development of mutual cooperation.

The two parties solemnly declare that the area should be kept free from any outside interference.

The Ministers of Foreign Affairs of Iran and Iraq met in the presence of the Algerian Foreign Minister on 15 March 1975 in Teheran to fix the details of work for the Joint Iraqi-Iranian Commission created to implement the decisions reached above by mutual agreement.

In accordance with the wishes of both parties, Algeria will be invited to all the meetings of the Joint Iraqi-Iranian Commission.

The Joint Commission will draw up its timetable and work-plan so as to meet, in case of need, alternatively in Baghdad and Teheran.

His Majesty the SHAHINSHAH has accepted with pleasure the invitation which has been conveyed to him, on behalf of H. E. President AHMED HASSAN EL-BAKR, to make an official visit to Iraq; the date of this visit will be fixed by mutual agreement.

Furthermore, H. E. SADDAM HUSSEIN has agreed to make an official visit to Iran on a date to be agreed between the two parties.

His Majesty the SHAHINSHAH and H. E. Vice President SADDAM

HUSSEIN wish to thank particularly and warmly President HOUARI BOUMEDIENNE who, acting from fraternal and disinterested motives, has facilitated the establishment of direct contacts between the leaders of the two countries and, as a result, has contributed to the establishment of a new era in relations between Iran and Iraq in the higher interest of the future of the region concerned.

Algiers, 6 March 1975

9. TREATY OF INTERNATIONAL BOUNDARIES AND GOOD NEIGHBORLINESS BETWEEN IRAQ AND IRAN SIGNED ON JUNE 13th, 1975

His Imperial Majesty the Shahinshah of Iran,
His Excellency the President of the Republic of Iraq,

Considering the sincere desire of the two Parties as expressed in the Algiers Agreement of 6 March 1975, to achieve a final and lasting solution to all the problems pending between the two countries,

Considering that the two Parties have carried out the definitive redemarcation of their land frontier on the basis of the Constantinople Protocol of 1913 and the minutes of the meetings of the Frontier Delimitation Commission of 1914 and have delimited their river frontier along the thalweg,

Considering their desire to restore security and mutual trust throughout the length of their common frontier,

Considering the ties of geographical proximity, history, religion, culture and civilization which bind the peoples of Iran and Iraq,

Desirous of strengthening their bonds of friendship and good neighborliness, expanding their economic and cultural relations and promoting exchanges and human relations between their peoples on the basis of the principles of territorial integrity, the inviolability of frontiers and non-interference in internal affairs,

Resolved to work towards the introduction of a new era in friendly relations between Iran and Iraq based on full respect for the national independence and sovereign equality of States,

Convinced that they are helping thereby to implement the principles and achieve the purposes and objectives of the Charter of the United Nations,

Have decided to conclude this Treaty and have appointed as their plenipotentiaries:

His Imperial Majesty the Shahinshah of Iran:

His Excellency Abbas Ali Khalatbary, Minister for Foreign Affairs of Iran.

His Excellency the President of the Republic of Iraq:

His Excellency Saadoun Hamadi, Minister for Foreign Affairs of Iraq.

Who, having exchanged their full powers, found to be in good and due form, have agreed as follows:

ARTICLE 1

The High Contracting Parties confirm that the State land frontier between Iraq and Iran shall be that which has been redemarcated on the basis of and in accordance with the provisions of the Protocol concerning the redemarcation of the land frontier, and the annexes thereto, attached to this Treaty.

ARTICLE 2

The High Contracting Parties confirm that the State frontier in the Shatt Al Arab shall be that which has been delimited on the basis of and in accordance with the provisions of the Protocol concerning the delimitation of the river frontier, and the annexes thereto, attached to this Treaty.

ARTICLE 3

The High Contracting Parties undertake to exercise strict and effective permanent control over the frontier in order to put an end to any infiltration of a subversive nature from any source, on the basis of and in accordance with the provision of the Protocol concerning frontier security, and the annex thereto, attached to this Treaty.

ARTICLE 4

The High Contracting Parties confirm that the provisions of the three Protocols, and the annexes thereto, referred to in articles 1, 2 and 3 above and attached to this Treaty as an integral part thereof shall be final and permanent. They shall not be infringed under any circumstances and shall constitute the indivisible elements of an over-all settlement. Accordingly, a breach of any of the components of this over-all settlement shall clearly be incompatible with the spirit of the Algiers Agreement.

ARTICLE 5

In keeping with the inviolability of the frontiers of the two States and strict respect for their territorial integrity, the High Contracting Parties confirm that the course of their land and river frontiers shall be inviolable, permanent and final.

ARTICLE 6

1. In the event of a dispute regarding the interpretation or implementation of this Treaty, the three Protocols or the annexes thereto, any solution to such a dispute shall strictly respect the course of the Iraqi-Iranian frontier referred to in articles 1 and 2 above, and shall take into account the need to maintain security on the Iraqi-Iranian frontier in accordance with article 3 above.

2. Such disputes shall be resolved in the first instance by the High Contracting Parties, by means of direct bilateral negotiations to be held within two months after the date on which one of the Parties so requested.

3. If no agreement is reached, the High Contracting Parties shall have recourse, within a three-month period, to the good offices of a friendly third State.

4. Should one of the two Parties refuse to have recourse to good offices or should the good offices procedure fail, the dispute shall be settled by arbitration within a period of not more than one month after the date of such refusal or failure.

5. Should the High Contracting Parties disagree as to the arbitration procedure, one of the High Contracting Parties may have recourse, within fifteen days after such disagreement was recorded, to a court of arbitration.

With a view to establishing such a court of arbitration each of the High Contracting Parties shall, in respect of each dispute to be resolved, appoint one of its nationals as arbitrators and the two arbitrators shall choose an umpire. Should the High Contracting Parties fail to appoint their arbitrators within one month after the date on which one of the Parties received a request for arbitration from the other Party, or should the arbitrators fail to reach agreement on the choice of the umpire before that time-limit expires, the High Contracting Party which requested arbitration shall be entitled to request the President of the International Court of Justice to appoint the arbitrators or the umpire, in accordance with the procedures of the Permanent Court of Arbitration.

6. The decision of the court of arbitration shall be binding on and enforceable by the High Contracting Parties.

7. The High Contracting Parties shall each defray half the costs of arbitration.

ARTICLE 7

This Treaty, the three Protocols and the annexes thereto shall be registered in accordance with Article 102 of the Charter of the United Nations.

ARTICLE 8

This Treaty, the three Protocols and the annexes thereto shall be ratified by each of the High Contracting Parties in accordance with its domestic law.

This Treaty, the three Protocols and the annexes thereto shall enter into force on the date of the exchange of the instruments of ratification in Teheran.

IN WITNESS WHEREOF the Plenipotentiaries of the High Contracting Parties have signed this Treaty, the three Protocols and the annexes thereto.

DONE at Baghdad, on 13 June 1975.

(Signed)
Abbas Ali Khalatbary
Minister for Foreign
   Affairs of Iran

(Signed)
Saadoun Hamadi
Minister for Foreign
   Affairs of Iraq

This Treaty, the three Protocols and the annexes thereto were signed in the presence of His Excellency Abdel-Aziz Bouteflika, Member of the Council of the Revolution and Minister for Foreign Affairs of Algeria.

(Signed)

10. PROTOCOL CONCERNING THE DELIMITATION OF THE RIVER FRONTIER BETWEEN IRAN AND IRAQ

Pursuant to the decisions taken in the Algiers communiqué of 6 March 1975,
The two Contracting Parties have agreed as follows:

ARTICLE 1

The two Contracting Parties hereby declare and recognize that the State river frontier between Iran and Iraq in the Shatt Al Arab has been delimited along the thalweg by the Mixed Iraqi-Iranian-Algerian Committee on the basis of the following:

1. The Teheran Protocol of 17 March 1975;

2. The record of the Meeting of Ministers for Foreign Affairs, signed at Baghdad on 20 April 1975, approving, *inter alia*, the record of the Committee to Delimit the River Frontier, signed on 16 April 1975 on board the Iraqi ship *El Thawra* in the Shatt Al Arab;

3. Common hydrographic charts, which have been verified on the spot and corrected and on which the geographical coordinates of the 1975 frontier crossing points have been indicated; these charts have been signed by the hydrographic experts of the Mixed Technical Commission and counter-signed by the heads of the Iranian, Iraqi and Algerian delegations to the Committee. The said charts, listed hereinafter, are annexed to this Protocol and form an integral part thereof:

Chart No. 1: Entrance to the Shatt Al Arab, No. 3842, published by the British Admiralty;

Chart No. 2: Inner Bar to Kabda Point, No. 3843, published by the British Admiralty;

Chart No. 3: Kabda Point to Abadan, No. 3844, published by the British Admiralty;

Chart No. 4: Abadan to Jazirat Ummat Tuwaylah, No. 3845, published by the British Admiralty.

ARTICLE 2

1. The frontier line in the Shatt Al Arab shall follow the thalweg, i.e., the median line of the main navigable channel at the lowest navigable level, starting from the point at which the land frontier between Iran and Iraq enters the Shatt Al Arab and continuing to the sea.

2. The frontier line, as defined in paragraph 1 above, shall vary with changes brought about by natural causes in the main navigable channel. The frontier line shall not be affected by other changes unless the two Contracting Parties conclude a special agreement to that effect.

3. The occurrence of any of the changes referred to in paragraph 2 above shall be attested jointly by the competent technical authorities of the two Contracting Parties.

4. Any change in the bed of the Shatt Al Arab brought about by natural causes which would involve a change in the national character of the two States' respective territory or of landed property, constructions, or techni-cal or other installations shall not change the course of the frontier line, which shall continue to follow the thalweg in accordance with the provisions of paragraph 1 above.

5. Unless an agreement is reached between the two Contracting Parties concerning the transfer of the frontier line to the new bed, the water shall be re-directed at the joint expense of both Parties to the bed existing in 1975 — as marked on the four common charts listed in article 1, paragraph 3, above — should one of the parties so request within two years after the date on which the occurrence of the change was attested by either of the two Parties. Until such time, both Parties shall retain their previous rights of navigaton and of use over the water of the new bed.

ARTICLE 3

1. The river frontier between Iran and Iraq in the Shatt Al Arab, as defined in article 2 above, is represented by the relevant line drawn on the common charts referred to in article 1, paragraph 3, above.

2. The two Contracting Parties have agreed to consider that the river frontier shall end at the straight line connecting the two banks of the Shatt Al Arab, at its mouth, at the astronomical lowest low-water mark. This straight line has been indicated on the common hydrographic charts referred to in article 1, paragraph 3, above.

ARTICLE 4

The frontier line as defined in articles 1, 2 and 3 of this Protocol shall also divide vertically the air space and the subsoil.

ARTICLE 5

With a view to eliminating any source of controversy, the two Contracting Parties shall establish a Mixed Iraqi-Iranian Commission to settle, within two months, any questions concerning the status of landed property, constructions, or technical or other installations, the national character of which may be affected by the delimitation of the Iranian-Iraqi river frontier, either through repurchase or compensation or any other suitable arrangement.

ARTICLE 6

Since the task of surveying the Shatt Al Arab has been completed and the common hydrographic chart referred to in article 1, paragraph 3, above has been drawn up, the two Contracting Parties have agreed that a new survey of the Shatt Al Arab shall be carried out jointly, once every 10 years, with effect from the date of signature of this Protocol. However, each of the two Parties shall have the right to request new surveys, to be carried out jointly, before the expiry of the 10-year period.

The two Contracting Parties shall each defray half the cost of such surveys.

ARTICLE 7

1. Merchant vessels, State vessels and warships of the two Contracting Parties shall enjoy freedom of navigation in the Shatt Al Arab and in any

part of the navigable channels in the territorial sea which lead to the mouth of the Shatt Al Arab, irrespective of the line delimiting the territorial sea of each of the two countries.

2. Vessels of third countries used for purposes of trade shall enjoy freedom of navigation, on an equal and non-discriminatory basis, in the Shatt Al Arab and in any part of the navigable channels in the territorial sea which lead to the mouth of the Shatt Al Arab, irrespective of the line delimiting the territorial sea of each of the two countries.

3. Either of the two Contracting Parties may authorize foreign warships visiting its ports to enter the Shatt Al Arab, provided such vessels do not belong to a country in a state of belligerency, armed conflict or war with either of the two Contracting Parties and provided the other party is so notified no less than 72 hours in advance.

4. The two Contracting Parties shall in every case refrain from authorizing the entry to the Shatt Al Arab of merchant vessels belonging to a country in a state of belligerency, armed conflict or war with either of the two Parties.

ARTICLE 8

1. Rules governing navigation in the Shatt Al Arab shall be drawn up by a mixed Iranian-Iraqi Commission, in accordance with the principle of equal rights of navigation for both States.

2. The two Contracting Parties shall establish a Commission to draw up rules governing the prevention and control of pollution in the Shatt Al Arab.

3. The two Contracting Parties undertake to conclude subsequent agreements on the questions referred to in paragraphs 1 and 2 of this article.

ARTICLE 9

The two Contracting Parties recognize that the Shatt Al Arab is primarily an international waterway, and undertake to refrain from any operation that might hinder navigation in the Shatt Al Arab or in any part of those navigable channels in the territorial sea of either of the two countries that lead to the mouth of the Shatt Al Arab.

DONE at Baghdad, on 13 June 1975.

(Signed)   (Signed)
Abbas Ali Khalatbary   Saadoun Hamadi
Minister for Foreign   Minister for Foreign
   Affairs of Iran   Affairs of Iraq

Signed in the presence of His Excellency Abdel-Aziz Bouteflika, Member of the Council Revolution and Minister for Foreign Affairs of Algeria.

(Signed)

$\mathcal{A}ppendix\ 2$

IDEOLOGICAL AND POLITICAL DOCUMENTS

1. SOME THEORETICAL PRINCIPLES OF ARAB UNITY AS APPROVED BY THE SIXTH NATIONAL CONGRESS OF THE ARAB BA'ATH SOCIALIST PARTY, OCTOBER 1963

*T*HE PARTY arose in circumstances where the traditional concept of Arab nationalism prevailed, and the call of Arab nationalism and unity was often used by the traditional political organizations as a demagogic instrument to mislead the masses with the object of perpetuating both fragmentation and backwardness.

The Arab Ba'ath Socialist Party was the first movement in the Arab homeland that really recognized the essence of the Arab cause and set it in its historical and revolutionary context:

a. In the first stage of its struggle, the Party affirmed the priority of Arab unity and gave it preponderance and moral precedence over socialism and freedom, considering that it was both erroneous and injurious to view or deal with the vital problems of the Arabs, both individually and as a whole, on any other basis than that of the axiom of "the unity of the Arab nation." The Party has always stressed that the idea of Arab unity must always accompany and direct the struggle of the Arab people for freedom and socialism.

The Party's insistence on the priority of unity was, from an objective point of view, a profound and admirable expression of the interests of the masses in particular and those of the Arab people in general, because the course of events and of development have proved that hopes of unity express, within a true historical framework, the masses' need for liberation.

b. The Party was the first to give Arab unity its true revolutionary dimension, seeing it as an important factor in making all real change in Arab society more profound, because the freedom for which every Arab region is striving for individually cannot be as profound, comprehensive and positively significant as that achieved by the Arab nation as a whole. Similarly, the material foundations of socialism can only be fully effective when its field is the whole Arab nation as an economic and human unity.

c. The Party was the first movement in the Arab homeland to link nationalist struggle to socialist struggle and to affirm that they were inseparable. It was this that transformed the struggle of the Arab nationalist from mere traditional bourgeois sloganeering into popular mass struggle. The practical result of this linking was that the call for Arab unity was turned into a sweeping mass movement and, thanks to this, unity was no longer merely a dream, but became a real and living reality embodied by the masses in their day-by-day struggle. Thus, nationalist struggle and socialist struggle evolved together, inseparably attached, each giving the other its energies and its impetus, each offering to the other its own wide horizons and profound scope.

The Party brought the call of Arab nationalism down from the sky of the aristocracy to the ground of the masses. It was thus transformed into a motive force that made the Arab people experience the problem of unity in their daily lives, and it became a basic moving force in the struggle of the Arab millions.

d. The Party was not content with presenting these themes as mere theory; they became the practical content of its policy and the incentive of its struggle. The Party was organized at the level of the Arab homeland, thus embodying the idea that the Arab countries are an indivisible unit; and it regarded unified and organized Arab action as the only serious solution of the problems of the Arab nation. Thus, from the start, the Party has been the historical movement that established as its point of departure an authentic concept of Arabism involving the absolute rejection of regionalism; and its day-by-day struggle has been a strict and radical rejection of regionalism at both the theoretical and the practical levels.

2

These are the positive aspects of the Party's basic principles as regards the issue of unity. However, these basic principles also have negative aspects.

a. In general the Party stated the problem of achieving unity correctly when it maintained that the unification of struggle is the way to unity.

Unity of struggle does indeed eliminate feelings of isolation and fragmentation; but it is not the objective instrument for the establishment of unity nor an adequate means of ensuring its safety and continuity.

The Party has always affirmed that Arab unity is not a mere agglomeration or coming together of the parts of the Arab homeland, but a cohesion and then fusion of those parts. Therefore unity is a revolution, with all the dimensions, meanings and levels implied by the word revolution; it is a revolution because it involves the elimination of regional interests that have lived, expanded and left their residues throughout the centuries. It is also a revolution because it confronts interests and classes that are opposed to and resist unity; also because unity is a revolution it must have its objective instruments, which are the vanguard popular revolutionary movements. However, the Party has never formulated theoretical guidelines showing the way to unity and indicating how it is to be achieved, and what safeguards are necessary for its protection and development. The effect of this was to be seen in the weakness of the theoretical and practical bases of the 1958 union [the formation of the United Arab Republic between Egypt and Syria], as a result of which there were inadequate safeguards for its protection against decline and collapse. The effects of this inadequacy also explain, to a great extent, the shock sustained by the Party in all regions, and in the Syrian region in particular, and the deviation or retrogression which led some people to doubt the very principle of unity.

b. The fact that the Party came into existence in disturbed historical conditions did much to determine the kind of slogans it employed at specific stages and its mode of political action. In order to transform unity from a dream anesthetizing the masses' will to revolt, into a national goal stimulating their day-to-day struggle, it was necessary for the Party, in the first stages of its struggle — which may be called the stage of making the masses nationally conscious — to concentrate constantly on unity, and stress its fundamental importance for the support of any other needs of the masses. This led the Party to adopt attitudes which might indeed, constitute a useful weapon in the context of the circumstances in which they were adopted; but such attitudes will become deviation, and endanger the cause of unity itself, if they are regarded as something absolute. In actual fact, these negative circumstances and this distorted and backward situation lasted a long time, making attitudes adopted because of the circumstances of a particular stage into part of the Party heritage, which molded the thinking of Party members at the local level, as well as the leadership itself, and transformed passive receptivity into positive action.

The fact that no complete theory was laid down for the Party at the start of its struggle and that it relied on experience to complement its theory and make it more profound, did indeed save the Party from ideological rigidity and intellectual petrifaction. But at the same time, it left the Party open to a passive receptivity to influences which were undefined and undisciplined by theory. As a result of the succession of battles it had to fight, the Party in many cases did no more than react to the events that confronted popular struggle. Although its sound nationalist principle and its belief that the economic, social and political situations were inseparable ensured that these reactions did not take the form of deviation, an exclusive reliance on this view is not good when the battle changes from a confrontation with the enemies of the nationalist and socialist cause, and becomes a matter of translating principles into reality at the stage of national construction.

c. From the start, the nationalist struggle of the Arab people has been faced with two challenges which, though they derive from mutually contradictory standpoints, coincide in their hostility to the Arab struggle. One is the colonialist reactionary challenge, which has striven to perpetuate fragmentation by provoking and reinforcing social, political and economic contradictions and by striking at the revolutionary movements which are the only objective instruments for the achievement of unity. The other is the challenge of local communism, which does, indeed, oppose colonialism, but agrees with it in combating unity and nationalist sentiment, even though its hostility has taken a different form from that of colonialism and its agents, the reactionaries. The ferocious hostility to the nationalist trend evinced by the local communist movement in all its attitudes, both practical and theoretical, led the Party to regard the nationalist trend as something practically sacred. For this challenge was extremely grave, especially as it came at a time when reaction had distorted the nationalist trend and made it a screen for its own objectives. The Party succeeded in making the nationalist trend the basic political force in the present Arab battle and the common denominator of all the parties and groups active in the Arab field, although for many of these the nationalist facade was no more than a misleading screen. The success achieved by the Party did have certain negative effects resulting from the ferocity of the battle and the character of its enemies; in some of its writings the Party presented an idealist concept of Arab nationalism which was open to an interpretation that was sometimes incompatible with both science and the development of history, so that for some party members, Arab nationalism became a petrified and frozen concept.

This is why, in some of the writings of that stage, which were characterized by antagonism to the deviation of the local communist movement and by mere passivity, the socialist cause was regarded as a branch of the nationalist cause; in the case of some people this obscured the reality of class struggle as having a true significance for and constituting a basic fighting principle of Arab nationalism.

If the writings, relevant to a specific stage, by which the Party confronted the local communist movement's hostility to the nationalist trend, are seen as expressing a constant attitude and a theoretical principle, the Party may be induced to take the position of arbitrator and mediator between the classes. Although such an attitude was reasonable in the first stages of nationalist struggle and could be justified under the circumstances prevailing at the time, it has no justificaiton whatsoever at the stage of socialist construction which the Party has now reached. Thus, should this attitude continue and become firmly entrenched, there is a danger of the Party becoming frozen in middle-of-the-road attitudes and its socialist impetus being paralyzed.

3

Arab unity is not a theorem requiring proof; it is a reality that stirs the profoundest feelings of the Arab masses from the [Arab] Gulf to the [Atlantic] Ocean. The important thing now is to define the social content of the Arab nationalist movement, then that of Arab unity, as being the practical "framework" of Arab nationalism.

The actual development of Arab struggle has affirmed the socialist, popular and revolutionary character of the fight for Arab unity:

a. The Arab nationalist struggle clashed with colonialism as having created fragmentation and being anxious to maintain and perpetuate it as a means of maintaining its influence and its monopolies in the Arab homeland.

b. The Arab nationalist struggle clashed with feudalism as being at once an obsolete mode of production and a political class, inasmuch as the feudal class is the one that is directly and openly the agent of colonialism.

c. The Arab nationalist struggle clashed with the national bourgeoisie, in view of the fact that the bourgeoisie of each region had grown up independently of and in isolation from those of the other regions, and that each of the regional bourgeoisies had turned the contradictions between themselves into inter-regional contradictions between one region and another. For this reason the struggle of the Arab nationalist movement found itself obliged to remove bourgeois obstacles as a means of transcending regional frontiers and creating its national unity.

For all these reasons the movement of Arab nationalism is the cause of the masses of the workers and peasants, the petty bourgeoisie and the revolutionary intellectuals, so that the course of Arab nationalism has become the Arabs' course towards socialism.

This is why Arab unity comes today within a true historical framework, and expresses the need of the masses for liberation and their desire that their forces should be set fully in motion to smash the obstacles that lie in the way of their advance.

Because the process of actually developing the nationalist movement has followed these new historical directions, the promotion of the movement for Arab unity requires resort to objective factors to build the foundations and outline the framework of this unity. Subjective and emotional factors are no longer capable of building a unity that can confront imperialism as a whole, and at the same time confront those internal class enemies whom unity deprives of their privileged positions, their influence and their supremacy.

The achievement of unity between regions in which fragmentation has left residues of backwardness and narrow interests is a colossal task, necessarily determined by commitment to ideology at the social, political and economic levels. This ideology must both honestly express the interests of the masses and depend on them as an organization. To ensure that unity enjoys the objective conditions required for a genuine new start, it must derive from masses who are conscious and politically formed, responsible and firmly organized; inasmuch as the spirit of democracy is belief in the masses, unionist struggle is necessarily democratic socialist struggle.

Comprehensive Arab unity is a revolutionary mass objective that must be realized in a conscious and sound manner. Unity must therefore be embodied in a democratic form, in the form of a scientific socialist trend, and of positive and effective participation by the organized masses.

In these new circumstances Arab unity is no longer merely a practical embodiment of the national unity of the people; it is also a driving force of Arab struggle at both the political and the social levels.

1. The desired Arab state will not resemble the traditional national states established on a purely national basis; regional bourgeois interests, in addition to feudalism and the monopolist classes, are now the enemies of unity, so that unionist struggle by the masses, by being obliged to remove these regionalist obstacles, creates socialism at the same time as it creates unity.

2. Arab unity is no longer the realization of a bygone past; it is an immediate necessity in the battle for Arab existence against colonialism in its old and new forms and against Israel. The only way to recover the usurped parts of the Arab homeland, to destroy colonialist monopolies and to close the door to neocolonialism once and for all, is unionist struggle.

Fragmentation and backwardness provide the natural atmosphere in which neocolonialism thrives. The contradiction and competition that are bound to exist between small artificial political entities make it easy for neocolonialism to infiltrate. Moreover, the policy of small states, however much they have been liberated, is always to a great extent merely a negative rejection of colonialist policy, and their cooperation with the socialist states is impaired by a sort of concealed fear of colonialism and a sort of complex vis-à-vis the socialist camp itself. Therefore the unitary state, which must of necessity be a large one, will be able to transform Arab policy, from being merely negative and defensive rejection of colonialism, into the exercise of a policy at the international level that is based on revolutionary principles, regardless of the repercussions of such a policy on the international camps. The weight, both quantitative and qualitative, of the large, unified Arab state will provide it with sufficient strength to strike just and legitimate revolutionary blows at the surviving positions of old colonialism, its monopolies and its agent, Israel, and this will close the door, once and for all, to infiltration by neocolonialism.

3. Unity will provide serious opportunities for a rapid upsurge of the Arab economy. Regional frontiers have been a basic factor in curbing contemporary economic development, for marketing is the converse of industrialization, and the fact that regional markets are so restricted is an important factor in impeding Arab economic development and preventing it from achieving its full potential; these frontiers are practically leading to the economic strangulation of the smaller Arab regions. The economic aspect of Arab unity provides

the objective conditions for the establishment of an economy of major dimensions and the setting up of major, advanced and modern industries, strong and efficient enough to stand up to foreign competition without the customs barriers required to protect small, backward and uneconomic industries. In addition to all this, the existing economic complementarity in our Arab homeland will provide an incentive for the rapid development of the Arab economy as a whole. The great and varied natural resources available in the Arab homeland will provide the objective conditions for an escape from subservience to the colonialist countries, because the decisive issue in economic development is not that of investment only, but of marketing and exchange. Arab unity will also eliminate competition and rivalry in the search for sources of foreign financing, eliminate unreasonable duplication of expenditure on similar projects and, finally, eliminate the unequal distribution of national resources and labor between the different regions of the Arab homeland.

For all these reasons unity means not only national salvation; it also means economic and social salvation, the elimination of backwardness, and rapid advance to catch up with the march of history.

4. Socialism is the real content of Arab unity, and the building of socialism makes unity the human and economic framework which is most consistent with the requirements of an all-embracing and radical socialist experience. Small countries cannot set out on the road to socialism on their own, because economic development (and industrialization in particular, which sets the material base of socialism) will always be threatened with stagnation and strangulation. Therefore, Arab unity and socialism are inseparable at both the historical and the economic levels.

5. The objective evolution of our present world is advancing rapidly towards large groupings of peoples; many states have been created on a multi-national basis, and political and economic groupings have started to crystallize as the first step towards deeper, more solid and stronger links, like the European Union and the European Common Market, the socialist camp and the bloc of African states. The attempt to tighten neocolonialist control of the backward countries, at a time when old colonialism is declining and collapsing, and when large international political and economic groupings are arising, makes Arab unity a weapon for the defense of the interests of the Arab people.

Thus, in addition to being an embodiment of Arab nationalism, Arab unity corresponds with the objective development of our contemporary world. It is a fundamental necessity for the confrontation of the new dangers; it is also the natural basis for the development of science and technology in the Arab homeland and for catching up with sweeping world developments in this field.

Arab unity is an indispensable basis for the establishment of a socialist society to confront the challenge of the new age — the age of the new industrial revolution — and the perils of neocolonialism.

6. The Arabs are one nation. Therefore Arab unity must be a complete

unity in the later stages of unionist struggle. The classical form of federation may be appropriate to the multi-national state, and may be merely a stage and a step towards full unity, because federation, if it is the final stage of unionist advance, is a form which maintains the regional residues that go along with bourgeois interests and bourgeois thinking. For unity to be real and complete it must have strong and effective leadership in the political, military, economic and cultural fields.

However, the popular foundation of unity requires the application of decentralization (or autonomy) in government, this being the practical application of socialist democracy. Decentralization in regional and local affairs is a democratic necessity, but need not necessarily be based on the present map of the Arab countries, nor need this map be taken as a basic principle or a basis for the application of decentralization. For the existing political entities have not always existed, nor are they natural; they are spurious, artificial and recent. The new framework for decentralized government will be determined in conformity with the conditions of production and the requirements of economic and social construction, so that it may be in harmony with the real and concrete interests of the masses of the Arab people.

7. For a genuine new start to be made on the basis of objective conditions, the concrete reality of the Arab situation must be affirmed; it must not be sidetracked and ignored. Long fragmentation has created varied regional conditions and a lack of uniformity in economic development, which are reflected in other aspects of life, in the political, social and cultural situation. Unionist construction must assimilate these conditions from the start, so that it may be able to overcome them and liquidate them in a gradual, balanced and sure manner through interaction between regions, for this is the only practical way of ensuring fusion.

8. Unity, in its democratic and revolutionary sense, must come as the culmination of Arab revolutionary struggle and as the fruit of the economic, social and political interaction between the various Arab revolutionary experiences, because to substitute expansionism for interaction and to dissolve authentic revolutionary experiences leads in practice to regional contradictions being aggravated and being manifested in the form of antagonism. This also furnishes the conditions for secessionist retrogression, as happened in Syria on September 28, 1961 [i.e., Syria's secession from the UAR as the result of a military coup]. This is even worse than fragmentation, because fragmentation is a sick state of affairs which is inherited, while secessionism is a step backwards, and negative steps and regionalist retrogressions have a great influence which is more dangerous than that of corrupt stagnation.

9. The socialist democratic character of the foundations of unity must be reinforced; this is essential to ensure that its structure is firmly established. The popular masses alone are untouched by regionalist residues, by their concomitant circumstances and the interests that give rise to them. The workers and peasants will lose nothing by the elimination of frontiers, whereas the

bourgeoisie and the bureaucracy will lose their real positions when the frontiers disappear. Regionalist fanaticism is a way of defending regional interests that are destroyed by unity, and Arab unity, in its concrete development, is both a nationalist and a socialist democratic revolution.

10. The organized revolutionary forces of the masses are the objective instruments which create, protect and entrench unity. Therefore the best and most firmly established form of unity is that which is the fruit of revolutionary mass struggle led by unified revolutionary forces, because the organic unity of the vanguard forces makes them better qualified and more able to adopt a unified and consistent attitude to the residues of fragmentation and to all other problems. However, objective conditions in the Arab homeland have created numerous progressive or revolutionary movements, and although all of them have a similar basic line, their characteristics and social composition, their different ideological levels and the residues left in them by fragmentation and regionalism create certain differences in their views of the problems of nationalist socialist struggle. However these differences do not lead to antagonism between them; it is a question of determining the limits between right and wrong.

The meeting of and interaction between the nationalist forces will eventually lead to the fusion of these forces on foundations that science and experience in struggle have proved to be the right ones. For the achievement of unity is conditional on the unification of the basic theoretical principles on which it is to be built, and on the unity of the methods of struggle that lead to its achievement. However, unification on the basis of imposing a preconceived framework derived from a single region leads, in practice, to sabotaging any real possibility of fusing the mass revolutionary forces. Inasmuch as unity will come about as the result of the meeting of these forces, this meeting must be on a democratic basis, on the basis of interaction, not compulsion, on the basis of eliminating partial and secondary differences through mutual criticism and self-criticism, mutual supervision and exchange of experiences. All attempts to build these relations on an undemocratic basis, on a basis of compulsion and annexation, will result not only in these partial differences developing into hostility between the different movements, but also in the course of unity being impeded and the liberated anti-imperialist Arab ranks being divided.

11. Arab unity will be achieved by stages, and this advance by stages towards the achievement of unity will not constitute a danger to comprehensive unity as long as it arises from certain objective conditions attendant on Arab struggle, and is not an expression of semi-secessionist and semi-regionalist theories. Partial unity can indeed be a danger to the nationalist cause when it is a substitute for comprehensive national unity, but it is a sound unionist step when it is merely a step along the road to comprehensive unity, securing the fusion of the revolutionary energies of two or more regions and paving the way for the creation of new conditions that will contribute to the achievement of further unionist steps.

2. THE RELATIONSHIP BETWEEN IDEOLOGY, STRATEGY AND
TACTICS: POLITICAL REPORT OF THE ARAB BA'ATH SOCIALIST
PARTY, TENTH NATIONAL CONGRESS, MARCH 1970

The political strategy of the Party aims, in a scientific and practical way, at developing Arab trends and tendencies towards the higher national aspirations of the Arab nation in its present stage of historical development. While trying to comprehend and absorb the dialectic peculiar to the present Arab trends and realities, it is also very much involved in controlling and directing the movement, helping it to gain acceleration in the proper direction, consolidating its achievements, safeguarding the correctness of its line, and enriching it with national and international experience.

Needless to say, the scientific and objective interpretation of social trends and movements is a prerequisite for their control. It would be necessary therefore, for any political strategy of a revolutionary and scientific nature to be closely associated with a scientific and revolutionary theory which can comprehend and comprehensively absorb the movement of society at a certain historical stage.

The overall and permanent strategy of the Arab Ba'ath Socialist Party is to build a socialist, democratic and unified Arab nation, thus fulfilling the aspirations of unity, freedom and socialism. It is a long-range strategy encompassing a whole historical era. As for the goals and targets of particular stages, it is necessary to define issues requiring action in the light of their national importance, urgency, and their impact on the future of the nation. Such matters of urgency include the Palestine problem, the imperialist invasion of the Arabian Gulf, liquidating foreign military bases in some Arab countries and the creation of new forms and formulas for integrationist action. On the social level, this involves the elimination of the remnants of feudalism and regression. A clear vision and understanding of the dialectical relationship between the national and the social levels, together with the present forms of struggle, is necessary for defining the strategy of each phase.

A clear and definitive ideological framework is basic for raising the strategy from the level of what is expedient to the level of the scientific and what is capable of comprehending the direction of historical change and the laws of social development.

Ideology is also a basic safeguard to political strategy, against the loss of vision in everyday tactics, or overestimating the importance of tactics at the expense of strategy, or divorcing tactics from strategy altogether.

The ideology of the Arab revolution as embodied by the Party is the theoretical framework of the Party's scientific interpretation of historical movement in Arab society. The basic factors governing the directions and the political strategy of the Party must of necessity be an application of the ideology within certain circumstances of time and place which takes into consideration the present forms of external and internal struggle and the real volumes and weights of the active political and social forces. While theory is a revelation of the historical context and developmental directions of Arab society within the wider human picture, political strategy tries to discover and analyze the main and secondary contradictions governing the direction of the masses' movement at a particular phase of history. The relationship between theory and political strategy is dialectical. For just as theory without strategy is only unorganized and ineffective thinking, so is political strategy without an ideological foundation. It is action lacking in the scientific, historical dimension. Consequently it becomes an experimental tactic devoid of dimensions and clear goals.

Tactics are a provisional plan of action consonant with objective and subjective circumstances of strategic clarity. They are at the same time an act of accommodation with circumstances not anticipated by strategy. In the absence of any relationship between theory and strategy, tactics become a de facto strategy. Tactics become a chronic disease whose most obvious symptoms are absolute submission to necessities without being able to envisage the phase or historical line of development of society. In such cases, norms of struggle degenerate and become a continuous practice of maneuver, gamble and incomplete solutions. Thus, the absence of theory leads to the absence of strategy and political work becomes continuous tactics.

The interdependence of political strategy and revolutionary ideology enables the Arab movement to forecast the moments of change, when secondary contradictions are liable to become primary ones, and consequently the movement is able to anticipate events with a capacity to reevaluate temporary alliances in time. Thus the revolutionary movement will never be out of step with events. It will not retreat or give up its position of leadership. It will not submit to expedient solutions which sap its revolutionary energy by arresting the development of struggle to the benefit of certain political leaderships whose interests are not served by the new phase of revolutionary work. While political strategy is helped by ideology to recognize and distinguish between phenomena and never lose itself in details, theory is enriched by political practice and direct contact with reality.

In theory, ideology creates the strategy. In practice, ideology is enriched and tested by revolutionary work which makes strategy a constant source of enrichment for theory and continuous rediscovery and development of the revolutionary idea through recognizable events. It also makes ideology a continuous process of discovering the general historical development of the nation and the age. In other words, ideology makes theoretical strategy. In practice, ideology is enriched and made clearer, while strategy itself is tested effectively and made more capable of bridging the gap between revolutionary thought and action.

The rewards of such a complete association between political strategy and theory depend a great deal on a third vital condition: the existence of revolutionary organization with genuine revolutionary thought, stable strategy and good discipline. The existence of this factor enables the Party to maintain high standards in carrying out its ideas and channeling events in the required direction. The party can then teach the masses and learn from them on a basis of mutual growth.

The vitality of association between political strategy and the ideological framework, the dynamism of such a relationship and its fertile effect depends on an organizational theory inspired in form and basic content by the ideology of the Party and in its details by political strategy. On this basis, the process of defining a phased strategy for the Party is a task with interrelated ideological, political and organizational facets.

National strategy reflects the analysis of the whole political and social phenomena at a certain phase in the development of Arab society, deriving from a revolutionary theory which enters into application under the control and direction of a central command.

Regional strategies, on the other hand, analyze the circumstances prevailing in individual Arab countries. They try to discover definite patterns and general laws governing the development of Arab society in those countries. The relationship between the national and regional strategies is in itself one of interdependence and mutual support. Regional strategies enrich the national strategy by the way they handle the local complications arising from the state of division of the Arab homeland. Likewise, the national strategy widens the revolutionary horizon of the regional strategies and makes them more effective and less pressed by the prevailing conditions and more drawn to the ideological and organizational form of the Party.

The Arab Ba'ath Socialist Party is a national socialist party, cognizant of the reality of the nation as a whole and based upon national strategy and organization. The greatest threat to the existence of the Party and its mission comes from the distortion of the national meaning. The meaning will be debased if unity comes to mean a mere gathering of separate units rather than actual unification.

Our Party is characterized by its insistence, from the beginning, on the reality of the nation and its unity, and by a rejection of the present state of division. For division is unrevolutionary and indeed antirevolution. The national strategy is a complete and original whole, and not a mere grouping of local strategies that are immersed in their daily, local circumstances. The national strategy does take into consideration the peculiar local circumstances and the degree of development of each country in relation to the others, and strives at the same time to create suitable conditions for uniform development. This is the central mission of the unified strategy which distinguishes our Party from the other Arab forces of revolution.

The regional strategy is, therefore, only a branch of the national mainstream. It is not a springboard to a national strategy. The meaningful existence of the Party depends on the fulfillment of this important formula. And it will not be possible to achieve such a formula without creating the conditions for cleansing the Party mentality of regional tendencies, of local reform as shown in local political practices which are contradictory to the national strategy. Those conditions can be summed up in the interrelationship of the subject of political strategy on one hand, and the complementary poles, the ideological and organizational frameworks on the other hand. It is, in other words, the unity between thought and leadership. It can be shown then, that any contradiction in the political and national strategy is an ideological and organizational deviation.

Stress on the national meaning of the Party is not only a reminder of the basic axioms from which the Arab Ba'ath Socialist Party sprang, nor is it just a warning against the mistakes and deviations committed during the previous phase of the Party's life; but rather it is an indicator of the new pinnacle which must be reached by the Party and the Arab struggle at the present stage as an expression of inevitable necessity.

The idea of unification in the previous phase was more philosophical in nature. The Party was preoccupied with molding its intellectual strategy until the Arab revolutionary ideology became the main wellspring of contemporary Arab revolutionary thought. In the present phase, after the defeat [of 1948 in Palestine], the need to give unity a strategic meaning and nature has become an objective necessity and a basic requirement for the struggle against the reactionary Zionist-imperialist alliance.

The new phase of the struggle requires — not only theoretically but practically — that unity be put forward as a base. For in this phase, it would be impossible for any single Arab country, whatever its resources may be, to meet the effects of the defeat and to prepare adequately at the same time for the fight, considering the size of the challenge facing the Arab nation. The national strategy must of necessity be both the foundation and the springboard.

The relationship of the political strategy to the ideological framework becomes even stronger as objective circumstances become better suited to a supreme revolutionary effort. There is no room at present, in the life of the Arab nation, for political work devoid of long-range revolutionary objectives. There is no justification for the existence of a regime or any political force if it has no role to play in creating the proper conditions for facing the disaster [in Palestine in 1948].

This phase, being the most revolutionary in contemporary Arab life, requires unity axiomatically as a minimum requirement — complete unity between political strategy and the ideological framework. This is a phase of ideological-strategic action. Revolutionary-ideological tools capable of absorbing the shock of defeat are required at this stage, as well as theoretical planning for the battle which will bring us victory. This phase is with us now.

Our Party, the Arab Ba'ath Socialist Party, is qualified to make its Tenth Congress, like the Ninth, a practical guide for the contemporary Arab revolution. This can be achieved by drawing up a national strategy which meets the objective requirements and needs of the contemporary Arab revolutionary struggle.

The clarification and definition of such a strategy must come as a result of analyzing the political realities of the Arab nation at present, defining the nature of the present phase and the main tasks to be carried at the Party level, the level of political struggle and by the guerrilla movement.

3. SELECTIONS FROM THE REPORT OF THE EIGHTH CONGRESS OF THE ARAB BA'ATH SOCIALIST PARTY IN IRAQ, JANUARY 1974: PAN-ARAB TASKS; THE ARABIAN GULF, THE ARABIAN PENINSULA AND THE RED SEA; INTER-ARAB RELATIONS; INTERNATIONAL POLICY

PAN-ARAB TASKS—TASKS IN THE COUNTRY AND IN THE ARAB HOMELAND

The Arab Ba'ath Socialist Party is the party of Arab revolution; wherever it exists, its struggle is in the framework of this revolution and for the achievement of its objectives. It is a single party led by a single leadership, the Pan-Arab Command. Its division into regional organizations, each operating in a separate Arab country, is a necessity imposed by the present division of the Arab homeland into individual states and by the practical requirements of revolutionary struggle. However, this is a transient situation which will disappear with the disappearance of those divisions.

Wherever the Party exists, whether in underground opposition or in power in a country, the essential aim of its existence and activity is to lead the Arab revolution in pursuit of its historic objectives of unity, liberty and socialism.

The political, economic and psychological consequences of the fragmentation of the Arab homeland, together with the special characteristics of the Party and the movement of Arab revolution in general, as well as many other factors, dictate the Revolution's operational strategy. It operates within the political and geographical framework of the different Arab countries, but always aims to remove regional barriers and develop unity so that a single united Arab state may emerge. An alternative method would be to prepare an uprising in one or another part of the homeland, rejecting all boundaries from the start, on the supposition that the revolution would spread until total liberation and unity were achieved. Clearly, each method implies different conditions, techniques and immediate results, even if, in the Party's view, both lead to the same goal, the establishment of a single democratic and socialist Arab state.

The theoretical and practical purpose of the Party's taking power in a single country is, therefore, to prepare a base for the Pan-Arab struggle. To begin with, the struggle will be waged within the framework of an interim, "regional" state whose task is to promote throughout the rest of the homeland the principles and objectives of the Party, and to put its moral and financial resources at the service of the aims of Arab revolution. It must do this under the Party's leadership, by means of ideological and organizational unity and the common political program of the Party's branches in different countries and of all forces and elements in the revolutionary movement, in order to realize the objectives of Arab revolution in unity, liberty and socialism.

Thus the revolution led by the Party in a single country has two functions. The first is urgently to carry out, within the political and geographical framework of that country, those tasks without which no genuine revolutionary base could be built there. The second is to work for Pan-Arab goals. Although these functions may differ formally and operate at different stages, dialectically and organizationally they are interdependent, two streams which flow into the same estuary: Pan-Arab revolution. The Party is the controlling and coordinating factor.

Once the Party holds power in a country, everything must be done to defend this revolutionary base of the Pan-Arab struggle. Its collapse would be a serious moral and material setback for the whole movement of Arab revolution. The Party and other revolutionaries are required to put all their intellectual, organizational and political potential at its service, in order to help the regional base overcome its difficulties, especially in the early phases, and to fulfill urgent domestic tasks. In this way, time will be gained to make the base a firm bastion where Arab revolution has a free hand. Within the limits imposed by circumstances and its own resources, the policy of the regional base must from the start demonstrate the Pan-Arab character of the revolution. Whenever possible it must increase its contribution to the Pan-Arab cause. It should thoroughly grasp the fact that tasks accomplished at the Pan-Arab level facilitate the accomplishment of tasks at the level of the individual country, as well as giving them their true revolutionary dimension. The converse is equally true, and enriches the experience of the regional base, enlarges its capabilities and gives it a terrain from which to work for its Pan-Arab obligations.

It is a mistake to draw rigid lines between national and Pan-Arab tasks, or to give abstract priority to either. The national tasks are an integral part of the Pan-Arab ones, and both are dialectically interconnected. To fulfill a national task, especially in the early days of the revolution, is to prepare the ground for a Pan-Arab task. Any priority must be judged by objective revolutionary criteria and determined by circumstances. To assert a priori the precedence of one over the other leads either to regionalism or to infantile adventurism. The Party must therefore be on its guard and see that both sorts of tasks are harnessed to ensure a healthy balance between them in all circumstances.

Take, for example, the national achievements of the Party since the revolution of 1968: the consolidation of the revolutionary government under the Party's leadership; the strengthening of Iraq's political and economic independence, especially by the nationalization of IPC [Iraq Petroleum Company] and of the shares held by America, Holland and the Gulbenkian family in the Basra Oil Company; the democratic advances, especially the peaceful solution of the Kurdish question; the formation of the Progressive Front; the social and socialist changes; and finally the establishment of a strong revolutionary army. All of these were interdependent with Pan-Arab tasks. Every advance in these domains consolidated the Revolution's power to influence the Pan-Arab scene, and enhanced the experience of the Party, which was thereby freed for further Pan-Arab struggle. The ground covered in fulfilling these tasks has reinforced the revolutionary base in Iraq, which has thus become a center radiating revolutionary and Pan-Arab ideals throughout the area, and a magnet for many Arab forces for liberation and progress, which it has supplied with the moral and material means to accomplish the immediate Pan-Arab tasks.

However, two vital matters must be underlined. First, the Party and the Revolution still have tasks to fulfill in Iraq which will help us to act on the Pan-Arab level. Second, all that we have achieved in Iraq under the leadership of the Party during the last five and a half years is, in relation to the tasks and responsibilities of Arab revolution, no more than the beginning of the road. Iraq is but one small area of the homeland in which we are struggling for liberation, unity and socialism.

THE ARABIAN GULF,
THE ARABIAN PENINSULA AND THE RED SEA

Until recently, the Arabian Gulf was under the direct control of British imperialism. Because of its vast area, its sparse population, its position on important sea routes and foreign control of most of its resources and facilities, the Gulf has always experienced immigration, whether casual or organized.

When its vast oil resources were discovered, British and American imperialists shifted the emphasis of their policies in the Gulf from its strategic military importance to this new and vital factor. In order to tighten their control over the area, they embarked on a long-term foreign immigration policy, as well as direct military occupation, holding the allegiance of local rulers and controlling all resources and facilities. Immigration, principally from Iran, was organized on a large scale, with the aim of changing the region's national character, as had been done for the same reason in Palestine. The intention was to isolate the area from its Arab environment and so prevent its liberation and its unification with neighboring Arab countries, especially Iraq.

From the 1960s in particular, the Ba'ath Party has been the most persistent of Arab movements in warning of the dangers threatening the Arabian Gulf. Recognizing that the focus of the conflict would be nationalism, it compared what was happening to developments in Palestine during the early stages of Zionist colonization.

During the 1960s, America and Britain made vigorous efforts to redeploy in the region. Superficially, British withdrawal was ensured and a degree of independence granted to existing entities, but in fact the political, economic and military grip of the imperialists was consolidated.

Although special considerations apply in the Gulf, such as the nationalist struggles prompted by Iranian penetration and designs, the issue is an integral part of the whole Arab cause, closely linked to its struggle for liberation, unity and progress.

Since this region, along with the rest of the Arabian Peninsula, Iraq and Iran, contains the largest oil reserves in the world, it has become the most important and sensitive for imperialists, especially since the energy crisis. Its oil is no longer simply a commercial commodity giving a good return on investment; it has become a major strategic product upon which the interests of imperialism, especially American imperialism, depend in international conflict. Upon it also depends the future of the West and Japan, which need energy. Thus, domination of this area and control of the situation, both there and in the rest of the Arab homeland, have become vital to American imperialism, which has concentrated unprecedentedly vast political, military and economic resources on the question. It is no longer possible, therefore, to isolate the conflicts and developments in the Gulf from those of the whole Arab homeland. Similarly, in spite of the specific characteristics of different parts of the homeland, it would be a mistake to determine the methods and dimensions of our riposte in terms of one part alone.

Imperialist attempts to undermine or modify the Arab character of the Gulf are part of the plan to arrange conditions in the Arab homeland in order to maintain the flow of oil and its supply lines from the Arabian Gulf, the Red Sea and the Mediterranean. Consequently, the imperialists' allies and lackeys in the area each have a part to play in the operation, despite existing and possible future contradictions among them which the Americans strive to settle by coordinating the different parties. But the role of the tools of imperialism is not confined to observing oil-supply contracts, keeping loyal regimes in place and protecting them from the winds of liberation and nationalization. They must also guarantee the safety of lines of communications. This double enterprise makes it necessary to circumscribe centers of revolution, primarily Iraq, and to work for their enfeeblement and fall. Since South and North Yemen occupy strategic positions controlling the entrance to the Red Sea, attempts must be made to isolate them, by bringing down the regime in the South and by imposing on the north a reactionary government in the pay of the imperialists. The plan also requires the control of conditions in Sudan, the encirclement of the Eritrean revolution, and the establishment of Ethiopian domination over the port of Djibouti. For all this, a great deal of air, sea and land armament is clearly necessary, and also massive expenditure on propaganda, buying up agents, fomenting coups d'etat, and organizing economic warfare in the region.

The enterprise has another aspect: the Palestinian issue, or what is called the Middle East crisis. Each aspect enumerated above has its place in the general plan whose object is to destroy the bastions of Arab revolution, or at least to circumscribe them as far as possible, undermine their strength, support right-wing pressures and trends against them, and if possible bring them down. The ultimate object is to impose an American settlement on the area.

When the Revolution of July 1968 occurred, the imperialist plans, for the Arabian Gulf in particular, were already in motion. Major advances had been made before the revolution could undertake its Pan-Arab responsibilities in this area. When it turned to the task, it had to take account of the following factors, which have in fact marked all the last five and a half years:

1. During the first stage of the Revolution, the Party was preoccupied with such crucial obligations as consolidating revolutionary authority under its leadership and other domestic tasks, and was thus unable to devote sufficient effort to influencing conditions in the Gulf effectively.

2. Since imperialist plans and the policies of former regimes had isolated Iraq, economic, political and cultural relations with countries in the area hardly existed at the time of the revolution, and had to be built up, almost from zero.

3. Political, economic, cultural and other activities needed to face up to [the imperialists'] aggressive ambitions could not flourish for reasons peculiar to the area, principally the weakness of the people's movements vis-à-vis the [national government] regimes. These regimes did not oppose the threats to the Arab character of the Gulf with an effective policy, in spite of the pressure of public opinion within the area and elsewhere in the Arab homeland. Iraq's initiatives in this domain met with anti-nationalist mistrust, on the false pretext of fear for our country, a pretext inspired by the imperialists and others whose design it was to keep the area apart from its biggest and most powerful Arab neighbor.

4. The threat to the countries of the Arabian Gulf grew greater at a time when the Revolution was deeply involved on both the military and political fronts with the Palestinian question and with resistance to Zionism and imperialism, so that Iraq's activities in the area were reduced in both scope and kind.

But the growing threat met only silence or indifference in the Arab world, due either to deliberate collusion or to ignorance and preoccupation with the Zionist enemy in the Palestinian arena. Some regimes used this pretext to close their ears to Iraq's urgent warnings of danger in the Gulf area. They withdrew from moral or even symbolic obligations, to the point of improving relations with Iran before and even after its occupation of the three Arab islands of Abu Musa and Greater and Lesser Tunb.

These regimes' alliance—especially at this point—with Saudi Arabia, which has an essential role in the imperialist plan for the Arabian Gulf, gave Saudi reaction a free hand and an effective political cover for it to exert great influence on the area, in collaboration with the Iranian regime and the reactionary regimes of the Gulf.

Other Arab regimes paid no attention to events in the Gulf, either willfully or from heedlessness, and were not prepared to participate in resistance to the danger. On the contrary, most tried directly or indirectly to suggest that Iraq's concern for this subject and its appeals for action were but a pretext for avoiding its obligations in the Palestinian arena.

The responsibility of the Party and the Revolution for the Arabian

Gulf arises from their Pan-Arab principles and aims. Furthermore, Iraq, as the most important and advanced Arab country in the area, and the one with the largest potential, must bear the heaviest burdens in protecting it against dangers and encroachment. At all events, we must stress once more the Arab character of the area, its Pan-Arab importance, and the reality of the dangers threatening it.

INTER-ARAB RELATIONS

In the course of the period under review, the Party and the Revolution concentrated their efforts on the two basic issues we have just discussed: Palestine and the Arabian Gulf. Our relations on the Pan-Arab level, whether official or unofficial, depended largely on attitudes to these two crucial and interrelated matters and their requirements.

But there are other factors in inter-Arab relations which, despite the lack of visible, short-term results, play a fundamental part in strengthening links with the masses in other Arab countries and in laying the foundations for Arab unity. The domain of economic, cultural and human relations as a whole constitutes the material, social, economic and psychological basis for Arab unity.

Most Arab governments, however, have been concerned solely with political questions, and agreement or disagreement on them, and have shown indifference to these vital aspects of the life of the Arab nation, its future and the union of its different parts. The Party and the Revolution have done all they could to overcome this situation, in order to facilitate the attainment of Pan-Arab objectives, by strengthening relations between different parts of the nation, between the masses everywhere, and in all fields.

The Party and the Revolution must lead the struggle for Arab unity not only on the level of propaganda and political action but also on all levels. In the next phase we must devote all possible economic and cultural resources and exert the greatest efforts to ensure maximum progress.

INTERNATIONAL POLICY

The basic considerations which underlie the Revolution's foreign policy are these:

1. The requirements of the Arab liberation struggle and its main issues, especially those of Palestine and the Arabian Gulf.

2. The need to protect the revolution in Iraq as a fighting base for the movement of Arab revolution in pursuit of its objectives of unity, liberty and socialism.

3. The belief that the Arab revolution is an integral part of world revolution, with which we must ally ourselves in the struggle against imperialism, aggression, plunder and racial discrimination, in order to guarantee

freedom, peace and human progress in the world, but, at the same time, taking every care, theoretical and practical, to safeguard the independence and distinctive features of Arab revolution.

4. Belief in the need to establish friendly relations between the Arab people and other peoples and states of the world, in accordance with our domestic and Pan-Arab interests and with the principles of brotherhood and cooperation between peoples.

With these considerations in mind, Iraq has been active in the international field, and in the last few years has established relations with various countries.

The Revolution has paid special attention to relations with neighboring and nearby countries, because of our long historical connections and the common interests and aspirations which unite us.

The Revolution has been anxious to establish neighborly and cooperative relations with Turkey, and these have recently developed satisfactorily. There was an interchange of top-level visits, including notably that of the President of the Republic, the Regional Secretary of the Party, to Turkey in 1972, which strengthened friendship between the countries and opened new prospects for cooperation.

Equally, the Revolution has been concerned to establish the closest friendly ties with Afghanistan, a long-standing friend of Iraq with whom we have been linked throughout history. Relations have developed well over past years. The foundations are stable and the prospect favorable for their expansion in all domains.

The Revolution has also been interested in establishing good relations with Pakistan, on account of long historical ties and in recognition of the attitude which it, among all Muslim states, has taken on the Palestinian question. However, in the period under review, circumstances did not allow these relations to develop as we desired. They have simply followed their normal course.

Since the revolution, relations with India have developed rapidly in many important fields, especially the economic and technical. India is the largest of the Asian countries close to Iraq. Long historical connections unite us. Moreover, our essential policies converge, especially in the struggle against imperialism and in adherence to the policy of non-alignment. We thus have a firm base for continued and developing relations in the interest of both peoples, in support of peace and stability, and in defiance of imperialism in the area.

In recent years relations with Iran have been tense, as a result of the Iranian government's hostile attitude, particularly after its unilateral abrogation of the 1937 treaty, its incitement of frontier incidents, and its intervention in Iraq's internal affairs. But, while the Revolution has kept its resolution to protect our legitimate rights and interests, and repel any attempt to threaten or violate them, it has been anxious to establish good neighborly relations and cooperation with Iran on a just basis, guaranteeing the common interests of both, in accordance with our long historical links. The Revolution has worked to solve the problems with Iran by peaceful means, and for its part has taken the necessary measures, including the restoration of diplomatic relations and an invitation to join in negotiating a settlement.

4. EXCERPTS FROM TAREQ AZIZ (MEMBER OF THE REVOLUTIONARY COMMAND COUNCIL AND DEPUTY PRIME MINISTER) ON ARAB-IRANIAN RELATIONS, AL-THAWRAH (BAGHDAD), MAY 1980

In April 1969, when the revolution in Iraq was in its first year, the Shah unilaterally declared the annulment of the 1937 treaty which regulated the borders and relations between the two neighboring countries. In order not to forget and shuffle the cards, when the Shah did this he said he was rectifying a situation imposed on Iran in British colonial days, and that as long as his regime had "got rid of" the colonialist domination, he was nullifying the treaty and demanding a new position on borders and relations. This is what the Shah said and no one else.

Since that date, and until March 1975, the Shah imposed an aggressive battle on revolutionary Iraq, using all political and military means as well as the media, and endeavored to intervene in Iraqi affairs. In January 1970, his intelligence plotted to overthrow the revolutionary regime, and used [the Kurdish leader Mustafa] Barzani to rebel against the revolution and stir up civil war.

At that time, the Shah, in his declaration against Iraq and in his intelligence activities, was hiding behind the religious question, playing the communal card, and mobilizing some of those who claimed to be from the religious circle. Anyone who wishes to study the truth can refer to these facts.

After six years of conflict, the Shah found that the idea of engulfing or fragmenting Iraq, or of aborting its national socialist revolution, would not succeed, and that the conflict with Iraq was a double-edged sword piercing his own country, as well as his armed forces and regime. It was then possible, in March, 1975, to reach agreement with him on the matters of coexistence and good neighborliness.

Then the Shah went and the new regime came. Without making accusations or debating the question, it is not impossible, objectively speaking, to understand the true intentions. Had Iraq any interest in harming Iran after the revolution whereby it would receive the same treatment? The answer is absolutely and emphatically not. The regime in Iraq is a national socialist regime, and believes in the principles and objectives of the Arab Ba'ath Socialist Party (ABSP). The latter's aims are not "national," but nationalist. Iraq, therefore, on principle, has no particular interest in any political or intellectual choice made by the Iranians, always provided that such choices do not arouse conflict between the two countries or stir up aggression against Iraq and the Arab nation. Furthermore, Iraq, with its revolutionary and socialist regime, is more at ease if its neighbors share similar principles and trends. This is because it provides for better cooperation in the area than if the regimes are apart intellectually, socially and politically, as well as in the nature of their relations and their position on international issues.

It is only natural for us to say that the option closest to the principles of the ABSP and the interests of Arab Iraq is for the political, social and intellectual option of the Islamic nations to be one in which their Islamic character is asserted. This is because when they do so they necessarily grow closer to the Arab nation, and join forces with the Arabs in their struggle against Zionism.

Of this there are living examples. When Turkey grew away from the spirit of Islam by virtue of secularism and affiliation to Western civilization, it simultaneously grew further apart from the Arabs. Not only this, but on several occasions, particularly in the 1950s, it was also used against the Arab nation and its liberation movement, and established relations with the Zionist entity which were detrimental to the Arab nation.

The same applies to Iran under the Shah, who attempted to constrain Iran to alienate itself from its Islamic character. Iran consequently became an enemy of the Arabs and an ally of their enemies. Because Pakistan, on the other hand, retained its Islamic character, even when a party to the Baghdad and CENTO Pacts, it remained close to the Arabs, supported their causes, and rejected any form of relations with the Zionist entity.

The revolution in Iran took place when Iraq was shouldering its responsibilities resulting from the Baghdad Summit and the National Joint Action Charter with Syria. In order to carry out these voluntarily chosen responsibilities in an effective manner, Iraq was therefore at that time in greatest need of calm and stability on its eastern borders. It was also in greatest need of any new force to add to the balance of power in the area against the Sadat-Zionist-American alliance.

So what possible political or economic benefit could Iraq gain from inflicting damage and injury on Iran? Absolutely none, as conflict leads only to losses which can in no way be offset by any measure of gain. Iraq could not enter into such a conflict unless coerced to do so in defense of its patriotic and national essence.

Since these are the bare objective facts, and since Iraq has, and is seen to have, a responsible and sensible leadership, which over twelve years has demonstrated a superior capacity for countering difficulties and overcoming traps, would it ever enter into a battle of this type unless forced to do so?

Some might say that Iraq brought up the question of the three islands, of Arabistan, and of the Shatt al-Arab agreements, prompting Iran to respond in this fashion. Yes, Iraq did indeed bring up these three issues, but is it so strange for Iraq to want the return of the three islands occupied by the

Shah of Iran with his military forces, his imperialist and expansionist arrogance, and the collusion of British colonialism and American imperialism? Is it not yet stranger still that the Iranian revolution, which came, it claims, to uproot the Shah's regime and undo his policies and misdeeds, did not declare from the first its resolve to rid these islands of the Shahanshah's colonialism?

What actually happened, after attempts by the new Iranian regime to avoid and ignore the question of these three islands, was that its leader, just as the Shah had done nine years earlier, openly declared the islands to be "Iranian," and said that he would not relinquish them. So who is to blame?

With respect to the Arabistan region, the Iranian peoples — after the revolution which toppled the Shahanshah's dictatorial and fanatic regime, which for years had imposed a purely racial Persian dominance, denied their national characteristics, and deprived them of their legal rights within Iran — demanded a change in the situation. The Arabs of the Arabistan area were among those who believed the revolution would grant their natural and legitimate rights, but the new leadership duped them in feud and hatred exactly as the Shah did. Let us not say more.

So whose position is it which creates surprise and inflicts harm? Is it that of Iraq, which supported the just demands of the Arab people of the Ahwaz area for autonomy within the framework of a united Iranian state? Or is the cause of astonishment the fact that the Iranian "revolution" is denying the Ahwaz inhabitants and other Iranian peoples their straightforward and fair demands, instead bringing them ruin and disaster? Was Iraq contradicting its principles and asking of others what it would not want for itself? Or is the Iranian "revolution" contradicting its words with its deeds?

Iraq believes it is only natural for the Iranian peoples to have a form of autonomy within the framework of a single Iranian state. This principle it applied to itself by granting the Iraqi Kurds a form of autonomy practiced within the framework of the one homeland. So who is contradicting whom, and who is harming whom?

Likewise, it is only natural for liberation revolutions destroying colonialist, dictatorial, and tyrannical regimes to present a new program declaring the end of colonial dominance, and of the repression and injustices of the defunct regime. It is acceptable for the revolution to ask for time to see its program through, and to discuss the nature and size of the demands made. But a revolution which denies these demands from the outset and maintains the previous status quo is not a revolution.

The same principle also applies to the question of the Shatt al-Arab. The circumstances of the conflict between Iraq and Iran have imposed a formula for the Shatt al-Arab which is incompatible with Iraq's historical rights and interests in the area. This occurred when Iran was ruled by an expansionist imperialist regime, which, in its aggression against the Arab nation and Iraq, had the total support of American imperialism. Why is it abnormal for the new "revolutionary" regime, which advocates fraternity with the Arabs, to consider reinstating the rights denied by the defunct regime.?

Who is contradicting himself here? Is it he who demands rights taken from him by a tyrannical oppressor? Or is it he who claims to have revolted against everything that oppressor represented, yet who continues to retain his hold over the latter's gains, namely the islands and Shatt al-Arab, follows the same policies towards the Iranian peoples, and flares up in anger and indignation each time it is mentioned to him?

It is not at all difficult for any fair and rational person to see just who is contradicting himself. The mass of accusations and attempts to create confusion cannot conceal the clear and simple facts as seen and understood by anyone who has reasoning and insight.

The truth, as history will show, is that Iraq, from its pure nationalist and principled premises, and from its penetrating view arising from its loyalty to principle, sensed very early on the spurious and contradictory nature of the statements made by the new Iranian leadership. It made sincere endeavors to uncover the truth and make it known to the Arab nation, and was first to do so. However, despite the accusations leveled at Iraq from certain brothers and relatives (we don't say enemies), what Iraq felt proved to be right, because the black and depressing truth emerged a few months later.

Iraq inflicted no battle or harm upon the Iranian "revolution." Instead, with all sincerity and every good intention, Iraq placed that revolution before its own responsibilities, only to be repaid with this resentment and injury which we see and experience.

Iraq, again with all good intentions, demanded that Iran, after the revolution, change the policies that were adversely affecting the Arabs, but the post-"revolution" rulers of Iran confirm that they and their predecessors are merely one and the same.

When making assertions, supported by fact and logic, that Iraq was not responsible for initiating the conflict with Iran, we are not aiming to throw light on the matter, but to rest our consciences and those of our brother Arabs, and to eliminate any likelihood of self-blame. Some may ask why we instigated the conflict when the revolution was in the process of being established, and was faced with so many challenges and difficulties.

The truth is, however, that it was the Iranian rulers themselves who decided the issue. They began boasting that they had started the conflict intentionally, to the extent that they no longer needed to hide this fact as they had done in previous months. Headed by the president of the republic, they have recently stated both clearly and frankly that they are now striving to "export the Iranian revolution," something which, as Bani-Sadr said, they consider vital to the survival and continuance of their "revolution." The Iranian president himself has also openly declared his refusal to have discussions or begin mediation towards solving the problems with Iraq.

Iran's campaign against Iraq is therefore nothing more than a result of the so-called "revolution export" plan. It is not a response to any determined stand or action supposedly taken by Iraq. Nor is it the effect of relations between the two countries. Were this the case, how would we be able to grasp the situation?

For the sake of the truth, we must discuss all probabilities without sensitivity, since anyone with confidence in himself and in the fact that truth is on his side is not afraid to look deeper into any possibilities or hypotheses.

Let us suppose that the Iranian leaders, who were helpless to counter the major issues brought to the surface by the revolution and who reached an impasse over the hostage question, are now endeavoring, under the theme of "exporting the revolution," to export their problems abroad as a way to divert attention from internal failure and to gain time, or as an attempt to restore the divided domestic front by stirring up an illusionary enmity. If so, is this the moral thing for them to do?

The Arabs sympathized with the Iranian revolution, and wished it success. They were glad it had declared its Islamic identity, as this meant a mutual approach and concerted efforts between them and Iran in the struggle against Zionism. Is it therefore grateful and moral for the Iranian rulers to consider their Arab neighbors' land a refuse ground on which to throw the remnants of their experiment, which is filled with conflict and contradiction? Has any friend of the Iranian rulers, singing their praises, said that this behavior of theirs, apart from the lack of morality and gratitude it displays, is a great miscalculation and a wrong appraisal? The Arab arena, even if suffering some problems, has no desire to become a refuse site for others, and indeed has the wherewithal to defend Arab territories capably with both honor and pride.

Even if the rulers of Iran found that they could keep themselves amused with their experiments inside Iran, would the situation in those countries bordering the Zionist entity, as well as in the Arabian Peninsula and Gulf countries, have allowed for such games and experiments? Or would the Zionist enemy—which has so far succeeded in removing Egypt from the battle and provoking communal strife in Lebanon—have exploited any opportunity provided by the Iranian scheming (where a thousand such opportunities will surely arise) to execute fully its scheme to dominate the area from the Nile to the Euphrates?

Iran's rulers are blinded by arrogance to an important fact. They are also blind to it because forces inside Iran are using all means to hide it, and because certain opportunists, who give them every praise, fail to explain the facts to their Iranian "friends." On the contrary, instead of bringing them to awareness and guiding them to the right path, they play on, and thus compound, their vanity and rashness.

What the Iranian rulers do not know is that, more than a year after the success of their revolution, they have turned their country into a stage for the game of covetous international powers. Neither do they realize that their capacity to amuse themselves with their contradictory and topsy-turvy experiments is based on two factors. The first is the continued flow of oil, and the second is that the international powers at loggerheads in the area are banking on the results which may arise from the unsettled situation in Iran. Once this has developed to the interests of one of those powers, these rulers will not be able to do much about it if they continue to follow this same policy and ignore what is happening.

Have Iran's friends made their associates aware of this, and told them to beware of deluding themselves? Have they told them to keep a close watch on the situation, and have they warned them that they themselves are preparing the favorable conditions for their country to be handed over, whether intentionally or otherwise, to these covetous international powers with their avidity for the area?

Let us move on to another hypothesis, and suppose that the Iranian rulers "have principles," and feel they are right to spread their experiment to other Islamic countries. Let us also hypothesize about their claim that, in so doing, they are aiming at destroying Zionism and imperialism.

For the export of any experiment to be legal and justified, and to persuade people that it will bring them strength and the ability to destroy powerful enemies like Zionism and imperialism, the engineers of any such experiment must first achieve outstanding and convincing successes in solving the problems and major issues they face. They must also succeed in creating the moral and material potential capable of meeting the dangers and challenges encompassing the experiment in question.

But have the rulers in Iran, who heatedly urge the export of their experiment to Arab countries, done this in Iran itself? The distinctive features of the Iranian situation now they have assumed control are as follows:

- the disintegration of Iran's military capability;
- the existence of several different centers of influence and decision, the lack of any real central power, and the sudden proliferation of disagreements and accusations amongst religious and political leaders;
- the eruption of conflicts between the Iranian peoples of non-Persian extraction and the ruling leaderships, and a complete inability to solve the problem of the different nationalities within Iran;
- the spread of anarchy and unrest, and the lack of security;
- the breakdown of production, the destruction of the economy, a horrendous increase in unemployment, and the absence of the majority of food products;
- chaos in relations with the countries of the region, and in international relations.

This is the picture of Iran today. Do her leaders want to export all this to Arab countries on the pretext of destroying Zionism and imperialism?

Let us imagine these leader have achieved their dreams of exporting their experiment to the whole of the Arab east, because logically speaking, the Zionist entity can only be resisted if geographically surrounded. Similarly, the

Arabian Peninsula and Gulf countries, because of their basic interests, can only effectively counter imperialism if they are given direction and guidance as to how to do so.

Let us imagine these dreams have been accomplished, and that the situation in these countries now resembles the "pioneering experiment" in Iran. Let us imagine that the Iraqi, Syrian and Jordanian armies have disintegrated, that factional, political and racial differences have erupted in the Arabian Peninsula and Gulf countries, that chaos and insecurity reign, that production has come to a standstill, and that sociopolitical contradictions have been kindled. Who then will be destroyed: Zionism and imperialism? or the Arab nation and all the gains of the Arab struggle? I doubt we will have much difficulty replying to the question.

Throughout the long years of open war, by sowing temptation and stirring up unrest, and through the various espionage networks, the media and counter-culture, Zionism has, with the backing of imperialist forces, strived to fragment the Arab homeland, and to create internecine war. The objective behind this is to cripple its capacity for revival, union, and the creation of a strong entity capable of resisting the Zionist entity and its expansionist projects. Even though Zionism achieved important goals by occupying the whole of Palestine and certain other Arab areas of land, inciting an explosive situation in Lebanon and drawing Sadat into the ranks of traitors, the Arab nation has not surrendered to the Zionist-imperialist scheming. It is still resisting and preparing itself to face the Zionist entity and its imperialist conspiracies.

Has the Iranian rulers' plan given the Arab nation additional strength in its battle, or has the execution of their plan, with or without their realization, achieved much of what Zionism and imperialism were aiming at?

The success of the Iranian leaders' plan to disintegrate Arab military power and cause communal and political conflict, with the resultant destruction of the existing entities, means that the "Jewish state" which has so far been an alien body in the Arab homeland rejected by the Arab national forces, will become legitimate. This will coincide with the designs some wish to see spread in the area. Should their plan meet with success, this Zionist entity will not only acquire the "legitimacy" it has lacked ever since its establishment, but will also assuredly and inevitably become the strongest client state of all in the Arab east. Likewise, the project of the separatist leaderships in Lebanon will acquire the legitimacy they still wish to acquire at any price.

So what benefit will the Arab nation gain from the plan to export the Iranian experiment in its struggle against Zionism and imperialism, even despite all the negative aspects of the current situation? In whose interests are Iran's rulers working when they urge this plan with such fervor? And who is inciting them?

Some might say we acknowledge the existence of corruption and negativity in the current Arab situation, and ask why, if we are revolutionaries struggling against these, we deny that the Iranian revolution is also making attempts to eliminate both? We do not deny anyone's role, but for any attempt to fight corruption and negativity to be laudable and effective, it must take this direction, and be capable of doing so.

As we have pointed out, the expected outcome of the Iranian plan is certain ruin, and this is what the Iranian revolution has so far achieved.

There is nothing in the Iranian experiment to confirm the ability of that experiment to build and unify in such a way as actively to uproot corruption, alter the negative aspects of society, and create an Arab revolutionary capacity which can effectively hinder Zionism and imperialism, and erase the effects of Zionism and imperialism in the Arab homeland.

Should we tackle corruption and negativity in the way suggested by the Iranian experiment? Is it to be dealt with by using destruction, dividing the people, and unleashing a pandemonium of contradictions? I don't think any Arab who is loyal and sincere would want this.

If Iran's rulers are really fighting corruption and negativity as they claim, why are they concentrating all their efforts against a regime which even our adversaries recognize as being honest, national and independent? This is in addition to the fact that these rulers are courting and allying themselves with corrupt regimes, which apart from being isolated from the people and surrounded with suspicion, are experiencing widespread feelings of Islamic revival running high against them.

However hard one might try to do so, one cannot find any justifiable excuses for the actions of Iran's rulers, nor foresee any beneficial results. Here we are not leveling accusations from an opposing position, but merely repeating what certain Iranian rulers have said of one another and of their activities. Indeed, the stream of contradictions and accusations reveal the kind of rulers controlling Iran's fate. They also reveal the country's unhappy state, and just what depths of despair and destruction the country, and even the entire area, may reach if these rulers should satisfy their whims and achieve their dreams.

The "Iranian revolution," which surprised all freedom-lovers when it was struggling against the Shah's regime, has lost its shine, and baffled its friends more than its enemies. Iran's rulers have now reached a stage for all sorts of dangerous and unfavorable situations to arise. This is so not only for Iran and its unfortunate peoples, who have not yet had the taste of freedom after years of being repressed, crushed and tyrannized, but also for the whole area, particularly the Arab nation, which is waging the fiercest and most delicate battle of modern times against the Zionist-imperialist alliance and the betrayal of the ruler of the largest Arab country.

Certain Arab officials and political circles are hiding their heads in the sand as an ostrich does, and behaving as if there is nothing to provoke concern and responsible action. Here we are not being completely frank, as we have no wish to insult, but merely to cement a loyal Arab stand on this issue, and uncover just some of the falseness of certain Arab positions. Above all, we wish to say that if any think that the revolution in Iraq, led by the ABSP and Saddam Hussein, is afraid for itself over the so-called "export of the Iranian revolution," they are suffering from a grave illusion.

The position in Iraq is not one of "authority" in the conventional sense, but a patriotic, national, socialist and democratic revolution comprising all walks of life, and immersing itself in all cells of society. Over twelve years of profound and comprehensive revolutionary change and sincere work to build the country and serve the people, a new Iraq has been created, felt by the millions to be their Iraq. The 17th–30th July revolution is their revolution, the Ba'ath party is their party, and Saddam Hussein is their man and leader.

The ABSP is not a conventional political organization, but is composed of cells of valiant revolutionaries, who came from the countryside in northern, southern, and central Iraq, as well as from the working class areas of the towns. They are experts in secret organizations. They are organizers of demonstrations, strikes, and armed revolutions, and are the champion challengers of oppressors and deviants. The Ba'athists were the people's hope in opposing the Baghdad Pact and Nuri Sa'id's tyranny. They were the knights of struggle against Qasim's dictatorship and against communist and anti-Arab tyranny. They created the first armed revolution led by a mass revolutionary party in the Arab homeland when they rose up in 1963, and they led the second revolution in 1968 against Arif's corrupt and reactionary regime. These are the Ba'athists, and so long as they are like this, there is no fear for them.

As for its leader, Saddam Hussein, he is not a politician who has inherited power or gained it through rigged elections. He is "the youth" who began his political struggle as a gun-carrying *feda'i* in Baghdad's Rashid Street to teach the anti-Arab dictator, Abdul-Karim Qasim, a harsh lesson. He is the fighter who was sentenced to death, led the secret civil and military cells of the Party after the counter-revolution of October 1963, entered prison in 1964, and escaped to continue his struggle and leading role until the triumph of the 17th–30th July revolution. He is the fighter, the organizer, the thinker and the leader.

Neither the Ba'ath Party, nor Saddam Hussein are afraid. If anyone imagined it possible to exploit the sectarian situation in Iraq to threaten her national unity, or to undermine the Arab character of the Iraqi people, they would be highly mistaken.

Iraq is a country with a long history within the framework of Arab history. Over thousands of years, its history has shown that it was always a fort of Arabism, and a fence defending invasions by the Persians and other covetous hordes. Were the Arab character of Iraq and the Iraqi people themselves liable to having their spirits broken, Iraq would have been shattered centuries ago, or in the modern age, twenty years ago during Qasim's rule and the communist tide. It would not have waited another twenty years for the Iranian rulers to come from outside her borders under the banner of the Ba'ath revolution and Saddam Hussein's leadership to injure its unity and Arab character.

Iraq, which has various Islamic sects and several religious denominations and nationalities, is an integral unit which is indivisible. All those who imagine they can somehow do harm are invited to try to do so if they wish.

The question is not one of fear for themselves on the part of the Party or the revolution because of events in Iran and her rulers' threats. Iraq, with its national responsibility, is afraid of the ills to which the Arab nation may be exposed with the situation the Iranian rulers want to impose on the area, and with the suspicious, opportunistic and contradictory stands adopted by certain Arab leaderships and political circles, who are behaving in such a way as to encourage the Iranian rulers to delude themselves and continue as they are, without any sense of responsibility.

Many ruling leaderships and political parties, in fact, are behaving in a highly illogical fashion towards the situation in Iran. Let us take some examples. A day has not yet passed since the Iranian "revolution" when Khomeini, Bani-Sadr, Qotbzadeh, or other rulers have not issued abusive statements condemning communism and the Soviet Union, and this is a well-known fact.

On the other hand, however, we find communist organizations, such as Na'if Hawatma's organization, the Iraqi Communist Party, and others, supporting these rulers who insult them in their press, and direct fabrication and slander against the revolution in Iraq, the revolutionary party, and its national revolutionary leadership.

To take another example, the Iranian media are conducting a malicious campaign against the ABSP and the nationalist ideology, and Bani-Sadr is openly accusing Arab nationalism, among other things, of being "Zionist." In Syria, a regime claiming to be of the ABSP and based on the "nationalist ideology" is disregarding the "ideological" insults, and allying itself with Iran's rulers against Iraq.

A third example is that Colonel Qaddafi stands accused of having liquidated Musa Sadr [the Lebanese Shi'i religious leader]. The Iranian leadership continues to blackmail the Libyan government and to stir the matter, which is barely kept silent a week when it flares up the next. After Qaddafi had been "cleared" of spilling Sadr's blood, the Iranians decided to form a supreme committee to reinvestigate, and then adjourned the matter. To date, the Iranian leaderships are refusing to have diplomatic relations with Libya, while Qaddafi himself continues to heap praise on the Iranian "revolution," and describe it as an extension of his own "revolution."

What is the explanation for this peculiar situation, and what is the intention behind this complicated process of shuffling the cards and building an intricate maze? Is it not strange that the three parties referred to, namely the communists, the Syrians and the Libyan regime, claim to be holders of "ideologies" ... and yet these "ideologies" of theirs are vilified day and night by the Iranian regime? Is it not also strange that these three "ideological" parties behave as if they are deaf and blind, heaping praise on and lending support to these rulers?

We shall not explain the positions of these "ideological" masters, as it is their responsibility to do so to those who belong to their "ideologies." However, we shall at least see one rather odd case which encourages the Iranians to be vain, reckless, suspicious and to continue with their damaging behavior, their sick dreams, and their dubious schemings. This is that when faced with such circumstances and examples, they find themselves incapable of tolerating Iraq's solid and adamant principled stand, this being in complete harmony with itself, its doctrine, and the interests of the Arab nation. They then become hysterical, as manifested in the statements and actions of those rulers today against Iraq and the Arab Gulf states, or in other words, against those Arab countries which are geographically close to them, because they find hypocrisy with the "far away" Arabs.

What is wanted of the area, the Arab nation, and the matter of its future in terms of unity, independence and liberating Palestine by shuffling the cards, and creating such mazes? The area has never before seen a process combining such complexity, blindness, spuriousness and hypocrisy.

Who is behind this wide and complicated process which has never before been paralleled? Who is responsible for making Islam reject and clash with revolutionary and socialist Arab nationalism?

How dare Bani-Sadr describe Arab nationalism as Zionism? Or was Arab nationalism not the banner under which the Arabs struggled against the Ottomans and their chauvinistic fanaticism? Or was not Arab nationalism, with its progressive liberation essence, as borne by the prime national strugglers, the ABSP, Jamal Abdul Nasser, and the Algerian revolution, the driving force of the masses against British and French colonialism and the military alliances? Or was not Arab nationalism the revolutionary force behind the Arab and Palestinian struggles against Zionism and imperialism?

Why then should anyone wish to distort and destroy it in this way, and in whose interest? How should we understand the alliance, sometimes open and sometimes covert, between movements using religion as a cover and certain parties and communist movements, when they have such obvious contrasts? What united them as one to deal a blow to Arab nationalism, and to entertain misgivings about the methods used for gaining national independence? Why are they rushing along so blindly and with such venom to destroy the national league, which united the nation, despite its differences, and unified the struggle against Zionism and imperialism?

Who is behind this complex process of shuffling the cards and creating a maze, with the aim of instigating conflict between those elements which are supposedly in harmony, and achieving harmony between those elements which are supposedly in contradiction? Which evil forces are behind the attempts to spread confusion among the Arab youth and masses?

What benefits are to be gained from all this by the nation? Is this the situation which will strengthen the nation in its struggle against Zionism? Or is it the situation which will lead to the fragmentation of the Arab nation, cause conflict to erupt, and spread the Lebanese experience over more parts of the Arab world, so that Zionism, which has reached the banks of the Nile with its conspiracies, will reach the banks of the Euphrates?

Does this situation strengthen the Arab nation's struggle against imperialism? Or will imperialism use it to increase its control over the small portions of land resulting from the fragmentation of the nation, and then the nation will lose its independence? Will hopes for unity and the liberation of Palestine be lost? And will the Arab nation return to the Mameluke period or the era of petty kings, and be distributed among the superpowers?

Why is all this venom being directed against Iraq and its sincere national leadership? Does this not indicate a pernicious attempt to injure Iraq and what it has represented in history, and what it today represents in the new life of the Arabs?

Iraq, led by the ABSP and Saddam Hussein, is the outstanding model of complete patriotic and national independence, economic independence, political independence and free will.

Iraq is the model of the patriotic and national rule which, without distinction, puts people on an equal footing. It spread national unity, security and stability, and provided the right conditions for the country to grow and flourish. All over Iraq everything has progressed: agriculture, industry, culture and services. The rates of development have increased in all fields, and the Iraqi is living a new life, and happy horizons are opening to each citizen and countryman.

Iraq is the country which watches over Arab interests, sacrificing its own interests for the nation's independence and sovereignty, and for the liberation of Palestine.

Iraq's leadership took the historic initiative of opposing the Camp David conspiracy and Sadat's treachery, and assumed responsibility for the Baghdad Summit, which it still continues to do. Iraq's leadership presented President Saddam Hussein's declaration on March 8th to protect Arab territory from foreign influence, and prevent the establishment of foreign military bases at a time when fervent imperialist attempts to spread influence over Arab territory were being made. Iraq's leadership, with the Charter for National Action, called for the relations of the Arab nation with its neighbors to be based on cooperation, good-neighborliness, and fraternity.

This is the model which Iraq today represents. So in whose interest is this poisonous venom directed against it? Is there an attempt to inflict punishment on Iraq because of what it has done and what it now represents in Arab life?

The Arab masses are suffering from many negative attitudes, and are being assailed by various forces aiming at distorting the picture before them, weakening their self-confidence, and pushing them into dangerous situations. But these masses, who are long in experience, are able to distinguish right from wrong, facts from lies, and truth from falsehood, even despite all attempts to shuffle the cards and weave intricate webs and mazes.

5. SELECTIONS FROM AYATOLLAH KHOMEINI, *ISLAMIC GOVERNMENT**

INTRODUCTION

Velayat-e faqih—the empowerment of the religious jurists—is a clear scientific idea that may require no proof in the sense that whoever knows Islamic laws and beliefs can see its axiomatic nature. But the condition of Muslim society, and the condition of our academic institutions in particular, has driven this issue away from people's minds so that today it needs to be proven again.

At its inception, the Islamic movement was afflicted by the Jews, who initiated a counter-activity by distorting the reputation of Islam, by assaulting it and by slandering it. This has continued to our present day. Then came the role of groups which can be considered more evil than the devil and his troops. This role emerged in the colonialist activity which dates back more than three centuries ago. The colonists found in the Muslim world their long-sought object. To achieve their colonialist ambitions, the colonists sought to create the right conditions leading to the annihilation of Islam. They did not seek to turn the Muslims into Christians after driving them away from Islam, because they do not believe in either. They wanted control and domination because during the Crusades they were constantly aware that the greatest obstacle preventing them from attaining their goals, and putting their political plans on the brink of an abyss, was Islam with its laws and beliefs and with the influence it exerted on people through their faith. This is why they assaulted Islam and harbored ill intentions toward it. The hands of the missionaries, the orientalists and of the information media — all of whom are in the service of the colonialist states — have cooperated to distort the facts of Islam in a manner that has caused many people, especially the educated among them, to steer away from Islam and to be unable to find accommodation with it.

Islam is the religion of the warriors who fight for right and justice, the religion of those seeking for freedom and independence and those who do not want to allow the infidels to oppress the believers.

But the enemies have portrayed Islam in a different light. They have drawn from the minds of the ordinary people a distorted picture of Islam and implanted this picture even in the academic institutions. The enemies' aim behind this was to extinguish the flame of Islam and to cause its vital revolutionary character to be lost, so that the Muslims may not think of seeking to liberate themselves and to implement all the rules of their religion through the creation of a government that guarantees their happiness under the canopy of an honorable human life.

---

*Ayatollah Khomeini. *Al-Hukumah al-Islamiyah* [Islamic Government]. 2d ed. Beirut: Dar al-Tali-ah lil taba'ah wa-al-Nashr, April 1979, pp. 7–92.

They claim that Islam has no relationship with organizing life and society or with creating a government of any kind and that it only concerns itself with the rules of menstruation and childbirth. It may contain some ethics. But beyond this, it has no bearing on issues of life and of organizing society. It is regrettable that all this has had its bad effect not only on the ordinary people, but also among university students and the students of theology. They misunderstand Islam and are ignorant of it. Islam has become as strange to them as it is for alien people. It has become difficult for the Muslim advocates to familiarize people with Islam. On the other side, there stands a line of the agents of colonialism to drown Islam with clamor and noise.

To distinguish the reality of Islam from what people have come to know about it, I would like to draw your attention to the disparity between the Koran and the Hadith books [on the Traditions of the Prophet Muhammad] on the one hand and the academic discourses on the other hand. The Koran and the Hadith books, which are the most important sources of legislation, are clearly superior to the theses written by religious interpreters and jurists, because the Koran and the Hadith books are comprehensive and cover all aspects of life. The Koran verses concerned with society's affairs are numerous compared to the verses concerned with private worship. In any of the detailed Hadith books, you can hardly find more than three or four sections concerned with regulating man's private worship and man's relationship with God and few sections dealing with ethics. The rest is strongly related to social and economic [affairs], to human rights, to administration and to the policy of societies.

You, the youth who are the soldiers of Islam, must examine more thoroughly the brief statements I am making to you, and throughout your lives must familiarize people with the laws and rules of Islam and must do so by every possible means: in writing, in speeches and in your actions. Teach the people about the catastrophes, tragedies and enemies that have engulfed Islam since its inception. Do not hide what you know from the people, and do not let people imagine that Islam is like present-day Christianity, that there is no difference between the mosque and the church, and that Islam can do no more than regulate man's relationship with his God.

At a time when darkness prevailed over the Western countries, when Indians were inhabiting America, when absolute regimes in the Roman and Persian empires were exercising domination and racial discrimination and resorting to the excessive use of force with total disregard for the public opinion and for the laws — at that time, God made laws which he revealed to the greatest prophet, Muhammad, may God's peace and prayers be upon him, so that man might be born under their canopy. Everything has its ethics and its laws. Before a man's birth and until the time he is lowered into his grave, laws have been drawn up to govern him. Social relationships have been drawn up and government has been organized, in addition to determining the duties of worship. Rights in Islam are advanced, complete and comprehensive. Jurists have often quoted the Islamic rules, laws and regulations on permissibles, punishment, jurisdiction, on regulating relations between states and peoples, on the principles of war and peace and on human rights.

Thus, Islam has treated every facet of life and provides a regulation for it. But the foreigners have whispered to the hearts of people, especially the [Western] educated among them: "Islam possesses nothing. Islam is nothing but a bunch of rules on menstruation and childbirth. Theology students never go beyond these issues in their training." It is true that some students pay greater attention to this, and they are wrong in doing so. For this helps the enemies to achieve their goals. This will please the imperialists who have worked for hundreds of years to plant the seeds of negligence in our academic institutions in order to achieve their aims [of exploiting us], our wealth and our resources.

At times, the imperialists whisper to the people: "Islam is deficient. Its judicial laws are not what they should be." To further deceive and mislead the people, the agents of the British tried, on the instructions of their masters, to import foreign laws in the wake of the well-known political revolution and of the establishment of a constitutional regime in Iran [1907]. When they wanted to draw up the country's basic law — meaning the constitution — those agents resorted to Belgian laws which they borrowed from the Belgian Embassy. A number of those agents, whom I do not wish to name, copied those laws and doctored their imperfections [by adding] some French and British laws, adding to them some Islamic laws for the purpose of camouflage and deception. The provisions in the [1907] constitution that define the system of government and establish the monarchy and the hereditary rule as a system of government for the country are imported from England and Belgium and copied from the constitutions of the European countries. These provisions are alien to Islam and are in conflict with it.

Does there exist in Islam monarchy, hereditary rule or succession to the throne? How can this happen in Islam, when we know that the monarchic rule is in conflict with the Islamic rule and with the Islamic political system? Islam abolished monarchy and succession to the throne. When it first appeared, Islam considered the sultanic systems of rule in Iran, Egypt, Yemen and of the Romans illegal. God's prophet, may God's prayers be upon him, sent messages to the king of the Romans (Hercules) and the king of Persia calling upon them to stop enslaving people and to free them to worship God alone because He alone is their master. Monarchy and succession to the throne are the ominous and null system of government against which al-Husayn, the master of martyrs, rose and fought. Rejecting injustice and refusing to submit to Yazid's succession and rule, al-Husayn [the eldest son of Imam Ali] staged his historic revolution and urged all the Muslims to follow suit. There is no hereditary monarchic system in Islam. If they consider this a defect in Islam, then let them say: Islam is defective. Added to this defect is the fact that Islam has failed to organize usury, disregarded alcohol drinking and failed to organize fornication and abomination. To correct these defects and to fill these voids, the ruling authorities — the foster child of colonialism — resorted to legislating laws organizing these matters, adopting such laws from England, France, Belgium and the United States. We know that all this is forbidden in our religious laws, and that one of the proud points of our Islam is that it is free of regulations organizing such matters.

At the outset of the so-called constitutional era, the British colonialism exerted efforts aimed at two things. One was to defeat the Russian influence in Iran, and the second was to oust and expel Islam from the sphere of application and import Western laws to replace the laws of Islam.

These foreign laws caused the Muslim society numerous problems. Experienced jurists are grumbling about them and whoever is involved in a judiciary or legal case in Iran, or in similar states, must spend a long life to win such a case. A proficient lawyer has told me: I can keep a case between two disputants in the courts all my life and it is most likely that my son will succeed me [to the case]. This fact does exist. Excluded from this are the illicit profits that people with influence gain from their cases through trickery, perfidy, bribery, deception and cheating. We find that the present judiciary laws intend for the people nothing but hardship. The case on which the Shari'a judge used to make a decision in two or three days now takes twenty years. During this time, a young man turns old for having to check with the judicial offices day and night, roaming their halls hopelessly and having to return to these offices and halls whenever he attempts to leave.

They write at times in their books and papers: The penalties of Islam are cruel and harsh. One of them has dared to say with utter impudence: "The harshness of these penalties is derived from the harshness of bedouin life. The harshness of the Arabs is what has caused these judgments to be harsh."

I wonder how these people think. They carry out the death sentence, under the pretext of the law, against several people for smuggling ten grams of heroin. I have learned that they executed some time ago ten persons, one after the other, for smuggling ten grams of heroin. When they legislate these inhumane laws under the pretext of preventing corruption, they see no harshness in them. I do not approve dealing in heroin, but I oppose death as a penalty for using it. Dealing in heroin must be fought but on a basis compatible with the dimensions of the crime.

Punishing an alcohol drinker with eighty whip lashes is harsh, but executing people for smuggling ten grams of heroin is not harsh when most forms of social corruption are caused by alcohol! Traffic accidents on the highways, incidents of suicide and even heroin addiction — according to some people — are the consequences of drunkenness and alcohol drinking. Yet, they do not ban alcohol because the West has permitted it. This is why they sell and buy alcohol with utter freedom. Woe to Islam from them!

If an alcohol drinker is to be given eighty lashes or an unmarried adulterer is to be punished with one hundred lashes and if a married adulterer or adulteress is to be stoned, you hear them scream: These are cruel and harsh sentences derived from the harshness of the Arabs, whereas the fact is that the provisions of the penal code in Islam came to prevent fornication, abomination and corruption in a great and vast nation. Now we find that corruption has reached the degree where our youths are lost in it, because this corruption has been advocated and has been provided with the necessary facilities. If Islam were to intervene at this moment and to punish an alcohol drinker by whipping him in the presence of a group of believers, these people will accuse Islam of cruelty and harshness. On the other hand, no objection must be made against the bloody massacres that have been taking place in Vietnam for fifteen years at the hands of the masters of these rulers, despite the exorbitant costs that are extorted from the pockets of peoples. If Islam wants to defend itself and to declare war to end corruption, they scream: Why has the war erupted?

All these are plans that were designed and drawn up hundreds of years ago and they are implementing them gradually. At the outset, they established a school somewhere. We did not lift a finger and we, and people like us, failed to prevent this. These schools increased gradually and now you find that they have advocates in all the villages. They have worked to lead our children away from their religion. Some of their plans are represented in keeping us as we are — backward, weak and miserable — so that they may exploit our resources, our minerals, our lands and our manpower. They believe that we must remain miserable and poor and with no knowledge of what Islam has legislated for dealing with poverty so that they, their agents and their lackeys may live in palaces and towers and enjoy a soft and luxurious life. Their plans have left their impact even on our religious and scientific academics, to the degree that if someone wishes to discuss the subject of Islamic government, he must resort to dissimulation or face the agents of colonialism, and to the degree that when the first edition of this book was published, it enraged the Shah's agents in Iraq* and exposed their character through the desperate moves that they made — moves that did them no good.

Yes, our situation has reached the degree that some of us consider the apparel of war and combat incompatible with valor and with justice, whereas our Imams [proudly] wore the apparel of war, carried the instruments of battle and engaged in war. Ali, the Amir [prince] of the Faithful, donned the apparel of war and carried a sword which had its own litter and so did [his sons] al-Hasan and al-Husayn. Had the opportunity risen, Imam Muhammad al-Baqir would have followed suit afterwards. How can wearing the apparel of war be incompatible with social justice and valor when we want to form an Islamic government? Can this be achieved with the turban and the cloak, considering that anything else is incompatible with valor and justice?

What we are suffering from currently is the consequence of that misleading propaganda whose perpetrators achieved their purpose and which has required us to exert great efforts to prove that Islam contains principles and rules for the formation of government.

*Khomeini was in exile in Iraq from 1963 to 1978. — TI

This is our situation. The enemies have implanted these falsehoods in the minds of people in cooperation with their agents, have ousted Islam's judiciary and political laws from the sphere of application and have replaced them by European laws in contempt of Islam for the purpose of driving it away from society. They have exploited every available opportunity for this end.

These are the destructive plans of colonialism. If we add to them the internal elements of weakness among some of our people, we find that the result is that people begin to grow smaller and to despise themselves in the face of the material progress of the enemies. When some states advance industrially and scientifically, some of us grow smaller and begin to think that our failure to do the same is due to our religion and that the only means to achieve such progress is to abandon religion and its laws and to violate the Islamic teachings and beliefs. When the enemies went to the moon, these people imagined that religion was the obstacle preventing them from doing the same! I would like to tell these people: The laws of the Eastern or the Western camps are not what led them to this magnificent advance in invading outer space. The laws of these two camps are totally different. Let them go to Mars or anywhere they wish; they are still backward in the sphere of securing happiness to man, backward in spreading moral virtues and backward in creating a psychological and spiritual progress similar to the material progress. They are still unable to solve their social problems, because solving these problems and eliminating hardship requires an ideological and moral spirit. The material gains in the sphere of overcoming nature and invading space cannot accomplish this task. Wealth, capabilities and resources require the Islamic faith, creed and ethics to become complete and balanced, to serve man and to avert him from injustice and poverty. We alone possess such beliefs, morals and laws. We should not cast aside our religion and laws just because somebody goes to the moon or makes something. These laws are directly related to man's life; they carry the nucleus of reforming society and securing happiness in this world and in the hereafter.

The ideas disseminated by the colonialists among us include their statement: "There is no government in the Islamic legislation and there are no government organizations in Islam. Assuming that there are important shari'a laws, these laws lack the elements to guarantee their implementation. Consequently, Islam is a legislator and nothing more." It is evident that such statements are an indivisible part of the colonialist plans that seek to divert the Moslems away from thinking of politics, government and administration. These statements are in conflict with our primary beliefs. We believe in government and we believe in the need for the prophet to appoint a caliph [successor] after him, and he did. What does the appointment of a successor mean? Does it mean a mere explanation of the laws? The mere explaining of laws does not require a successor. It would have been enough for the Prophet, God's prayers be upon him, to disseminate the laws among the people and then lodge them in a book and leave it with the people to consult after him. The need for a successor is for the implementation of the laws, because no law without an executor is respected. In the entire world, legislation alone is not enough and cannot secure the happiness of people. There must be an executive authority and the absence of such an authority in any nation is a factor of deficiency and weakness. This is why Islam decided to establish an executive power to implement God's laws. The person in charge is the one who implements the laws. This is what the Prophet, may God's prayers be upon him, did. Had he not done so, he would not have completed his mission. The appointment of a successor after him to implement and uphold the laws and to spread justice among the people was an element complementing the Prophet's mission. In his days, the prophet, may God's prayers be upon him, was not content with explaining and conveying the laws. He also implemented them. He punished, cut off the thief's hand, lashed and stoned and ruled justly. A successor is needed for such acts. A successor is not the conveyor of laws and not a legislator. A successor is needed for implementation. Here is where the importance of forming government and of creating and organizing executive agencies emerges. The belief in the need for forming government and for creating such agencies is an indivisible part of the belief in governance. Exerting efforts for and seeking this goal are an aspect of the belief in governance.

You must show Islam as it should be shown. Define governance to the people as it is. Tell them: We believe in governance; that the Prophet, God's prayers be upon him, appointed a successor on the orders of God; that we believe in the need for forming government; and that we seek to implement God's order and rule to manage people, run their affairs and care for them. The struggle for forming government is a twin to the faith in governance. Write and disseminate the laws of Islam and do not conceal them. Pledge to apply an Islamic rule, rely on yourselves and be confident of victory.

The colonialists prepared themselves more than three centuries ago and started from the zero point. They have accomplished what they wanted. Let us now start from scratch. Do not allow the Westerners and their followers to dominate you. Familiarize the people with the truth of Islam so that the young generation may not think that the men of religion in the mosques of Qum and al-Najaf believe in the separation of church from state, that they study nothing other than menstruation and childbirth, and that they have nothing to do with politics. The colonialists have spread in school curricula the need to separate religion from the state and have deluded people into believing that the ulema of Islam are not qualified to interfere in political and social affairs. The lackeys and followers of the colonialists have echoed these words. In the Prophet's time, was religion separated from the state? Were there at the time theologians and politicians? At the time of the caliphs and the time of Ali, the Amir of the Faithful, was the state separated from religion? Was there an agency for religion and another for the state?

The colonialists and their lackeys have made these statements to isolate religion from the affairs of life and society, and to tacitly keep the ulema of Islam away from the people and drive people away from the ulema, because the ulema struggle for the liberation and independence of the Moslems. When their wish for separation and isolation is realized, the colonialists and their lackeys can take away our resources and rule us. I tell you that if our sole concern is to pray, to implore and mention God and never go beyond, colonialism and all the agencies of aggression will never oppose us. Pray as you wish and call for prayer as you wish and let them take what God has given you. The final account is to God and God is the only source of strength and might. When we die our reward will come from God — if this is our thinking, then we have nothing to be concerned with or to fear.

It has been said that a commander of the British occupation of Iraq heard a *muezzin* call for prayers and asked about the harm that such a call causes the British policy. When he was told that there was no harm, the commander said: "Let him say whatever he wants as long as he does not broach us." If you do not deal with the colonialist policy and if your study of the laws does not go beyond the theological framework, they will not bother you. Pray as you wish. They want your oil, so what do they care about your prayers. They want our minerals, and they want to open our markets for their goods and capital. This is why we find the lackey governments obstruct the industrialization of the country, being content at times with assembly plants and nothing else. They do not want to rise to the level of human beings because they fear the human beings. If they find a human being somewhere, they are terrified by him because this human being is progressive and advanced and can influence people and society in a manner that destroys all that the enemy has built and that shakes the earth under the thrones of tyranny, treason and lackeyhood. This is why when they see a human being at any time, they plot against him to kill him, to paralyze him, to oust him or to accuse him of being a politician. This clergyman is a politician! But was not the Prophet, God's prayers be upon him, a politician? Is there anything shameful in being a politician? All these things are said by the enemy's agents and lackeys to keep you away from politics and from society's affairs and to prevent you from fighting the authorities of treason and tyranny so that they may have a free hand, may do what they like and may plunder whatever they want without any opposition or any obstruction.

NEED FOR GOVERNMENT

Need for Executive Agencies

An aggregation of laws is not sufficient to reform society. For a law to be an element for reforming and making people happy, it requires an executive authority. This is why God, may He be praised, created on earth, in addition to the laws, a government and an executive and administrative agency. The great Prophet, may God's prayers be upon him, headed all the executive agencies running the Muslim society. In addition to the tasks of conveying, explaining and detailing the laws and the regulations, he took care of implementing them until he brought the State of Islam into existence. In his time, the Prophet was not content with legislating the penal code, for example, but also sought to implement it. He cut off hands, whipped and stoned. After the Prophet, the tasks of the caliph were no less than those of the Prophet. The appointment of a caliph was not for the sole purpose of explaining the laws but also for implementing them. This is the goal that endowed the caliphate with importance and significance. The Prophet, had he not appointed a caliph to succeed him, would have been considered to have failed to convey his message. The Muslims were new to Islam and were in direct need for somebody to implement the laws and to make God's will and orders the judge among people to secure their happiness in this world and in the hereafter.

In truth, the social laws and regulations need an executor. In all countries of the world, legislation alone is not enough and cannot secure people's happiness. The legislative authority must be followed by an executive authority, which is the only authority that can bring to people the fruits of just legislation. This is why Islam decided to establish an executive authority side by side with the legislative authority, and appoint a person to implement [the legislation], in addition to teaching, disseminating and explaining.[1]

Methods of the Great Prophet, May God's Prayers be Upon Him

We learn from the Prophet's doings and sayings and from his conduct that it is necessary to form government, first because he himself formed a government. History attests to this. The Prophet assumed the leadership in managing society. He appointed rulers [*walat*] for the provinces, acted as a judge to settle the disputes among people and sent ambassadors outside the borders of his state, to the chiefs of tribes and to kings. He concluded treaties and he led wars. Consequently, he implemented all the laws of Islam.

Second, he appointed, on orders from God, a successor to carry out these tasks after him. This appointment of a successor indicates clearly the need for the government to continue after the Prophet. Considering that this appointment of a successor was on orders from God, then the continuation of government and of its agencies and organizations is also ordered by God.

Need for Continued Implementaton of Laws

It is obvious that the need for implementing the laws was not exclusive to the Prophet's age, and that this need continues because Islam is not limited by time or place. Because Islam is immortal, it must be implemented

---

[1] The Koranic verse "O you believers, obey God, obey the Prophet and obey those in charge among you" requires us to obey those in charge. The people in charge after the Prophet are the Imams who have been entrusted with explaining the Islamic laws and rules and with disseminating them among the Muslims and other peoples of the world. The Imams have also been entrusted with implementing these laws and rules. The just *faqihs* have been required to carry out these tasks after the Imams.

Editor's note: The numbered footnotes are reproduced here just as they appear in the original text of Khomeini's book. I apologize to any readers inconvenienced by the fact that full bibliographic information is not always provided. — TI

and observed forever. If what was permissible by Muhammad is permissible until the day of resurrection and what was forbidden by Muhammad is forbidden to the day of resurrection, then Muhammad's restrictions must not be suspended, his teachings must not be neglected, punishment must not be abandoned, tax collection must not be stopped and defense of the nation of the Muslims and of their lands must not be abandoned. The belief that Islam came for a limited period and for a certain place violates the essentials of the Islamic beliefs. Considering that the implementation forever of laws after the venerable Prophet, may God's prayers be upon him, is one of the essentials of life, then it is necessary for government to exist and for this government to have the qualities of an executive and administrative authority. Without this, social chaos, corruption, and ideological and moral deviation would prevail. This can be prevented only through the creation of a just government that runs all aspects of life.

In regard to the existence of government, it was proven by logic and law that what was necessary during the days of the Prophet, may God's prayers be upon him, and during the reign of the Amir of the Faithful, Ali ibn Abi Talib, peace be upon him, is still necessary to this day. To explain this to you I shall raise the following question: More than one thousand years have passed since the disappearance of Imam al-Mahdi [the messiah]* and thousands more years may pass before there is a need for the appearance of the awaited Imam. During this long period should we suspend all Islamic laws and people can do as they wish? Wouldn't chaos result from such a thing? The laws that were called for by the Prophet of Islam, may God's prayers be upon him, who worked very hard for twenty-three years to spread them, explain them and implement them, was all that for a limited term? Did God limit the age of the religious laws [shari'a] to two hundred years, for example? Should Islam lose everything after the disappearance [of the Imam]? To accept this, in my opinion, is worse than believing Islam is plagiarized. Nobody who believes in God or the afterlife can say we should not defend the cities of the homeland, or that it is permissible not to pay *zakat* [alms tax] or *khumis* [one-fifth tax] or other taxes; nor will he call for suspension of the penal code of Islam, or freeze convictions and fines. Thus, anyone who exhibits the opinion of calling the formation of the Islamic government unnecessary is denying the need to execute Islamic laws. Thus, he is calling for its suspension and freezing. It follows from this that he denies the comprehensiveness and the eternalness of the Islamic religion.

In Time of the Amir of the Faithful

No Muslim doubted the need for the continued presence of the government after the Prophet, may God's prayers be upon him. All agreed on this. The disagreement was on who should follow. The government was present

---

*The twelfth Imam of the Shi'i sect. Shi'i doctrine believes that he will return to restore justice in the world.

after the Prophet, especially in the time of Ali, the Amir of the Faithful, with all its administrative and executive agencies. There is no doubt about this.

Veracity of Islamic Laws

The essence of the Islamic laws is another proof of the need for forming government. They show us that they are designed for the formation of a state with an administration, with a sound economy and with a high culture.

First, provisions of the Islamic canonical law contain various laws for a complete social system. Under this system, all of man's needs are met, beginning with the relationships of neighborliness, of children and tribe and with fellow citizens, with all aspects of family and married life and ending with legislation concerning war and peace, international relations, penal laws, commercial, industrial, and agricultural rights. The canonical law also regulates legal matrimony and what the couple eats when married and in the period of nursing. Islam regulates the duties of the parents who are entrusted with bringing up the children, the relationship of husband with wife and wife with husband and the relationship of each of them with the children. In all these spheres, Islam contains laws and regulations to raise perfect and virtuous human beings. Islam promulgates the law, keeps it alive, implements it and works intrinsically for it. It is well known to what degree Islam has devoted attention to society's political and economic relations so as to create a well-mannered and virtuous human being.

The venerable Koran and the noble Suna contain all the rules and regulations to make human beings happy and to lead them toward perfection.

Al-Kafi's book contains a chapter entitled: "Explanation of All That People Need in the Book and the Suna." The book explains everything. The Imam [al-Kafi] swears, according to some Hadiths, that all that people need is undoubtedly found in the Book and the Suna.

Second, when we thoroughly examine the nature of the provisions of the canonical law closely, it becomes certain to us that it is impossible to implement them except through a government with capable agencies. I will give you a few examples and the faithful brothers will have to explore the rest:

1. Financial Laws

The financial taxes legislated by Islam do not contain anything to indicate that they were legislated to gratify the poor, especially the *sadah* [descendants of the Prophet] among them. They indicate that their legislation was for the purpose of securing the expenditures of a major sovereign state.

For example, the one-fifth tax (*khumis*) is an enormous source of income that yields to the treasury enormous revenues, which constitute the larger part of this treasury. In our creed, one-fifth is collected for all gains, benefits and profits, whether from agriculture, commerce, minerals or treasures. A vegetable vendor participates in paying the one-fifth tax if he earns that which is in excess of his annual supply needs, as specified by the teachings of the shari'a on expenditure and spending. A ship's captain and a prospector for minerals and treasures also participate and pay to the imam or the Muslim ruler one-fifth of the surplus profits so that he may forward them to the treasury house. It is obvious that this enormous resource is for the purpose of managing the affairs of the Muslim state and of meeting all its financial needs. If we were to calculate one-fifth of the profits of the Muslim state or of the entire world, if it were Muslim, it would become obvious to us that these enormous funds are not for the purpose of meeting the needs of a *sayyid* [descendant of the prophet] or of an education seeker, but for a greater and broader purpose, i.e., for meeting the needs of an entire nation. When a Muslim state is established, then such a state must use the help of the one-fifth tax, of the alms tax [*al-Zakat*], the tax on non-Muslims[2] [*al-Jiziyah*] and the land tax [*al-Kharaj*].

When have the direct descendants from the Prophet been in need of such sums of money? The one-fifth tax collected from the Baghdad market is enough for the needs of all these descendants, for the expenses of all the theological academics, and for all the poor Muslims, not to mention the markets of Teheran, Islampol [Constantinople], Cairo and other markets. Such an enormous budget is intended for running the affairs of a major nation, for meeting the important essential needs of people and providing for the public health, educational, cultural, defense and development needs.

The coordination required by Islam in collecting, safeguarding and spending funds guarantees freedom of the public treasury from injustice and abuse. The treasury does not belong to the head of state, to the officials or to the government members. Any privileges may be abused. The nation's treasury is for all the people alike.

Should we throw this enormous wealth into the sea? Should we bury it in the ground until al-Hijjah [the messiah] comes or should we distribute it to fifty or five hundred thousand Hashimites [descendants of the Prophet]? If this money is given to them, would they not be astounded and amazed? Don't we know that the right of the Hashimites to this money goes only to the degree of what they need to spend purposefully and moderately? All that there is to the matter is that the Hashimites should take only their need and nothing more of the one-fifth tax. The Hadith says that these people should return to the Imam what exceeds their annual needs, and that the Imam should help them when what they take from the treasury house is not enough for their annual needs.

If we examine the revenues collected through the tax imposed on the followers of the Book, and through the land tax, we would find that there is an enormous wealth that cannot be taken lightly. The ruler or the governor [*wali*] must impose on the followers of the Book a tax compatible with their financial

---

[2] This is a tax collected annually from the followers of the Book [the Bible], [*dhimiuin* or *ahl al-dhimmah*] namely the Jews and the Christians. These people live under the protection of the Muslim state and are exempted from the one-fifth tax and the alms tax. They are also exempted from carrying arms to defend the Muslim state. They benefit from the state agencies in the same manner as Muslims do.

capacity. He must also impose a land tax on lands utilized under the supervision of the state, and this revenue must go to the [state] treasury [*bayt al-mal*]. All this requires the formation of special agencies, careful accounts, management and records and foresight so that there may be no chaos. All this indicates clearly the need to form government because these financial legislations cannot be realized until after completing and stabilizing the government administration.

2. Defense Laws

On the other hand, we find that the laws governing war [*jihad*] and defense of the Muslims to secure the nation's independence and dignity also indicate the need for forming government.

Islam has dictated the need for preparing and being fully ready and alert, even in peace time, according to His words, may He be praised: "Prepare for them all the force and the horses you can muster so that you may scare away the enemies of God and your enemies." Had the Muslims adhered to the meaning of this Koranic verse and had they been ready to fight under all circumstances, it would not have been possible for a handful of Jews to occupy our land and to damage and burn our al-Aqsa mosque* without being faced with any resistance. All this came about as an inevitable result of the failure of the Muslims to carry out God's instruction and their failure to form an upright and reliable government. Had the current Muslim rulers tried to implement the laws of Islam, abandoning all their differences, putting aside their disputes and their division and uniting in one hand in the face of the others, the bands of Jews and the puppets of America and Britain would not have been able to attain what they have attained, regardless of how much America and Britain support them. The reason for this is, of course, the fact that the Muslim rulers are unfit and unqualified.

The verse "prepare for them all the force you can muster... " orders that we be fully prepared and alert so that the enemies may not subject us to the worst forms of torture. But we did not unite; we split into factions, our hearts were disunited and we did not prepare, and so the oppressors went beyond all limits in tyrannizing us and inflicting injustice upon us.

3. Laws on Strictures, Blood Money and Penalties

These laws cannot be established without government authorities. Through these authorities, blood money is collected from the culprit and paid to the victim, restrictions are established and punishment is placed under the supervision and control of the judge.

Need for Political Revolution

At the early stage of Islam, the Umayyads and those supporting them tried to obstruct the stability of the government of Imam Ali ibn Abi Talib, even

---

*A Muslim holy shrine in Jerusalem burned after Israeli occupation of the Arab sector.

though it was a government that pleased God and the Prophet. With their hateful efforts, the method and system of government changed and deviated from Islam because the methods of the Umayyads were in complete contradiction with the teachings of Islam. The Abbasids came after the Umayyads and followed the same path. The caliphate changed and turned into a sultanate and a hereditary monarchy. The rule became similar to that of the emperors of Persia and Rome and the pharaohs of Egypt. This situation has continued until our present day.

The shari'a and reason require us not to let governments have a free hand. The proof of this is evident. The persistence of these governments in their transgressions means obstructing the system and laws of Islam, whereas there are numerous provisions that describe every non-Islamic system as a form of idolatry and a ruler or an authority in such a system as a false god. We are responsible for eliminating the traces of idolatry from our Moslem society and for keeping it away from our life. At the same time, we are responsible for preparing the right environment for bringing up a faithful generation that destroys the thrones of false gods and destroys their illegal powers because corruption and deviation grow on their hands. This corruption must be wiped out and erased and the severest punishment must be inflicted upon those who are responsible for it. In His venerable book, God describes Pharaoh as "a corrupter." Under the canopy of a pharaonic rule that dominates and corrupts society rather than reforms it, no faithful and pious person can live abiding by and preserving his faith and piety. Such a person has before him two paths, and no third: Either be forced to commit sinful acts, or rebel against and fight the rule of false gods, trying to wipe out or at least reduce the effect of such a rule. We only have the second path open to us. We have no alternative but to work for destroying the corrupt and corrupting systems and to destroy the symbol of treason and the unjust among the rulers of peoples.

This is a duty with which all Muslims wherever they may be are entrusted — a duty to create a victorious and triumphant Islamic political revolution.

Need for Islamic Unity

On the other hand, colonialism has partitioned our homeland and has turned the Muslims into separate peoples. When the Ottoman state appeared as a united state, the imperialists sought to fragment it. The Russians, the British and their allies united and fought the Ottomans and then shared the spoils, as you all know. We do not deny that most rulers of the Ottoman state lacked ability, competence and qualifications, and many of them ruled the people in a despotic, monarchic manner. However, the imperialists were afraid that some pious and qualified persons would, with the help of the people, assume leadership of the Ottoman state and [would safeguard] its unity, ability, strength and wealth, thus disappointing the hopes and aspirations of the imperialists. This is why as soon as World War I ended, the colonialists partitioned the country into mini-states and made each of these mini-states their satellite. Despite this, a number of these mini-states later escaped the grip of colonialism and its agents.

The only means that we possess to unite the Muslim nation, to liberate its lands from the grip of the colonialists, and to topple the agent governments of colonialism is to seek to establish our Islamic government. The efforts of this government will be crowned with success when we become able to destroy the heads of treason, the idols, the human images and the false gods who disseminate injustice and corruption on earth.

Thus the formation of a government is for the purpose of preserving the unity of the Muslims after it is achieved. This was mentioned in the speech of Fatimah al-Zahra', may peace be upon her, when she said: "In obeying us lies the nation's order and our imamhood is a guarantee against division. ... "

Need for Rescuing the Oppressed and Deprived

To achieve their unjust economic goals, the imperialists employed the help of their agents in our countries. As a result of this, there are hundreds of millions of starving people who lack the simplest health and educational means. On the other side, there are individuals with excessive wealth and broad corruption. The starving people are in a constant struggle to improve their conditions and to free themselves from the tyranny of the aggressive rulers. But the ruling minorities and their government agencies are also seeking to extinguish this struggle. On our part, we are entrusted to rescue the deprived and the oppressed. We are instructed to help the oppressed and to fight the oppressors, as the Amir of the Faithful [Ali] instructed his two sons in his will: "Fight the tyrant and aid the wronged."

The Muslim ulema are entrusted to fight the greedy exploiters so that society may not have a deprived beggar and, on the other side, someone living in comfort and luxury and suffering from gluttony. The Amir of the Faithful [Ali] says: "By Him Who split the seed and created the breeze, were it not for the presence of the Omnipresent, the presence of the proof of the existence of the Victory Giver, and were it not for God's instructions to the ulema not to condone the oppression of a tyrant nor the suffering of the wronged, I would let matters go unchecked and would get the end mixed up with the beginning, and you would find this world of yours less significant to me than a goat's sneeze."[3]

How can we today tolerate to keep silent on a handful of exploiters and foreigners who dominate with the force of arms when these people have denied hundreds of millions of others the joy of enjoying the smallest degree of life's pleasures and blessings? The duty of the ulema and of all the Muslims is to put an end to this injustice and to seek to bring happiness to millions of

[3]Nahju al-Balaghah, 1/41

people through destroying and eliminating the unjust governments and through establishing a sincere and active Muslim government.

The Need for Formation of Government in Hadith

This need has already been proven by the dictates of reason and of the shari'a, by the Prophet's life and by the life of the Amir of the Faithful and through the meaning of many Koranic phrases and Hadiths. As an example of this need, we will cite the edification [spiritual instruction] related by Imam al-Rida:

> "'Abd-al-Wahid ibn Muhammad ibn 'Abdus al-Nisaburi al-'Attar said, [and] Abu-al-Hasan 'Ali ibn Muhammad ibn Qutaybah al-Nisaburi said, [and] Abu Muhammad al-Fadl ibn Shathan al-Nisaburi said:* If somebody asks, Tell me, is it possible that the Wise appoints [rulers]? and if somebody asks, Why did He appoint people in charge and order that they be obeyed—
>
> It has been said [it was done] for many reasons, one of them the fact that people have been ordered to observe certain strictures and not to violate them, because violating the restrictions corrupts people. This could not be established and realized without appointing a trustee over the people to watch over circumstances, and prevent them from violating what is banned to them. Without this, nobody would abandon his benefit and pleasure so that he may not corrupt others — this is what the incorrect version [of the Hadith] says, whereas the correct version is: Nobody would abandon his pleasure. The reasons also include the fact that we find no sect or group that lived and survived without values and a leader to manage their inevitable religious and secular affairs. In His wisdom, God would not leave the people without that which He knows they must have and without which they cannot survive, that with which to fight their enemy, to divide their rewards, to unite them and to deter the oppressor among them from doing others an injustice. The reasons also include the fact that if He did not appoint for the people an imam, trustee, preserver and pacifier, the nation would be obliterated, religion would disappear, laws and rules would be changed and the heretics would add to them and the atheists would detract from them and would have attributed this to the Moslems because we have found people to be deficient and imperfect, regardless of their inclinations and their various states. Had He not set up a trustee and a preserver, the first Prophet would not have appointed one and people would have degenerated as we have demonstrated; laws, rules and faith would have changed and this would have led to the corruption of all mankind."[4]

You can see that the Imam cites several aspects as proof of the need for the presence of a person in charge to govern people. The reasons that he mentioned are present at all times. Consequently, it is necessary to form the

---

* This is the typical form used in tracing back the authority and authenticity of a Hadith. — TI

[4] 'a lail alshari' 1/183 Hadith 9.

Islamic government at all times because violating the restrictions of God, seeking personal pleasure, spreading corruption on earth and disregarding the rights of the weak are things that are present at all times and are not confined to a specific time. This is why the Divine Wisdom dictated that people live justly within the restrictions imposed upon them by God. This Wisdom is constant and everlasting. Therefore, the presence of a person in charge of the Islamic laws and rules is essential because such a presence prevents injustice, violation and corruption and because this person carries the trust, guides people to the straight path and thwarts the heresies of the atheists and of the pertinacious. Wasn't the caliphate given to the Amir of the Faithful for this purpose? These reasons and needs that made Imam Ali take charge of the people are present currently, with one difference, namely that the Imam is specifically specified as the man in charge, whereas in our days the personality of the legitimate ruler has been defined through defining his identity, qualities, and qualifications in a general manner.

If we want to immortalize the rules of the shari'a in practice, to prevent violation of the rights of weak people, to prevent corruption on earth, to apply the shari'a laws justly, to fight the heresies and the deviations decided upon by the sham parliaments and to prevent the influence and intervention of the enemies in the affairs of the Muslims, we must form the government because all this is carried out by a government led by a trustworthy and pious ruler who commits no injustice, deviation or corruption.

Previously, we did not work and did not rise together to form a government to destroy all the traitors and corrupters. Some of us have displayed timidity even in the theoretical sphere and have failed to call for Islam and for spreading its laws. Perhaps some of us have been preoccupied with propagating [the views of the corrupt ruler]. As a result of all this, all these conditions have come into existence; the influence of the Islamic law in the Muslim society has diminished; the nation has been afflicted with division, weakness and degeneration; the rules of Islam have been obstructed; the situation has changed and the colonialists have used all this as an easy opportunity, brought foreign laws to which God has given no power, spread their poisoned cultures and thoughts and disseminated them among the Muslims. All this because we lost the leader who is entrusted with the affairs of the Muslims and because we lost the formation of good government. All this is obvious.

ISLAMIC SYSTEM OF GOVERNMENT

Its Distinction From All Other Political Systems

The Islamic government is not similar to familiar forms of government. It is not a despotic government in which the head of state dictates his opinion and tampers with the lives and property of the people. The Prophet, may God's prayers be upon him, and Ali, the Amir of the Faithful, and the other Imams had no power to tamper with people's property or with their lives. The

Islamic government is not absolute but constitutional. However, it is not constitutional in the popular sense of the word, which means representation in the parliamentary system or in the people's councils. It is constitutional in the sense that those in charge of affairs observe a number of conditions and rules outlined in the Koran and in the Suna and represented in the necessity of observing the system and of applying the dictates and laws of Islam. This is why the Islamic government is the government of the Divine Law. The difference between the Islamic government and the constitutional governments, both monarchic and republican, lies in the fact that the people's representatives or the king's representatives are the ones who codify and legislate whereas the power of legislation is confined to God, may He be praised, and no one else has the right to legislate and no one may rule by that which has not been given power by God. This is why Islam replaces the legislative council[5] by a planning council that works to run the affairs and work of the ministries so that they may offer their services in all spheres.

In the view of the Muslims all that is mentioned in the Koran and in the Suna is believed and obeyed. This submission facilitates the state's responsibilities, whereas when the majorities in the constitutional, monarchic or republican governments legislate something, the government has to exert efforts later to compel people to obey, even if such obedience requires the use of force.

The Islamic government is the government of the law and God alone is the ruler and the legislator. God's rule is effective among all the people and in the state itself. All individuals—the Prophet, his successors and other people—follow what Islam, which descended through revelation and which God has explained through the Koran and through the words of his Prophet, has legislated for them.

The venerable Prophet, may God's peace and prayers be upon him, was appointed ruler on earth by God so that he might rule justly and not follow whims. God addressed the Prophet through revelation and told him to convey what was revealed to him to those who would succeed him. The Prophet obeyed the dictates of this order and appointed Ali, the Amir of the Faithful, as his successor. He was not motivated in this appointment by the fact that Ali was his son-in-law and the fact that Ali had performed weighty and unforgettable services, but because God ordered the Prophet to do so.

Yes, government in Islam means obeying the law and making it the judge. The powers given to the Prophet, may God's peace and prayers be upon him, and to the legitimate rulers after him are powers derived from God. God ordered that the Prophet and the rulers after him be obeyed: "Obey the Prophet and those in charge among you." There is no place for opinions and whims in the government of Islam. The Prophet, the Imams and the people obey God's will and shari'a.

The government of Islam is not a monarchy, not a shahinshahdom

---

[5] The legislative council is one of three powers in all states in modern ages. These are the legislative power, the judiciary power and the executive power (cabinet).

and not an empire, because Islam is above squandering and unjustly under-mining the lives and property of people. This is why the government of Islam does not have the many big palaces, the servants, the royal courts, the crown prince courts and other trivial requirements that consume half or most of the country's resources and that the sultans and the emperors have. As you all know, the life of the great Prophet was a life of utter simplicity, even though the Prophet was the head of the state who headed it, directed it and ruled it by himself. This method continued to a degree after him and until the Umayyads seized power. The government of 'Ali ibn Abi Talib was a government of reform, as you know, and 'Ali, peace be upon him, lived a life of utter simplicity while managing a vast state in which Iran, Egypt, Hejaz and Yemen were mere provinces under his rule. I do not believe that any of our poor people can live the kind of life that the Imam lived. When he had two cloaks, he gave the better one to Qanbar, his servant, and he wore the other. When he found extra material in his sleeves, he cut it off. Had this course continued until the present, people would have known the taste of happiness and the country's treasury would not have been plundered to be spent on fornication, abomina-tion and the court's costs and expenditures. You know that most of the corrupt aspects of our society are due to the corruption of the ruling dynasty and the royal family. What is the legitimacy of these rulers who build houses of enter-tainment, corruption, fornication and abomination, and who destroy houses which God permitted to be raised [mosques] and in which His name is men-tioned? Were it not for what the court wastes and what it embezzles, the country's budget would not experience any deficit that forces the state to borrow from America and England, with all the humiliation and insult that accompany such borrowing. Has our oil decreased or have our minerals that are stored under this good earth run out? We possess everything and we would not need the help of America or of others if it were not for the extravagance of the court and for its wasteful use of the people's money. This is on the one hand. On the other hand, there are state agencies that are not needed and that consume money, resources, paper and equipment. This is a waste banned by our shari'a because such waste escalates the people's problems, wastes their time and efforts and consume monies of which they are in need. In Islam — during its rule — justice was dispensed, restrictions established and disputes settled with utter simplicity. The judge saw to it that all this was done by a handful of persons with some pencils and a little ink and paper. Behind all this, the judge directed people to work for an honorable and virtuous life. But now, only God knows the number of the justice offices, bureaus and employees — all of which are futile and do the people no good, not to mention the hardship, difficulties, waste of time and monies, and, consequently, the loss of justice and rights that they cause the people.

Qualifications of a Ruler

The qualifications that must be present in a ruler emanate from the nature of the Islamic government. Regardless of the general qualifications, such as intelligence, maturity, and a good sense of management, there are two important qualifications:

1. Knowledge of the Islamic law.
2. Justice.

1. Knowledge of the Islamic Law

In view of the fact that the Islamic government is a government of law, it is a must that the ruler of the Muslims be knowledgeable in the law, as the Hadith says. Whoever occupies a [public] post or carries out a certain task must know as much as he needs within the limits of his jurisdiction and the ruler must be more knowledgeable than everybody else. Our Imams proved their worthiness of the people's trust by their early search for knowledge. What the Shi'ite ulema criticized others for revolves mostly around the level of knowledge attained by our ulema — a standard that the others failed to rise to.

Knowledge of the law and of justice are among the most important mainstays of the imamate. If a person knows a lot about nature and its secrets and masters many arts but is ignorant of the law, then his knowledge does not qualify him for the caliphate and does not put him ahead of those who know the law and deal with justice. It is an acknowledged fact among Moslems since the first day and until our present day that the ruler or the caliph must know the law and possess the faculty of justice with a sound faith and good ethics. This is what a sound reason requires, especially since we know that the Islamic government is an actual embodiment of the law and not a matter of whims. A person ignorant of the laws is not qualified to rule because if he imitates in his decisions, his rule will have no dignity and if he does not imitate, he will be unable to carry out the laws, assuming he is totally ignorant of the laws. It is an acknowledged fact that "the jurists are rulers over the kings." If the sultans are pious at all, then all they have to do is proceed in their decisions and actions on the advice of jurists. In such a case, the real rulers are the jurists and the sultans are nothing but people working for them.

Naturally, it is not the duty of any civil servant whatever his task to know all the laws and to study them deeply. It is enough for such a person to familiarize himself with the laws relevant to his function or to the task entrusted to him. This is how matters proceeded in the time of the Prophet and of the Amir of the Faithful. The supreme ruler knows all the Islamic laws and the emissaries, envoys, governors and provincial rulers are content to know the laws and legislation pertaining to their tasks and refer to the sources of legislation designated for them on matters that they do not know.

2. Justice

The ruler must have the highest degree of faith in the creed, good ethics, the sense of justice and freedom from sins because whoever undertakes to set the strictures, to achieve the rights and to organize the revenues and expenditures of the treasury house must not be unjust. God says in His precious book: "The unjust shall not have my support." Thus, if the ruler is not just, he cannot be trusted not to betray the trust and not to favor himself, his family and his relatives over the people.

The Shi'a view of who is entitled to rule the people is known since the death of the Prophet and until the time of the disappearance [of the Shi'ite leader]. To the Shi'a, the imam is a virtuous man who knows the laws and implements them justly and who fears nobody's censure in serving God.

Ruler in Time of Absence

If we believe that the laws concerning the establishment of the Islamic government are still valid and that the shari'a denounces chaos, then we must form the government. Reason dictates that this is necessary, especially if an enemy surprises us or if an aggressor who must be fought and repelled attacks us. The shari'a has ordered us to prepare for them all the force that we can muster to scare God's enemy and our enemy, and it encourages us to retaliate against those who attack us with whatever they attack us. Islam also calls for doing justice to the wronged, for restoring his rights and for deterring the unjust. All this requires strong agencies. As for the expenses of the government that is to be formed for the service of the people — the entire people — these expenses come from the treasury house whose revenues consist of the land tax, the one-fifth tax and the tax levied on Jews and Christians and other resources.

Now, in the time of absence [of the Imam al-Mahdi] there is no provision for a certain person to manage the state affairs. So what is the opinion? Should we allow the laws of Islam to continue to be idle? Do we persuade ourselves to turn away from Islam, or do we say that Islam came to rule people for a couple of centuries and then to neglect them after that? Or do we say that Islam has neglected to organize the state? We know that the absence of the government means the loss and violations of the bastions of the Muslims and means our failure to gain our right and our land. Is this permitted in our religion? Isn't the government one of the necessities of life? Despite the absence of a provision designating an individual to act on behalf of the imam [al-Mahdi] in the case of his absence, the presence of the qualities of the religious ruler in any individual still qualify him to rule the people. These qualities, which are knowledge of the law and justice, are available in most of our jurists in this age. If they decide, it will be easy for them to create and establish a just international government that cannot be matched.

Rule of Jurists

If a knowledgeable and just jurist undertakes the task of forming the government, then he will run the social affairs that the Prophet used to run and it is the duty of the people to listen to him and obey him.

This ruler will have as much control over running the people's administration, welfare and policy as the Prophet and Amir of the Faithful had, despite the special virtues and the traits that distinguished the Prophet and the

Imam. Their virtues did not entitle them to contradict the instructions of the shari'a or to dominate people with disregard to God's order. God has given the actual Islamic government that is supposed to be formed in the time of the absence the same powers that he gave the Prophet and the Amir of the Faithful in regard to ruling, justice and the settlement of disputes, the appointment of provincial rulers and governors, the collection of taxes [on non-Muslims], and the development of the country. All that there is to the matter is that the appointment of the ruler at present depends on locating someone who has both knowledge and justice.

Subjective Rule

The above-mentioned must not be misunderstood. One should not assume that the qualifications of the jurist to rule elevates his status to that of the Prophet or of the Imams. This discussion here is not related [to the issues of] status and rank but is concerned with the practical task [of rule]. Rule here means governing the people, running the state and executing the laws of the shari'a. This is a difficult task under which those qualified for it buckle without being raised above the level of men. In other words, rule means the government, the administration and the country's policy and not, as some people imagine, a privilege or a favor. It is a practical task of utmost significance.

The rule of the jurist is a subjective matter dictated by the shari'a, as the shari'a entrusts [an adult] with guardianship over one's children. The task of a guardian over an entire people is not different from that of the guardian over children, except quantitatively. If we assume that the Prophet and the Imam had been guardians over children, their task in this respect would not have been very different quantitatively and qualitatively from the task of any ordinary person designated as a guardian over those same children. Their guardianship over the entire nation is not different practically from the guardianship of any knowledgeable and just jurist in the time of absence.

If a just jurist capable of establishing the restrictions is appointed, would he establish the restrictions in a manner different from that in which they were established in the days of the Prophet or of the Amir of the Faithful? Did the Prophet punish the unmarried fornicator more than one hundred lashes? Does the jurist have to reduce the number to prove that there is a difference between him and the Prophet? No, because the ruler, be he a Prophet, an Imam or a just jurist, is nothing but an executor of God's order and will.

The Prophet collected taxes — the one-fifth tax, the alms tax, the tax on the Christians and the Jews and the land tax. Is there a difference between what the Prophet and the Imam collected and what the present-day jurist should collect?

God made the Prophet the custodian of all the faithful and his domain included even the individual who was to succeed him. After the Prophet, the Imam became the custodian. The meaning of their rule is that their orders are legitimate and are applicable to all and that the appointment of, control over and, when necessary, dismissal of judges and governors was in their hands.

The jurist has this same rule and governance with one difference, namely that the rule of the jurist over other jurists is not so that he can dismiss them or appoint them because the jurists in the state are equal in terms of qualifications.

Therefore, the jurists must work separately or collectively to set up a legitimate government that establishes the strictures, protects the borders and establishes order. If competence for this task is confined to one person, then this would be his duty to do so corporeally; otherwise the duty is shared equally. In case of difficulty in forming that government, the [attribution] to rule does not disappear. The jurists have been appointed by God to rule and the jurist must act as much as possible in accordance with his assignment. He must collect the alms tax, the one-fifth tax, the land tax and the tax from Christians and Jews if he can, so that he may spend all this in the interest of the Muslims. If he can, he must implement the divine strictures. The temporary inability to form a strong and complete government does not at all mean that we should retreat. Dealing with the needs of the Muslims and implementing among them whatever laws are possible to implement is a duty as much as possible.

Nascent Rule

Confirmation of rule and governance for the Imam does not mean stripping him of the status which he occupies with God and does not make him like other rulers. The Imam has a commendable status, a sublime rank and nascent rule to whose control all the particles of this universe are subject. It is one of the essentials of our creed that our Imams possess that which no favored king and no dispatched prophet possesses. According to the narrations and the Hadiths we have, the Great Prophet and the Imams were before the creation of this world lights and God set them around His throne and gave them a status and a place that only God knows. The angel Jibra'il [Gabriel] says in the tales of al-Mi'raj [the Prophet's midnight journey to the seven heavens]: "Had I come a hair's breadth nearer, I would have been burned." The Imams are quoted as having said: "We have with God states that no favored king nor a dispatched prophet approaches." Such a place is held by Fatimah al-Zahra', peace be upon her, not because she was a caliph, a ruler or a judge, because the place of rule, caliphate or amirate is something else. When we say that Fatimah was not a judge, a ruler or a caliph, then this does not mean that she does not possess that favored status, and it also doesn't mean that she was an ordinary woman, like the women we have. If somebody says that the Prophet is above the faithful, then he has given the Prophet a place beyond that of being a ruler or a governor of the faithful. We do not object to this and we rather support it, even though this is something that only God knows.

Government Is a Means for Achieving Sublime Goals

Running state affairs does not give those in charge of running them a higher place and status because the government is a means for implementing the laws and for establishing the just Islamic system. Government is deprived of all value if it comes to be considered a goal sought for itself. The Amir of the Faithful once said to Ibn 'Abbas, while the Amir was mending the sole of a shoe: "What is the worth of this sole?" Ibn 'Abbas said: "It has no value." The Imam said: "By God it is worth more to me than being your ruler, unless I set matters aright or prevent an injustice."[6] The Imam was not seeking power nor was he fond of it. He says: "By Him Who split the seed and created the breeze, were it not for the presence of the Omnipresent and of the presence of the proof of the existence of the Victory Giver and for God's demand from the ulema not to condone the injustice of a tyrant and the suffering of the wronged, I would let matters go, would mix up its end with its beginning and you would find this world of yours less significant to me than a goat's sneeze."

Governing is not an end in itself. It is a means of value as long as its goal is noble. If sought as a goal, and if all means are used to attain it, then it degenerates to the level of a crime and its seekers come to be considered among the criminals. Our Imams did not have the opportunity to take charge of affairs, even though they waited for this opportunity to the end of their lives. The just jurist must wait for opportunities and must exploit them to form and organize a wise government intended to carry out God's order and to establish a just system, even though this may require strenuous efforts from them. No excuse for [avoiding this responsibility] will be acceptable. The jurist's taking charge of people's affairs as much as possible represents in itself obedience to God's order and a performance of the duty required by the shari'a.

To prove that government is a means and not a goal we mention what the Amir of the Faithful said in the speech that he made in the Prophet's mosque after he was given the pledge of allegiance by the people: "God, You know that what we have done was not to compete for power nor to seek the ephemeral things of life, [but] rather to restore the landmarks of your religion and to achieve reform in your land so that the wronged among your worshippers may gain security and that your obstructed strictures may be carried out."

Qualities of the Ruler Who Achieves These Goals

In this same speech, the Imam [Ali] identifies the qualities that must be present in the ruler who wants to achieve the sublime goals. The Imam said: "God, I am the first to deputize, to hear and to answer, preceded to prayer only by the Prophet of God, may God's peace and prayers be upon him. You have taught that the ruler must not be a womanizer, and must not be bloodthirsty, a seeker of gains, of governance and of leadership of the Muslims. He

---

[6] *Najh al-Balagha,* Vol. 1, p. 80.

must not be greedy because he will covet what they possess, must not be ignorant because he will mislead them with his ignorance, must not be arrogant because he will alienate them with his arrogance, must not be fearful of states because he will favor some over others, must not be a taker of bribes because he will cause rights to be lost and must not obstruct the Suna because he will cause the nation to perish."

All this revolves, as you can see, around the ruler's knowledge and justice. They are two conditions that must be present in the Muslim ruler, as the Imam indicated when he said: "And he must not be ignorant because he will mislead them with his ignorance." In these words, the Amir of the Faithful refers to the first condition. In the rest of his Hadith, he refers to justice which means that the ruler must follow the example of the Amir of the Faithful in his rule, his relations and his association with the people. We have learned from the decree issued [by the Imam Ali] appointing Malik al-Ashtar governor of Egypt that these instructions apply to all governors, rulers, provincial governors and jurists in every age and place.

Successors of the Prophet Are Just Jurists.

Ali, the Amir of the Faithful, said that the Prophet of God said thrice: "God have mercy upon my successors." So he was asked: "O Prophet of God, who are your successors?" He said: "Those who come after me, transmit my statements and my laws and teach them to the people after me."[7]

Shaykh al-Saduq, may God have mercy upon him, mentions this narration in *Jami' al-Akhbar,* in *'Uyun Akhbar al-Rida* and in *al-Majalis* [all Hadith books] in five different versions, or at least in four versions because two relaters have a common name. When this narration is mentioned unquoted, it does not include the phrase "and they will teach them to the people after me." When quoted from various sources, the narration contains the phrase "and will teach them to the people" in some versions and "will teach them" in other versions.

Our discussions on this Hadith will focus on two assumptions:

1. Let us assume that this narration was relayed by *al-ahad* [people who misquoted the original statements of the Prophet] and that the phrase "and will teach them" was added to the Hadith, or assume that the phrase was in fact there but was dropped—and this is a more feasible assumption because we cannot accuse the three relaters of collusion to add this phrase, considering that there was no tie binding them, that one of them lived in Balakh, the other

---

[7] The author of *Wasa'il al-Shi'a* [Methods of the Shi'ite] mentions this Hadith in the "Book of the Judiciary," in the eighth chapter concerning the qualities of the modern *qadi* [judge] and also in detail in Chapter 11, Hadith 7. This Hadith is also mentioned in *Ma'ani al-Akhbar Wa al-Majalis* [Meaning of Messages and of Councils] in two versions and by a number of narrators, some of whom share the same name. It is also mentioned in three different versions in *'Uyun Akhbar al-Rida* [Sources of Good News].

in Nisabur and the third in Maru, that they lived very far apart and that they did not know one another. Therefore, we can say decisively that the phrase "and will teach them" in the version relayed by al-Saduq was dropped by the scribes or that al-Saduq forgot it.

2. Assume that there are two versions, one of them without the phrase "and they will teach them" and the other containing it. Let us assume that this phrase is present in the Hadith. The Hadith still does not include decisively those whose sole preoccupation is to relay the Hadith only without study and examination and without interpretation, without making conclusions and without the ability to reach a realistic judgment. We cannot describe such relaters as being qualified for the succession as long as they are mere transmitters or scribes of the Hadith who hear it and relay it to the people. We say this while acknowledging the value of the service that they offer Islam. The mere transmission and relay of the Hadith is not something that qualifies the transmitter or relater to succeed the Prophet because some transmitters and relaters might be the embodiment of the phrase "there may be a transmitter of jurisprudence who is not a jurist." This does not mean that there are no jurists among the transmitters and relaters because many are the transmitters who are jurists, such as al-Killaini, Shaykh al-Saduq and his father who were jurists who taught the people. When we differentiate between Shaykh al-Saduq and Shaykh al-Mufid, we do not mean by this distinction that Shaykh al-Saduq was not a jurist or that he was a lesser jurist than Shaykh al-Mufid.

How can we say this when it is said that Shaykh al-Saduq explained the religious fundaments and subsidiaries in one session? The difference between the two is that Shaykh al-Mufid exerts more efforts to make conclusions and examine the narrated versions of the Hadith more carefully and closely.

This Hadith is intended for those who seek to spread the sciences and laws of Islam and to teach them to the people, as the Prophet and the Imams taught and graduated thousands of ulema. If we say that Islam is an international religion, and this is clear and obvious, then the ulema of Islam must spread and disseminate the laws of this religion in the entire world.

Assuming that the phrase "teach them to the people" is not part of the Hadith, let us examine what the Prophet's phrase "God have mercy upon my successors who will come after me and relate my statements and my laws" means.

For this purpose, the Hadith does not mean the relaters to the exclusion of the jurist because the Prophet's law is the law of God and whoever wants to disseminate it must know all the divine laws, must be able to distinguish the correct Hadiths from the false ones, must be familiar with the general and with the particular and with what is absolute and what is restricted and must be able to combine them knowledgeably and rationally. He must also know the versions related under conditions forcing the Imams to resort to dissimulation, and preventing them from demonstrating the real judgments in certain cases. A Hadith transmitter who has not reached the rank of interpretation and who is just entrusted with transmitting the Hadith

cannot reach the truth of the law. In the opinion of the Prophet, such a transmitter of the Hadith is of no consequence. It is well known that the Prophet did
not want the people to be content with saying, "The Prophet, may God's peace
and prayers be upon him, said. ... " or "The messenger of God is quoted as
having said. ... " The Prophet did not want the people to be content with this,
regardless of the way the Hadith was quoted and related. The quotation "God
will make a jurist of whoever preserves for my people forty Hadiths," and other
quotations that glorify those who seek to spread the Hadith, are not intended to
mean the relater who does not understand what he relates and who perhaps is
transmitting to someone who understands more than him. These quotations
are intended for those who teach people the real laws of Islam. This cannot be
done except by a learned jurist who reaches the actual laws and derives them
from their sources in accordance with the criteria set for him by Islam and by
the Imams themselves. These interpreters of religion are the successors to the
messenger of God. They spread the Suna and the sciences of Islam and teach
and convey them to the people. This is why they deserve the Prophet's invoca-
tion in God's mercy for them.

There is no doubt then that the Hadith "God have mercy upon my
successors ... " has nothing to do with those who merely transmit the Hadith
without any jurisprudence because the mere scribing of the Hadith does not
qualify a person to succeed the Prophet. Those referred to are the jurists of
Islam who simplify the teachings and ethics of Islam and who combine justice
and true religion with their jurisprudence and knowledge.

A jurist distinguishes those who may be quoted from those who may
not be quoted. There are among the relaters of the Hadith those who have
falsified Hadiths of the Prophet. A relater like Samrah ibn Jandab falsifies
Hadiths that undermine the prestige of the Amir of the Faithful, Ali. There are
perhaps relaters who do not refrain from transmitting thousands of [false]
Hadiths praising unjust rulers and their conduct through the aides of ignorance and the ulema of the court, in order to glorify the sultans and justify
their actions. Such a thing is happening at present, as you can see. I do not
know why some people cling to two weak Hadiths in contrast to the Koran in
which God orders Moses to rise in the face of Pharaoh, who is a king, and in
contrast to the many Hadiths that order that the unjust be fought and resisted.
The idle ones among the people are the ones who put aside all this to cling to
two Hadiths that honor kings and justify cooperating with them. If such
people were truly religious, they would cite these two weak Hadiths* along
with the Hadiths that are opposed to the unjust and to their supporters. Such
relaters of the Hadith are unjust because they align themselves with the
enemies of God, because they steer away from the correct teachings of the
Koran and the Suna and because their gluttony, and not their knowledge, is
what made them do such a thing. The love of glory motivates some people to
march with the bandwagon of tyrants.

*Hadiths whose authority and authenticity are in question. — TI

Therefore, dissemination of Islam's laws and sciences is a task performed by just jurists who can differentiate right from wrong and who are aware of the pious lives which the Imams sustained. This piety led to the preservation of the creed from obliteration and not to the preservation of personal interest.

There is no reason to doubt that the transmission [of the Hadith] indicates that the jurist is the ruler and the successor in all affairs. The succession referred to in the phrase "God have mercy upon my successors" is no different from the succession referred to in the phrase "Ali is my successor."

The phrase "those who come after me and relay my statements" describes the character of the successor and does not explain the meaning of the succession because at the outset of Islam, succession was a clear concept. It was clear even to the person asking the question who did not ask the Prophet about the meaning of the succession but rather asked him: "Who are your successors?"

Nobody considered the position of a caliph [successor] in the days of the Amir of the Faithful and in the days of the Imams following him as a position of interpretation solely. Rather, the Muslims interpreted this position as a position of rule and governance and of carrying out God's orders and they cited too many proofs to be mentioned here in support of their interpretation. But why do some of us pause before the meaning of the phrase "God have mercy upon my successors?" Why do these people think that the succession to the Prophet's position is confined to a certain person? In view of the fact that the Imams were the successors to the Prophet, then other ulema may not rule and manage the affairs of people and let the Muslims remain without a legitimate ruler, let the laws of Islam remain idle and let the borders of the Muslims remain open for the enemies. This thinking and this position are far from Islam because it is a devious thinking which Islam disavows.

Muhammad ibn Yahya, citing Ahmad ibn Muhammad who quoted Ibn Mahbub who quoted 'Ali ibn Abi Hamzah, said: "I heard Abu-al-Hasan Musa ibn Ja'far, peace be upon him, say, 'When the faithful dies, the angels, the lands in which he worshipped God and the gates of heaven towards which he rose with his actions weep for him and he leaves in Islam an irreparable loss because the jurists are the fortress of Islam as the city's wall is its fortress.'"[8]

A Look at the Text of This Hadith

The same chapter of al-Kafi's book contains another version of this Hadith which says "when the faithful jurist dies ... " whereas the first part of this version of the Hadith does not contain the word "jurist." But it is indicated by the last part of the previous Hadith which says "because the faithful jurist ... " that the word "jurist" was [inadvertently] omitted from the first part of the Hadith, considering that this word is compatible with the Prophet's phrase

[8] Al-Kafi, *Fadl al-'Ilm* [Virtues of Knowledge], "Loss of Ulema" chapter, Third Hadith.

"loss for Islam" and his use of the word "fortress" and similar words compatible with the status of faithful jurists.

On The Meaning of the Hadith

His [Imam Abu-al-Hasan Musa ibn Ja'far] words "because the faithful jurists are the fortresses of Islam ... " are an assignment to the jurists to preserve Islam with its creeds, laws and systems. This statement was not made by the Imam in praise or commendation, or as part of the general courtesy acknowledged among us, like when I tell you that you are the authoritative source of Islam and you reciprocate with something similar.

If a jurist isolates himself from the people and their affairs and lives in a corner of his house, if he fails to preserve and disseminate the laws of Islam, to exert efforts to reform the affairs of Muslims and if he does not care for Muslims, can he be considered a fortress of Islam or a wall protecting it?

If the government head sends a person to a small area and orders him to tend and preserve it, does this man's duty permit him to stay in his home locking its doors, so the enemy may roam as he pleases and to wreak corruption on that area, or does his job require him to exert all his efforts to tend and preserve what he is entrusted with?

If you say we will keep some of the laws, then I will ask you this question: Will you carry out the strictures and apply the penal code of Islam? No! Then you will have created a crack in the edifice of Islam that should have been repaired and mended or should have been prevented from occurring in the first place.

Will you defend the borders and safeguard the security and independence of the lands of Islam?

No, we beseech God to do this!

Here, another side of the edifice has collapsed, in addition to the side that had already collapsed.

Will you collect the dues of the poor that are imposed by God on the money of the rich and give these dues to those who deserve them in implementation of what God has ordered?

No! This is not our concern. God willing, this will be achieved at the hands of others.

What remains of the edifice? The structure is about to be ruined. In this regard, you are like Shah Sultan Husayn and Asfahan.

What fortress of Islam are you? As soon as one of you is entrusted with preserving something, he declines! Is what is meant by the fortress of Islam your current situation?

His words that "the jurists are the fortresses of Islam" means that they are entrusted with preserving Islam with all their power. Preserving Islam is one of the most important, absolute and unconditional duties. This is what the religious academies and councils must think of thoroughly so that they may prepare themselves with agencies, resources and conditions under which the laws, creeds and rules are preserved and safeguarded, as the great prophet and the guided Imams preserved Islam.

We have been content with discussing a few rules concerning succession and we have discussed numerous aspects and details of this issue. Much of what we have discussed is strange to us. Islam in its entirety has become alien to us and what remains of it is its name only. Its penalties have been disregarded and the penalties specified by the Koran are recited as mere phrases. Only the form of Islam remains. We read the Koran for nothing more than to recite it well. As for the corrupt social situation, the spread of corruption throughout the country under the eyes and ears of the governments or with their support for and with their dissemination of fornication and abomination, this is something with which we are not concerned. It is enough for us to understand that there are certain strictures concerning adulterers and adulteresses. As for implementing these strictures and others, this is not our concern!

We ask: Is this how the great Prophet was? Was the Prophet content with reciting and singing the phrases of the Koran without establishing its strictures and implementing its rules? Were the Prophet's successors content with relaying the shari'a rules to the people and then letting people do whatever they wished to do? Did not the Prophet and his successors after him implement the strictures on lashing, stoning, jailing and banishing? Study again the works concerning strictures, penalties and blood money to find that all this is of the essence of Islam. Islam came to organize society through the just government that it establishes among the people.

We are entrusted with preserving Islam. This is one of the most important duties and is perhaps a no less important duty than praying and fasting. This is the duty for which noble blood was shed. There is no nobler blood than that of [Imam] al-Husayn which was shed for the sake of Islam. We must understand this and explain it to the people to understand it. You will be the Prophet's successors if you teach the people and familiarize them with the truth of Islam. Do not say we will leave this until al-Hijjah [the expected messiah], may peace be upon him, appears. Would you stop praying while waiting for al-Hijjah? Wouldn't you be saying what other people have said, namely: "We must wait until sins spread so that al-Hijjah may appear!" This means that if abomination does not spread, then al-Hijjah will not appear! Do not be content with sitting here and discussing private matters. Study the various laws deeply. Spread the facts of Islam. Write and publish what you write because this will influence people, God willing. I have tried this myself.

Jurists Are the Trustees of Prophets

Ali, citing Abih who quoted al-Nawfali who quoted al-Sukuni who quoted Abi 'Abdallah, said: "The messenger of God, may God's prayers and peace be upon him and upon his kinsmen, said: 'The jurists are the trustees of the prophets, unless they enter the world.' He was asked: 'O messenger of

God, what does their entering the world mean?' He said: 'Follow the sultan. If they do so, then beware of them for your religion.'"[9]

We cannot examine the Hadith in its entirety because this requires a long discussion. We must examine closely the phrase "the jurists are the representatives of the prophets."

We must first know the duties, functions, power and the works of the prophets and the messengers so that we may then know the assignments entrusted to the jurists by the prophets.

Aims of the Missions

By the dictates of reason, the aim behind the dispatch of messengers is not confined to explaining the laws and rules that they receive by revelation. The prophets were not only assigned to carry out these laws among the people with utter sincerity and the prophets were not content to entrust the jurists with explaining the issues that they learned from them. The phrase "the jurists are the trustees of the prophets" does not mean that the jurists are entrusted only to relate what the prophets said. The most important thing with which the prophets were entrusted was to establish a just system in society and to implement the laws. All this can be concluded from God's words: "We have sent our messengers with the evidence and we have sent down with them the book and the scales so that they may establish justice among people."[10] The real aim of sending the prophets was to establish justice among people and to organize their lives in accordance with the criteria of the shari'a. This can be done only by a government that implements the laws. The same way this government is embodied in the person of the prophet or the messenger, it is also embodied in the Imams and in the learned, faithful and just jurists after them, because governing people and establishing right and a just system is required in all cases.

When God says "Know that one-fifth of what you gain is for God, the prophet and for his kinsmen"[11] and when He says "Take alms from their monies"[12] and when He gives other such orders, then this does not mean that the prophet is not only entrusted to convey this to the people, but is also

---

[9] Al-Kafi's book, *Fadl al-'Ilm* [Virtues of Knowledge], Chapter 13, Hadith 5. This Hadith is also included in what al-Niraqi related. Al-Nuri also transmitted the Hadith in Chapter 38 of the book *Mustadrak al-Wasa'il*, Hadith 8, citing the book *al-Nawadir* by al-Rawandi, who quotes correctly Imam Musa ibn Ja'far and the book *Da'a'im al-Islam* [Mainstays of Islam], Chapter 11 on the qualities of the judge, and also quoting Hadith 5 from Imam Ja'far ibn Muhammad. Al-Kafi's book itself contains another Hadith to this effect, citing Abi 'Abdallah, peace be upon him, who said: "The ulema are trustees, the pious are fortresses and the prophets are masters."

[10] *Al-Hadid.*

[11] *Al-anqal,* 43.

[12] *Al-Tawbah,* 104.

ordered to act upon it and implement it. He is ordered to collect these taxes from the people who should pay them so that he may spend them in the interest of the Muslims. He is ordered to spread justice among the people, to establish the strictures, to protect the borders of the Muslims, to guard the country against the enemies and to prevent anybody from exploiting the nation's treasury. The venerable Koran says: "Obey God, obey the Prophet and obey those in charge among you. ... [13] This means that we must not only believe what they have told us but must also act upon it and obey it because this pleases God. God says in another part of His book: "Take what the Prophet has brought you, refrain from what he had ordered you to refrain from and have the fear of God."[14] Obedience to the Prophet is obedience to God, because the Prophet does not speak out of whims but out of revelation. If the Prophet orders that Usamah's campaign be joined, then nobody would be disobedient to the messenger when the messenger is given charge of the affairs of Muslims and assigned to run their affairs, to direct and guide them and to appoint for them provincial rulers, governors and judges, and to dismiss them if necessary.

Jurists are Representatives of Messengers in Commanding the Army, Managing Society, Defending the Nation and Adjudicating Among People.

The above-mentioned Hadith in which the jurists are trusted by the messengers makes it a condition that the jurists refrain from worldly desires because a jurist whose concern is to amass ephemeral things is not just, is not trusted by the Prophet and does not implement his laws. The just jurists are the only ones qualified to implement the laws and rules of Islam, to establish Islam's strictures and to protect the borders of the Muslims. In any case, the prophets have entrusted the jurists with all the powers to which they themselves were authorized and have trusted them with that which they themselves were trusted with. Thus, the jurists are the ones who collect the taxes to spend them in the interests of the Muslims and they are the ones who correct whatever corruption there is in the affairs of Muslims. The Prophet was charged with implementing the laws and establishing the system and so are the jurists to whom the rule belongs and on whose shoulders fall the burdens of implementing the laws, establishing God's stricture, fighting his enemies and eliminating every source of corruption.

Law-Abiding Government

In view of the fact that the government of Islam is the government of law, only the jurist, and nobody else, should be in charge of the government. He is the one to undertake what the Prophet undertook, without adding any-

[13] *Al-Nisa'*, 63.
[14] *Al-Hashr*, 7.

thing to it or striking away from it. He is the one to establish the strictures as the prophets established them, to govern as God has ordered, to collect the excess monies of people as this was done in the days of the Prophet and to organize the treasury and be trusted with it. If the jurist violates the dictates of the shari'a laws, God forbid, then he is dismissed voluntarily for lacking the element of trustworthiness. The supreme ruler is, in fact, the law, and all must live under its canopy. People are born free and are free in their legal actions. Nobody has a right over somebody else and nobody may, when the law is implemented, force anybody to sit anywhere or to go anywhere unjustly. The government of Islam reassures and secures the Muslims and does not take away their reassurance and security like the governments under which the Muslim lives in fear, expecting them to attack his home at any moment and to take away his life, his money and all he possesses, as you can see with your own eyes. Such a thing happened in the days of Mu'awiyah who killed people on mere suspicion and accusation, jailed people for long times, banished them from the country and would unjustly drive people out of their homes for no reason other than their saying God is our God. Mu'awiyah's government did not represent the Muslim government or resemble it closely or remotely. If God wills the Muslim government to arise, and this is not beyond God's will, then everybody will be reassured about his life, his money, his kinsmen and his possessions, because no ruler is empowered to carry out among the people acts in violation of the stipulations of the glorious Islamic law. This is what the word "trust" means. It is well known, as already pointed out, that trust is not confined to honesty in relaying, transmitting or interpreting only but also includes honesty in action, in application and in implementation, even though honesty in transmitting and interpreting is of great importance. The Prophet and the Amir of the Faithful spoke and acted upon their words and God trusted them with His message. God trusted the messengers and the jurists to speak out, to work, to hold prayers, to collect taxes, to order good deeds and prohibit evil deeds and to run the people's affairs justly. Islam considers the law an instrument and a means for achieving justice in society and a means for polishing man morally, ideologically and practically. The task of the prophets was to embody the law, to adjudicate among people when they disagree, to run their affairs and to lead them toward their happiness in this world and in the hereafter.

We have already mentioned in this discussion that Imam al-Rida said: "Had He not appointed for them a trusted and pacifying Imam, the nation would have perished...."[15] In this same Hadith, he says: "The jurists are the trustees of the messengers." It is concluded from the two quotations that the jurists are the ones who should lead the march of the people so that Islam may not perish. The obliteration of Islam and the obstruction of its strictures are actually due to the fact that the jurists in the Muslim countries have not been able to rule the people. Experience has confirmed the Imam's opinion as

---

[15]*'Ilal al-Shara'i'* [Causes of Laws], 1/172, Hadith 9.

stated in the phrase: "Had He not appointed an Imam ... the nation would have perished."

Hasn't Islam been obliterated? Isn't Islam obliterated now? Have not the laws of Islam been obstructed in the countries of Islam? Are Islam's laws observed and is its system followed? Isn't the situation one of chaos? Is Islam this ink on paper? Do you think that the sole aim of our religion is to have its laws collected in al-Kafi's book and then be shelved away? Will Islam be preserved if we kiss the Koran, put it on our heads and recite its phrases with a beautiful voice day and night?

Islam has reached this tragic end because we have not thought of organizing society and of bringing it happiness through a Muslim government. Unjust and corrupt laws violating the teachings of Islam have been applied to the Muslims—laws that God has given no power. Islam has almost been obliterated and forgotten in the minds of some of the esteemed gentlemen, to the degree that some of them have gone as far as interpreting the phrase "the jurists are the trustees of the prophets" to mean honesty in transmitting the issues. They have also gone as far as interpreting the Koran and Hadith phrases which indicate that the jurists should rule the people in the age of absence as phrases which mean that the jurists should only explain the issues and the laws! Is this honesty? Isn't it the duty of the trusted representatives to keep the laws of Islam actually alive and to guard them against negligence and obstruction? Isn't it the duty of a man trusted with a country not to let the aggressors move without being punished? Isn't it his duty to prevent chaos, to fight heresies and falsehoods and to strike the hands of those who tamper with the people's lives and properties? Yes, this is what trusteeship requires and what the trust given to the messengers themselves required.

Who Should Be Trusted With Tasks of the Judiciary?

Muhammad ibn Yahya, citing Muhammad ibn Ahmad who quoted Ya'qub ibn Yazid who quoted Yahya ibn Mubarak who quotes 'Abdallah ibn Jamilah who quoted Ishaq ibn 'Ammar who quoted Abi 'Abdallah, peace be upon Him, said: "The Amir of the Faithful, God's prayers be upon him, said to Shurayh: 'O Shurayh you have taken a position that only a prophet's guardian or a villain takes.'"[16]

This Shurayh occupied the post of a judge for nearly fifty years. He flattered, praised and applauded Mu'awiyah and flattered Mu'awiyah with praise he did not deserve. This position that he took was tantamount to destroying what the government of the Amir of the Faithful had built. But [Imam] Ali could not dismiss Shurayh because he was appointed by Ali's predecessor and, therefore, the Amir of the Faithful was not empowered to dismiss him. However, Ali did watch him and did prevent him from violating the rule of the shari'a.

[16]*Wasa'il al-Shi'a* [Methods of the Shi'ite], "Book of Judiciary," Chapter 3, Hadith 2; *Man La Yahduruhu al-Faqih,* Part 3, page 4.

The Judiciary is the Concern of the Just Jurist

Even though there has been disagreement on the issue of rule and even though some ulema, such as al-Niraqi and al-Na'ini, may he rest in peace, expressed the belief that the jurist has the same tasks as those of the Imam in the spheres of government, administration and policy, while others said that the rule of the jurist is not as comprehensive as that of the Imam — even though there has been disagreement on this, I do not find that there has been any disagreement on the fact that the position of a judge is exclusively for the just jurist, considering that the quotation mentions the "Prophet, villain and guardian." It is well known that the jurists are not prophets and there is no doubt that they are not villains. By necessity, the description "guardian" applies to them. Because the word "guardian" is used predominantly by the Amir of the Faithful, the first guardian, we find that some people do not accept this quotation as a proof of our issue. We have already said that nobody should imagine that the position of rule elevated the status of the Imams, because governing the people and running their affairs was nothing more than carrying out a duty, setting matters aright, reforming society and spreading justice among people. The Imams had high positions and ranks that only God knew. Their appointment or non appointment to the caliphate neither elevated nor lowered their ranks, because this position of rule is not what raises the status of a person or makes him important. Whoever is a pious jurist is qualified to occupy this position as a part of his duties in life.

In any case, we understand from the Hadith that the jurists are the Prophet's guardians after and in the absence of the Imams and that they were entrusted to carry out whatever the imams were entrusted to do.

There is another Hadith that supports our issue and which is perhaps better supported and more indicative. This Hadith was weakly transmitted by al-Killini. However, al-Saduq transmitted it, quoting Sulayman ibn Khalid, who is correct and authoritative.

"Citing several of our colleagues who quoted Suhayl ibn Ziyad, who quoted Muhammad ibn 'Isa, who quoted Abi 'Abdallah al-Mu'min, who quoted Ibn Makan, who quoted Sulayman ibn Khalid, who quoted Abi Abdallah, may peace be upon him, as saying: Follow the government because government belongs to an imam who is knowledgeable in the affairs of the judiciary and just among Moslems, to a prophet (or like a prophet) or to a prophet's trustee." This quotation was also transmitted by al-Saduq, quoting Sulayman ibn Khalid.[17]

You can see that whoever governs or dispenses justice among the people must be an imam knowledgeable in the laws and the rules and must be

---

[17] *Al-Wasa'il*, "Book of Judiciary," Book 3, Hadith 3, 18/7, modern edition.

just. These qualities are present only in a prophet or a prophet's trustee. I have already demonstrated that it is axiomatic that the position of the judiciary can only be held by the just jurist. A jurist means a person knowledgeable in the Islamic creeds, laws, rules and ethics, i.e., he is a person who is familiar with all that the Prophet brought. The Imam confined the judiciary to a prophet or a prophet's trustee.

Knowing that the jurist is not a prophet, then he is a prophet's trustee. In the age of the absence, the jurist, and nobody else, is the imam and leader of the Muslims and the person dispensing justice among them justly.

Who Is the Authority on the Affairs of Life?

The third narration is [an announcement] signed by al-Qa'im al-Mahdi, the twelfth Imam, and we will present this narration, explaining the way to benefit from it:

The book *Ikmal al-Din Wa Itman al-Ni'mah* [Perfection of Religion and Completion of Blessing], cites Muhammad ibn 'Isam who quoted Muhammad ibn Ya'qub who cites Ishaq ibn Ya'qub as having said: "I asked Muhammad ibn 'Uthman al-'Umari to dispatch for me a message in which I had asked about issues that posed a problem for me. The answer came signed by our master, Sahib al-Zaman, may peace be upon him, who replied: 'As to what you have asked about, may God guide and strengthen you. ... '" This continues until the master says: "As for the events that have taken place, refer to the transmitters of our statements because they are my authority to you and I am God's authority. As for Muhammad ibn 'Uthman al-'Umari, may God be pleased with him and with his father before him, he has my confidence and his book is mine."[18]

Naturally, what is meant by the intended events is not the canonical laws and issues. The inquirer knew his authority on these issues and laws. People referred to the jurist when they had a problem with any of the canonical laws and rules. This used to happen even in the days of the Imams themselves, because people were far from the Imams and lived in provinces other than that in which the Imam lived. The inquirer, who lived at the outset of the age of the absence of the Imam and who was in contact with his deputies and who was corresponding with the Imam and asking for his opinion, was not asking for the authority on interpretation because he knew this well. He was asking about the authority on the contemporary social problems and on the developments in the people's lives. Because it was impossible to refer to the Imam due to the latter's absence, the inquirer wanted to know the authority on the changes in life, on society's developments and on transient events and did not know what to do. His question was a general question that was not addressed

---

[18]*Al-Wasa'il*, 18/101, "Book of the Judiciary," Chapter 11, Hadith 9, related by Shaykh al-Tusi in the book *al-Ghaybah* [Absence] and al-Tubrusi related it in the book *al-Ihtijaj* [Protect].

to a certain authority and the answer was also general and befitting the question. The answer was, as you know: "Refer to the transmitters of our statements because they are my authority to you and I am God's authority."

What does God's authority mean? What do you understand from it? Does God's authority mean that if the ruler, peace be upon him, transmits information about the Prophet, then we must accept this information as we accept Zarrarah's information? Does God's authority lie in explaining issues and laws only? When the Prophet said, "I have appointed Ali, peace be upon him, as your authority," does this mean, "I will go and leave behind Ali with you to explain and clarify issues and laws to you?" What does it mean?

God's authority means that the Imam is the reference to the people on all affairs of life and that God has appointed him and entrusted him to take every action capable of benefitting the people and making them happy. The same applies to the jurists. They are the nation's reference and leaders. God's authority is the man appointed by God in charge of the affairs of the Muslims. His actions and his statements are a writ to the Muslims that must be implemented and that must not be allowed to be disregarded in establishing the strictures, collecting the one-fifth, alms, the land and the gains taxes and in spending these taxes. This means that if you refer to the tyrant rulers in the presence of the authority, then you will be held accountable and will be punished for your action on the day of resurrection. God, may He be praised, gives the authority to the Amir of the Faithful to pursue those who rebelled against Him and disobeyed His order. God also objects to Mu'awiyah and the Umayyad and Abbassid rulers, their aides and their supporters for usurping what was not their right and for holding a position to which they were not qualified.

God brings to account unjust rulers and every government deviating from the teachings of Islam. He makes them account for what they gained, for how they spent the monies of the Muslims, for the monies they wasted on coronation ceremonies and on the twenty-fifth centennial anniversary of the rule of sultans in Iran. What will they say when they are brought to account? Perhaps he [the Shah] will apologize and say, "Our special circumstances made this inevitable and called for building the biggest palaces and for excessive and unchecked extravagance in coronation anniversaries and similar occasions for the sake of fame and reputation in the world!" He will be asked: "Was not Ali a good example for you? Was he not a ruler of the Muslims and the Amir of a vast nation? Have you done for the people more than the Amir of the Faithful did for them? Did you want to elevate Islam to a status to which Ali had not elevated it? Which of the two states is bigger—yours or his? Your state was nothing more than a single province in his state which included Egypt, Iraq, Hejaz and Yemen. Despite all this, don't you know that his office was in the mosque and that his judiciary platform was in one of the mosque's corners? Didn't you know that he gathered his armies and troops in the mosque to start their march and their movement from that mosque? Didn't you realize that they marched to war confident of themselves and with prayers filling their hearts? Didn't you know how they marched and advanced and how God gave them victories?"

Jurists are nowadays the authority of the people as was the Prophet their authority. Whatever was delegated to the Prophet has been delegated to the Imams and to the jurists after them. The jurists are the authority on all matters, issues and problems. They have been authorized to govern, rule and run the affairs and politics of people and to collect taxes and spend them. God will bring to account and punish whoever disobeys them.

This narration that we have cited has a clear significance. If it does not reach the degree of a proof of our opinion, then at least it supports and backs up what we believe.

Phrases From the Venerable Koran

There is another narration that supports our topic of discussion, even proves it. This is 'Umar ibn Handhalah's Concurrence, which contains a phrase from the Koran. Let us now review some phrases of the Koran and study them somewhat so that we may proceed to this narration and others.

> God doth command you to render back your trusts to those to whom they are due, and when ye judge between man and man, that ye judge with justice. Verily how excellent is the teaching which He giveth you! For God is He Who heareth and seeth all things.
>
> O ye who believe! Obey God, and obey the Apostle, and those charged with authority among you. If ye differ in anything among yourselves, refer it to God and His Apostle, if ye do believe in God and the Last Day. That is best, and most suitable for final determination.[19]

Some people believe that what is meant by the trust is that money which people deposit with an individual as a trust, and the shari'a laws with which God has trusted the people and whose observance and application is considered as returning the trust to its owners. The former is a people's trust and the latter God's trust. Others interpret the trust as the imamate. This is contained in the meanings of some Hadiths which show that what is meant by this phrase is we, the Imams. God ordered the Prophet to return the trust — meaning the imamate — to its people, meaning the Amir of the Faithful who should give it to those succeeding him and so on.

The verse also states: "If you rule among people, then rule justly." This is addressed to those who hold in their hands the reins of affairs and is not intended for the judges alone; they are not the entire government. It is well known that modern states have three authorities of which the government and the state agencies are formed, namely: the judiciary authority, the legisla-

---

[19] *Al-Nisa'* [The Women], 58 and 59.

tive authority and the executive authority. God's words "if you rule ... " are addressed generally to all the individuals of whom these government authorities consist. A just government is one of the components of the trust which must be delivered to its owners and the owners must take the best care of this government. This government must work in accordance with the laws and with the noble shari'a. A judge in this government must rule justly and fairly, not tyrannically and unjustly and he must derive his rulings from religion. This government's legislative authority derives from shari'a teachings and the general and comprehensive rules and laws and never exceeds them or violates them. The executive authorities must operate as religion wants them to operate so that they may bring the people happiness and drive away the ghost of poverty, starvation and backwardness from them. These authorities must also establish the boundaries, safeguard security and order—all with moderation and balance and without exaggeration or negligence.

After cutting off a thief's hand, the Amir of the Faithful, may peace be upon him, used to show the thief compassion, treat him kindly, dress his hand and immerse it in oil. A thief thus came to have the greatest love for him. When the Amir heard that Mu'awiyah's army raided al-Anbar and that his men seized Christian and Jewish women and took away their earrings and their bracelets, he felt profound grief and sadness and said: "Should a man die of sadness after this, he would not be blamed and would be a worthy man to me."[20] With these strong emotions, the Amir used to carry his sword when necessary to cut off the heads of those wreaking havoc on earth. This is justice.

God's messenger is a just ruler. If he orders that a position be occupied or that a corrupting group of people be wiped out, he rules justly because if he fails to do so, he would be violating justice and because his rule is always in harmony with the requirements of the interests of Muslims, rather with the requirements of human life in its entirety.

The supreme ruler must consider the public interests. He must not pay attention to emotions and must not fear anybody's censure in serving God. This is why we find that many of the selfish private interests were wiped out due to concern for the public interest. We also find that Islam fought various groups of people for the harm they caused. The Prophet, may God's peace and prayers be upon him, annihilated the Bani Qurayzah Jews to the last man, because of the harm he realized they were causing the Muslim society, his government and all the people. The ruler's courage and his reputation in God's eyes lie in his implementation of God's orders and in establishing His strictures without being subject to emotions or to whims and also lie in his compassion, kindness, sympathy and concern for people. These two qualities make the ruler a refuge to which the people resort. As for the fear and anxiety that we witness these days, they are the result of the illegitimacy of the actual governments and because government these days gives the idea of domination, selfishness and tyranny. But in a government like the Imam's or in any true

[20]*Nahj al-Balagha*, Vol. 1, p. 69.

Islamic government, there is no fear and no grief among the people and a man is fully secure, unless he betrays, behaves unjustly or violates God's strictures.

The Hadith says that His words, may He be praised, "return the trusts to their owners" pertain to the Imams, that His words, "if you rule among the people..." pertain to the amirs and that His words, "obey God" are a general address to all the Muslims ordering them to obey those in charge, meaning the Imams, to learn from them and to obey their orders.

You have already learned that what is meant by obedience to God is to follow His orders in all the laws of the shari'a, both the laws pertaining to worship and to other affairs, that obedience to the Prophet means following all his orders, including those pertaining to organizing and coordinating society and those pertaining to preparing the material and moral force to defend it, and that this obedience is also obedience to God. Your obedience to the messenger means obeying the instructions he issues to you. If he instructs you to join Usamah's army, to take position on the borders, to pay or to collect taxes and to associate with people kindly, then you must not disobey. God ordered us to take what the Prophet has allowed us and to refrain from what he has ordered us not to do. God has also ordered us to take orders from the people in charge, namely the Imams, peace be upon them, keeping in mind that obeying the messenger and obeying those in charge is obedience to God because our obeying them reflects our obedience to God's order that we obey them.

The last part of the verse states: "Should you quarrel over something, refer to God and the Prophet if you believe in God and the hereafter. This is better for you." Disputes among people may be over legal issues on which the judge must decide in accordance with evidence and faith. The dispute may not be over a legal matter. It may be a penal issue—an issue of an injustice, attack, murder, theft of something else. In such cases, the matter must be referred to the authorities concerned so that they may act upon these penal or dual — meaning both legal and penal — cases and must issue their sentences in accordance with what the shari'a orders.

The Koran instructs us to refer all these cases, be they legal or penal, to the Messenger in his capacity as the head of the state. He, in turn, is ordered to establish what is right and what is false. After the Messenger come the Imams and after them come the just jurisprudents.

God, may He be praised, then says: "Have you not seen those who claim that they believe in what has been revealed to you and what was revealed before you wishing to seek the ruling of the false god which they have been ordered to disavow."[21] What is meant by the false god is every judiciary or governmental authority that bases its rulings on that which God has given no power and every authority that acts unjustly, sinfully and aggressively. God has ordered us to disavow such a thing and to rebel against every unjust government, even if this causes us hardships and difficulties.

---

[21] *Al-Nisa'*, 63.

Ban on Seeking Arbitration of Unjust Rulers

In the first part of his answer to the inquirer's question, the Imam prohibited altogether referring to the unjust rulers in legal or penal cases. This means that whoever refers to them is seeking the judgment of the false god which God has ordered us to disavow. The shari'a orders us not to follow what the unjust rulers order: "He takes it unjustly, even if it is his proven right." A Muslim is prohibited from seeking the arbitration of false gods on a debt that somebody owes him and if he collects his debt in accordance with their rule and sentence, then he is not permitted to dispose of what he is given. Some jurisprudents have said that even in in-kind cases, it is not permitted to take the repossessed article, such as a cloak, and to dispose of it if it is regained in accordance with their order and rule.

This is a political ruling that urges the Moslems to stop referring to the tyrannical authorities and their judiciary agencies, so that they may go out of business when the people desert them and so that the door may be opened for the Imams and for those appointed by the Imams to dispense justice among the people. The true purpose of this narration is that the tyrannical rulers must not be a reference on people's affairs because God has prohibited referring to them and has ordered that they be abandoned and isolated and that they and their rule be disavowed because of their tyranny, injustice and deviation from the straight path.

Muslim Ulema Are Authorities on All Matters

According to what the Imam has been quoted to say, the authority is the person who relates the Imams' Hadiths, knows their proscriptions and their prescriptions, and examines their rulings thoroughly in accordance with the interpretive criteria at his disposal. In his answer to the question cited in the narration, the Imam left nothing ambiguous or unclear. He required as a condition in the authority, in addition to relating the Hadith, that he know what is permissible and what is forbidden and that he be discerning and perceptive because a Hadith relater who is not discerning and perceptive is not an authority.

Position of Ulema Is Always Preserved

We believe that the position that the Imams granted the jurisprudents is still preserved for the jurisprudents. We cannot imagine the Imams to be forgetful or negligent and we believe that they were familiar with all that was in the interest of the Muslims. The Imams were aware that this position of the jurisprudents would not vanish after their death. If the Imam knew that the appointment was meant to be for his lifetime, then he should have drawn the attention of the people to this fact and would have explained to them that the position of the jurisprudents is dependent on the life of the Imams and that the jurisprudents are to be dismissed after the death of the Imams.

Therefore, in accordance with this narration, the ulema were appointed by the Imam for government and for judgment among the people and their position is still preserved for them. We do not find it likely that the Imam who came after Imam [Jafar] al-Sadiq dismissed the jurisprudents from this position because this is a weak and improbable likelihood. The Imam, peace be upon him, prohibits referring to the unjust rulers and judges and considers referring to them tantamount to referring to the false god. He clings to the Koran phrase in which God orders that the false god be disavowed. If the succeeding Imam dismissed those jurisprudents from their position and did not appoint others, then to whom should the Muslims refer in their disputes and conflicts?

We are confident that Imam Musa ibn Ja'far could not have revoked what Imam al-Sadiq had ordered in this regard and in other spheres. He could not have prohibited referring to the just jurisprudents, could not have ordered that the rule of the false god be consulted or could have accepted the loss of rights, properties or lives. The Imam does not revoke the general bases which his predecessor has explained and advocated. However, an Imam can change rulers or judges in his lifetime if the public interest requires such a change. This is not considered a revocation of what the predecessor adopts.

6. CONSTITUTION OF THE ISLAMIC REPUBLIC OF IRAN, DECEMBER 3rd, 1979*

In the name of God, the compassionate, the merciful.

We sent aforetime our apostles with clear signs
And sent down with them the Book and balance that
men may stand forth in justice [quote from the Koran].

INTRODUCTION

The Constitution of the Islamic Republic of Iran explains the cultural, social, political, and economic institutions of the community of Iran based on Islamic principles and standards which are a reflection of the heartfelt desires of the Islamic community. The essence of the great Islamic Revolution of Iran and the process of the struggle of the Muslim people from the beginning to victory which was crystallized in the explicit and striking slogans of all classes of the people were characterized by this basic desire, and

*Reprinted from the *Middle East Journal* 34, no. 2 (Spring 1980): 184–204.

now our nation, with all its being, is in the vanguard of this great victory seeking to achieve this desire.

The special founding nature of this revolution vis-à-vis other movements in Iran in the last century, both the religious school [mektebi] and Islamic, is that the Muslim people of Iran, after experiencing an antidespotic constitutional movement and an anticolonialist movement nationalizing the oil, have acquired valuable experience showing that the main cause and lack of success of these religious school movements was the absence of struggles.

Although in the recent movements, Islamic ideology and the leadership of the fighting clergy played the main and basic roles, nevertheless these movements quickly headed toward stagnation because their struggles departed from the noble principles of Islam. Now since the awakening of the people to the exalted and exemplary leadership of his great eminence, the Ayatollah Imam Khomeini, the urgent need to follow the line of the noble philosophic and Islamic movement has been recognized. And this time the country's struggling clergy who were always in the front rank of the people's movement, as well as writers and intellectuals, have found new impetus by following his leadership. (The latest movement in Iran began in the Hegira lunar year of 1382 which corresponds to the Hegira solar year of 1341.) [1341 is 1963 A.D.]

THE VANGUARD OF THE REVOLUTION

The protest of the smashing of Imam Khomeini in connection with the American plot, "The White Revolution," which was a ploy to stabilize the foundations of the colonialist government and strengthen Iran's political, cultural, and economic ties with world imperialism was the cause of the monolithic movement of the nation and afterward of the great and bloody Islamic revolution in June 1963 which in truth was the starting point of the blossoming of this glorious and widespread uprising which established and confirmed the centrality of the Imam Khomeini as the Islamic leader. Despite his absence from Iran after the protest to the shameful law of capitulation (immunity of American citizens), the strong ties of the nation with the imam became perpetual, and the Muslim nation, especially the dedicated intellectuals and fighting clergy in banishment or prison were undergoing continuing torture and execution.

In these circumstances, the aware and responsible elements of society were engaging in soul-searching in the strongholds of the mosques, the seminaries of religious scholars and universities. And with the inspiration of the revolutionary school and the fruit of Islam, they began the relentless and fruitful struggle of raising the level of combative and religious school awareness and vigilance of the Muslim nation. The colonialist regime that crushed the Islamic movement with the ferocious attack on the Fezieh University, as well as all the vociferous clubs which started the revolution took the most murderous measures to quell the revolutionary rage of the people. And in these circumstances, firing squads, widespread tortures, and long imprisonments were the price our Muslim nation paid to show its resolve to continue the struggle. The blood of hundreds of young men and women flowed in the execution yards at dawn as they shouted "Allah Akbar." Or they were hit by bullets in the sidestreets or bazaars as they furthered the Islamic Revolution of Iran, distributed the persistent statements and messages of the imam on various occasions, and proclaimed the resolution of the Islamic nation ever wider and deeper.

ISLAMIC GOVERNMENT

The plan of the Islamic government is based on religious authority which was introduced by Imam Khomeini at the height of the strangulation and suffocation on the part of the colonialist regime and created the new characteristic motivation of the Muslim people and widened the noble path of the struggle of the school of Islam which, in turn, expedited the struggle of the dedicated Muslim fighters both inside and outside the country.

It is in this line that the movement continued until finally the strong dissatisfaction and rage of the people, due to daily increasing pressure and strangulation inside the country, caused the struggle to be taken up by the fighting clergy and students on the worldwide level that strongly shook the rule of the regime and forced it to reduce its pressure and strangulation. It forced the regime, so to speak, to open the political field inside the country until it thought the degree of safety had been achieved to prevent the certain fall of the regime. However, the nation which was excited, aware, and resolute in the unwavering and undauntable leadership of the imam rose victoriously and unanimously on all sides.

The rage of the people: Publication of the letter insulting the holiness of the clergy, especially Imam Khomeini on 7 January 1977 by the regime hastened this movement and caused the rage of the people to explode all across the country. In order to control the spreading of the people's rage the regime tried to suppress this protest uprising by shedding blood, but this only quickened the blood in the veins of the revolution and the tempo of the revolution in the coming weeks and the 40-day commemorations of martyrs and increased the fervor and solidarity of this movement all across the country. It also perpetuated the movement of the people in all the country's organizations by means of a general strike and participation in street demonstrations to bring down the colonialist regime as well as encouraging active participation and widespread solidarity of both men and women from all classes and religious and political groups in this struggle in a striking fashion. Women in particular joined actively in this great and widespread holy war. In particular, mothers holding children rushed into the squares in front of machine guns. They were a large and determining societal group in this struggle.

THE PRICE THE NATION PAID

After one year the outburst of the revolution and persistent struggle cost more than 60,000 martyrs, hundreds of wounded and injured, as well as billions of *tomans* in property damage to the champions of independence, freedom, and Islamic government. And this great movement which offered security, unity, and certainty stirred feelings and excitement which led to victory and success in smashing all the calculations, dealings, and arrangements of imperialism so that, in turn, the new high season of peoples' revolutions was ushered into the world.

The 10th and 11th of February 1979, the days when the shah's establishment fled and the domestic despotism and the foreign intermediaries based on it were defeated, were also the days when the glad tidings of the great final victory of the Islamic government, long sought by the Muslim people, came. As one man, the Iranian nation, with the inspiration and teaching of Islam and its leadership in matters of the Islamic republic, made their final and definite decision to create the new order of the Islamic republic and proclaimed it in Order 97/2.

At present, the Constitution of the Islamic Republic of Iran, which is the proclamation of all the political, social, cultural and economic ideals and relations of our society, should be the guide to solidify the bases of the Islamic government and the new framework and plan of the order of government to replace the ruins of the previous order of the idolators.

STYLE OF GOVERNMENT IN ISLAM

From the viewpoint of Islam, the government does not arise from the notion of classes and mediation among persons or groups but is a crystallization of political idealism based on religious community and concord which provide its organization — which through the process of ideological transformation turns its path toward the final goal (movement toward God). Our nation which during its revolutionary experience was cleansed of the mist and corrosion of the idolators and foreign ideological influences returned to the noble worldview of Islam. And now it is on that basis that it is building its model (equal) society with Islamic norms, principles, and mission as its constitution which reflects the beliefs of the movements and the conditions and values found in Islam.

In regard to the Islamic contents of the Iranian Revolution which was a movement for the victory of all oppressed people over the arrogant, the Constitution provides the basis for trying to perpetuate this revolution both at home and abroad. This is especially so with regard to expanding international relations with other Islamic movements and people to pave the way to form the world unity of followers (Your community is one community, and I am your lord whom you are to worship) and to perpetuating the struggle to save the deprived nations under tyranny throughout the world.

Regarding the character of this great movement, the Constitution guarantees help to abolish any kind of ideological, social, or economic despotism and provide the way to break the system of despotism by entrusting the fate of the people to their own hands. (He releases them from their heavy burdens and yokes which are on them.)

In creating the political positions and foundations for shaping society on the basis of interpretation of the Book, the pious men became responsible for ruling and administering the nation. (The earth will be inherited by my pious followers.) And the legislation that will make norms to administer society will be based on the Koran. Therefore, careful and serious views are urgently needed in the field of Islamic justice, piety, and obligations (just jurists), that is, since the purpose of sovereignty is to make people grow toward the divine order. Until the ground has been prepared and the talents have blossomed to glorify the dimensions of God's ways and have become known to the people (to emulate God's morality), this cannot be active participation and involvement by all social elements in the process of transforming society.

Regarding this subject, the Constitution provides for such participation by all circles in decisionmaking in determining the fate of all persons in society in order to perfect every person. The responsibility for growth and advancement belongs to the leadership which will have all the rights to govern the oppressed. (And we wish to be gracious to those who were being depressed in the land, to make them leaders in faith and heirs.)

THE RESPONSIBILITY OF THE JUST JURIST

So as to assure the permanent security of the Constitution, the rights of clerical leadership is [sic] under all conditions to be the leadership recognized by the people. (The course of affairs is in the hands of those who know God and who are trustworthy in matters having to do with what He permits and forbids.)

The just jurist is equipped to insure that the various organizations do not deviate from their true Islamic duties.

ECONOMY, A MEANS NOT AN END

In strengthening the economic structures, the basis is the people's need for growth and perfection, not anything else in the economic order such as concentration of wealth and profiteering. In materialistic schools the economy is its own goal and, for this reason, in cycles of growth, the economy is a factor of destruction, corruption, and decay. However, in Islam, the economy is a means intended to be a part of the work of improvement — and the means cannot become the end.

From this viewpoint, the Islamic economic program is to provide a suitable field for creativity of human diversity and, in this respect, provide equal opportunities to create work for all persons and to satisfy the need to perpetuate the movement to perfection according to Islamic rule.

WOMEN IN THE CONSTITUTION

In creating Islamic social foundations, all the human forces that had up to now been in the service of foreign exploitation will be accorded their basic identity and human rights. And in this regard it is natural that women, due to the greater oppression that they have borne under the idolatrous order, will enjoy more rights.

The family unit is the foundation of society and the main institution for the growth and advancement of mankind. Agreement of faith and ideals in forming the family, which is the basic organ in the national perfection and growth movement, is the main foundation which provides the potential for achieving these goals. It is the principal duty of the Islamic government to regard women as the unifying factor of the family unit and its position. They are a factor in bringing the family out of the service of propagating consumerism and exploitation and renewing the vital and valuable duty of motherhood in raising educated human beings to take their part in the various fields of active life. As a result, motherhood is accepted as a most profound responsibility in the Muslim viewpoint and will, therefore, be accorded the highest value and generosity.

ARMY OF THE BOOK

In organizing and equipping the country's defense forces, attention should be paid to the fact that faith and the Book are the norms. Therefore, in conformity with this goal, the Islamic Republican Army and the Revolution Guards Corps will be responsible not only for defending the borders, but also for the mission stated in the Book, of holy war in the way of God and fighting to expand the rule of God's law in the world. (Against them make ready your strength to the utmost of your power, including steeds of war, to strike terror into the hearts of the enemies of God and your enemies, and others besides them whom ye know not. God knoweth them.)

THE JUDICIARY IN THE CONSTITUTION

The question of the judiciary with respect to guarding the people's rights in line with the Islamic movement for the purpose of preventing deviation within the Islamic community is a vital matter. In this regard, the creation of a judicial system based on Islamic justice and consisting of just judges who are acquainted with precise religious norms must be provided for. Because of the fundamental sensitivity and precision of this system in the Book, it is necessary that it be removed from any unsound relationships and connections. (And when you judge between man and man, judge with justice.)

EXECUTIVE POWER

Due to its special importance with regard to enforcing Islamic orders and regulations for the purpose of achieving just relations in ruling society and the urgency that this vital function will have in building the foundations leading to the final goal, the executive power must open the way for creation of an Islamic society. As a result, it must be surrounded by all kinds of rules and mores that will lead to this goal or that would be useful from the Islamic viewpoint. To this end, the bureaucratic system that was the basis of the idolatrous rule will be abolished in order for the executive system to be put into practice with ever more and faster efforts to implement administrative obligations.

PUBLIC RELATIONS MEDIA

Public relations media (radio and television) should be used for perfecting the Islamic Revolution and in serving to propagate Islamic culture. In this matter they should promote healthy exchanges of various ideas and strictly refrain from propagating and spreading harmful and antirevolutionary notions.

In light of the legal principles that regard freedom and human dignity as the main points of their aims, and which posit the road of development and perfection of the individual as the responsibility of all, it is necessary that the Islamic community elect wise and pious managers with firm views. They will serve actively to build the Islamic society with the hope that in building the ideal Islamic society they will be able to show the example of matryrdom and self-sacrifice to the people of the world. (Thus, we appointed you a central nation that you might be witnesses to the people.)

REPRESENTATIVES

The Assembly of Experts which is composed of representatives of the people, formulated the Constitution on the basis of studying a draft of the proposals of the government and all the suggestions made by various groups of people. The Constitution is composed of 12 chapters which contain 175 articles. It was completed on the eve of the 15th century of the advent of the great Prophet of God and the anniversary of the redemptive school of Islam, with the goals and motives described above and in the hope that this century will be the century of a world rule by the heretofore oppressed and the complete defeat of the arrogant.

POSTSCRIPTS

Several verses and quotations are cited below as examples of the documents used as basic principles of the Constitution.

Law

Right is not due to one unless he is governed by it, and it is not applied to anyone to whom it is not applicable.

Human Rights

They are of two types: Either your brothers in religion or your peers in morality, immune from wrongdoing and judges of weaknesses.

Helping the Oppressed

Be an enemy to the oppressor and a friend to the oppressed. (The Way of Eloquence)

Brotherly Unity

1. O ye people, we have created you from a male and a female, and have made you into peoples and tribes that ye might know one another.
2. The noblest of you in the sight of God is he who is most righteous. (The Surah of the Inner Apartments)
3. O ye people, since your Lord is one, and since your Father is one, there is no preference for Arab above alien, nor for alien above Arab, nor for black above red, nor for red above black, except in righteousness. (Sayings of the Prophet)

The Possibility of Public Pleading

And convoke a general council for them. A nation will never be blessed in which the right of the weak is not taken for him from the strong who is heedless. (The Way of Eloquence)

Liberties

Be not the slave of another, for God hath created thee free.

Do No Harm

There is no oppression and no oppressor in Islam. (Sayings of the Prophet)

Follow What Is Best

Then proclaim the news to My servants, those who hear the word and follow what is best in it. (The Surah of the Crowds, verse 18)

Trustworthiness and Justice

1. God commands you to repay what you hold in trust to those to whom it is due, and, when ye judge among people, to do so with justice. (The Surah of the Women, verse 58)

2. God commands justice and doing good. (The Surah of the Bee, verse 90)

3. That men may stand forth in justice. (The Surah of Iron, verse 25)

4. Stand forth for justice as witness for God, even against your own selves or your parents and your kin. (The Surah of the Women, verse 135)

5. Let not the hatred of others toward you cause you to do injustice. Be ye just, for justice is next to piety. (The Surah of the Table, verse 9)

Equality

1. In the law of equality there is life for you, O ye men of understanding. (The Surah of the Cow, verse 179)

2. Should anyone attack you, then attack ye him even as he has done unto you. (The Surah of the Cow, verse 194)

Take Away Difficulty, Obstacles, and Restraints

1. God intends facility for you, and does not want to send you difficulty. (The Surah of the Cow, verse 185)

2. Nor has He imposed any restraint on you in religion. (The Surah of the Pilgrimage, verse 78)

3. God does not wish to impose restraint on you. (The Surah of the Table, verse 6)

4. But if one is forced by necessity, without willful disobedience, not transgressing due limits, then he is guiltless. (The Surah of the Cow, verse 173)

Enjoining What Is Acceptable

1. The men and women who believe help one another; they enjoin whatever is acceptable and forbid whatever is abominable. (The Surah of Repentance, verse 71)

2. Let there arise from among you a people who will call for righteousness, who will enjoin whatever is acceptable and forbid whatever is abominable. (The Surah of Al 'Imran, verse 104)

The Special Qualities of Leadership

1. Is not He, then, who shows the way to truth more worthy to be followed than he who does not show the way unless it is shown to him? (The Surah of Jonah, verse 35)

2. God has chosen him above you and has imbued him abundantly with knowledge and strength. (The Surah of the Cow, verse 247)

3. God has given it to the imams of justice to appoint themselves by the weakness of the people. (The Way of Eloquence)

4. The courses of affairs are in the hands of the religious scholars, whose office it is to say what is permissible and what is forbidden. (The Gift of Intellects)

5. It is not fitting that the one who has power over the [word illegible] the blood, the spoils, the judgments, and the imamate of the Muslims be an avaricious man, for his desire would be in their wealth; nor an ignorant man, for he would lead them astray with his ignorance; nor a brutish man, for he would cut them to pieces with his brutishness; nor a man who fears nations, for he would favor one people above another; nor a man who is venal in judgment, for he would go forward and stop with rights, disregarding the divisions; nor a man who sets the Sunnah at nought, for he would bring the nation to destruction. (The Way of Eloquence)

6. Your labor is not a morsel for you to taste, but a trust for you to wear about your neck. (The Way of Eloquence)

7. In the sight of God, the most desirable of His worshipers is a just imam who has been guided and who guides, and therefore He has established a clear Sunnah and suppressed dark heresies. (The Way of Eloquence)

The Essence of Obedience

1. Those who transgress the limits of God are the oppressors. (The Surah of the Cow)

2. There is no obedience in a creature who disobeys his Creator.

The Army a Source of Strength

1. Against them make ready your strength to the utmost of your power, including steeds of war, to strike terror into the hearts of the enemies of God, your own enemies, and others whom ye may not know. (The Surah of the Spoils of War, verse 60)

2. For the soldiers, by the grace of God, are the protectors of the people, the pride of the rulers, the glory of the faith, and the ways to safety, and the people cannot be established except with them. (The Way of Eloquence)

Consultation

1. Consult them in the matter. (The Surah of the Family of 'Imran, verse 3)

2. Their affair being consultation among themselves. (The Surah of Consultation, verse 38)

3. He who keeps stubbornly to his own opinion perishes, but he who consults others shares in their wisdom. (The Way of Eloquence)

Free Instruction

Do not take a fee for instruction. (Imam Sadiq')

Property

1. Do not give to foolish men the property which God has made to be a means of support. (The Surah of the Women, verse 5)

2. O ye who believe! Eat not up your property among yourselves in vanities, but let there be trade among you by mutual consent. (The Surah of the Women, verse 29)

Common Property

1. It is He who hath created for you all things that are on earth. (The Surah of the Cow, verse 29)

2. O ye people! Eat of what is on earth that which is lawful and good. (The Surah of Repentance, verse 71)

3. The earth is God's, to give as a heritage to such of His servants as He pleaseth. (The Surah of the Heights, verse 128)

4. They ask thee about the spoils of war. Say, "The spoils are for God and His Prophet." (The Surah of the Spoils of War, verse 1)

5. The people are sharers in three things: water, fire, and grass.

6. Thee and the monopolization of what is for all of the people equally. (The Way of Eloquence)

7. This property is neither for me nor for thee, but is a spoil for the Muslims and the clamor of their swords. Hadst thou partaken in their warfare, the same fortune would have been for thee, but since thou has not, the fruits of their efforts shall be for no mouths but theirs.

The Behavior of Non-Muslims

God does not forbid you to vindicate and to deal justly with those who have not fought against you in religion or driven you out of your homes, for He loves those who deal justly. (The Surah of the Woman To Be Examined, verse 8)

In the name of God, the clement and the merciful.

CHAPTER I
GENERAL PRINCIPLES

Principle 1

The Government of Iran is an Islamic Republic, endorsed by the Iranian nation by an affirmative vote of 98.2 percent of the majority of eligible voters, in a referendum held on the 10th and 11th of Farvardin, of the year 1358

Hijri Shamsi [solar year], coinciding with 1st and 2d of Jamadi-ol-Avval, of the year 1399 Hijri Qamari [lunar year] based on its ancient belief in the administration of truth and justice of the Koran, following its victorious Islamic Revolution, under the leadership of the high exalted religious authority, the Great Ayatollah Imam Khomeini.

Principle 2

The Islamic Republic is a system based on the belief in:

1. One and only God (There is no God but God); appropriation to Him the faculty to rule and implement the divine law, and the necessity to obey His orders.

2. Divine inspiration and its fundamental role in the interpretation of laws.

3. Resurrection and its constructive role in the evolutionary course leading mankind toward God.

4. God's justice in creation and divine laws.

5. Religious leadership and continuous guidance, and its fundamental role in the permanency of Islam's Revolution.

6. Compassion and the high value of human beings, and freedom coupled with a sense of responsibility before God.

These aims are to be achieved by:

a) Efforts exerted on a continuous basis by clerical jurists meeting all requirements, based on the Book and Traditions of the Impeccables [the Prophet, his daughter, and the 12 Imams], may God's blessings be upon them.

b) Utilization of human advanced scientific and technical means and experiences, and efforts to improve them.

c) Negation of all kinds of oppression, tolerance of oppression, dominance and acceptance of dominance.

These concepts will secure justice, as well as political, economic, social and cultural independence, and national interdependence.

Principle 3

The Islamic Republican Government of Iran will be charged with the duty of putting into effect, with all existing possibilities, the following means and methods, in order to attain the goals mentioned in Principle 2:

1. Creation of a favorable environment for the development of moral virtues, based on faith, piety, and waging struggle against all kinds and symptoms of corruption and vice.

2. Raising the level of the general knowledge of the public in all fields, by a correct use of the press, the mass media and other means.

3. Free education and physical training at all levels, and creation of facilities for the generalization of higher education.

4. Strengthening the spirit and zeal for research and initiative power in all fields, i.e., scientific, technical, cultural and Islamic, by means of establishing research centers, and encouraging researchers.

5. Complete expulsion of colonialism, and prevention of foreign influence.

6. Elimination of all kinds of despotism, autocracy and monopolism.

7. Securing and safeguarding of political and social freedoms within the limits of law.

8. Participation of all the people in determining their political, economic, social and cultural destiny.

9. Elimination of inadmissible discriminations, and creation of fair possibilities for all, in all financial and moral fields and affairs.

10. Creation of a correct administrative system, and elimination of unnecessary organizations.

11. Complete reinforcement of the foundations of national defense by means of public military training, for the preservation and safeguarding of the independence, territorial integrity and Islamic system of the country.

12. Laying the groundwork for a sound and just economy, based on Islamic regulations, aimed at creating comfort, elimination of poverty and all kinds of deprivations dealing with food, housing, jobs, hygiene, and generalization of social insurances.

13. Securing of self-sufficiency in scientific, technical, industrial, agricultural and military affairs, and the like.

14. Securing of the rights of the people on an all-out basis, men and women alike; creation of judicial security for all based on justice, and equality of all before the law.

15. Expansion and strengthening of Islamic brotherhood and public cooperation among all of the people.

16. Adoption of a foreign policy based on Islamic standards and criteria; brotherly commitment to all Muslims, and unsparing support to the underprivileged and oppressed peoples of the world.

Principle 4

All civil, penal, financial, economic, administrative, cultural, military, political, etc., laws and regulations should be based on Islamic rules and standards. This principle will absolutely or in general be dominant over all of the principles of the Constitution, and other laws and regulations as well, and any determination in this connection will be made by the religious jurists of the Council of Guardians.

Principle 5

During the absence of the Glorious Lord of the Age [the missing twelfth Imam of the Shi 'ite sect], may God grant him relief, he will be represented in the Islamic Republic of Iran as religious leader and imam of the people by an honest, virtuous, well-informed, courageous, efficient administrator and religious jurist, enjoying the confidence of the majority of the people as a leader. Should there be no jurist endowed with such qualifications, enjoying the confidence of the majority of the people, his role will be undertaken by a leader or council of leaders, consisting of religious jurists meeting the requirements mentioned above, according to Principle 107.

Principle 6

The affairs of the country should be administered in the Islamic Republic of Iran by relying upon public opinion, expressed through elections, i.e., election of the president of the republic, deputies of the National Assembly, members of councils, and the like, or by plebiscite, anticipated for cases specified in other principles of this Constitution.

Principle 7

According to the instructions of the holy Koran, consultations should be held in all affairs, and therefore the National Assembly, the Provincial Council, urban, city, local, rural councils and the like are considered to be organs where decisions should be made for the administration of the affairs of the country.

The occasions, formation, limits of rights and powers, as well as the functions of the councils will be specified and defined by this law and other laws emanating from it.

Principle 8

In the Islamic Republic of Iran an invitation for accomplishing good deeds, a positive command and prohibition of doing evil are concepts to be adopted by all the people, and is in the meantime a mutual undertaking to be observed and implemented by the government toward the people, and by the people toward the government. Conditions, limits and quality will be specified by law.

Principle 9

In the Islamic Republic of Iran, freedom, independence, unity and the territorial integrity of the country are inseparable from each other and their preservation and safeguarding is the duty of the government and the people. No individual, or group, or authority has the right to harm even slightly the political, cultural, economic, military and territorial independence of Iran by exploiting the name of freedom, and no authority will have the right to eliminate legal freedoms, even by enacting rules and regulations on the excuse of preserving the independence and territorial integrity of the country.

Principle 10

The family being the fundamental unit of the Islamic society, all regulations, rules and planning for its comfort and preservation of its holiness and the stability of family relationships should be based on Islamic standards and moral concepts.

Principle 11

According to the Koran, all Muslims are of the same and one single religious community, and the Islamic Republican Government of Iran is bound to base its general policies on the coalition and unity of the Islamic nations, and it should exert continuous efforts in order to realize the political, economic and cultural unity of the Islamic world.

Principle 12

The official religion of Iran is Islam, and the sect followed is Twelver Shi'ism (Ithna 'Ashari). This principle is never subject to change. Other Islamic denominations also, such as Hanafi, Shafi'i, Maliki, Hanbali and Zaydi, enjoy complete respect. The followers of these sects are free to perform their religious rites, based on their religious jurisprudence. They are also officially recognized as such in the courts, in connections with lawsuits dealing with religious teachings and personal affairs (such as marriage, divorce, hereditary disputes, wills, etc.). In any area where the majority of the population should consist of the followers of any of these sects, local regulations within the power possessed by the councils will be based on the regulations of that denomination.

Principle 13

The Iranian Zoroastrians, Jews and Christians are the only recognized minorities, who, within the limits of the law, are free to perform their religious rites and ceremonies, and will act in personal matters and religious teachings in accordance with their religious regulations.

Principle 14

According to the Koran, the Islamic Republican Government of Iran and the Muslims as well are bound to treat non-Muslims with good moral conduct and Islamic justice, and to observe their fundamental rights. This principle will be applicable to those who do not get involved in anti-Islamic activities and in conspiracies hatched against the Islamic Republic of Iran.

CHAPTER II
THE OFFICIAL LANGUAGE, SCRIPT, CALENDAR AND FLAG
OF THE COUNTRY

Principle 15

The official and common language and script of the people of Iran is Persian [Farsi]. Official documents, correspondence and statements, as well as textbooks, must be in this language and script. However, the use of local and nationality languages in their press and mass media is allowed. The teaching of their literature in their schools, along with Persian language instructions is also permitted.

Principle 16

The language of the Koran and Islamic studies and instructions are in Arabic, and Arabic totally permeates Persian literature. Therefore, Arabic must be taught in all classes and fields of study beginning with the completion of elementary school to the conclusion of secondary school.

Principle 17

The origin of the official calendar of the country is the journey [Hijran] of the Prophet of Islam (May God's Greetings and Blessings Be Upon Him). Hijri solar and Hijri lunar calendars are both recognized. However, the government bases its operations on the Hijri solar calendar. The official weekly day of rest is Friday.

Principle 18

The official flag of Iran is comprised of green, white and red colors with the specific insignia of the Islamic Republic and the words "God Is Great."

CHAPTER III
NATIONAL RIGHTS

Principle 19

The people of Iran regardless of ethnic and tribal origin enjoy equal rights. Color, race, language and the like will not be cause for privilege.

Principle 20

All citizens of the nation, whether men or women, are equally protected by the law. They also enjoy human, political, economic and cultural rights according to Islamic standards.

Principle 21

The government is responsible for guaranteeing the rights of women in all areas according to Islamic standards and must provide the following:

1. The creation of favorable environments for personal growth and restoring her material and intellectual rights.
2. Protection of mothers, especially during pregnancy and child rearing period, as well as the protection of orphans.
3. The formation of qualified courts for the protection of relatives and preservation of the family unit.
4. Creation of a special insurance for widows, old women and destitute women.
5. Granting of guardianship to worthy mothers, to avoid envy, and in the absence of a lawful guardian.

Principle 22

Reputation, life, property, rights, dwelling and vocation of individuals are immune from trespassing except in circumstances prescribed by law.

Principle 23

Interrogation of people for their beliefs is forbidden. No one can be attacked or reprimanded for holding certain beliefs.

Principle 24

Publications and the press are free in the expression of topics unless it is contrary to Islamic precepts or public rights. The law will provide the details.

Principle 25

Inspection and failing to deliver letters, retention and divulging telephone conversations, revealing telegraph and telex messages, censoring, refusing to communicate messages, tapping and investigating is forbidden, unless ordered by law.

Principle 26

The formation of parties, groups, and political and professional associations, as well as Islamic or recognized minority religious associations is free, provided they do not harm the principles of freedom, sovereignty, national unity, Islamic standards and the foundation of the Islamic Republic. No one may be prevented from joining these groups or be forced to join any one of them.

Principle 27

Unarmed assemblies and marches are permitted provided they do not violate the precepts of Islam.

Principle 28

Every person has the right to choose the profession he wishes, provided it is not in contravention of Islam, public interest and the rights of others.

It is the responsibility of the government to consider the needs of the society for diversified occupations. It must create, for all individuals, the possibility of employment and equal opportunities for obtaining it.

Principle 29

The right to enjoy social security benefits, such as those for retirement, unemployment, old age, disability, lack of support, being stranded, as well as circumstances which create the need for medical services, treatment and professional care, through insurance, etc. is a public right.

The government must, according to law, utilize national revenues and income obtained from individual contributions and provide the aforementioned services and financial support for every individual in the country.

Principle 30

It is the responsibility of the government to provide free educational and training means for all through high school and also develop means within acceptable limits for free higher education.

Principle 31

A suitable dwelling, according to need, is the right of every Iranian person and family. The government is responsible for providing this, on a priority basis, to those who need it the most, in particular the peasants and agricultural workers.

Principle 32

No one may be arrested except in accordance with and by the manner prescribed by law. Once an arrest has been made, the nature of the accusation and the reasons for the actions taken must be immediately communicated and explained to the accused in writing. Within a maximum of 24 hours, preliminary documents must be referred to the appropriate legal authorities. Prompt steps must be taken for trial procedures, whereupon the accused will be punished according to the law.

Principle 33

No one may be banished from his dwelling, deprived of residing in his chosen place or forced to reside in a particular location, unless prescribed by law.

Principle 34

Every individual has the right of recourse to competent courts in order to seek justice. All people of the nation have the right of access to such courts and no one may be prevented from referring to a court to which he is legally entitled.

Principle 35

In all courts, both parties have the right to select their own lawyers and if they are not able to do so, steps must be taken to provide them with a lawyer.

Principle 36

Sentencing for punishment and the execution of such a sentence must be carried out solely by competent courts and in accordance with the law.

Principle 37

An individual is considered innocent, and no one is presumed guilty according to the law, unless his guilt has been proved by a competent court.

Principle 38

Any type of torture to obtain confession or acquire information is forbidden. Forcing people to testify, confess or take an oath is not permitted and such testimony, confession and taking an oath is null and void. The punishment for violating this principle will be prescribed by law.

Principle 39

Violating the dignity and honor of a person who has been apprehended, detained, arrested or exiled in accordance with the law is forbidden under any circumstances and is liable to punishment.

Principle 40

No one may utilize his own rights as a means of putting pressure on others or encroaching upon public interest.

Principle 41

Holding Iranian citizenship is the fundamental right of every Iranian. The government may not deprive any Iranian of his citizenship, unless requested by the individual or if the person becomes the citizen of another country.

Principle 42

Foreign nationals may become Iranian citizens according to the limitations of the law. The citizenship of such individuals may be revoked only when government grants them citizenship or if they themselves request it.

CHAPTER IV
THE ECONOMY AND FINANCIAL AFFAIRS

Principle 43

The economy of the Islamic Republic of Iran is based on the following regulations, in order to achieve independence in national economy, uproot poverty and impoverishment and fulfill growing human needs, while preserving its independence:

1. Securing basic needs: housing, nourishment, clothing, hygiene, medical care, education and vocational training and establishing a suitable environment for all to start a family.

2. Securing opportunities and possibilities for employment for all in order to achieve full employment, offering employment opportunities to able workers who are unemployed, making use of the cooperative system in providing interest-free loans and other legitimate means which will not result in the concentration and circulation of wealth in the possession of specific individuals or groups and which will refrain from turning the government into a major absolute employer. These measures must be accomplished while considering the dominant needs of the developing national economy in every stage of its growth.

3. Organizing the economic structure of the country in such a way that the procedures, tasks and work hours will be such that every individual, in addition to exerting professional effort, will have the opportunity and enough energy for intellectual, political and social self-improvement and an active participation in the leadership of the country as well as to improve skills and demonstrate creativity.

4. Regard for independent job selection, so as to refrain from forcing individuals into a specific position and prevent profiteering from the labor of others.

5. Forbidding the harming of others, as well as monopolizing, speculation and usury and other futile and unlawful dealings.

6. Forbidding extravagance and dissipation of all forms in all matters pertaining to the economy, whether in spending, investment, production, distribution, or services.

7. Learning from scientific, technical and educational skills of experts to improve and develop the economy of the country.

8. Preventing foreign economic domination of our country's economy.

9. Emphasizing increased agricultural, animal and industrial production in order to secure public needs and bring the country to a self-sufficient state and rid it of dependency.

Principle 44

The economic system of the Islamic Republic of Iran consists of three sectors: governmental, cooperative and private, with systematic and sound planning.

The governmental sector consists of all major industries, foreign trade, major mines, banking, insurance, power production, dams and major water-carrying networks, radio and television, postal, telegraph and telephone system, air, sea, land and railroad transportation and others similar to the above, which in the form of public ownership are at the disposal of the government.

The cooperative sector establishes and assigns the cooperative companies and organizations which have been created in cities and villages in accordance with Islamic regulations.

The private sector consists of those portions of agriculture, animal husbandry, industry, trade and services which supplement the activities of the governmental and cooperative sectors.

Ownership in these three sectors shall be protected by the laws of the Islamic Republic as long as this ownership is in conformance with the other essentials of this chapter, does not depart from Islamic precepts, promotes economic growth and development for the country and does not harm the society. The details regarding the standards, procedures and conditions for all three of these sectors will be determined by law.

Principle 45

Public property such as wastelands and abandoned lands, mines, seas, lakes, rivers, and other public waterways, mountains, valleys, forests, swamps, natural groves, pastures without boundaries, inherited land with no heir, unowned property, and public property which has been confiscated from usurpers, belongs to the Islamic government and shall be put to public use. The details and method of use for each one of these regulations will be determined by law.

Principle 46

Everyone shall enjoy the benefits of his legitimate business and labor and no one may, because he is the owner [of a particular type of business], deprive others of the opportunity to do the same job.

Principle 47

Personal property obtained through legitimate means is honored. The details for this will be determined by law.

Principle 48

There should be no discrimination with regard to benefits to be gained from the use of natural resources, the utilization of public funds on the provincial level, and the distribution of economic activities among the provinces and various regions of the country. This is so that every region will have within its reach capital and opportunity to fulfill its needs and develop its skills.

Principle 49

The government is responsible, after investigation, verification and establishing proof in accordance with the law, for confiscating wealth obtained from robberies, extortion, bribery, embezzlement, theft, gambling, from activities that take advantage of pious property, contract work and governmental deals, from the sale of wastelands and those belonging to others, and from houses of ill-repute and other illegal places. It should be returned to its lawful owner, and if there is no lawful owner available, it should be assigned to public use.

Principle 50

Protecting the environment in which the present generation lives and in which future generations shall live and prosper is considered a public responsibility in the Islamic Republic. Therefore industrial activities, and other activities which may pollute the environment or ruin it to the point where it cannot be restored, are forbidden.

Principle 51

No taxes shall be levied except in accordance with the law. The law will determine the instances when tax exemptions and reductions may occur.

Principle 52

The annual national budget shall be prepared by the government as determined by law and submitted to the National Consultative Assembly for review and approval. Any alteration in the figures of the budget shall also be subject to the procedures set by law.

Principle 53

All revenues received by the government shall be transferred into the accounts of the treasury and all disbursements shall be within the approved allocations in accordance with the law.

Principle 54

The National Court of Accounts shall be directly under the National Consultative Assembly and its organizations and operations in Tehran and provincial centers shall be determined by law.

Principle 55

The Court of Accounts shall inspect and audit all the accounts of ministries, government organizations and companies as well as other organizations which in one way or another benefit from the country's general budget, as stipulated by law. It shall insure and see to it that no expenditure shall exceed the approved allocation and that every allocation is used for the purpose specified. The court shall collect the various accounts, documents, and papers, according to law, and shall submit to the National Consultative Assembly a budget settlement for each year, together with its own views. This report must be made available to the public.

CHAPTER V
THE RIGHT OF NATIONAL SOVEREIGNTY AND THE POWERS
PERTAINING THEREUNTO

Principle 56

The absolute ruler of the world and humanity is God and He alone has determined the social destiny of human beings. No one shall take away this God-given right from another person or make use of it to serve his personal or group interests. The nation will use this God-given right to act according to the manner determined by the following principles.

Principle 57

The powers arising from the right of national sovereignty are: the legislative power, the judicial power, and the executive power. These powers shall always remain independent of each other, and, according to this law, the link between them will be provided by the president.

Principle 58

The National Consultative Assembly is vested with authority to exercise power on behalf of the legislative power. The assembly will be composed of the elected representatives of the people, and its resolutions, after passing through certain phases to be specified in subsequent principles, will be communicated to the executive and judicial branches for implementation.

Principle 59

In dealing with very essential issues of an economic, political, social and cultural nature, legislative power might be exercised by holding a referendum and referring the issue directly to the people for a judgment. The request for a referendum should be approved by a vote comprising two-thirds of the representatives of the assembly.

Principle 60

The duties of the executive branch, with the exception of the tasks delegated directly by this law to the leadership, will be performed by and through the president, the prime minister and the ministers.

Principle 61

The powers of the judicial branch will be exercised by the courts of the Justice Department, which are to be convened based on Islamic rules and standards, and will be engaged in solving and passing judgment on lawsuits, preserving the rights of the public, expanding and implementing justice and setting up and establishing divine limits.

CHAPTER VI
LEGISLATIVE POWER

Part 1: National Consultative Assembly

Principle 62

The National Consultative Assembly will be composed of the people's representatives, who are to be elected by a direct and secret ballot. Conditions affecting eligibility of voters and candidates, as well as voting procedures will be determined and specified by a separate law.

Principle 63

The term for the membership of the National Consultative Assembly is 4 years. The elections of each term should be held before the expiration of the previous term, so that the country may never remain without an assembly at any time.

Principle 64

The number of the members of the National Consultative Assembly is 270, and after every 10 years, should an increase be registered in the population of the country, one representative will be added to the number of representatives of each constituency for every increase in population of 150,000 people. The Zoroastrians and Jews will each have one representative, the Assyrian and Chaldean Christians will together have one representative, and the Armenian Christians of the south and the north will each elect one representative. Should the size of the population of each of the minorities show an increase after 10 years, they will have an additional representative for each additional 150,000 persons. Regulations for holding elections will be determined and compiled by law.

Principle 65

After elections are held, the sessions of the National Consultative Assembly will be considered legal by the presence of two-thirds of the total number of the representatives at the assembly, and the drafts and bills presented will be ratified in accordance with the internal regulations approved by the assembly, with the exception of cases for which a special quorum is specified by the Constitution. In order to have the internal regulations approved, it would be necessary to have the consent of two-thirds of the representatives present at that particular session.

Principle 66

Matters dealing with the election of the speaker, the Presidium members of the National Assembly, the number of commissions, the term of their incumbency and other affairs relating to the hearings and disciplinary regulations of the assembly will be determined by the internal regulations of the assembly.

Principle 67

At the first session of the assembly the representatives will take the following oath, and then sign the text of the pledge, as follows:

"In the name of God, the compassionate, the merciful.

"In the presence of the holy Koran, I do swear in the name of God the almighty, and based on my humane honor, I do pledge to be the guardian of the inviolability of Islam, of the gains of the Islamic Republic; to safeguard the trust given me by the nation as an honest and trustworthy person; to observe honesty and piety while performing my duties as a representative; to be always bound to the independence and elevation of the country, preservation of the rights of the people, and to render my services to the people of the country; to defend the Constitution, and to have in mind the independence of the country, the freedom of the people, and the interests of the people in all statements made by me, as well as in all writings and expression of opinions."

The representatives of the religious minorities will take the oath by mentioning the name of their holy book. The representatives not present at the first session will take the oath at the first session they attend afterwards.

Principle 68

During a war, and if the country is occupied militarily, at the proposal of the president, by the approval of three-fourths of the representatives, and by the endorsement of the Council of Guardians, the elections of the occupied areas or all of the country will be stopped for a certain period of time, and should a delay be caused in convening a new assembly, the former assembly will continue its operation.

Principle 69

The National Consultative Assembly will hold open sessions, its discussions will be made public by radio broadcasts, and the minutes will be published in the official newspaper. In conditions of an exceptional nature, should the observance of the security of the country necessitate, at the request of the prime minister, one of the ministers, or 10 representatives, the assembly will convene behind closed doors. The issues approved at such a session will be considered valid when ratified by three-fourths of the representatives, in the presence of the members of the Council of Guardians. The reports containing the minutes of those sessions should be made public through the press after the elimination of the exceptional circumstances.

Principle 70

The president, the prime minister, and the ministers will be authorized to attend the sessions of the National Consultative Assembly together or individually. They may also have their aides and advisers accompany them. If deemed necessary by the representatives, the president, the prime minister and the ministers are bound to be present at the assembly and may request permission to make statements and give explanations. The invitation extended to the president to be present at the assembly should be approved by a majority of the representatives.

Part 2: Powers and Authority of National Consultative Assembly

Principle 71

The National Consultative Assembly is authorized to enact laws concerning all issues of a general nature, within the limits set down in the Constitution.

Principle 72

The National Consultative Assembly is not authorized to enact laws contradicting the principles and commandments of the official religion of the country, or the Constitution. The determination of this (as mentioned in Principle 96) is entrusted to the Council of Guardians.

Principle 73

The interpretation of the ordinary laws is a duty of the National Consultative Assembly. This does not mean that judges are deprived of the right to interpret laws while making efforts to establish justice.

Principle 74

Bills are submitted to the National Consultative Assembly after being approved by the Council of Ministers. Resolutions could be brought up for discussion at the National Consultative Assembly by the proposal of at least 15 representatives.

Principle 75

Resolutions, proposals and amendments presented by the representatives in connection with bills that would result in the reduction of public income or increase of general expenses, can be brought up for discussion at the National Consultative Assembly provided they contain ways and means to remedy the income reduction or secure funds for new expenses.

Principle 76

The National Consultative Assembly is authorized to conduct investigations and verifications in connection with all the affairs of the country.

Principle 77

Pacts, contracts, accords and international agreements should be approved by the National Consultative Assembly.

Principle 78

Any changes in the borders and frontiers are prohibited, with the exception of minor adjustments based on the interests of the country which are made on the condition that they are not of a unilateral nature or detrimental to the independence and territorial integrity of the country. They must be approved by four-fifths of the representatives in the National Consultative Assembly.

Principle 79

Imposition of martial law is prohibited. In time of war and under circumstances that necessitate such restrictions, the government will be authorized to establish temporary restrictions with the approval of the National Consultative Assembly. In no case could their duration exceed 30 days. Should the circumstances requiring the restrictions continue to exist, the government will be bound to obtain a new authorization from the assembly.

Principle 80

The receiving and granting of loans or aids, domestic and foreign, by the government, should be done with the approval of the National Consultative Assembly.

Principle 81

Granting concessions to foreigners for establishing corporations and firms dealing with commercial, industrial, agricultural, mineral affairs and services, is absolutely prohibited.

Principle 82

The employment of foreign specialists by the government is prohibited, unless deemed necessary, in which case it may be done with the approval of the National Consultative Assembly.

Principle 83

Buildings and government properties considered to be precious national possessions, are not transferable to others. This can only be done with the approval of the National Consultative Assembly, on the condition that a property is not considered valuable.

Principle 84

Every representative is accountable to the entire nation, and is authorized to express his views in connection with all domestic and foreign issues.

Principle 85

Membership in the assembly is a possession of the person in question and cannot be transferred to some other person. The assembly cannot authorize a person or board to make laws. In case of necessity it can empower its commissions, in accordance with Principle 72, to enact certain laws. In such cases those laws will be implemented on a tentative basis during a period of time determined by the assembly, and it will be up to the assembly to examine them for a final approval.

Principle 86

While performing their duties as deputies, the representatives of the assembly will be completely free in expressing their views or voting moves, and they will not be liable to prosecution or arrest because of the views expressed at the assembly or the votes cast while performing their duties as representatives.

Principle 87

The Council of Ministers, after its formation and introduction to the assembly, and prior to any move or action, should obtain a vote of confidence from the assembly. Likewise, when it faces difficult and controversial issues during its incumbency it can request the assembly to express its view in the form of a vote of confidence.

Principle 88

Whenever a representative asks a question relating to the duties of a minister, the minister is bound to be present at the assembly and answer the question. The reply should be given in a period not exceeding 10 days, unless there is a plausible reason for delay, to be determined by the assembly.

Principle 89

Representatives of the assembly can in cases deemed necessary interpellate the Council of Ministers of each minister [sic]. Interpellation can be proposed in the assembly if it has the signatures of ten of the representatives.

The Council of Ministers, with the interpellated minister, must be present in the assembly ten days after the date that the interpellation was proposed, in order to answer it. They are required to demand a vote of confidence from the assembly. If the Council of Ministers or the minister in question is not present to reply to the interpellation, then the representatives who have proposed it will explain it. If the assembly finds it appropriate to do so, it will announce the lack of a vote of confidence.

If the assembly does not arrive at a vote of confidence, then the Council of Ministers or the minister will be dismissed. In both cases, the interpellated prime minister or minister cannot be a member of the Council of Ministers that would be formed immediately after that.

Principle 90

Anyone who has a complaint about the modus operandi of the assembly, the executive or the judiciary force can, in writing, give his complaint to the assembly. The assembly is responsible for investigating these complaints and arriving at a satisfactory response. If the complaint is related to the executive or judiciary force, the assembly is responsible for demanding an investigation and getting a satisfactory answer from these forces, and then announcing the results in due time. In cases where the complaint is related to the public, the result should be announced to the public.

Principle 91

For the purpose of guarding the precepts of Islam and the constitution and in order to avoid any contradiction between them and the laws of the assembly, a Council of Guardians will be formed with the following members:

1. Six just and religious persons who are knowledgeable of the requirements of the times and the daily problems. The selection of this group is in the hands of the leader of the Leadership Council.

2. Six lawyers in different branches of law. From among the Muslim lawyers, those who have been introduced to the National Consultative Assembly by the High Council of the Judiciary, will be voted on by the Assembly.

Principle 92

The members of the Council of Guardians are elected for a 6-year term. But after 3 years, half of the members shall be changed and new members will be elected in their place by means of a lottery.

Principle 93

The National Consultative Assembly has no legal validity without the presence of the Council of Guardians, unless the credentials of the representatives have been approved [by the Council of Guardians] and six lawyers from among the members of the Council of Guardians have been elected [to the National Consultative Assembly].

Principle 94

All the sanctioned laws and regulations of the National Consultative Assembly must be sent to the Council of Guardians. The Council of Guardians is responsible, within ten days of the receipt of them, to investigate them so that they will conform with the Islamic standards and the constitutional laws.

And if they find any contradiction, they will be returned to the assembly for revision. Otherwise, the laws are ratified.

Principle 95

If the Council of Guardians decides that 10 days is not enough for investigation and expressing of opinion, then stating a given reason, it will request a 10-day extension.

Principle 96

The majority of the six religious members of the Council of Guardians decides whether a national assembly law is in contradiction with Islamic decrees. And the majority of all the members of the Council of Guardians decides whether a constitutional law is in contradiction with the Islamic decrees.

Principle 97

To expedite the work, members of the Council of Guardians can attend the assembly and listen while a bill or a legal project is being discussed. When an urgent project or bill is put before the assembly, they must attend that session and express their opinions.

Principle 98

The Council of Guardians is responsible for interpreting the constitutional law. This interpretation can be given after three-fourths of the members have approved it.

Principle 99

The Council of Guardians is responsible for supervising the presidential election, the elections of the National Consultative Assembly and the referendum.

CHAPTER VII
COUNCILS

Principle 100

In order to further social, economic, development, public health, cultural, and educational programs as well as other welfare matters through popular cooperation and in keeping with local circumstances for administering these affairs, every rural area, district, township, or province will elect from its citizens members for councils for the village, district, township, and province.

The qualification of the electors and those who are elected, the limits of their duties, and privileges, the manner of their election, and the supervision of the said councils and their associated offices should be according to the principles of national unity, territorial integrity, rule of the Islamic Republic, and sovereignty of the central government as determined by law.

Principle 101

To prevent discrimination and to gain cooperation in planning development and welfare programs for the provinces and to supervise their coordination, a Supreme Council of the Provinces will be organized composed of representatives of each province.

The organization and duties of this council will be determined by law.

Principle 102

The Supreme Council of the Provinces has the right to make plans within the limits of its duties and submit proposals to the National Consultative Assembly, either directly or through the government. These plans will then be studied by the assembly.

Principle 103

The governors, commanders, district chiefs, and other authorities that are appointed by the government are obligated to obey the councils' decisions as long as they fall within the limits of the councils' powers.

Principle 104

In order to guarantee Islam a role and insure cooperation in preparing programs, and to coordinate progress in the activities of production units — both industrial and agricultural — councils composed of representatives of workers, villagers, and other employees and managers will be organized to operate in educational, administrative, and service units. These councils will thus be comprised of representatives of the members of these units.

The manner of organizing these councils and the limits of their duties and privileges will be determined by law.

Principle 105

The decisions of the councils should not violate the standards of Islam or the laws of the country.

Principle 106

The councils may not be dissolved unless they deviate from their legal duties. The process for determining such deviation, the manner in which the councils are dissolved, and the method by which they are reconstituted will be determined by law.

If opposition to dissolution of a council is justified, a complaint will be submitted to the competent court, and the court will be obligated to investigate it outside the docket sequence.

CHAPTER VIII
THE LEADER OR THE LEADERSHIP COUNCIL

Principle 107

Whenever one of the jurists who fulfills the conditions mentioned in Principle 5 of the law is recognized by a decisive majority of the people for leadership and has been accepted — as is the case with the Great Ayatollah Imam Khomeini's high calling to the leadership of the revolution — then this leader will have charge of governing and all the responsibilities arising from it. Otherwise, experts elected by the people from all those qualified for leadership will be investigated and evaluated. Whenever a candidate who has outstanding characteristics for leadership is found, he will be introduced to the people as leader. Otherwise, 3 or 5 candidates who fill the conditions for leadership will be appointed members of the Leadership Council and introduced to the people.

Principle 108

The law regarding the number and qualifications of experts, the manner of their election, the internal regulation of their sessions and the fixing of their terms has to be prepared by the primary jurists of the Council of Guardians and approved by the majority of their votes before the final approval of the revolutionary leader. Thereafter, any kind of change and revision of this law is within the competence of the Council of Experts.

Principle 109

The qualifications and attributes of the leader or members of the Leadership Council:

1. The necessary competence in theology and piety to deliver formal legal opinions and authority.

2. Enough political and social insight, boldness, strength, and managerial ability to lead.

Principle 110

Duties and powers of leadership:

1. Appointing the jurists on the Council of Guardians;
2. Appointing the highest judicial authorities of the country;

3. Command of all the armed forces as follows:
   A. Appointing and dismissing the chief of the general staff;
   B. Appointing and dismissing the commander-in-chief of the Islamic Revolution Guards Corps;
   C. Organizing the High Council for National Defense which will be composed of the following seven members:
      — president of the republic
      — prime minister
      — minister of defense
      — chief of the general staff
      — the commander-in-chief of the Islamic Revolution Guards Corps
      — two advisers specified by the leader;
   D. Naming the commanders-in-chief of the three armed forces at the suggestion of the High Council for National Defense;
   E. Declaring war and mobilizing the armed forces at the suggestion of the High Council for National Defense.
4. Signing the order [formalizing] the election of the president after he has been elected by the people. Approving the competence of candidates for the presidency with regard to the qualifications specified by this law. Confirming them before the Council of Guardians before the elections and confirming the president's first term;
5. Dismissing the president of the republic in consideration of the good of the country after an order is issued by the Supreme Court charging him with violating his legal duties toward the National Consultative Assembly and relieving him of his political competence;
6. Pardoning or reducing the sentences of convicts within the limits of Islamic standards, pursuant to the suggestions of the Supreme Court.

Principle 111

Whenever the leader or one of the members of the Leadership Council becomes incapable of performing his legal duties of leadership or loses one of the qualifications mentioned in Principle 109, he will be removed from his position. This action is within the purview of the experts mentioned in Principle 108.

Regulations for calling a meeting of the experts to investigate cases arising from this principle will be formulated in the first session of the experts.

Principle 112

The leader or members of the Leadership Council are equal before the laws with all other citizens of the country.

CHAPTER IX
EXECUTIVE POWER

Part 1: The Presidency

Principle 113

The president is the holder of the highest official power next to the office of leader. He is responsible for carrying out constitutional laws and for organizing the relationships among the three powers. He will also be the chairman of the executive power except for those affairs that are directly related to the leader.

Principle 114

The president is elected for a 4-year term by the direct vote of the people. He can be reelected for only one additional term.

Principle 115

The president must be elected from among men of political and religious distinction. He must: be of Iranian origin; be an Iranian citizen; be an administrator and efficient; be loyal, with a good past history; be pious; be a believer in the foundation of the Islamic Republic of Iran and in the official religion of the country.

Principle 116

Candidates for the presidency must officially announce their candidacy before the beginning of the election. The way in which the election will be carried out to elect a president will be determined by law.

Principle 117

The president will be elected by an absolute majority of the votes, but if in the first round none of the candidates obtains such a majority of votes, a second election will be held on the following Friday. Only the two candidates who had the most votes can run for the second election. However, if these candidates decide not to run, the two candidates who had the next largest number of votes in the first round will be introduced for this second round of elections.

Principle 118

According to Principle 99, the Council of Guardians will be responsible for supervising the election of the president. But prior to the initial creation of the Council of Guardians, the responsibility lies with the board of control which specifies the law.

Principle 119

The election of the new president must be carried out at least one month prior to the termination of the term of the incumbent president. In the interim period between the election of the new president and the conclusion of the term of the incumbent, the incumbent will carry out the duties of the presidential office.

Principle 120

If one of the eligible candidates dies in the 10 days prior to the elections, the elections will be delayed for 2 weeks. If between the first and the second round of the election, one of the two candidates with the most votes dies, the election time will be extended for 2 more weeks.

Principle 121

At the National Consultative Assembly, in the presence of the head of the Supreme Court and the members of the Council of Guardians, the president will take the following oath and sign it: "In the name of God the compassionate, the merciful.

"I, the president, swear on the Koran and before the people of Iran that I will be the guardian of the official religion, of the order of the Islamic Republic and of the constitutional laws. I shall use all my talents and competence to perform the duties I have undertaken. I will dedicate myself to the elevation of the country, propagation of religion and character, and support of the spread of right and justice. I shall avoid any kind of self-interest, protect freedom, respect the people and respect the rights that the constitution has recognized for the people. I will not hold back from any step that will protect the boundaries and the political, economic, and cultural independence of the country. With the help of God and obedience to the prophet, as a devout and trustworthy guardian, I will guard the power entrusted to me by the people and I shall entrust that power to the men elected after me by the people."

Principle 122

The president is responsible before the people for the limits of his authorities and duties. The manner of investigation for such an infringement is determined by law.

Principle 123

When a law of the assembly has been made or a referendum has been completed through legal procedures and has been presented to the president, he is responsible for signing it and handing it over to responsible authorities for execution.

Principle 124

The president will nominate a person as prime minister and after obtaining a vote of endorsement from the National Consultative Assembly, he will issue the oath of office to the prime minister.

Principle 125

After the approval of the National Consultative Assembly, the signing of treaties, conventions, written agreements and contracts between the Government of Iran and all other governments and the signing of agreements related to international unions [as published] is the responsibility of the president or his legal representative.

Principle 126

After laws and decrees have been approved by the Council of Ministers, the president will be informed of them. If he finds them illegal, he will send them back to the Council of Ministers for revision, only after having mentioned his reasons.

Principle 127

Whenever the president finds it necessary, the Council of Ministers will meet in his presence and under his leadership.

Principle 128

The president will sign the accreditation of ambassadors and will receive letters of accreditation from the ambassadors of other nations.

Principle 129

Bestowal of national medals is the responsibility of the president.

Principle 130

In the case of absence or sickness of the president, a council with the name of Temporary Council of the Presidency will be formed. This council will consist of the prime minister, the head of the national assembly and the head of the Supreme Court, and it will carry out the duties of the president; this is on condition that the absence of the president will be no longer than 2 months.

Also, in case of dismissal, or when the term of office of the previous president has been completed and due to certain obstacles the new president has not been elected, this council will be responsible for carrying out the duties of the president.

Principle 131

In case of death, resignation, or sickness that lasts more than 2 months, the dismissal of the president or any other such crisis, the Temporary Council of the Presidency is responsible for making arrangements so that a new president may be elected within the next 50 days. Within this period, the temporary council is responsible for all duties and authorities of the president, except in the matter of referendums.

Principle 132

While the duties of the president are being performed by the temporary council, the government cannot be interpellated, nor can it receive a vote of nonconfidence, nor can any steps be taken for the revision of the constitutional laws.

Part 2: Prime Minister and Ministers

Principle 133

The ministers will be appointed according to the suggestion of the prime minister and with the approval of the president. They shall then be introduced to the parliament for a vote of confidence. The number of ministers and their authorities shall be determined by law.

Principle 134

The prime minister shall head the Council of Ministers and he will supervise the work of the ministers, and taking the necessary advice, he will coordinate government decisions. With the cooperation of the ministers, he will select government policies and execute the laws. The prime minister is responsible to the assembly for the actions of the Council of Ministers.

Principle 135

The prime minister stays in office as long as he has a vote of confidence from the assembly. The letter of resignation of the government should be handed to the president. The prime minister will continue with his duties until the appointment of the next government.

Principle 136

Dismissal and appointment of a new minister by the prime minister has to be approved by the president. A vote of confidence on the new minister has to be obtained from the parliament. If half of the members of the Council of Ministers (cabinet) are changed after receiving a vote of confidence from the parliament, the government must ask again for a vote of confidence from the parliament.

Principle 137

Each minister is responsible to the assembly for his own special duties, but in affairs that have been approved by the Council of Ministers, he will be held responsible for the action of others.

Principle 138

In addition to being responsible for the compilation of laws for various cases, the Council of Ministers, or a single minister, also has the right to compile laws in regard to administrative duties, safeguarding the execution of the laws and regulating administrative organizations. Each of the ministers, within the limits of his duties, and with the sanction of the Council of Ministers, has the right to formulate regulations and issue circulars, but the content of these regulations must not be in disagreement with the content and the spirit of the laws.

Principle 139

Resolving of litigation related to public and government possessions, or its referral to a judge, in each case is subject to the approval of the Council of Ministers, and the assembly must be informed of it. When the claimant is a foreigner, or in important internal matters, the case must be approved by the assembly. The importance of the case is determined by law.

Principle 140

Accusations related to ordinary crimes made by the president, the prime minister or the ministers will be investigated in the public courts of the Ministry of Justice.

Principle 141

The president, prime minister, ministers and government employees are not allowed to hold more than one government job. They are also forbidden to have any other job in organizations all or some of whose capital belongs to the government and public institutions, nor are they allowed to be a representative of the national assembly, an attorney with the Ministry of Justice, a legal advisor, head, managing director or member of the board of directors in various private organizations, except for cooperative associations and organizations of the administration (government). Teaching positions at universities and research institutes are excepted from these institutions.

The prime minister may, when necessary, undertake the duties of certain ministries on a temporary basis.

Principle 142

The Supreme Court will investigate the wealth of the leader, members of the Leadership Council, president, prime minister, the ministers, and their wives and children before and after holding office, lest their wealth has increased contrary to the law.

Part 3: The Army and Revolution Guard

Principle 143

The Army of the Islamic Republic is responsible for safeguarding independence and territorial integrity and keeping order in the Islamic Republic.

Principle 144

The Islamic Republican Army must be an Islamic army. It must be a popular and religiously educated army and it must accept worthy people who will be faithful to the goals of the Islamic Revolution and will be self-sacrificing in the attainment of those goals.

Principle 145

No foreign person will be accepted for membership in the army or regular forces.

Principle 146

Establishment of any kind of foreign military bases in the country is forbidden, even though those bases are to be used for peaceful purposes.

Principle 147

The government in time of peace must utilize the personnel and technical equipment of the military for relief operations, educational and productive purposes and in a crusade for reconstruction.

This should be done with total observance of religious justice and only to the extent that it does not harm the combat readiness of the military.

Principle 148

Personal use of military equipment and use of military personnel as servants, chauffeurs and for other such tasks is prohibited.

Principle 149

Promotion and demotion in military ranks is done according to the law.

Principle 150

The Islamic Revolution Guard Corps that was formed in the first days of the victory of this revolution will remain active in order to continue its role as the guardian of the revolution and its offshoots. The limit of this force's duty and the scope of its authority in relation to the duties and scope of authority of other armed forces will be determined by law, with emphasis on cooperation and brotherly harmony.

Principle 151

According to a noble verse of the Koran, "Make ready your strength to the utmost of your power, including steeds of war, to strike terror into the hearts of the enemies of God and your enemies and others besides them whom ye know not. God knoweth them."

The government is responsible for providing military training programs and facilities for all the people of the country, in accordance with the laws of Islam, so that all the people will always have the capability to defend the country and the order of the Islamic Republic of Iran with arms. Possession of arms must be with the permission of competent authorities.

CHAPTER X
FOREIGN POLICY

Principle 152

The foreign policy of the Islamic Republic of Iran is founded on the basis of ending any type of domination, safeguarding the complete independence and integrity of the territory, defending the rights of all Muslims, practicing nonalignment with respect to the dominating powers and maintaining mutual peaceful relationships with nonbelligerent nations.

Principle 153

Any type of agreement that allows a foreign power to dominate the natural resources, or the economic, cultural, military and other affairs of the country is forbidden.

Principle 154

The Islamic Republic of Iran considers its goal to be the happiness of human beings in all human societies.

It recognizes the independence, freedom and rule of right and justice for all people of the world. Therefore, while practicing complete self-restraint from any kind of influence in the internal affairs of other nations, it will protect the struggles of the weak against the arrogant, in any part of the world.

Principle 155

The Islamic Republic of Iran can give political asylum to those who seek it unless they have been recognized as traitors according to the laws of Iran.

CHAPTER XI
JUDICIARY FORCE

Principle 156

The judiciary is an independent force that supports individual and social rights and is responsible for bringing about justice. It is also responsible for carrying out the following duties:

1. Investigating and passing judgment on cases of injustice, transgressions and complaints; resolving lawsuits and settling conflicts; and making decisions and taking necessary steps in those probate matters that are regulated by the law.

2. Restoring public rights and expanding justice and legal freedoms.

3. Supervising the enforcement of laws.

4. Discovering crime; prosecuting, punishing and reproving the criminal, and bearing the responsibility for carrying out the prescriptions and regulations of the Islamic penal code.

5. Taking appropriate steps to prevent crime and reform criminals.

Principle 157

A council named "The High Council of the Judiciary," will be formed to carry out the responsibilities of the judiciary. This council is considered to be the highest judicial office and its duties are as follows:

1. Forming necessary organizations in the Ministry of Justice to deal with the responsibilities contained in Principle 156.

2. Preparing bills having to do with the judiciary that are suitable for an Islamic Republic.

3. In accordance with the law, exercising the responsibility of hiring just and worthy judges, appointing and dismissing them, changing the location of their tours of duty, assigning them jobs and other such administrative affairs.

Principle 158

The High Council of the Judiciary consists of five members:

1. Head of the Supreme Court of Justice.
2. Attorney General.
3. Three religious and just judges, chosen by the judges of the country.

According to the law, the members of this council are elected for 5 years and can be reelected. The qualifications for the electors and the elected will be determined by law.

Principle 159

The Ministry of Justice is the official place to which complaints of injustice will be referred. The formation of courts and the determination of their competency are subject to the rule of law.

Principle 160

The minister of justice has the responsibility for all the problems related to the relationship between the judiciary and the executive and legislative forces. He is selected from candidates that the High Council of the Judiciary has suggested to the prime minister.

Principle 161

The Supreme Court of the country is formed on the basis of laws that are determined by the High Council of the Judiciary. It is responsible for supervising the correct enforcement of laws in the courts of the land, for creating unity in judicial policy, and for carrying out, according to the law, the responsibilities that have been given to it.

Principle 162

The head of the Supreme Court and the attorney general must be just, religious jurists [mujtahid] and must have knowledge of judicial matters. The leadership, in consultation with the Supreme Court judges, will appoint them to those offices for a period of 5 years.

Principle 163

Qualifications of the judge will be determined by law according to the standards of religious jurisprudence.

Principle 164

A judge cannot be, temporarily or permanently, dismissed from the office that he is holding without a trial and proof of crime and violations that are considered as grounds for dismissal. Nor can his place of duty or his job be changed unless it is in the interest of society and is carried out with the unanimous approval of the members of the High Council of the Judiciary. Periodic transfers of the judges will occur according to rules determined by law.

Principle 165

Trials will be held openly and the public is allowed to attend unless the court decides that an open trial is incompatible with public sense of chastity and order or both adversaries request that the trial not be held openly.

Principle 166

The decrees of the courts must be supported by the articles of law and they must be methodical.

Principle 167

The judge is responsible for trying to find the statute for each dispute in the codified laws, and if he does not find it, relying on reputable Islamic sources or judicial decrees, he must pass judgment on the matter. He cannot, by using the excuse of silence, deficiency, abridgment or contradiction of the codified laws, avoid investigation and passing of a judgment.

Principle 168

Investigations of political and press crimes are to be held in the courts of the Ministry of Justice, openly in the presence of a jury. Defining the political crime, the manner in which the jury will be selected, their authority and qualifications will be determined according to Islamic standards.

Principle 169

If a law is enacted after an action or lack of action has occurred, then that action or lack of action cannot be considered as a crime.

Principle 170

The judges of the court are dutybound to refrain from executing governmental decisions that are contrary to Islamic laws and regulations and that are outside the limits of the executive power.

Principle 171

If an individual receives any material and spiritual damage due to the fault or mistake of the judge, in the subject matter, in the passing of the judgment, or in the verification of the judgment, then the guilty party, when shown his guilt, will be responsible for those damages. Otherwise, compensation for the damage will be provided by the government and, in either case, the loss of honor of the accused will be reinstated.

Principle 172

For investigation of crimes related to special military or disciplinary duties, committed by members of the army, gendarmery, police force or Islamic Revolution Guard, a military tribunal will be formed in accordance with the law. But if these individuals commit common crimes or crimes that are dealt with by the Ministry of Justice, then their crimes shall be investigated in public courts. The Provost Marshall and military courts are part of the public judiciary and come under its principles.

Principle 173

With a view to attending to the complaints, criticisms and objections of the people concerning state officials, units, regulations and the administration of their rights, a court named the Court of Administrative Justice has been created under the supervision of the High Judicial Council. The law defines the limits of the jurisdiction and authority of this court.

Principle 174

On the basis of the right of supervising the judicial power, with regard to proper conduct of affairs and correct legal procedure in the administrative systems, an organization called the General National Investigative Organization has been created under the supervision of the High Judicial Council. The law defines the jurisdiction and functions of this organization.

CHAPTER XII
MASS MEDIA

Principle 175

In the mass media (radio and television), freedom of dissemination and information according to Islamic principles should be assured. These media will be supervised by a joint judicial (the Higher Judicial Council), legislative and executive body. The law defines the plan of this supervision.

The Constitution of the Islamic Republic of Iran was formulated in 12 chapters, comprising 175 principles. The final review of the Constitution was approved by at least two-thirds of the total membership of the assembly on the 24th day of the month of Aban of the year 1358 of the solar Hijri calendar, corresponding to the 24th day of the month of Dhu-al-Hijjah of the year 1399 of the lunar Hijri year.

7. INTERIM CONSTITUTION (1970) OF THE REPUBLIC OF IRAQ AND ITS AMENDMENTS

The Revolutionary Council has decided, in its session convened on 16-7-1970, on the promulgation of the new Interim Constitution and its publication in the official Gazette.

Ahmed Hassan Al-Bakr
Chairman of the
Revolutionary Command Council

PART ONE
THE REPUBLIC OF IRAQ

Article 1

Iraq is a sovereign people's democratic republic; its principal aim is to achieve the United Arab State and establish the socialist system.

Article 2

The people are the source of power and its legality.

Article 3

(a) The sovereignty of Iraq is an indivisible unit.
(b) The land of Iraq is an indivisible unit and no part of it may be relinquished.

Article 4

Islam is the religion of the State.

Article 5

(a) Iraq is part of the Arab Nation.
(b) The people of Iraq are formed of two principal nationalities, the Arab nationality and the Kurdish nationality. This Constitution shall recognize the national rights of the Kurdish people and the legitimate rights of all minorities within the unity of Iraq.

Article 6

The Iraqi nationality and its rules shall be organized by the law.

Article 7

(a) Arabic is the official language.

(b) The Kurdish language shall be the official language, beside the Arabic language, in the Kurdish region.

Article 8

(a) Baghdad is the capital of the Republic of Iraq, and it may be shifted by a law.

(b) The Republic of Iraq shall be divided into administrative units which shall be organized on the basis of decentralization.

Article 9

The flag and the emblem of the Republic of Iraq and the rules pertaining to them shall be defined by a law.

PART TWO

SOCIAL AND ECONOMIC BASES OF THE REPUBLIC OF IRAQ

Article 10

Social solidarity is the foremost foundation for the society. Its implication is that every citizen shall perform fully his duty towards the society and that the society shall ensure to the citizen his full rights and freedoms.

Article 11

The family is the nucleus of society. The State shall guarantee its protection and support, and shall foster maternity and childhood.

Article 12

The State shall undertake planning, directing and guiding the national economy for the aim of:

(a) Establishing the socialist system on scientific and revolutionary principles.

(b) Achieving the Arab economic unity.

Article 13

National resources and substantial instruments of production are the property of the People, and the central authority of the Republic of Iraq shall invest them directly in accordance with the requirements of the general planning of the national economy.

Article 14

The State shall ensure, promote and support all kinds of cooperation in production, distribution and consumption.

Article 15

Public properties and the properties of the public sector shall have special inviolability, which the State and all citizens of the nation have to maintain and watch over for their security and protection. Any subversion thereof or violation thereon shall be deemed as subversion to the structure of the society and a violation on it.

Article 16

(a) Ownership is a social function which shall be exercised within the limits of the society's aims and the State's programs in accordance with the provisions of the law.

(b) Private ownership and individual economic freedom shall be ensured within the limits of the law and on the basis of not investing them in what contradicts or impairs the general economic planning.

(c) Private property shall not be expropriated except for the public interest and in accordance with just compensation under the rules defined by the law.

(d) The maximum amount of agricultural land that may be privately owned shall be defined by the law and the surplus shall be deemed as the property of the people.

Article 17

Inheritance is an ensured right which shall be defined by the law.

Article 18

Real estate ownership is forbidden to non-Iraqis except what is excluded by a law.

PART THREE
BASIC RIGHTS AND DUTIES

Article 19

(a) Citizens are equal before the law, without discrimination because of race, origin, language, social category or religion.

(b) Equal opportunities for all citizens shall be guaranteed within the limits of the law.

Article 20

(a) The accused is innocent until he shall be proved guilty through legal trial.

(b) The right of defense is sacred in all stages of investigation and trial in accordance with the provisions of the law.

(c) Sittings of courts shall be convened openly unless the court decides to convene *in camera*.

Article 21

(a) Penalty is personal.

(b) There shall be no offense or penalty except on the act deemed by the law as an offense at the time of its commission. More severe penalty than the penalty enforced at the time of committing the offense may not be applied.

Article 22

(a) The dignity of man is maintained. Exercise of any form of physical or psychological torment shall be prohibited.

(b) No one may be arrested, detained, imprisoned or searched except under the provisions of the law.

(c) Homes are inviolable. They may not be entered or searched except under the rules defined by the law.

Article 23

Privacy of mail, telegraphic and telephone communications shall be guaranteed, and they may not be disclosed except for justice and security needs in accordance with the limits and the rules provided by the law.

Article 24

A citizen may not be prevented from travel outside the country or from returning thereto and no restriction may be imposed on his moving and residence inside the country except in the case defined by the law.

Article 25

Freedom of religions, beliefs and exercise of religious ceremonies shall be guaranteed, provided that this should not contradict the provisions of the Constitution or the law and should not infringe the morals and public order.

Article 26

The Constitution shall guarantee freedom of opinion, publication, meeting, demonstration, forming of political parties, unions and societies in accordance with the aims of the Constitution and within the limits of the law. The State shall endeavor to provide the means required for practicing these freedoms, which are in accordance with the nationalist and progressive line of the Revolution.

Article 27

(a) The State shall abide by combating illiteracy and ensure the right of free education in various elementary, secondary and university levels, for all citizens.

(b) The State shall endeavor to make elementary education compulsory, expand vocational and technical education in cities and villages and particularly promote evening education which enables the popular masses to relate science to labor.

(c) The State shall guarantee freedom of scientific research, promote and reward distinction and creation in all intellectual, scientific and technical activities and various phenomena of popular genius.

Article 28

Education shall aim at raising and developing the general cultural level, developing the scientific thinking, kindling the spirit of research, fulfilling the requirements of economic and social development programs, creating a free nationalist and progressive generation solid in structure and character, which esteems its people, its homeland and its legacy, sympathizes with the rights of all the nationalities, and struggles against the philosophy of capitalism, exploitation, reaction, Zionism and colonialism for achieving Arab unity, freedom and socialism.

Article 29

The State shall endeavor to provide the means of enjoying the achievements of modern civilization for the masses of the people and distribute the progressive output of modern civilization to all citizens.

Article 30

(a) Public office is a sacred trust and a social service, whose stature is the loyal obligation aware of the interests of the masses, their rights and freedoms in accordance with the provisions of the Constitution and the law.

(b) Equality in filling public posts shall be guaranteed by the law.

Article 31

(a) Defense of homeland is a sacred duty and an honor bestowed to the citizen. Service of the flag is compulsory and the law shall organize the manner of its performance.

(b) The Armed Forces are the property of the people, and they are the people's tool for preserving their security, defending their independence, protecting the people's and the homeland's safety and unity, and achieving their national and nationalist aims and aspirations.

(c) The State, alone, shall undertake the establishment of the Armed Forces, and no body or group shall be entitled to establish military or semi-military formations.

Article 32

(a) Work is a right which the State shall undertake to provide to every citizen capable of it.

(b) Work is an honor and a sacred duty imposed on every capable citizen. It is required by the necessity of participation in building the society and its protection, development and prosperity.

(c) The State shall undertake to improve conditions of work and promote the standard of living, skills and culture of all working citizens.

(d) The State shall undertake to provide wider social insurance for all citizens in case of sickness, disability, unemployment or old age.

(e) The State shall endeavor to organize the program and ensure the necessary means which enable the working citizens to spend their leaves in an atmosphere that helps them to improve their health standards and develop their cultural and technical abilities.

Article 33

The State shall undertake to protect public health through the continuous expansion of free medical services whether in prevention, treatment or medication throughout the cities and villages.

Article 34

(a) The Republic of Iraq shall grant political asylum for all who struggle and are persecuted in their own countries because of their defense of the principles of human liberation, which the Iraqi people have affirmed in this Constitution.

(b) Political refugees shall not be extradicted.

Article 35

Payment of financial taxes is a duty imposed on all citizens. Financial taxes may not be imposed, amended or levied except by a law.

Article 36

Any activity which contradicts the aims of the people defined in this Constitution and any act or conduct aiming at crumbling the national unity of the masses of the people, provoking racial or sectarian or regional bigotry among their ranks, or violating their progressive gains and achievements, shall be prohibited.

PART FOUR
THE INSTITUTIONS OF THE REPUBLIC OF IRAQ

Chapter One—The Revolutionary Command Council

Article 37

The Revolutionary Command Council is the supreme body in the State, which has undertaken since the 17th of July 1968 the responsibility of achieving the people's public will by stripping off the power from the reactionary, dictatorial and corrupt system and restoring it to the people.

Article 38

The Revolutionary Command Council shall exercise by the majority of two thirds of its members the following responsibilities:

(a) Elect the Chairman from among its members, who shall be designated as the Chairman of the Revolutionary Command Council and shall, as a rule, be the President of the Republic.

(b) Elect the Vice Chairman from among its members, who shall be designated as Vice Chairman of the Revolutionary Command Council and shall take the place of the Chairman, as a rule, with his capacities defined in the previous paragraph, in case of his official absence or when his exercise of his constitutional responsibilities becomes difficult or impossible, for any legal reason.

(c) Select new members to the Council from among the regional leadership of the Arab Ba'ath Socialist Party provided that its members shall not exceed twelve.

(d) Decide on the resignation of the Chairman or the Vice Chairman or one of the Council's members.

(e) Release any of its members from membership in the Council.

(f) Charge and send to trial the members of the Revolutionary Command Council, the deputies of the President of the Republic and the Ministers.

Article 39

The Chairman, the Vice Chairman and the members of the Revolutionary Command Council shall take the following oath before the Council:

"I swear by Almighty God, by my honor and belief to preserve the Republican regime and abide by its Constitution and laws, foster the people's interests, safeguard the homeland's independence and safety and the integrity of its lands and endeavor with full sacrifice and loyalty to fulfill the Arab Nation's aims of unity, freedom and socialism."

Article 40

The Chairman, Vice Chairman and members of the Revolutionary Command Council shall enjoy full immunity and any measure may not be taken against any one of them except by prior permission from the Council.

Article 41

(a) The Revolutionary Command Council shall convene at the invitation of its Chairman or Vice Chairman or one third of its members. Its sessions shall be convened under the presidence of the Chairman or the Vice Chairman and the presence of the majority of its members.

(b) Meetings and discussions of the Revolutionary Command Council are confidential; their disclosure shall be subject to constitutional inquiry before the Council. Announcement, publication and notification of the decisions of the Council shall be performed in the manner provided for in this Constitution.

(c) Laws and resolutions shall be approved in the Council by the majority of its members, except in cases otherwise provided for in this Constitution.

Article 42

The Revolutionary Command Council shall exercise the following responsibilities:

(a) Promulgate laws and resolutions which have the power of the law.

(b) Issue resolutions required by the necessities of applying the provisions of the enforced laws.

Article 43

The Revolutionary Command Council shall exercise, by the majority of its members, the following responsibilities:

(a) Approve the affairs of the Ministry of Defense and public security, initiate laws and adopt resolutions concerning them in respect to organization and jurisdictions.

(b) Declare a general mobilization, either partially or fully, declare war, accept armistice and conclude peace.

(c) Approve the draft of the general budget of the State and the independent and investment budgets appended thereto and the credit of the final accounts.

(d) Ratify international treaties and agreements.

(e) Provide the Statute of the Council, define its duties, approve its budget, appoint its officials and specify remunerations and allowances of the Chairman, the Vice Chairman, the members and the officials.

(f) Prepare the rules for the trial of its members as regards forming the court and the procedures which must be followed.

(g) Authorize its Chairman or the Vice Chairman to exercise some of the Council's responsibilities which are provided in this Constitution, except legislative responsibilities.

Article 44

The Chairman of the Revolutionary Command Council shall undertake the following:

(a) To preside over the sessions of the Council, represent it, administer its sessions and order expenditure therein.

(b) To sign all laws and resolutions promulgated by the Council and authorize their publication in the official Gazette.

(c) To supervise the works of the Ministers and institutions of the State, call the Ministers for conferring on the affairs of their Ministries, question them when necessary and inform the Revolutionary Command Council thereof.

Article 45

The Chairman, the Vice Chairman and the members of the Revolutionary Command Council shall be responsible before the Council in case of any violation of the Constitution, or for failing to uphold the obligations of the Constitutional oath or for any act or conduct which the council deems detrimental to the honor of the office which he exercises.

Chapter Two—The National Assembly

Article 46

The National Assembly shall be composed of the representatives of the people in all its political, economic and social sectors. Its formation, manner of membership, process of work and its jurisdictions shall be defined by a special law, namely, the National Assembly Law.

Article 47

The National Assembly must convene two ordinary sessions each year. The Chairman of the Revolutionary Command Council is entitled to call the Assembly for a special session whenever required, and the meeting shall be confined to the subjects for which it is convened. Sessions of the National Assembly shall be convened and concluded by a resolution issued by the Revolutionary Command Council.

Article 48

Sessions of the Assembly shall be convened publicly unless it is decided to convene some of them *in camera* in accordance with the rules defined in its law.

Article 49

(a) Members of the National Assembly may not be questioned over the opinions and suggestions they introduce during their exercise of the tasks of their posts.

(b) None of the members of the Assembly may be pursued or arrested for an offense committed during the holding of sessions without the Assembly's permission, except in case of being held in the act of crime.

Article 50

The National Assembly shall undertake to:

(a) Provide its internal Statute, specify its duties, approve its budget and appoint its personnel. Remunerations and allowances of its President and members shall be defined by a Law.

(b) Draw up the rules for charging and trying its members in case of their committing one of the acts specified in Article 55 of this Constitution.

Article 51

The National Assembly shall consider the draft laws proposed by the Revolutionary Command Council within a period of fifteen days from the date of their arrival at the bureau of the National Assembly's Presidency. If the Assembly approves the draft, it shall be submitted to the President of the Republic, to promulgate it. But if the Revolutionary Command Council insists on its opinion in the second reading, the draft shall be returned to the National Assembly to be presented in a joint sitting of the Council and the Assembly. The decision issued by the majority of two-thirds shall be considered final.

Article 52

The National Assembly shall consider within a period of fifteen days the draft laws forwarded to it by the President of the Republic. If the Assembly rejects the draft, it shall be returned to the President of the Republic with a statement of the reasons for rejection. But if the Assembly accepts the draft, then it shall be submitted to the Revolutionary Command Council; and if the Council approves the draft, it shall then be liable for promulgation. But if the National Assembly amends the draft, then it shall be submitted to the Revolutionary Command Council; and if it approves the draft, it shall be liable for promulgation. But if the Revolutionary Command Council rejects the amendment or makes another amendment, it shall be returned again to the National Assembly within one week. If the National Assembly adopts the opinion of the Revolutionary Command Council, the draft shall be submitted to the President of the Republic for promulgation. But if the National Assembly insists, in the second reading, on its opinion, then a joint session of the Council and the Assembly shall be held, and the draft adopted by the majority of two-thirds shall be considered final, and it shall be submitted to the President of the Republic for promulgation.

Article 53

The National Assembly shall consider the draft laws submitted by one quarter of its members in affairs other than military, financial and public security affairs.

If the Assembly approves the draft law, it shall be forwarded to the Revolutionary Command Council for consideration within fifteen days from the date of its arrival at the bureau of the Council. If the Revolutionary Command Council approves the draft, it shall be submitted to the President of the Republic for its promulgation.

But if the Revolutionary Command Council rejects the draft, it shall be returned to the National Assembly.

If the Revolutionary Command Council makes amendment in the draft, it shall be returned to the National Assembly. If the latter insists on its opinion, in the second reading, then a joint session of the Council and Assembly shall be held under the Presidency of the Chairman of the Revolutionary Command Council or his deputy, and the draft adopted by the majority of two-thirds shall be considered final, and shall be submitted to the President of the Republic for its promulgation.

Article 54

(a) Deputies of the President of the Republic and the Ministers and those who are in ranks similar to them shall be entitled to attend the sessions of the National Assembly and participate in discussions.

(b) The National Assembly may, upon the approval of the President of the Republic, call the Ministers in order to make an inquiry or request an explanation.

Article 55

The President of the National Assembly and every member in it are held responsible before the Assembly in case of any violation of the Constitution, for failing to uphold the obligations of the Constitutional oath, or for any act or conduct which the National Assembly deems detrimental to the honor of the office which he exercises.

Chapter Three—The President of the Republic

Article 56

(a) The President of the Republic is the Head of State and the Commander-in-Chief of the Armed Forces, and shall exercise executive power directly or with the assistance of his deputies and Ministers, in accordance with the provisions of this Constitution.

(b) The President of the Republic shall promulgate the necessary ordinances for exercising his powers as prescribed in this Constitution.

Article 57

The President of the Republic shall exercise the following responsibilities:

(a) Preserve the independence of the country and the integrity of its lands, protect its interior and exterior security and foster the rights and freedoms of all citizens.

(b) Declare full or partial emergency and terminate it in accordance with the law.

(c) Appoint deputies of the President of the Republic and the Ministers and release them from their posts.

(d) Appoint civil and religious judges and all civil and military officials of the State, promote them, terminate their services, retire them and grant medals and military ranks in accordance with the law.

(e) Submit the draft of the general budget of the State and the independent and investment budgets appended to it, accredit the final accounts of these budgets and refer them to the National Assembly for discussion.

(f) Submit the general plans of the State in all economic and social affairs, which are prepared by the concerned Ministries, and refer them to the National Assembly.

(g) Conclude and grant loans and supervise organizing and administering currency and trust.

(h) Supervise all public utilities, official and semi-official institutions and the public sector organizations.

(i) Direct and supervise the work of the Ministries and state organizations, and coordinate them.

(j) Hold negotiations and conclude international agreements and treaties.

(k) Accept diplomatic and international representatives in Iraq and demand their withdrawal.

(l) Appoint and accredit Iraqi diplomatic representatives to Arab and foreign capitals and to international conferences and organizations.

(m) Issue special amnesty and ratify capital punishments.

(n) Supervise the good application of the Constitution, laws, resolutions, judicial judgments and development projects all over the Republic of Iraq.

(o) Authorize one or more of his deputies with some of his constitutional powers.

Article 58

The deputies of the President of the Republic and the Ministers shall be held responsible before the President of the Republic for their works, and he is entitled to refer any one of them to trial, in accordance with the provisions of the Constitution, for functional errors committed, for taking advantage of, or abusive use of, his powers.

Article 59

The deputies of the President of the Republic and the Ministers shall take the following oath before the President of the Republic before proceeding with their official tasks:

"I swear by Almighty God, by my honor and faith to preserve the Republican regime, abide by its Constitution and laws, guard over the people's interests, safeguard the country's independence, its safety and the integrity of its lands and endeavor with full sacrifice and loyalty to achieve the aims of the people."

Chapter Four—Jurisdiction

Article 60

(a) The judiciary is independent and no power shall be exercised over it except the law.

(b) Right to litigation shall be guaranteed to all citizens.

(c) The law shall define the manner in which the courts shall be organized, and their levels and jurisdictions, and it will specify stipulations for appointing civil and religious judges, transferring and promoting them, bringing charges against them and retiring them.

Article 61

The law shall define the offices of the Public Prosecutor, stipulations for appointing public prosecutors and their deputies, and the rules for transferring and promoting them, bringing charges against them and retiring them.

PART FIVE
GENERAL PROVISIONS

Article 62

(a) No one shall be a member in the Revolutionary Command Council and no one shall be a deputy to the President of the Republic or Minister except whoever is Iraqi by birth and from Iraqi parents by birth also.

(b) Members of the Revolutionary Command Council, deputies to the President of the Republic and the Ministers shall not exercise a free profession or a commercial business or purchase from the State properties, sell to the State some of their properties or barter for them during their tenure in office.

Article 63

(a) The provisions of this Constitution shall be in force until the Permanent Constitution is promulgated.

(b) This Constitution shall not be amended except by the Revolutionary Command Council by the majority of two-thirds of its members.

Article 64

(a) The laws shall be published in the official Gazette and shall come into force right from the date of their publication except otherwise provided therein.

(b) Laws shall not have retroactive effect except if otherwise provided therein, and this exclusion shall not include criminal laws and laws of taxes and financial dues.

Article 65

This Interim Constitution, and the laws and rules of jurisdiction shall be promulgated and executed under the name of the people.

Article 66

All laws and resolutions of the Revolutionary Command Council enforced prior to the promulgation of this Constitution shall remain valid and they may not be amended or abrogated except through the manner provided in this Constitution.

Article 67

The Chairman of the Revolutionary Command Council shall undertake promulgating this Constitution and its publication in the official Gazette.

ANNEX (1)
AMENDMENT TO THE INTERIM CONSTITUTION
RESOLUTION NO. 567

Article 2

The provision of Article (53) of the Interim Constitution shall be abrogated and substituted by the following provision:

"Article 54: The National Assembly shall consider draft laws presented by one-quarter of its members in affairs other than military matters and public security affairs.

"If the Assembly approves the draft law, it shall be submitted to the Revolutionary Command Council to consider it within fifteen days from the date of its arrival at the Council's bureau.

"If it is approved by the Revolutionary Command Council, it shall be submitted to the President of the Republic for promulgation.

"But if the Revolutionary Command Council rejects or amends it, the draft shall be returned to the National Assembly. If the latter insists on its opinion, in the second reading, a joint session of the Council and the Assembly shall be convened under the presidency of the Chairman of the Revolutionary Command Council or his deputy. The draft issued by the majority of two-thirds shall be considered final and shall be submitted to the President of the Republic for promulgation."

Article 3

Paragraph (a) of Article (56) of the Interim Constitution shall be abrogated and substituted by the following:

"Article 57(a): The President of the Republic is the President of the State and the Commander-in-Chief of the Armed Forces. He shall undertake executive power directly or through the Council of Ministers."

Article 4

Article (57) of the Interim Constitution shall be abrogated and substituted by the following:

"Article 58: The President of the Republic shall directly exercise the following responsibilities:

(a) Preserve the independence of the country and integrity of its lands, protect its interior and exterior security and foster the rights and freedoms of citizens.

(b) Supervise the good application of the Constitution, laws, resolutions, judgments of jurisdiction and development projects in all parts of the Republic of Iraq.

(c) Appoint deputies for the President of the Republic and release them from their posts.

(d) Appoint the Ministers and release them from their posts.

(e) Appoint the judges, *qadhis* (justices) and civil and military officials of the State, and terminate their services in accordance with the law.

(f) Appoint and accredit Iraqi diplomatic representatives at the Arab and foreign countries and in international conferences and organizations.

(g) Grant military ranks and medals in accordance with the law.

(h) Hold negotiations and conclude international agreements and treaties.

(i) Accept diplomatic and international representatives and demand their withdrawal.

(j) Ratify capital punishments and issue special amnesty.

(k) Direct the control of the work of the Ministries and general institutions and coordinate them."

Article 5

The following shall be added to the Interim Constitution, and the subsequent Articles and Chapters shall be renumbered accordingly.

Chapter Four—The Council of Ministers

"Article 60:

(a) The Council of Ministers shall consist of the Ministers who are presided over by the President of the Republic.

(b) The President of the Republic shall call the Council of Ministers for meeting and conduct its sessions."

"Article 61:

The Council of Ministers shall exercise the following responsibilities:

(a) Organize draft laws and refer them to the concerned legislative authority.

(b) Issue administrative regulations and decisions in accordance with the law.

(c) Appoint civil officials of the State and promote them, in accordance with the law.

(d) Submit the general plan of the State.

(e) Submit the general budget of the State and the budgets appended to it.

(f) Conclude and grant loans, and supervise organizing and administering currency.

(g) Declare a full or partial emergency and terminate it in accordance with the law.

(h) Supervise general utilities and official and semi-official institutions."

Article 6

This resolution shall come into force as from the date of its publication in the official Gazette.

Ahmed Hassan Al-Bakr
Chairman of the
Revolutionary Command Council

ANNEX (2)
AMENDMENT TO THE INTERIM CONSTITUTION
RESOLUTION NO. 247

In accordance with paragraph (b) of Article (63) of the Interim Constitution,

The Revolutionary Command Council has decided, in the name of the people, in its session convened on 11/3/1974, to amend the Interim Constitution promulgated on July 16, 1974 as follows:

Article 1

The following paragraph shall be added to Article (8):
"(c) The area whose majority of population is Kurdish shall enjoy autonomy in accordance with what is defined by the law."

Article 2

This constitutional amendment shall come into force as from the date of its publication in the official Gazette.

Made at Baghdad on the 17th Safar, 1394 Hejra, coinciding with the 11th March, 1974.

Ahmed Hassan Al-Bakr
Chairman of the
Revolutionary Command Council

8. STATEMENT OF DR. SAADOUN HAMADI, MINISTER FOR FOREIGN AFFAIRS OF THE REPUBLIC OF IRAQ, BEFORE THE SECURITY COUNCIL OF THE UNITED NATIONS, OCTOBER 15th, 1980

Mr. President, allow me first to extend to you and the other members of the Council my sincere thanks for having given me the opportunity to participate in this meeting.

As one of the founding members of the United Nations, Iraq has strongly adhered in its international relations to the purposes, principles and rules of the Charter of the United Nations. As we are a member of the non-aligned movement, the principles of non-alignment constitute the cornerstone of our foreign policy. We have not simply pledged ourselves to those principles but have also translated them into action in our international relations. Whether in our region or in the world area, our policy has always been the preservation of international peace and security, as well as the avoidance of world economic catastrophe. But this policy absolutely rejects any form of interference from any quarter, irrespective of its pretext. Hence, we cannot agree to any attempt or action to interfere in the internal affairs of our country contrary to the legally established norms of state conduct.

Having said that, permit me to state that the problem with which the Council is concerned should be regarded in its proper perspective. Otherwise we are liable to overlook some of its important dimensions, and consequently no viable solution is likely to emerge. The problem is neither new nor simple. It goes back over 460 years of history. It is not a mere border problem or a minor conflict over navigational rights. It is much wider than that. Historically it is established that, since 1520, eighteen treaties have been concluded by the "Persian state" with its western neighbors concerning its relations therewith, including the question of borders, only to be terminated by the said state, whether by word or by deed. We are neighbors of Iran and have shared with the Iranian people cultural, religious and humanitarian ties. We have for some time been convinced that the policies and actions of the successive regimes in Iran are clearly those of territorial expansionism. I shall not bother the Council with a detailed historical account. I need only recall one fact of very recent history. All of us witnessed the visions of power and domination of the Shah, which were not confined to the Arab Gulf area but extended also to the Indian Ocean and beyond. And today we all know that President Bani-Sadr of Iran has declared that between Muslim countries there are no borders. That is not meant to indicate a policy of free and open relations among Islamic states, because the Iranian government claims that many Islamic countries belong to Iran — countries such as Bahrain, Yemen and Oman — and even the capital of my country.

The Iranian government and its representatives claim that since the Islamic Republic was established in Iran, my government has adopted a hostile attitude towards the new regime. That allegation is utterly baseless. Khomeini was given refuge in Iraq for about fifteen years, and he was given full moral and material support for over seven years. Iraq welcomed the new regime from the very early days, in every sense.

On 5 April 1979, the president of the Republic of Iraq addressed to Khomeini a telegram of congratulations on the occasion of the declaration of the Islamic Republic. In that telegram our president expressed, on behalf of the people and government of Iraq and on his own behalf, "sincerest congratulations" to Khomeini and the "neighborly and friendly peoples of Iran, hoping that the new republican regime will open wider opportunities to serve the friendly Iranian peoples in a manner that promotes Iran's role in the service of peace and justice in the world and forges the strongest relations of friendship with the Arab countries in general and Iraq in particular."

To that telegram we received two answers from Khomeini — a nice one, through the Ministry of Foreign Affair, and another one published by the Pars News Agency and some newspapers between 19 and 21 April 1979, expressing an entirely different attitude in a hostile tone and with improper language. So we pursued the matter through diplomatic channels to seek clarification. We were told by Prime Minister Bazargan and Foreign Minister Yazdi that the former telegram was the official one and that an investigation would be carried out to find out how the second version appeared. We considered the matter settled, although the outcome of that investigation was not communicated to us and we did not see any official correction in the Iranian press later on.

Despite that unhappy incident we continued our official contacts. My government addressed to the Bazargan government a note in which it expressed its earnest intention to establish the closest fraternal ties and cooperative relations with neighboring peoples and countries, especially with Iran, on the basis of respect for sovereignty, non-interference in internal affairs and respect for the legitimate aspirations of peoples in accordance with principles they have chosen of their own free will.

The note also expressed the view that Iraq had a special interest in relations between the people of Iraq and the neighboring peoples of Iran and Turkey; for those people were not merely neighbors but brothers, with whom the Arab Nation in general and the Iraqi people in particular were related by old Islamic ties and a common history stretching over hundreds of years. In addition, the people of Iraq, who had struggled for years against colonial domination, corrupt monarchy and exploitation, had achieved their victory through the revolution of 17 July 1968 led by the Arab Ba'ath Socialist Party. Hence the people of Iraq looked with sympathy upon and supported the struggle waged by the friendly and neighborly Iranian people for freedom, justice and progress. It felt joy and pride when the Iranian people achieved victory in those respects. In the same vein, similar satisfaction was expressed in the note regarding the statements and positions of Prime Minister Bazargan, which emphasized the Islamic character of some of the popular trends in Iran, because such had been the principled and practical position of the Arab Ba'ath Socialist Party. Such a trend was considered by Iraq an important positive transformation in the region which would contribute to promoting its independence and development. Finally, the note went on to express Iraq's sincere hope for prosperity for the friendly and neighborly Iranian people and for strong relations of fruitful cooperation between Iraq and Iran of a kind that would promote common bonds, serving the mutual interests of both countries and strengthening freedom, peace and stability in the region.

Later on my government extended an invitation to Prime Minister Bazargan to visit Iraq and discuss bilateral relations and bases for mutual cooperation. The same invitation was renewed by the Iraqi vice-president of the Revolutionary Command Council during the month of Ramadan—in July and August 1979—in a telegram on the religious occasion. I should say for the record that Mr. Bazargan was also cooperative and tried to strengthen relations between the two countries.

Even after our relations became tense, the president of the Republic of Iraq, in two meetings with Mr. Yazdi in Havana last year, clearly expressed his willingness to meet with the Iranian leaders at the highest level to resolve our differences peacefully. I reaffirmed the same thing to Mr. Yazdi when I met with him last year here at the United Nations. Minister Yazdi said that they would consider the matter in Teheran, but nothing happened.

Now let us ask what was the outcome of all those efforts, which surely cannot by any criterion be considered hostile?

Prime Minister Bazargan resigned, and with him went Foreign Minister Yazdi. So the arena was left free for Khomeini and his followers. At that time, Khomeini reached the point of unmasking the true intentions of his Islamic revolution, by deciding to export it to Iraq and the Arab Gulf region.

Under his auspices, and with his blessings, a meeting was held at Qum of the leaders of the reactionary and sectarian al-Da'wa Party — which means the "Call Party." The decision was reached to overthrow our government through subversion, sabotage and terrorism by the so-called *Joundi el Imam* — that is, the "Imam's Soldiers," meaning the militants of the al-Da'wa Party. The idea was that after enough terror had reigned in Iraq to destabilize its government, then a popular uprising would bring it down. Here Khomeini was obviously thinking that what he had achieved in Iran could be secured in Iraq as well.

The task of the so-called Joundi el Imam—the Imam's Soldiers—was carried out by Iranian infiltrators and residents in Iraq as well as by first-generation Iraqis of Iranian origin. We witnessed all over our country, and particularly in the central and southern parts, acts of sabotage and terrorism of mounting magnitude. Such acts were committed at al-Thawra and Khadhumain in Baghdad, and in cities like Kerbala, Najaf, Amarah, Basra and Naserriyah. They consisted of hurling explosive materials on the masses during religious and national occasions, throwing nitric acid in the faces of people attending prayers at mosques, poisoning food and water prepared for the pilgrims to the holy shrines in Kerbala, Najaf and Khadhumain, and the like. At al-Thawra in Baghdad — a heavily populated working-class quarter — the terrorist attack claimed many lives, and a number of Iranian terrorists were caught. The Iranian ambassador, Mr. Doa'i, met with me personally later to plead for the release of the terrorists, and we responded positively.

All those acts were directed from Qum, as daily instructions were issued to al-Da'wa agents through Khomeini's broadcasting stations from Teheran, Qasr Shirin, Ahwaz, Abadan and Kurdistan. Those stations also issued instructions to manufacture local bombs for use in killing innocent citizens. The Iraqi security forces seized considerable amounts of money, arms, bombs, poisons and explosive materials in the hideouts of the said criminal group.

The most cruel terrorist act was the throwing of bombs at a huge student gathering at the Mustansiriyah University in Baghdad on 1 April 1980, where an attempt was made to assassinate Mr. Tareq Aziz, a member of the Revolutionary Command Council and the Deputy Prime Minister. During the terrorist act lives were lost, and many persons were injured. Similarly, bombs were thrown from the Iranian school at Waziriya Street on the funeral procession of those innocent persons who had been murdered in the previous incident, on 5 April 1980, in which some Iranian diplomats took part. In addition, an attempt was made on 12 April 1980 on the life of the Minister of Culture and Information, in front of his ministry.

In all those incidents, Iranians were caught who fit the description of Joundi el Imam, which I mentioned earlier.

We reacted to those acts of terrorism by expelling Iranian residents from our country. Our action was prompted by reasons of internal security, as no state in the world could be expected to condone acts against its internal security by foreigners residing within it.

It is worth noting that, parallel with the acts I have just described, the Barzani followers [Kurdish rebels] — now harbored in and supported by Iran — began to commit similar acts of terrorism in the northern part of our country. In addition, the Khomeini authorities began to prevent the return of Iraqi Kurds from Iran to Iraq, and to persecute any remnants of families, when some members had succeeded in returning to their homeland. All those acts were accompanied by a formidable public media propaganda campaign unprecedented in its fanatical and sectarian religious overtones. Iraq, in fact, was not alone in witnessing such acts. Similar actions were attempted in Kuwait, Saudi Arabia, Bahrain and the United Arab Emirates.

Khomeini's scheme through the so-called Islamic revolution was to destabilize the region by inciting sectarian religious strife. We in Iraq refuse such a medieval ideology. Our concept is secular, and we do not mix together affairs of state and religion. Revolutions cannot be imposed from the outside against the free will of the people. We are bound to stand against Khomeini's theories and practices, in defense of our security, well-being and independence.

The Khomeini authorities accuse us of fomenting civil strife in Iran among the national minorities. Those authorities have lost sight of the fact that the Arabs, Kurds, Turkomans and Baluchi, and the other national minorities in Iran, contributed to the national struggle which brought the downfall of the Shah. It was natural, therefore, that those minorities expected the so-called Islamic revolution to grant them their national aspirations. What inherent hostility could we possibly have had towards Iran or the Iranian people, or Khomeini for that matter, had it not been for the most dangerous of all forms of interference in our internal affairs?

Iraq has placed before the Council, in document S/9323, dated 11 July 1969, some historical facts and details regarding the legal status of the Iraqi-Iranian border up to 1969. That document will be brought up to date and presented to the Council in order to show that the policy of territorial expansion is a cardinal policy of successive Iranian governments. That policy has always followed the same pattern: first, an Iranian allegation; then, a denial of legal obligations, to be followed by a new legal instrument designed to secure a territorial gain for Iran; then the same sequence repeating itself.

The Algiers Agreement of 6 March 1975 was no exception to that pattern. The political situation in our region during the period prior to that date witnessed the emergence of the Shah in Iran as the policeman of the region. The expansionist plans and pretensions of the Shah were met by us with a firm adherence to sovereignty, full independence and noninterference in the internal affairs of state. Neither ideologically nor pragmatically did we fit into the picture; hence the reactionary rebellion of Barazani was adopted as the means for a solution.

The idea was to disrupt our national unity in order to overcome our resistance. The Shah provided huge quantities of sophisticated armaments to Barazani. The Iranian army gave important logistical support to the rebellion.

Israel for its part armed and trained Kurdish rebels under Barazani from 1965 to 1975, and also provided them with instructors. This was reported by the *New York Times* of 29 September 1980, which published a report on the disclosure of what it termed as the "tightly suppressed secret" by Menachem Begin on the date just mentioned. The report indicates that the Israeli assistance started under Eshkol and grew under Golda Meir and Rabin, and that the last Israeli instructor left when Barazani was evacuated in 1975. While our people were valiantly fighting against the rebellion, a new factor emerged in relation to the balance of the military situation, namely, the October 1973 war. With a view to creating the appropriate conditions that would enable us to participate in the battle together with our Arab brethren, my government decided to seek a political settlement with Iran through peaceful means. Consequently, when the late president of Algeria, Houari Boumedienne, offered to mediate, we accepted.

Against that political background the Algiers Agreement was negotiated and concluded in the form of a package deal. It had both political and juridical aspects. The spirit of the agreement was that the parties decided "in all sincerity" to conclude it with a view to reaching "a final and permanent solution to all the problems existing between the two countries," and that the arrangements agreed upon were "in application of the principles of territorial integrity, the inviolability of borders and non-interference in internal affairs." The elements of the package deal were the definitive demarcation of land frontiers on the basis of legal agreements between the two countries; the delimitation of water frontiers in the Shatt al-Arab according to the thalweg line; the restoration of security and mutual trust along the common boundaries and the commitment to exercise a strict and effective control over them with a view to putting an end to all acts of infiltration of a subversive character, no matter where they originated. The most fundamental obligation which the two parties assumed and which indicated the package-deal nature of the agreement was paragraph (4) thereof, in which the parties considered the three elements just mentioned as "integral elements of a comprehensive solution. Hence, any impairment of any of their components shall naturally be contrary to the spirit of the Algiers agreement."

In order to translate those arrangements into more concrete instruments, a joint Iraqi-Iranian Ministerial Commission was established in which Algeria participated and a Treaty of International Boundaries and Good Neighborliness, along with three Protocols and Annexes, were signed in Baghdad on 13 June 1975. In that connection it is worth noting that article (4) of the Treaty on International Frontiers and Good Neighborliness explicitly consecrated the package-deal nature of the Algiers Agreement.

Upon the coming into force of the Treaty on Boundaries, Iran acquired sovereignty over half of the Shatt al-Arab, hence securing an early advantage. In return Iraq did not receive the land areas that Iran had trespassed on contrary to its international obligations. This was the situation when the Shah was toppled from power. Upon the installation of the new regime in

Teheran, the government of Iraq saw fit to allow the new government a period of grace before pressing for the completion of the process of the return of areas belonging to Iraq.

Notwithstanding Iraq's positive attitude towards the changes in Iran, Teheran's new rulers soon revealed their enmity towards Iraq through their official pronouncements and information media. They began to display Iran's renewed intentions of territorial ambitions and aggressive expansionism.

I should like to quote here a few examples of the scores of statements made by high-ranking Iranian officials and directed against Iraq and the Arab countries.

On 21 March 1980, in a statement delivered by Khomeini's son on behalf of his father, he declared that: "We must do our utmost to export our revolution to other parts of the world and renounce the concept of keeping the revolution within our own boundaries."

On 3 April 1980, Ghotbzadeh, then the foreign minister of Iran, declared that Aden and Baghdad belonged to Iran. On 9 April he further added that his government had decided to overthrow the Iraqi government. Bani-Sadr, the President of Iran, in an interview with *Al-Nahar Al-Arabi wal Dawli,* in its issue 151 of 24 March 1980, stated that Iran would not evacuate nor return the three Arab islands it had occupied by force in 1971, and that the Arab states of the United Arab Emirates, Qatar, Oman, Kuwait and Saudi Arabia were not independent states.

Khomeini was quoted in the *Jumhuri Islami* dated 19 April 1980 as saying that "the Iraqi people should liberate themselves from the claws of the enemy; it is the duty of the Iraqi people and army to turn against this un-Islamic party in Iraq." In an interview with Radio Monte Carlo on 30 April, Ghotbzadeh denied the Arabs the right to reclaim the three islands of Abu Musa and the Tunbs in the Arabian Gulf because, he said, all the countries around the Gulf are historically part of Iranian territory. In an interview in the *Al Khaleej* newspaper of 1 May, Ghotbzadeh was asked whether he did not consider Khomeini's statement to the effect that, if Iraq continued in its policies he, Khomeini, would go to Baghdad to liberate the Iraqi people, as interference in the internal affairs of Iraq. Ghotbzadeh replied: "This could not be considered as interference in Iraq's affairs since we consider the Islamic nation as one, and the Imam (Khomeini) is a religious leader; he is thus a leader for the Iraqi people and all Islamic peoples; as he feels responsible for Iran, so he feels responsibility towards Iraq."

In addition, the present Iranian government committed another grave violation of the Algiers Agreement. While the said agreement enjoined Iran to restore security and trust along its common boundaries with Iraq, and to exercise strict and effective control for the purpose of putting an end to all infiltrations of a subversive character, the Iranian government openly violated this fundamental obligation. It brought over and offered refuge in Iran to the remnants of the former rebels against Iraq, namely, the sons of Barazani and his followers.

With the explicit support of the ruling authorities in Iran, those groups used Iranian territory as a base for threatening and interfering in the internal security and national integrity of Iraq. Repeated Iraqi demands for the return of Iraqi lands were not only frustrated but also met by new territorial claims, as I have indicated.

Unlike the Ayatollah Khomeini, Iraq still has faith in this international organization. Iraq has, in fact, twice brought complaints against Iran before this Council. The first was in 1971 when Iran occupied by force the three strategic Arab islands in the Arabian Gulf, and that complaint was brought on behalf of the sheikhdom of Ras al-Khaima. It is sad to have to state that the failure of the Security Council to effect Iranian withdrawal from the occupied islands served to encourage the Shah and his successors to pursue their dream of establishing Persian hegemony over the whole of the Arabian Gulf.

Iraq's second complaint before this Council was made in 1974, after Iranian acts of aggression committed across the same borders as are the cause of the present conflict. Again United Nations mediation failed to stop Iranian expansionist ambitions and Iran engaged, as I have already stated, in blatant military interference in northern Iraq.

The prelude to the present conflict was not limited to what I have mentioned so far. There were not less than 57 violations of Iraqi air space by Iranian military aircraft between the period 23 February 1979 to 28 May 1980. In addition to the repeated Iranian artillery fire at Iraqi territories and border police posts, there were more than fifteen intensive Iranian bombardments between 26 August 1979 and 3 June 1980. Most of the bombardments originated from the Iraqi lands withheld by Iran, namely, Zain-al-Qals, Saif Saad and Maimak. Iraqi and foreign vessels navigating the Shatt al-Arab were often subjected to attacks by Iran. All those incidents and violations were the subject of numerous official notes delivered to the Iranian Foreign Ministry and the Iranian embassy in Baghdad, to which no Iranian replies were received.

Declarations were made in official circles in Iran that Iran no longer considered itself bound by the Algiers Agreement. On 19 June 1979, Mr. Sadiq Tabatabai, the political assistant to the Iranian Ministry of the Interior, said that Iran did not implement the Algiers Agreement. In a statement broadcast by Iran's television network on 15 September 1980, General Falahi, deputy joint chief of staff of the Iranian army, said that Iran did not recognize the Algiers Agreement and that the areas of Zain-al-Qals and Saif Saad were Iranian, as was Shatt al-Arab. The latest statement was that of President Bani-Sadr himself. He was reported by Teheran Radio on 17 September 1980 to have said the following to the French news agency: "On the political plane, Iran has not fulfilled the Algiers Agreement signed with Iraq in 1975. ... The Shah's regime itself did not fulfill it."

All our persistent efforts through diplomatic and political channels to persuade Iran to fulfill its obligations were in vain. Consequently we were left with no choice but to reassert our rights under international law by taking possession of our lands. In response to the intention of the Iranian government, which it had made clear by word and deed, to terminate the Algiers Agreement of 6 March 1975, my government decided to consider the said agreement as terminated on the grounds of the provisions of paragraph (4) thereof, to which I referred earlier.

In announcing that decision we strongly emphasized that we had no territorial ambitions in Iran. Furthermore, we openly declared that we had no intention whatsoever of waging war on Iran or extending the scope of the conflict beyond the limits of defending our sovereignty and legitimate rights.

The response of the government of Iran to this legitimate position was to escalate the situation to total war through indiscriminately hostile acts involving the use of force against Iraqi and foreign vessels in Shatt al-Arab. Iran started bombing civilian centers and economic establishments inside our country. Consequently, my government was left with no choice but to direct preventive strikes against military targets in Iran. There was, to borrow from a well-known [legal] case (*The Caroline,* 1837), "a necessity of self-defense, instant, overwhelming, leaving no choice of means and no moment of deliberations." In taking those actions my government clearly and openly declared that Iranian civilian targets would not be the object of military strikes unless Iran continued to strike at such targets in Iraq. Thus, our actions involve "nothing unreasonable or excessive, since the act justified by the necessity of self-defense must be limited by that necessity and kept clearly within it" (ibid.).

Iraq does not stand for war, nor does it believe in the use of force in international relations. Iraq, as its record proves, and particularly in its frontier relations with Iran, has always adhered strictly and honorably to the letter and the spirit of its international commitments. But at the same time Iraq does not accept any form of threat or aggression against its sovereignty and dignity, and we are ready to make all the sacrifices necessary for the preservation of our legitimate rights and vital interests.

Concern has been expressed regarding the repercussions of the recent events on the world economic interests which might be adversely affected. Let me point out at once that Iraq is anxious to protect, within the limits of its ability, the economic interests of other nations. Any attempt to widen the character and scope of our problem with Iran would endanger the situation. Such an attitude would invite further foreign intervention in our part of the world, which we earnestly want to keep outside the sphere of influence and rivalry of the big powers, in the interest of international peace and security and world economic prosperity.

It is well known to the Council and the international community as a whole that Iraq has responded favorably and positively to the various appeals addressed to it and the efforts made to stop the fighting and move towards a peaceful settlement of the present conflict. We have cooperated with the Security Council from the outset and have participated in its deliberations. Our response to this Council's resolution 479 of 28 September 1980 was prompt and positive; our President informed the Secretary-General on 29 September 1980 that, "We naturally accept the above-mentioned resolution ... and declare our readiness to abide by it if the Iranian side does likewise" (S/14203, annex). He added, "We hope that the Security Council will take the necessary measures to urge the Iranian side to abide by that resolution." (ibid.)

Iran officially rejected the call of the Council. Moreover, in response to the goodwill mission undertaken by the president of Pakistan and secretary-general of the Islamic Conference, we offered a unilateral cease-fire from 5 to 8 October, which actually went into effect at dawn on 5 October. Iran's response was a large-scale attack on land and sea and in the air.

I should like finally to reaffirm before the Council that Iraq does not stand for the use of force in international relations. We firmly believe in the peaceful settlement of disputes. We fully realize that as a developing country we need to utilize all our energies and resources for social and economic development. But at the same time we cannot remain idle in the face of any encroachment upon our legitimate sovereign rights in the totality of our territories, or upon our security, peace and well-being.

9. STATEMENT OF MOHAMMAD ALI RAJAI, PRIME MINISTER OF THE ISLAMIC REPUBLIC OF IRAN, BEFORE THE SECURITY COUNCIL OF THE UNITED NATIONS, OCTOBER 17th, 1980

No one can cry out his indignation unless he has been a victim of aggression. We have come here at a time when our country is engaged in a war which was initiated by the cruel, despotic government of Iraq. We are here at a time when our Imam and our people have been greatly saddened by the many deaths that have been caused by the earthquake in Algeria. We regret the fact that the war has made it impossible for us to give the aid and the assistance that we would have liked to give to Algeria and to our Muslim brothers of Algeria.

I have come here straight from the front. The spectacle of the dead and the wounded would have moved the most heartless of men. I saw that spectacle with my own eyes. The land-to-land missiles which struck the city of Dezful demolished a large part of the city and many of the courageous population perished. In Dezful, more than thirty babies are in the hospital, babies who are less than six months old. I have seen those babies and they are fighting for their lives.

The army of Saddam Hussein, using ridiculous pretexts—and perhaps it really should be added that they are no pretexts at all—has committed an act of aggression against our country. It has destroyed centers of production, the economy and towns including hospitals and schools, and it has killed innocent people.

The whole world must know that Saddam's army has acted without mercy, without pity, like Hitler's armies. To prolong his cruel regime, Saddam Hussein has engaged twelve divisions and more than two thousand five hundred tanks, as well as large quantities of weapons and hundreds of war planes. He has used them to attack the people of our country — this at a time when the Islamic Republic was entering into a period of reconstruction.

Yesterday, during my flight, I learned that at Kermanshah, following a bombing against schools and universities, those buildings and the hospital were hit, and more than one thousand school children and civilians were victims of that raid. Iraq's Ba'athist army, which has no understanding whatsoever of humanity, spared no effort in those inhuman acts. They have plundered; they have even been guilty of rape. In the occupied areas, they have imprisoned all adult men and have in that way taken many war prisoners, some of whom have been tortured and others killed in the prisons.

We would appeal to the conscience of the people of the entire world, in particular to the Muslim people, with whom we share a common ideology and common values. It is for them to pass judgment. It is surprising that those who profess belief in dignity remain aloof and say nothing and in the face of this open aggression declare their neutrality in international forums.

How can the representatives of those people speak of neutrality? We know that many revolutionaries have already come here to the Security Council and have asked that the rights of their peoples be defended. But in the final analysis, it is always the people themselves who have defended their rights, by fighting the aggressor with their own hands.

Our oppressed but heroic people, inspired by the potent ideology of Islam and under the leadership of Imam Khomeini, will continue to fight and will determine their own future. The resistance of the Iranian armed forces and the Iranian people in the face of the enemy has amazed the entire world. Our people are resolute and determined to fight, even if the people's war must be prolonged. We will not only expel the aggressor, but we will allow the friendly fraternal people of Iraq to become aware of the tyrannical and dependent nature of Saddam Hussein's regime.

They will then be able to deal a lethal blow to American imperialism, which directly or indirectly has been helping the Ba'athist government of Iraq. The United States with its AWACS aircraft in Saudi Arabia controls the movements of Iranian troops and passes all information on to Iraq. It also misleads Iranian pilots.

We warn all those who, through the port of Aqaba in Jordan, send arms and munitions and spare parts to Iraq so that all those weapons can be used to attack and bomb the anti-imperialist and revolutionary people of Iran that our people are determined to survive. Our people will protect the Islamic and humanitarian revolution. They will remain free. They will live and with the help of God, they will win.

The superpowers wish to impose a new Israel on the Middle East. The crimes of the United States that have been committed against the people of Palestine and southern Lebanon should have been enough, but today they are trying to create a new Israel under the banner of an Arab nationalism. The Zionists in Israel were sufficiently criminal, but another government led by Saddam Hussein has now been given a mandate to destroy humanitarian values and pursue its own ambitions. Saddam has brought destruction to the whole area. All those who help him will die in that destruction, as will he.

The true aim of the Iraqi regime and its masters is not to gain a few kilometers of territory. What they are trying to do is to mutilate the revolutionary movement of the Islamic Iranian people. They wish to destroy the Islamic Republic. They want to prevent the completion of the bond that mankind has begun to forge in Iran. They are trying to prevent us from building a free Iran on the foundation of Islamic and humanitarian values, for any victory for Iran spells the defeat of all the forces of evil throughout the world.

The dispossessed people of the world, as well as all those who have lost confidence in both the left and the right, must realize that our Islamic revolution has opened up a new path for all the disinherited people of the world. The Iranian revolution acquired independence, thanks to the power of the people, and our people will guarantee their future by sacrifice and through self-sufficiency.

We believe that the true winner of the war will be the revolutionary faith of the people, not arms and munitions. That is why we firmly declare that in this war, which has been imposed upon us, the Islamic revolutionary faith of our people will prevail. It is not the American AWACS or the Russian Tupolevs that will bring about this victory. In this war, we are defending not only our territorial integrity and our economy, but also human dignity and the honor of our Muslim people. We are leading mankind towards true humanitarian values.

We know that this war which has been imposed upon us will end with the victory of the forces of good over the forces of evil. We shall show the world that we can rely on our own strength, without allying ourselves with the colonialism of the East to fight the colonialism of the West, and that we will make every sacrifice to guarantee our independence.

The Tabas raid, the planned coup d'etat and the armed invasion of Saddam Hussein have shown the superpowers that in their relations with the Islamic Republic any resort to force is doomed to failure. That war has aleady cost us thousands of martyrs, thousands of wounded. Material reparations cannot compensate for that.

We are looking forward to the day when the criminal Saddam Hussein will be judged by a revolutionary tribunal in Iraq, to the day when he will be punished for his deeds. We are looking forward to the day when the people of Iraq will rid themselves of him. Let all the oppressed people of the world learn this lesson: that dignity and independence cannot be obtained without sacrifice, for God is with the deprived.

Let us now review the pretexts advanced by the Saddam regime for launching an aggression against Islamic Iran. Saddam, mercenary of the oppressors of the world, recognizing that he himself was responsible for the military attack against Iran and its territorial integrity, invoked the non-applicability of the articles of the agreement concluded in 1975 as a pretext, to whitewash this open aggression. It should be pointed out that, following the Algiers negotiations at the conference of the OPEC countries which was held from March 4 to 6, 1975, a treaty concerning the frontiers of the state and good neighborly relations, with three annexed protocols, was concluded on June 13, 1975, and four more complementary agreements were entered into on December 26, 1975. A document serving as a final, comprehensive settlement of the outstanding questions was signed on the same date, and there was an exchange of the instruments of ratification between Iran and Iraq. All these agreements and documents were duly registered with the Secretariat of the United Nations. All these instruments make it perfectly clear that Iraq's totalitarian regime admitted at the time that it had no more claims regarding its rights and that the disputes had been terminated.

The people of the world must also know that the regime of the Islamic Republic of Iran, since immediately after the victory of the revolution, although it might have called for a review of all the agreements that had been concluded, has never strayed from the terms of the treaty that I have mentioned; and that it is those who governed the people of Iraq when the treaty was being prepared and whose signatures appear on the treaty who were the ones who violated the provisions of the treaty. Moreover, the treaty itself provided for the means of settling whatever disputes might arise between the two parties.

Let me now turn to a possible explanation for the abrogation of the treaty by Iraq. Perhaps the best explanation is that the Iraqi regime is acting irrationally, in an inhuman manner, or perhaps that it is blindly following its masters, namely, the superpowers, not so as to make changes in the borders but to deal a lethal blow to the Islamic revolution in Iran.

Even before the unilateral announcement that the treaty had been abrogated by Saddam Hussein, there were instances of flagrant violations and here are a few: first, continual interference in the internal affairs of Iran since the victory of the Islamic revolution; secondly, the violation of articles pertaining to the security of borders by the continual dispatch of mercenaries and Ba'athist agents and armed groups into the provinces of Kurdistan, Kermanshah, Elam and Khuzistan, and the provision of assistance to anti-revolutionary elements in the provinces I have just mentioned and also in Sistan and Baluchistan; thirdly, the provision of assistance to persons sought in Iran for having committed crimes against the population during the Shah's regime, and guarantees that those individuals would have all material means and the use of propaganda to weaken the regime of the Islamic revolution. They now have two radio stations on Iraqi territory, it should be added, and are engaging in propaganda against the Iranian regime.

Now let me turn to the true aims of Iraq in its aggression against Iran and consider the nature and position of the Iraqi regime vis-à-vis the Islamic revolution and the role of the superpowers.

Why did the Baghdad regime reject the treaty and commit aggression against Iran? What were its aims and purposes?

First, the very nature of the regime should be clarified, and we should briefly review the positions taken by Saddam Hussein in respect to the Islamic revolution. The Ba'athist party in power in Iraq is made up of the supporters of the notorious Michel Aflaq. He was a Freemason and a cunning Zionist. He diverted the anti-Zionist, anti-imperialist struggles of the Muslim people and of the disinherited Arab people, and he founded institutions that were in appearance natio ialist and socialist, but were, in fact, inspired by racist ideals. After the victory of Abdul Nasser in Egypt and his attacks on the interests of the puppet regimes in the Arab Middle East — in view of the fact that the reactionary regimes (such as those of King Husain and King Hasan, for example) we ? not in a position to counter those attacks individually—the West, in order to fight against Nasser and Nasserism, undertook to set up so-called leftist regimes whose slogans sounded much more conservative than those of King Husain-type regimes. One of those regimes, as the Council is aware, was the Ba'athist regime in Iraq.

The history of the struggle of the Arab Muslim people shows that this regime, which today is using its full military might to destroy the Islamic revolution, never sent its troops to combat the invaders of Jerusalem, except, perhaps, at the last moment, when the war was already over. That party, notwithstanding its anti-Zionist slogans, never took any practical action to combat the interests of Zionism. Is there really any need to add that it will never do so?

Inside the country the Iraqi regime has taken dictatorship and oppression to such limits that is has even dared to imprison and kill Ayatollah Mohammad Baqir Sadr and his sister. The prisons are full of honest Muslim prisoners. The position of the regime of Saddam Hussein vis-à-vis the Iranian revolution has been hostile from the start and is aimed at preventing the achievements of the Islamic revolution. The entire world will recall that right at the very beginning of the revolution in Iran, the Baghdad regime forced Imam Khomeini to leave Iraq. The friendly fraternal relations of Saddam Hussein with the Shah's Iran changed right after the victory of the revolution, and its relations with Iran became imbued with a hostility that cannot ever be compared with the kind of hostility that that regime feels towards Israel. The publicity machine used by Saddam and his mercenaries was set in motion against the Islamic revolution. Iraq became the land of asylum and the center of activities of the lackeys of the United States and the Pahlavi regime and notorious torturers such as anti-revolutionaries from the right and the left in Iran joined the material and moral support of the Ba'athists in Iraq. As I have said, radio broadcasting stations called "Iranian stations against the revolution" were set up in Iraq.

We call on the people of the world to ask why the Iraqi regime, which says that it is fighting against the United States, had friendly relations with the Shah's regime, the valet of the United States, whereas its position is hostile to a regime that is truly fighting to destroy the vital and strategic interests of imperialism, and in particular those of the United States and international Zionism, a regime that was even the victim of direct intervention by the United States when diplomatic relations were broken off and an economic embargo was put into effect. Why is Saddam's position so hostile towards Iran? If Iraq is really hostile to the United States and if that hostility goes beyond mere declarations of intent, why did it never dare attack the Shah's army, which was entirely controlled by American military advisers, while today it is attacking an army that has only recently freed itself from the American yoke? Is this not, in fact, an American mission with an anti-American appearance?

These tactics are not at all mysterious to the people of the world. Recently we saw another puppet regime — that of Ian Smith in Zimbabwe — using the same tactics and rising up against its masters.

The position of Iraq, which is hostile to Iran, is only a reflection of the hostility of the superpowers, first and foremost the United States, towards the Islamic Republic of Iran. From this rostrum we declare to all the people of the world that Iraqi military aggression is construed by us as an integral part of the continual attempts at international aggression against our revolution. We wish to repeat that Iraq's aggression is in reality the aggression of the forces of evil and is the work of the great Satan and the lesser Satan. We ask the people of the world, and in particular, the Arab Muslim people, to pause and ponder, and we trust that they will find an answer to the questions which I am about to ask.

First, how is it that Iraq's regime, even assuming that there was a territorial dispute with Iran, before having recourse to the good offices of Algeria, which presided over the reconciliation of the two countries, engaged in a widescale military attack on the land of the Islamic Republic of Iran?

Secondly, together with that attack, how is it that today Iraq's aggression goes beyond changes in borders and has as its object the invasion of our provinces, in particular, the oil province of Khuzistan?

And, together with that attack, how is it that all the counter-revolutionaries outside Iran went to Iraq, where it was made possible for them to conduct their activities on Iraqi territory?

How is it that the United States sees in that attack an opportunity for their hostages to be freed?

How is it that Iraqi aggression coincides with the end of the separatist claims in Kurdistan and with the installation of the government of the Islamic Republic?

Finally, how is it that in this war the puppet regimes par excellence which are entirely dependent on the United States, such as those of Jordan, Egypt, Morocco and so on, are the primary port of entry for Iraq, and the airports of Jordan today are accommodating Iraqi planes? The Egyptian pilots and crews are playing a particularly active role in Iraq, and units of the Jordanian army are at present stationed there.

Considering all these points can we still consider the war of the Iraqi regime with Iran a war of claims that are exclusively territorial in nature? Are we not entitled to consider that this war is part of the fight of the superpowers against the Islamic revolution? During these days of warfare, while blood is being shed, we are witnessing a build-up of the military agreements between European governments and countries of the Middle East. We are also greatly surprised these days to see that America, which had refused to take part in the Olympic games in Moscow because of the Soviet Union's military aggression in Afghanistan, is today readily agreeing to engage in new SALT negotiations. Does that not explain why Soviet weapons are being shipped through American Jordan to Iraq and the regime of Saddam Hussein?

Let me now set forth our position on the war, and let me speak now about the outcome of the conflict. The people of the world are well aware of the fact that the war between Iran and Iraq is a war that has been imposed upon us. The regime of the Islamic Republic never would have dared use its forces and its weapons against an Islamic country with an unpopular regime at a time when the fight should have been against the invading regime in Jerusalem, which has subjected our Palestinian Arab brothers to international Zionism, and deprived them of all their property and all their rights in the occupied territories and in southern Lebanon.

Unfortunately, Iraq's recent aggression has taken a very heavy economic and military toll on the Muslim people of both countries. Bullets which were intended to be used against the invaders of Islamic territories are today being used to kill our Muslim brothers, with the aim of slaking the thirst, satisfying the ambitions, of a single individual to serve the interests of the forces of evil.

The Ba'athist government of Iraq, after occupying part of our territory, after killing civilians, innocent people, after destroying our facilities, our factories, our towns, asks for a cease-fire today in order to deceive international public opinion. Regrettably, some countries have wittingly or unwittingly supported that request. We wish to declare that a fair end to this war can be found only if the aggressor is vanquished and punished. That is our final position. For if a country that has been devastated, a country that has been the victim of aggression, accepts a cease-fire, that will only serve to consolidate the position of the aggressor; it will only serve to condone the act of aggression.

Our people are today in mourning for the thousands of school children killed during an Iraqi raid against the schools of Kermanshah. That is the best reason for condemning the Ba'athist regime. We have seen that regime go so far as to bomb a hospital in Abadan. Eight wounded persons died, and, as a result of the bombing, more than forty persons who had been working in the hospital were seriously wounded; today, they are in the very beds that had been occupied by most of the victims. That is but one reason, but we could cite so many more, for condemning the Ba'athist regime of Iraq.

In conclusion, I should like to explain in a few words why we are here. Islam and historical experience have taught us that we cannot overcome difficulties unless we rely on God's will and the will of the people. In view of what I have just said, the members of the Security Council will readily understand that we are not here to ask the Council for anything at all; we are here to convey the facts, to expose what is actually happening in our country.

We are perfectly aware that the Security Council, in view of the veto of the major powers, and in view of the existence of other difficulties, is not in a position truly to help the oppressed and disinherited people of the world. Moreover, history shows us that the Security Council, even if upon occasion it has adopted resolutions on matters of principle under the pressure of world public opinion, has been unable to ensure their implementation owing to the opposition of one major power or another. The failure to implement the resolutions of the Council—for example, those on Israel or the racist regime of South Africa—are particularly enlightening.

We are here for the sole purpose of making the voice of the Muslim and revolutionary people of Iran heard. We are here to warn the people of the entire world about the dangers that overthrowing the Iranian revolution would entail, about the impact that that would have on the struggles of other oppressed people. We are here to urge, once again, the great powers and the forces of evil to put an end to their plots against the Islamic revolution, to realize that the noble, divine Iranian revolution, born of and nourished by the blood of thousands of martyrs, will never be vanquished.

The decision of the Council, whatever it may be, will not change anything for us. Our people, with the help of God, will fight Saddam and his oppressive regime with their own hands. Our people will win. With the help of God, the people of Iraq will in the near future be liberated once and for all from this cruel oppressor. Very soon the people will see the oppressors of the world disappear; they will see that in the last analysis it is those who have the truth on their side who will win.

Selected Bibliography

DOCUMENTS AND GOVERNMENT PUBLICATIONS

Bank Melli. *The Persian Gulf: A Name Born with History.* Teheran: Bank Melli Press, 1970.

Embassy of the Republic of Iraq, London. "Saddam Hussein on the Conflict with Iran." Statement of a press conference held on 10 Nov. 1980.

Hussein, Saddam. *On Social and Foreign Affairs in Iraq.* London: Croom Helm, 1979.

Imperial Iranian Embassy, London. "Some Facts Concerning the Dispute between Iran and Iraq over the Shatt al-Arab. The Boundary Line Between Iran and Iraq." July 1969.

Lorimer, J. G. *Gazetteer of the Persian Gulf, Oman and Central Arabia.* 2 vols. Shannon: Irish University Press, 1970.

Ministry of Foreign Affairs, Baghdad. "The Iraqi-Iranian Dispute: Facts v. Allegations." October 1980.

Ministry of Foreign Affairs, Baghdad. "Factual Study Concerning the Iraqi-Iranian Boundary." August 1969.

Ministry of Foreign Affairs, Baghdad. "The Iraqi-Iranian Conflict: Documentary Dossier." January 1981.

Ministry of Foreign Affairs, Teheran. "British Official Documents Shed New Light on the Question of Shatt al-Arab." 9th Political Department, September 1969.

Ministry of Foreign Affairs, Teheran. *Iran's Foreign Policy: A Compendium of the Writings and Statements of His Imperial Majesty Shahanshah Aryamebr.* N.d.

Ministry of Islamic Guidance, Teheran. "Selected Messages of Imam Khomeini Concerning Iraq and the War Iraq Imposed upon Iran." March 1981.

Pahlevi, H.I.M. Muhammad Reza Shah. *Mission For My Country.* New York: McGraw-Hill, 1961.

United States Congress, House of Representatives. *New Perspectives on the Persian Gulf.* Ninety-third Congress, 1st Session, June 6, July 17, 23, 24, and Nov. 28, 1973. Washington, D.C., 1973.

ARTICLES

Ahmad, Eqbal, ed. "The Iranian Revolution." Special Issue, *Race & Class* 21, no. 1 (Summer 1979).

Akhtar, S. "The Iraq-Iranian Dispute over the Shatt-el-Arab." *Pakistan Horizon* 22, No. 2 (1969): 213–21.

Banani, Amin. ed. "State and Society in Iran." Special Issue, *Iranian Studies* 11 (1978).

Beaujard, Lt. Col. "Etat de Forces Aeriennes dans le Golfe Persique." *Revue de Defence Nationale* 27 (December 1971): 1912–14.

Bill, James A. "Iran and the Crisis of '78." *Foreign Affairs* (Winter 1978/79): 323–42.

Bloomfield, Lincoln P. "Law, Politics, and International Disputes." *International Conciliation* 516 (January 1968).

Dawisha, A. I. "Iraq: The West's Opportunity." *Foreign Policy* 41 (Winter 1980–81): 134–53.

D'Encausse, Hélène Carriere. "L'Iran en Quete d'un Equilibre." *Revue Francaise de Science Politique* 17, no. 2 (April 1967): 213–36.

Drambyantz, G. "The Persian Gulf: 'Twixt the Past and the Future,'" *International Affairs* (Moscow) 10 (October 1970): 66–71.

Edmonds, C. J. "The Iraqi-Persian Frontier: 1639–1938." *Asian Affairs* 62 (New Series Vol. 6) Part 2 (June 1975): 147–54.

Floor, Willem M. "The Revolutionary Character of the Iranian Ulama: Wishful Thinking or Reality." *International Journal of Middle East Studies* 12, no. 4 (December 1980): 501–24.

Gordon, Edward. "Resolution of the Bahrain Dispute." *American Journal of International Law* 65, no. 3 (July 1971): 560–88.

Halpern, Manfred. "Perspectives on U.S. Policy: Iran." *School of Advanced International Studies Review* 6, no. 3 (Spring 1962): 25–30.

International Legal Materials: Current Documents 8, No. 3 (May 1969): 478–96.

Ismael, J. S., and T. Y. Ismael. "Social Change in Islamic Society: The Political Thought of Ayatollah Khomeini." *Social Problems* 27, no. 5 (June 1980): 601–19.

Kelly, J. B. "The Legal and Historical Basis of the British Position in the Gulf." St. Anthony's Papers. *Middle East Affairs* (1958): 119–40.

Khadduri, Majid. "Iran's Claim to the Sovereignty of Bahrayn." *American Journal of International Law* 45, no. 5 (October 1951): 631–47.

Lauterpacht, E. "River Boundaries: Legal Aspects of the Shatt al-Arab Frontier." *International and Comparative Law Quarterly* 9 (1960): 208–36.

Lissitzyn, Oliver J. "Treaties and Changed Circumstances (Rebus Sic Stantibus)." *American Journal of International Law* 61 (1967): 895–922.

MacDonald, Charles G. "Iran's Strategic Interests and the Law of the Sea." *The Middle East Journal* 34, no. 3 (Summer 1980): 302–22.

Marlowe, John. "Arab-Persian Rivalry in the Persian Gulf." *Journal of Royal Central Asian Society* 51, Part I (January 1964): 23–31.

Melamid, Alexander. "The Shatt al-Arab Boundary Dispute." *Middle East Journal* 20, no. 3 (Summer 1968): 351–57.

Page, Stephen. "Moscow and the Persian Gulf Countries, 1967–1970." *Mizan* (London) 13, no. 3 (October 1971): 72–88.

Sterkina, G. "Behind the Screen of the Islamic Pact." *International Affairs* (Moscow) 4 (April 1966): 86–87.

Sullivan, Robert R. "The Architecture of Western Security in the Persian Gulf." *Orbis* 14, no. 1 (Spring 1970): 71–91.
Yaminsky, P. "USSR-Iran: Way of Friendship and Cooperation." *International Affairs* (Moscow) 1 (January 1971): 68.

BOOKS AND MONOGRAPHS

Achoube-Amini, Ramatollah. *Le Conflit de frontiere Irako-Iranien.* Paris, 1936.
Adamiyat, Fereydoun. *Bahrein Islands: A Legal and Diplomatic Study of the British-Iranian Controversy.* New York: Praeger, 1952.
Agwani, Mohammed Shafi. *Politics in the Gulf.* New Delhi: Vikas, c. 1978.
Albaharna, Husain M. *The Legal Status of the Arabian Gulf States.* New York: Oceana, 1968.
Albert, David H., ed. *Tell The American People: Perspectives on the Iranian Revolution.* Philadelphia: Movement for a New Society, 1980. 174.
Al-Izzi, Khalid. *The Shatt al-Arab River Dispute in Terms of Law.* Baghdad: Ministry of Information, 1972.
Algar, Hamid. *Religion and State in Iran, 1785 to 1906.* Berkeley: University of California Press, 1970.
Amin, Abdul Amir. *British Interests in the Persian Gulf.* Leiden: Brill, 1967.
Amirie, Abbas, and Hamilton A. Twitchell. *Iran in the 1980s.* Teheran: Institute for International Political and Economic Studies, 1978.
Amuzegar, Jahangir, and Ali Fekrat. *Iran: Economic Development under Dualistic Conditions.* Chicago: University of Chicago Press, 1971.
Banisadr, Abolhassan. *The Fundamental Principles and Precepts of Islamic Government.* Translated from the Persian by Mohammad R. Ghanoonparvar, 1981. Lexington, Ky.: Mazda, 1982.
Batatu, Hanna. *The Old Social Classes and the Revolutionary Movements in Iraq.* Princeton: Princeton University Press, 1978.
Behn, Wolfgang. *The Iranian opposition in exile: an annotated bibliography of publications from 1341/1962 to 1357/1979 with selective locations.* Wolfgang Behn. Wiesbaden: Harrassowitch in Komm., 1979.
Bill, James A. *The Politics of Iran: Groups, Classes, and Modernization.* Columbus, Ohio: Merrill, 1972.
Binder, Leonard. *Iran: Political Development in a Changing Society.* Berkeley: University of California Press, 1962.
Blucher, Wipert von. *Zeitenwende in Iran. Erlebnisse und Beobachtungen.* Biberach an der Riss: Koehler & Voigtlander, 1949.
Browne, Edward G. *The Persian Revolution of 1905–1909.* Cambridge: At the University Press, 1910.
Busch, Briton Cooper. *Britain and the Persian Gulf, 1894–1914.* Berkeley and Los Angeles: University of California Press, 1967.
Center for Strategic and International Studies, Georgetown University. *The Gulf: Implications of Britain's Withdrawal.* Washington, D.C. Special Report Series, No. 8, 1969.
Chubin, Shahram, and Sepehr, Zabih. *The Foreign Relations of Iran: A Developing State in a Zone of Great-Power Conflict.* Berkeley: University of California Press, 1974.

Copeland, Miles. *The Game of Nations: The Amorality of Power Politics*. New York: Simon and Schuster, 1969.

Cottam, Richard W. *Nationalism in Iran*. Pittsburgh: University of Pittsburgh Press, 1964.

Denman, D. R. *The King's Vista*. Berkhamsted, Herts: Geographical Publications Ltd., 1973.

Devlin, John F. *The Ba'th Party: A History From its Origins to 1966*. Stanford: Hoover Institution Press, 1976.

Edmonds, C. J. *Kurds, Turks and Arabs*. London: Oxford University Press, 1957.

Fatemi, Nasrollah S. *Diplomatic History of Persia, 1917–1923: Anglo-Russian Power Politics in Iran*. New York: Moore, 1952.

Firzili, Nicola, ed. *The Iraq-Iran Conflict*. Paris: Editions du Monde Arabe, 1981.

Fischer, Michael M. J. *Iran: From Religious Dispute to Revolution*. Cambridge, Mass.: Harvard University Press, 1980.

Foster, Henry A. *The Making of Modern Iraq: A Product of World Forces*. Norman, Okla.: University of Oklahama Press, 1935.

Gabbay, Rony. *Communism and Agrarian Reform in Iraq*. London: Croom Helm, 1978.

Graham, Robert. *Iran: The Illusion of Power*. New York: St. Martin's, 1979.

Hairi, Abdul-Hadi. *Shi'ism and Constitutionalism in Iran*. Leiden: Brill, 1977.

Halliday, Fred. *Iran: Dictatorship and Development*. New York: Penguin, 1979.

———. *Arabia without Sultans*. London: Penguin, 1974.

Hamzavi, Abdol Hossein. *Persia and the Powers: An Account of Diplomatic Relations, 1941–1946*. London: Hutchison, 1946.

Heikal, Mohamed. *The Cairo Documents: The Inside Story of Nasser and His Relationship with World Leaders, Rebels, and Statesmen*. New York: Doubleday, 1973.

Herrmann, Georgina. *The Iranian revival*. Oxford: Elsevier-Phaidon, 1977.

Hirszowicz, Lukasz. *Iran, 1951–53: Nafta, Imperializm, Nacjonalizm* (Iran, 1951–53: Oil, Imperialism, Nationalism). Warsaw, 1958.

Hurewitz, J. C. *The Middle East and North Africa in World Politics: A Documentary Record*, 2 vols. New Haven, Ct.: Yale University Press, 1975.

Ismael, Tareq Y. *The Middle East in World Politics*. Syracuse: Syracuse University Press, 1974.

———. *The Arab Left*. Syracuse: Syracuse University Press, 1976.

———. *The Iraq-Iran Conflict*. Toronto: The Canadian Institute of International Affairs, Behind the Headlines Series, 39, 1981.

Ivanov, M. S. *Noveyshaya Istoriya Irana* (The Recent History of Iran). Moscow: Nauka, 1965.

———. *Iran Sevodnya* (Iran Today). Moscow: Nauka, 1969.

———. *Rabochiy Klass Sovremennovo Irana* (The Working Class of Contemporary Iran). Moscow: Nauka, 1969.

Jabbari, Ahmad, and Robert Olson, eds. *Iran: Essays on a Revolution in the Making*. Lexington, Ky.: Mazda, 1982.

Johansen, Baber. *Islam und Staat*. Berlin: Argument-Verlag, 1982.

Kapur, Harish. *Soviet Russia and Asia, 1917–1927: A Study of Soviet Policy Towards Turkey, Iran, and Afghanistan*. Geneva: Michael Joseph, Ltd., for Geneva Graduate Institute of International Studies, 1966.

Kazemzadeh, Firuz. *Russia and Britain in Persia, 1864–1914: A Study in Imperialism*. New Haven, Ct.: Yale University Press, 1968.

Keddie, Nikki R., with a section by Yann Richard. *Roots of Revolution, An Interpretive History of Modern Iran*. New Haven, Ct.: Yale University Press, 1982.

Keddie, Nikki R. *Religion and Rebellion in Iran: The Tobacco Protest of 1891–1892*. London: Frank Cass, 1966.

Kelly, J. B. *Britain and the Persian Gulf, 1795–1880*. New York: Oxford University Press, 1968.

Kerr, Malcolm H. *The Arab Cold War: Gamal Abd al-Nasser and his Rivals, 1958–1970*. 3rd ed. New York: Oxford University Press, for the Royal Institute of International Affairs, 1971.

Khadduri, Majid. *Independent Iraq*. London: Oxford University Press, 1951.

———. *Republican Iraq: A Study of Iraqi Politics Since the Revolution of 1958*. London: Oxford University Press, 1969.

———, ed. *Major Middle Eastern Problems in International Law*. Washington, D.C.: American Enterprise Institute of Public Policy Research, 1972.

———. *Socialist Iraq: A Study in Iraqi Politics since 1968*. Washington, D.C.: The Middle East Institute, 1978.

Khalatbary, Abbas. *L'Iran et Le Pacte Orientale*. Paris: Predone, 1938.

Lederer, Ivo J., ed. *Russian Foreign Policy: Essays in Historical Perspective*. New Haven, Ct.: Yale University Press, 1962.

Lenczowski, George. *Russia and the West in Iran, 1918–1948: A Study in Big-Power Rivalry*. With a Supplement, 1954. Ithaca, N.Y.: Cornell University Press, 1949, 1954.

———. *Soviet Advances in the Middle East*. Washington, D.C.: American Enterprise Institute for Public Policy Research, 1971.

———. ed. *Iran under the Pahlavis*. Stanford, Calif.: Hoover Institution Press, 1978.

Little, Tom. *South Arabia: Arena of Conflict*. London: Pall Mall, 1968.

Longrigg, Stephen H. *Iraq, 1900 to 1950: A Political, Social and Economic History*. London: Oxford University Press, 1953.

———. *Oil in the Middle East. Its Discovery and Development*. 3rd ed. London: Oxford University Press, 1968.

Luard, Evan, ed. *The International Regulation of Frontier Disputes*. London: Thames and Hudson, 1970.

Marayati, Abd'al. *A Diplomatic History of Modern Iraq*. New York: Robert Speller, 1961.

Marlowe, John. *The Persian Gulf in the Twentieth Century*. New York: Praeger, 1962.

Martin, Bradford E. *German-Persian Diplomatic Relations, 1873–1912*. The Hague: Mouton, 1959.

Mejcher, Helmut. *Die Politik und das Ol im Nahen Osten, I. Der Kampf der Machte und Konzerne vor dem Zweiten Weltkrieg*. Stuttgart: Klett-Cotta Verlag, 1980.

Monroe, Elizabeth. *The Changing Balance of Power in the Persian Gulf*. New York: American Universities Field Staff, 1972.

Nakhleh, Emile A. *Arab-American Relations in the Persian Gulf*. Foreign Affairs Study no. 17. Washington, D.C.: American Enterprise Institute for Public Policy Research, 1975.

Nirumand, Bahman. *Iran: The New Imperialism in Action*. Translated from the German by Leonard Mins. New York: Monthly Review Press, 1969.

Nollau, Gunther, and Hans Jurgen Wiehe. *Russia's South Flank: Soviet Operations in Iran, Turkey, and Afghanistan*. New York: Praeger, 1963.

Pachachi, Nadim. *The Role of OPEC in the Emergence of New Patterns in Government-Company Relations*. London: Royal Institute of International Affairs, 1972.

Ramazani, Rouhollah K. *The Persian Gulf: Iran's Role*. Charlottesville: University Press of Virginia, 1972.

———. *The Foreign Policy of Iran: A Developing Nation in World Affairs, 1500–1941*.

Charlottesville: The University Press of Virginia, 1966.

———. *Iran's Foreign Policy, 1941–1973: A Study of Foreign Policy in Modernizing Nations*. Charlottesville: The University Press of Virginia, 1975.

Rizvi, Saiyid Athar Abbas. *Iran: Royalty, Religion and Revolution*. Canberra: Ma'rifat, 1980.

Sadeeg, Javad. *Nationalities and Revolution in Iran*. New York: Distributed by Pathfinder Press, 1974.

Saleh, Zaki. *Mesopotamia [Iraq], 1600–1914: A Study in British Foreign Affairs*. Baghdad : al-Ma'aref, 1957.

Sanghvi, Ramesh. *Shatt al-Arab: The Facts Behind the Issue*. London: Transorient, 1...

Shuster, W

Sluglett, Pe

Stephens, I

Stocking, C

Sykes, Sir

Wilson, Sir

Yar-Shater,

Zabih, Sep

———. *Ira*

Zonis, Mar

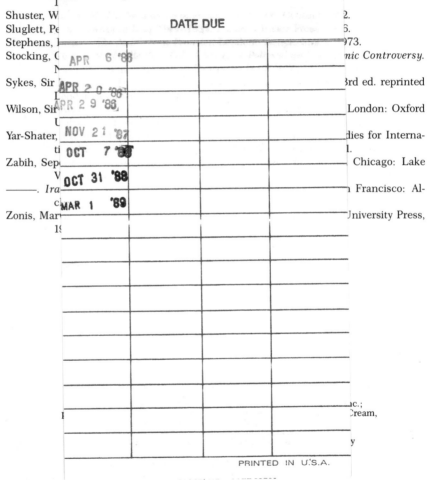

DATE DUE

APR 6 '86

APR 2 0 '86

APR 2 9 '86

NOV 2 1 '87

OCT 7 '87

OCT 31 '88

MAR 1 '89

PRINTED IN U.S.A.

S U
PRESS

"I gotta run." Cam skipped down the steps. "Nice to see you again, Bree."

His mom didn't let it go. "What kind of places?"

"We went smelt dipping with Kate and Neil on Friday." This conversation was taking an odd turn, and Darren wanted it back on track.

"How'd you do?" His dad's eyes lit up. "I haven't been dipping in years."

"We got close to our limits." Darren scanned the streets. An old man walked his dog. Churchgoers heading home. No one to worry about.

"I've never done anything like that before, and it was fun," Bree added.

"You poor thing." Monica laughed. "Darren's more at home outside than in. I've gotta run. Chamber meeting with Brady."

"On Sunday?" Darren knew it didn't matter the day. His sister had had a crush on the chamber of commerce president for a while now. The guy didn't know what he was in for. Or maybe he did, and that's why he'd never asked Monica out.

"As good a day as any other." Monica got all prickly as if daring him to make something of it.

He raised his hands in surrender. "Fine."

"Good," Monica sparred back.

His mom intervened. "Come on, let's go where it's warm instead of clogging up the church steps."

"Bye." Monica elbowed him in the ribs before bolting.

"Supposed to get even colder." His dad stood on the wide church steps and surveyed downtown.

"Not expected to warm up for a few days yet." Usually in a rush to leave, today Darren wasn't in a hurry to head for his empty home. He followed his father's gaze over Maple Springs. The leaves on the trees were still young with that spring-green crayon color. Main Street lay sleepy on this cold morning before the town swelled with summer residents and tourists.

"As long as it doesn't snow on Mother's Day, I'm good." His mom tucked her arm into the crook of Darren's elbow. "Come to breakfast with us. It's your favorite place."

Simply called Dean's Hometown Grille, the tiny restaurant was right around the corner and probably packed. He used to go there a lot with Tony. Darren swallowed hard. Maybe he wasn't feeling *that* brave.

"Hey, isn't that your girlfriend over there?" Cam had exited the church and pointed.

Darren spotted Bree walking toward them from across the street. "She's not my girlfriend."

His mom's eyes widened. "Why didn't you tell me you're seeing someone?"

"Darren's got a girlfriend? Will wonders never cease?" His sister Monica joined the gawkers. "Who is she?"

"Just a friend." There was no use correcting them. They wouldn't believe him, anyway.

Bree waved and crossed the street. Pretty in dark leggings and a long sweater, she headed straight for them with a smile that made those dimples flash. She wore the same brown knitted hat, and her hair was gathered into one long, fat braid.

His pulse kicked up a notch. *Great. Just great.*

When Bree stood at the base of the church steps, she smiled again. "Morning Darren, Cam."

"Meet my family. Some of them, anyway." Darren should have left when he'd had the chance.

"So, this is where you go to church. I go to the Bay Willows chapel." Before he could stop the inevitable, Bree extended a hand toward his mom. "Hi, I'm Bree Anderson."

"Helen Zelinsky." His mom eagerly returned the handshake. "And this is my husband, Andy. My daughter Monica, and you've met Cam."

"Last night at Darren's," Cam added.

His mom gave him that questioning look Darren knew to answer. "Bree is helping out with the wild edibles class at Bay Willows."

"Oh." His mom's eyes widened a bit more before focusing back on Bree. "How's he doing?"

"Wonderful. He really knows his stuff." Bree gave him a nod. "I saw Stella at services this morning, and we're looking forward to hunting for fiddleheads."

Darren nodded. "They can be elusive, but they're out there."

They fell into an awkward silence.

"Well, I'd better get back home." Bree dipped her head.

"We're headed for breakfast around the corner. Please, join us." His mom used her *don't-refuse-me* tone.

Darren could have kicked his mom, but letting Bree walk away would open up a can of questions he didn't feel like answering. He'd feel safer if she joined them. "You won't be sorry. The food's plain but good."

"Yeah?" Bree looked as if she weighed his words.

He meant it, and threw out a ready excuse. "Buying your breakfast is the least I can do considering your help with the class."

"Showing me the area is more than enough thanks."

His mom jumped on that like his beagles swarmed after hearing a scraped plate. "Are you moving here permanently?"

Bree laughed. "Oh, no. My parents have a summer cottage here—"

"I agreed to show her the nontouristy places before she leaves," Darren interrupted.

"Nice."

Bree glanced at him. Looking uncomfortable. Maybe she didn't want to go and couldn't say no.

Darren knew how she felt. His mom was a formidable force. In fact, his entire family could be intimidating because of the sheer number of them. "If you're busy—"

"No, no plans right now." Bree kicked at the sidewalk.

"Let's go, then." Darren gestured for her to walk next to him.

They followed his parents down the block and turned toward the diner. His mom stopped when they came to his brother's glass shop. "My eldest son, Zach, owns this store."

Bree peeked inside the window decorated with blown glass ornaments of all shapes and sizes. "I heard about this place from Stella. She loves it."

"He's closed on Sundays, but have Darren bring you in for a tour," his mom offered.

"I'll have to stop in regardless." Bree pulled back from the window and they resumed walking. "How many brothers and sisters do you have?"

"Six and three."

Bree gave him a wide-eyed look. "And I thought it was bad with only one sister to drive me nuts."

Darren chuckled. "You don't get along?"

"We do. It's just that, well, she's the one who did everything right. While I…"

"You what?"

Bree shrugged, looking uncomfortable again. "I'm still finding my way."

Darren's arm brushed against Bree's, and it seemed natural to take hold of her hand. She didn't pull away. Her hand felt small in his, delicate. The pads of her fingers were tough. Those calluses proved her strength. Bree didn't give herself enough credit.

He looked down at her and smiled.

She smiled back.

What was he doing? This sure felt like the start of a relationship hanging out with his folks. Bree must have felt it, too, because she looked thoughtful. Maybe her hesitation in accepting the invitation to breakfast was wrapped up in how right it felt to hold her hand. How right *they* felt together.

He let go. "So, were you just out walking?"

"Yes. After church I like to walk and meditate on the message, you know? Let it sink in."

"Huh." Darren couldn't remember this morning's sermon. He held open the door to the tiny restaurant that served only breakfast and lunch.

A staple in town for plain home cooking, Dean's Hometown Grille had been owned by the same woman for years. Once inside, Darren was hit with the familiar smell of strong coffee, cinnamon rolls and bacon grease. It had been a while.

They grabbed a booth, and Darren let Bree slide in first. His mom watched his every move as if he might fall and she wanted to be there to catch him. He wasn't five. At thirty-five, Darren was old enough to learn from his mistakes. He hoped Bree wouldn't be one of them.

Linda, the owner, delivered four water-filled glasses. She pulled an order pad from the pocket of her red-checkered apron and a pencil from the bun of her gray hair. "Well, I'll be. Darren Zelinsky, I thought maybe you'd moved away."

"Never." He smiled.

Linda, as well as half of Maple Springs, knew why he'd stayed away from town. It was no secret that Raleigh and Tony lived in a posh apartment overlooking the public beach.

Linda gave him a friendly pat. "Good to have you back. Now, what can I get you?"

After giving their orders, Darren shifted, all too aware of Bree, who'd wedged herself into the corner to give him plenty of room. He heard her stomach rumble and chuckled. "Hungry?"

"Starved."

Proof that her hesitation to join them hadn't been about her appetite. "Ever been here before?"

"Once with my father, but my mother thinks the food is too greasy for anyone's good."

"Don't let Linda hear you."

"I'll remember that." Bree sipped her water.

"What kind of things are you interested in seeing while you're here?" Darren's mom got down to business.

"It all started with the wild edibles class. Roaming the woods is a novel experience for me."

His mom glanced at him.

"She's a cellist heading to Seattle in a few weeks for two years," Darren explained.

"With a symphony?" His mom looked even more impressed as Bree filled her in. "Oh, I'd love to hear you play."

Their breakfasts arrived. "Let's pray." Darren's father said the blessing before digging in.

"Well, I'm playing in a string quartet for the Mother's Day brunch at the Maple Springs Inn."

His mom looked at him. "Oh, Darren, we should go."

Not a chance. "Maybe."

"If you're looking to try new things, you should come by the sugar shack and check out our maple syrup," his dad offered.

"You make maple syrup?" Bree had that kid-in-a-candy-store look in her eyes. The same look she'd had when she spotted her first morel and scooped up her first net of smelt.

He liked that expression. Maybe too much. It made him want to show her things that would make her look like that again. And again.

"You'll have to come out and see. We had an excellent harvest of sap this year," his mom added.

"Oh, I'd love to."

"Then we'll set a date. And maybe you can bring your cello. We'll make you play for syrup. How's that?"

Bree laughed. "That sounds wonderful."

Darren concentrated on his biscuits and gravy. He was sunk. Bringing Bree to his parents' smacked of a romantic relationship. But then, he'd held Bree's hand while they walked here. What was that? "Maybe we can make a class out of it."

His mother nodded. "Sure. Your dad would love to give a tour, and there are morels in the woods. When do you want to do this?"

"How about a week from this Tuesday? We were going to look for white morels anyway. Might as well scour our own woods." Darren liked this idea. There'd be protection in numbers. It'd be a work-related outing. That's all it'd be.

That's what he'd make it.

Tuesday afternoon, Bree growled when her phone whistled with an incoming text interrupting her cello practice. If it was Philip after she'd told him to stop, she'd scream. Laying aside her bow, she grabbed the phone and her breath caught.

It was Darren.

I've got your sweater. Will bring to class.

She ran her finger over the screen and texted back.

Thanks. See you later this afternoon.

He didn't reply. There was no need.

She tipped her head back and closed her eyes. Darren couldn't be labeled a charmer, but there was something about him—something unsettling in how a simple thing like holding his hand had turned her upside down. Maybe she should look at him like a test that needed passing, proving her resolve. Was God testing her?

She'd almost let Philip talk her out of applying for the music residency. He'd said she wasn't good enough because she didn't play in the top-tier, more prestigious orchestras. It wasn't as if she didn't worry about that same thing, but she'd get nowhere if she didn't try. A man worth his salt wouldn't hold her back. He'd encourage her to reach her potential.

What kind of man was Darren?

Taking up her bow, Bree practiced. She played classics, she played modern pieces, even one of her own compositions, but her thoughts kept wandering toward today's class. Scouring the woods for ramps and fiddleheads promised adventure. And dirt.

When she finally glanced at the clock on the stand next to her bed, she had to hurry to pack her cello into its case. She slipped on a pair of thick socks, followed by the hiking boots she'd purchased. Next she threw on a thick fleece shirt and over that her gold windbreaker, a hat and gloves and headed downstairs.

"Your practice sounded good, Bree." Her mother was bundled up on the couch with a throw blanket.

The gas fireplace hummed instead of snapping and crackling with real fire. The carefully controlled flames twisted inside a fake log cage, giving off only a modest amount of heat. Bree stared at it, lost for a moment. It did the job but was nothing special. Clean and convenient. Easy to flip a switch instead of working hard for the real thing.

Bree wanted real fire in her life. Would Seattle provide it?

"Did you hear me?"

Bree shook loose her thoughts. "What?"

"You okay, honey? You're not coming down with something, are you? This cottage is drafty, and with cold weather like this, it's a wonder both of us aren't sick."

Bree smiled. "I'm fine. I'm heading out for class."

"Let me know how it goes. I heard pretty good feedback overall, but—"

"But what?"

Her mother clicked her tongue. "Ed thinks this DNR guy is a know-it-all."

Bree laughed out loud. "How well do you know Ed?"

She smiled, understanding her meaning. "Well enough, I suppose. Even so—"

"Don't worry. I'll give you a full report." Bree grabbed a basket and left.

Ed. What a character. Maybe she should tell Darren. But to what end? She didn't want to cause any rifts or trouble. Maybe it'd be better to let it go for now and see how things went. Darren had already proved he could handle someone like Ed.

Ten minutes later, when she walked into the community room, Darren greeted her with a ready smile. "Glad to see you dressed warm. With this cold snap, we might have a light group."

His wide smile turned her inside out. Not good.

Bree set down her basket and lifted her foot onto the chair with a clunk. "Check these out."

Darren laughed. "Good job on the boots. I have your sweater in the van. You might need the extra layer. It's cold."

"I think I'll be okay."

She heard Stella's voice followed by several others as people arrived. After waiting only a few minutes, Bree knew Darren was surprised when everyone showed, bundled up and with baskets in hand. Even Ed, who grumbled about the weather, seemed eager to go.

In no time, they loaded up into the van and set out. Bree sat in the passenger seat again. Everyone else had slipped into the same seats as last week. "Where to? Same woods?"

"No." Darren took a turn and headed south, and then took another turn eastward according to the compass on the dash. "Different land. Loaded with trillium and ramps. And further in are fiddleheads. I've found them there before."

Bree had heard of fiddleheads when she'd traveled out east.

She and Philip had gone with her parents to Vermont one spring weekend for a fine art show. Her folks had come home with a prized painting. Bree had returned with yet another reason why Philip wasn't right for her. At the bed-and-breakfast where they'd stayed, Bree had wanted to try fiddleheads. Philip had given her so much grief about eating something that grew like a weed that she finally gave up. She didn't bother ordering any and missed her opportunity to try something new. Something different.

She'd always given in instead of standing her ground. Today she'd look for fiddleheads, and if she found some, she'd eat them. But ramps she wasn't familiar with.

"What are ramps?" she asked.

"They're a wild leek and taste like a cross between an onion and garlic."

"Oh." Simple.

After a few twists and turns on what Darren called "seasonal roads," and more bumps and jostling that led to laughter, they finally came to a stop. Bree got out and looked around. These woods were dense. The ground was covered with white trillium flowers, and a few purple ones dotted the carpet of white.

"Beautiful." She breathed in the cold spring air, feeling a zip of boldness. She felt alive. More alive than ever before.

"Remember, ladies, no picking the trillium. They are protected plants." Darren opened the doors at the back of the vehicle. "Please gather round the van for instruction and tools."

"Ooh, tools. What did you bring?" Stella tried to peek over his shoulder but couldn't.

"Small planting shovels for loosening the soil around the ramps." Darren stepped aside. "Grab a whistle lanyard along with a shovel. Remember to stay in pairs. If you get turned around—"

"We know—use the whistle and you'll find us." Ed's voice dripped sarcasm.

Bree glanced at Darren.

He took it in stride. "Right. And if you'll look at the book on page five…"

They were already wandering away.

"Come on, folks, let's stay together." Darren

kept his voice even, but several ignored him and kept walking.

Bree gathered her courage and blew her whistle. Hard. "Don't you want to know what we're looking for?"

Everyone stopped. Darren jiggled his finger in his ear as if she'd blown out his hearing. "Thanks, I think."

Stella grinned at her. "She's right. Get back here, Ed. Connie. Let's find out what they look like."

"I know what they look like," Ed spat back.

"Then we'll follow you." Darren slipped the edibles booklet back into the pocket of his official-looking canvas jacket.

He seemed calm, but Bree felt tension in him. And she noticed that the tops of his ears were red. This man held back his anger instead of giving it full vent. He had control.

"But we'll meet at the van in twenty minutes and move to the next spot." Darren's stern voice warned against argument.

Ed gave him a nod.

Bree wasn't sure why Ed wanted to challenge Darren, but at least the class was moving toward a clump of green leaves with purplish stems that disappeared into the dirt.

"These are wild leeks," Ed said and waited.

"Correct." Darren bent and used his garden shovel to pry around them, loosening the dirt and bringing up slender white bulbs at the end of those pink-purple stems. "And that's all there is to it."

"Wow, easy. And look how many there are." Connie scanned the area.

"I'm thinking of a potato-leek soup recipe I have." Stella took Bree's hand. "Come with me. We'll have a bunch in no time."

Bree laughed. The tense moment was forgotten as everyone spread out and started digging up ramps. An oniony scent filled the air along with everyone's chatter. She spotted Darren on his cell phone, so at least they had coverage out here. Bree had turned hers off.

"Did you enjoy smelt dipping?" Stella asked.

"I did." The fingertips of Bree's gloves were crusted with dirt. She should have grabbed her mom's garden variety instead of these knitted ones.

"And?" Stella wiggled her eyebrows.

Bree glanced at Darren, who was out of earshot, digging up a few ramps of his own. "And nothing. He's a nice guy and so are his friends."

"But?"

Bree appreciated her elderly friend's attempt at kind matchmaking, but it was a moot point. "I'm leaving soon, remember? I can't get involved."

"You like him—"

"As a friend, Stella. As a friend." Bree needed to keep that in mind. She didn't know what the next two years held but knew she had to go. God had given her this opportunity, maybe to find real purpose. She needed fire in her life, not convenient settling for the easier route. Falling for Darren might be easy and full of exciting fire, but living here would be neither. What could she really do here with her music?

Twenty minutes went by fast, and Bree's basket was indeed full when she heard Darren announce they needed to load up.

No one had ventured far, so they quickly climbed in the van. Darren headed deeper into the woods, bouncing along an even rougher road. The surrounding trees thinned, and scrubby pines popped up along with mounds of old brown ferns. A creek sliced through a small field with twists and turns.

"Wow, we're really out here." Bree had no idea where they were. She exited the van with the rest of the group, anxious to find these elusive fiddleheads.

Darren got out too, and scowled. "Okay, folks, let's stick close. The weather's going to turn."

Bree looked up. Sure enough, dark clouds had rolled in and the temperature had dropped. The light gurgling sound of that creek reminded her of smelt fishing and cold water, making her shiver. She blew her breath out in long white tendrils of mist. "It's really cold."

"That's snow." Darren had everyone's attention as he nodded toward the clouds.

"You're kidding." Bree looked up. "But it's May."

"Let's make this quick, before we all freeze." Stella stamped her feet. At least everyone had the sense to wear boots and coats. Not everyone wore hats and gloves, though.

"That okay with everyone?" Darren asked. "Ed?"

"If we must." He looked like he'd sucked on a sour lemon.

"Yup," Connie said.

"Your call," the other elderly gentleman agreed.

Darren went over what they were looking for in the booklet and then elaborated. "There will be several fronds, or fiddleheads, shooting up from the base. Pick only three, and leave the rest so we don't kill the plant. Look for a brown papery coating. I'll try to find the first one, but it's anyone's game here. If you do find one, whistle so we can all see it."

They split up with instructions to meet back at the van in twenty minutes.

Of course, Darren found the first one. "Right here, folks. This is a fiddlehead. And there are several more along there, toward the creek."

Bree forgot all about the cold, jogged toward a field filled with them and picked. Only three per plant. Bree hoped everyone else followed the rules. The immature ferns were a pretty spring green with a grassy scent. Delicate. Wild. She'd try these and find out what she'd missed out on in Vermont.

She made room in her basket for the fiddleheads when the first snowflake fell. Another, and then another. Bree pulled out her phone and took a picture of her basket of goodies with fat snowflakes nestled amid the greens before they melted.

She looked up and noticed that everyone had already gathered around the van. With a sigh, she picked up her basket and walked back. The snow fell heavier now. The flakes stuck to her eyelashes. But it was beautiful and quiet. So very quiet.

At the van, she noticed a hush had settled over all of them as they stood and watched it snow across a pretty field filled with fiddleheads near a small stream.

Darren did a head count. "Where's Connie?"

Bree looked at Stella. And everyone looked at Ed.

"She wasn't with me." Ed raised his hands in surrender. "I'm not her keeper."

Bree glanced at Darren.

"Everyone get in the van and stay there. I'll do a quick sweep."

"Can I help?" Bree asked.

"Stay in the van." Darren gave her a nod. "Keep them in there, Bree."

She nodded. He didn't need more people getting lost. Not out in weather like this. She flicked on her phone—still bars but only a couple in this spot.

"Come on, let's do what he said and get in the van. We'll be warmer in there." She hoped that proved true, because Darren hadn't left her the keys.

She watched him disappear over a small hill. They were on their own, but then, so was Connie.

Chapter Seven

Darren walked a large half circle, calling out Connie's name to no avail. The snow fell and stuck in places. A snowy ground cover would soon mask tracks, making his search more difficult. He'd started by following many sets of footprints that had become a few and then one. Someone had walked this way. He hoped it was Connie.

He shuddered to think what might happen if she kept moving, wandering farther away. He hoped she had sense enough to stop and wait, knowing they'd look for her, but the fact that she hadn't blown her whistle worried him. What if she'd fallen? With an older woman, that was all too possible. Add in the temperature drop, and he had to find her—fast.

He checked his watch. He'd been searching fifteen minutes with no success. He prayed everyone stayed in that van.

His cell phone buzzed with an incoming text message. From Bree.

Connie is here. Safe and sound.

Darren texted back.

Good. Be there shortly.

Shaking his head, he made his way back. Spotting a small red thing sticking out of the snow at the base of a tree, Darren knew why Connie hadn't used her whistle. He stooped over and picked it up. The string of the lanyard was broken.

Nice. He gritted his teeth. She'd have had access to another whistle if she'd stayed in a pair as he'd instructed.

Darren rubbed his forehead. But then, he'd rushed them with the threat of snow. He'd counted all of them in the field, and then his attention had snagged on Bree taking pictures of her basket. Was that when Connie had wandered off?

This incident wasn't going to look good to Bree's mom. Nor did he look forward to entering it in his daily field report, but he wouldn't shirk his duties. Connie's mishap was his own fault. He was dealing with older people who needed reminding to stay in pairs because of the dangers out here. Many of the missing person searches he'd been part of had found folks a mile or less from where they'd started out.

He'd do better. Blowing out his breath, Darren made quick time back to the van. The windows were steamed up with so many in there. He noticed Bree's passenger window and one in the back had been rolled down some to let in fresh air. Smart girl.

Without a word, he climbed in the driver's side, started the van and cranked up the front and rear defrosters.

"Darren, I'm so sorry," Connie said.

"Not much of a tracker, are you?" Ed sneered.

"Ed—" Bree and Stella chorused together, ready to jump all over the guy.

Darren raised his hand to quiet everyone, then turned and faced them. "All the more reason to stay in pairs. Got it?"

He looked at Connie. She held something in her hand besides her basket of ramps and fiddle-heads. She'd picked a couple of jack-in-the-pulpits. Those wildflowers, which happened to be protected on state lands, were the reason she'd veered away from the group.

Staring down Ed, he reiterated the serious-ness of the situation. "Let's use this as a re-minder of how easy it is to get turned around out here. Agreed?"

"Absolutely, Darren." Stella led the group in agreement.

Even Ed nodded, but he didn't look impressed.

Darren didn't care. The old guy was impossible to please. He'd encountered Ed's type several times in the woods, especially during hunting season. Men who weren't going to let the DNR tell them how to do things.

He glanced at Connie, and the woman looked so forlorn that Darren gave her an encouraging smile. At least she'd apologized instead of giving him that air of snobbishness he expected from Bay Willows residents. It dawned on him that there wasn't much of that with this group. Not much at all.

He'd bust her about those flowers, but only a warning. It'd be bad form to ticket one of his class attendees.

"Okay, let's get back to town." He didn't say any more but glanced at Bree.

She gave him a proud smile. She had his back.

He could count on her, and that realization broke something deep inside. She'd chiseled a hole in the shell he'd built around his heart. A year and a half of careful construction, and Bree had rammed through with one look, one smile. Dangerous, maybe, but it felt good.

Bree stayed behind to help Darren clean up the community room kitchen from their preparations of fiddleheads and ramps. She'd finally tried them, and while the ramps were super flavorful, the fiddleheads didn't live up to all the hype.

"Could you introduce me to your mom?" Darren dried off the frying pan and placed it in the cupboard.

Bree stopped wiping off the counter. "Yeah, sure. What's up?"

Darren looked pensive. "I'd like to let her know what happened today. I'd rather she didn't hear it secondhand."

From her. Is that what he meant? Bree nodded. "Sure, we can walk over there right now."

"I'll drive."

It wasn't far. Was it meeting her mother that had Darren looking so uncomfortable? Silly. Her parents were nice people. Although her father wasn't around. He'd returned home in order to work in Detroit for the week. They exited the building and climbed back into the van.

"Where should I go?"

"Drive straight for two blocks and take a left toward the lake." Bree pointed. "We're on the corner in a white cottage with green trim."

When he didn't say anything, Bree tried to lighten the mood a little. "She won't bite."

Darren tipped his head. "Who?"

"My mother. She's a reasonable woman. Well, most of the time."

He chuckled. "It's not that." He pulled in front of her parents' cottage and stared out over the bay.

Small, insignificant snowflakes fell and disappeared as soon as they hit the ground. Nothing like the heavier snow they'd had earlier while on state land.

Bree waited.

He shrugged. "There are a lot of memories here."

"Of Raleigh?"

Darren nodded.

"What happened?" Bree knew what Kate had said, and Stella, too, but Bree wanted to know why. Maybe Darren didn't know the answer to that. "I mean, if you care to share."

He looked at her. "It's old news. I can't believe you didn't hear about it. She took off with my best man the night before our wedding, right after rehearsal."

Hearing him say it in such a matter-of-fact way made her wince because of the pain in his eyes. This was a wound that still festered. "I'm so sorry."

"In hindsight, we probably wouldn't have worked." He made a sweeping gesture. "I can't provide all this."

"This?" Bree didn't miss the bitterness in his voice.

"I live a simple life and I like it that way."

Bree felt her hackles go up when she remembered Neil's comment about Darren's dislike of the summer resorters. "Not everyone who comes up here is a jerk, you know. This isn't *Lifestyles of the Rich and Famous*. We're just people who've made a tradition of summering here."

"People with a lot more cash than I'll ever have." Darren didn't sound envious at all, just disappointed. As if the summer community had let him down.

Was that because of Raleigh? Or a pattern of actions by some of the more arrogant wannabes who also summered here? She'd run into a few of them, too, but that didn't mean she painted everyone with the same broad stroke.

Her parents had pushed Philip with her because of the security his career provided. They wanted her settled with the promise of being taken care of. She'd grown up with an expectation of financial security, and maybe too much emphasis was made on that sort of stability.

By accepting the music residency, Bree had placed her trust in God's provision. She had faith that she'd find the right path through this opportunity, but it wasn't about the money. Her music had never been about the money.

"Come on, then. I'll show you how the other half lives." She gave him a smirk.

He laughed, getting the joke, and his tension eased.

They weren't rich. Very few in Bay Willows

could have been called seriously wealthy, but many were secure or they couldn't have maintained two homes. Many of the cottages here had been handed down and kept in the family. A long-standing tradition of summering up north in a beautiful place that was void of the employment options found elsewhere.

Bree glanced at Darren as he walked up her parents' porch steps. The man oozed a different kind of security. A woman could depend on him to do the right thing. That kind of stability was harder to find. That kind of strength lasted.

She slipped past him, walked inside, set down her basket of edibles and pulled off her hat and windbreaker. "Would you like something to drink? Coffee? Or pop?"

"No. I'm good." He looked determined and a little antsy.

"I can take your coat."

He refused that, too. "I won't be long."

Of course not. He didn't want to socialize with her kind. Now who was the snob? Bree nearly laughed at the thought. She brought him into the living room, where her mother sat in a wingback chair with her foot propped up on an ottoman stacked with pillows. "Mom, this is Darren Zelinsky, the conservation officer facilitating your class."

Her mother glanced over the rim of her reading glasses, and then her face brightened into a smile. She reached out her hand. "Nice to meet you. Sorry, I'd get up, but I just got situated."

Darren returned the handshake. "No problem, Mrs. Anderson. I thought I'd touch base and let you know how your class is progressing."

"Wonderful. Please, sit down, and call me Joan."

Darren did as asked but didn't relax. He leaned forward, bracing his elbows on his knees. "Today we had an incident I wanted you to be aware of."

Concern flashed across her mother's face. "What happened?"

Bree sat down, too, but kept quiet.

"One of the ladies got turned around in the woods. It could have been a bad situation, especially with this weather, but fortunately, she found her way back before too long. She'd lost her whistle and veered away from her partner. We have to stay in pairs."

Bree watched her mother digest that information, feeling like a school-age kid sitting in on a parent-teacher conference.

"Yes, of course." Her mother nodded agreement and glanced at her. "Bree, was there anything you could have done to prevent this?"

Bree had been caught with her head in the clouds once again. She opened her mouth, but Darren cut her off before she could speak.

"Your daughter has been a big help, but keeping everyone safe is my responsibility."

Her mother's eyes narrowed. "Thank you for telling me. I'll be walking with only a cane in a couple days, so I should be able to join you for the next class."

"About that." Darren pulled out the schedule from inside his jacket. "My parents have offered to give a tour of their maple syrup operation, and their nearby woods should be loaded with tan and white morels, so I've made that change."

"Wonderful. That works very well."

"Good." Darren rose to his feet. "I won't keep you. Thank you, Joan."

"I'll walk you out." Bree led Darren back out onto the front porch. "Thanks for that, but you didn't have to come to my rescue."

"I stated a fact. I'm responsible for everyone in that class."

"Yeah, but if I hadn't been taking pictures, I might have seen Connie wander off." She rubbed her arms.

"They're adults, Bree. And old enough to follow instructions. Instructions made clear that first day." His voice softened. "Do you think your mom is okay with that?"

Bree nodded. Surely this wouldn't impact the promotion he was after. It wasn't his fault Connie wandered away.

"You should go inside. It's cold out here."

Bree still felt like she'd failed him somehow. "Okay. See you next week?"

"Next week. And be sure to bring your cello. My mom wants to hear you play."

"Why not take her to brunch on Mother's Day? I'm playing in a string quartet."

He got a funny look on his face. "I don't really do that sort of thing."

Bree laughed. "Yeah, well, I don't smelt dip either, and I found out that I liked it. A lot."

His blue eyes looked uncertain, thoughtful. "I'll think about it."

"Do that." Bree had expected him to decline outright, but he didn't, and that made her smile. She had a hunch he'd be there.

She watched him climb into the van and waved as he pulled out.

He waved back.

She sighed and headed inside.

Her mother was up with her crutches, waiting for her. "Bree, what's going on? What was that all about?"

"Darren wanted you to hear about Connie getting lost from him. It wasn't a big deal. Connie found her way back in like ten minutes."

Her mother watched her closely.

"What?"

"Darren is a handsome man." Her mother made it sound like some huge problem.

"So?"

Her mother's gaze bore into hers. "So, you're spending a lot of time with him. Why?"

"We're just friends."

She didn't believe that for an instant.

"This is my vacation, Mom. Maybe the last one for a long time. Darren's showing me around because I've never been anywhere up here. He's fun and that's it. Nothing to worry about."

"Okay." Her mother didn't question her further. She peeked in the basket of ramps and fiddleheads. "Let's see what we can make for dinner with what you brought home this week."

Bree breathed easier, but a knot settled between her shoulder blades. One she'd have to stretch out before she practiced her cello. She didn't want anything more than friendship with Darren. Sure, she had a bit of a crush on him, but that was no doubt temporary. As her mother had pointed out, he was a handsome man. Who wouldn't find him attractive?

That didn't mean she'd let this attraction grow into something that'd knock her off track. Bree had hit the snooze button on her biological clock because a husband and kids were quicksand. She had plenty of years yet, but for the first time in a long while, she considered the tick of that internal clock. Darren struck her as the kind of guy who'd want kids. What if he was that someone special she'd miss out on to pursue her dreams.

Bree wanted no more regrets.

She'd dated Philip on and off for close to two

years, and she'd known him for years before that. It had taken her forever to figure out finally that he wasn't right for her. After only a couple of weeks, how could she even consider Darren a candidate for life?

Engaged after only a month.

Bree had thought that kind of thing ridiculous before a pair of bright blue eyes made almost anything seem possible. And completely impossible.

His day off and Darren sat at his dining room table entering the last few days' worth of field reports. Bree's words rang through his thoughts. *They're just people.*

Covering what had happened to Connie in his report made him think long and hard. When push came to shove, Bree was right. They were just people who summered here. They got lost and made mistakes like anyone else. There was no reason to treat them differently.

Growing up, he'd hated that many who summered here acted like they somehow owned Maple Springs. Sure, every merchant depended on the summer crowd spending dollars to survive. The entire town looked for ways to make Maple Springs more attractive to tourists. More wasn't always better. He might live way out in the woods, but Maple Springs was his hometown and he wanted to protect it. It was the reason he'd gone for the supervisor position a couple of years ago, only to come in second. Had he been overlooked because of his attitude toward the tourists?

He ran his hands through his hair and then stretched. Bree's sweater, folded as neatly as he could manage, lay at the end of the table. She'd forgotten to grab it from the van the other day, so he brought it back inside where it would stay clean. He wouldn't know how to wash something delicate like that. He'd probably ruin it.

He'd ruin a lot of things if he let his feelings for Bree get out of hand before she left.

He looked out his windows, where the sun shone and the temperatures had climbed back toward spring. He had a dozen things to do but didn't want to. Neil was at work, and his brothers were, too. Well, not Cam. On this Friday afternoon, Darren wanted to go somewhere. He didn't care where as long as he was with Bree.

His beagles snoozed on the floor in a puddle of sunshine streaming in through the windows.

The forecast called for climbing temperatures into the weekend and beyond. The elk would be moving today after the cold snap, no doubt getting out into the meadows to graze on the new growth.

He glanced at Bree's sweater, grabbed his phone and texted her.

Are you busy?

After a few seconds he got a text back.

Practicing. What's up?

He typed.

Want to see the elk?

YES!

He smiled. She was easy to please. Another difference from his ex and pretty much every other woman he'd dated. There was a sense of wonder in Bree he liked bringing out. It had nothing to do with tangible gifts. He simply showed her what he loved about Northern Michigan and she responded in kind. Like a real friend would, with no expectations or pressure for more.

Only, he wanted more.

Ignoring the warning bells in his head, he texted back.

I'll pick you up in half an hour.

Great. I'll be home. And bring my sweater. LOL.

He chuckled as he pocketed his phone, shut down his laptop and gathered up her sweater. He brought it to his nose, but her soft floral scent had long since worn off.

Grabbing two harnesses with leashes, he said, "Come on, dogs. Let's go for a ride."

Mickey and Clara perked their ears, but that was it. Neither moved. It had been a long while since he'd taken them for a ride in the truck.

He slapped a hand against his thigh. "Come on, I mean it."

They got up quick and shot past him, down the stairs.

Darren loaded his truck with a blanket across the backseat while his dogs did their business. Then they all climbed in and headed for Maple Springs. Less than twenty minutes later, he pulled near the driveway of the Anderson cottage and glanced out over the bay. The water looked aqua followed by the deeper blue of an open Lake Michigan beyond.

Bree stood outside on the porch. She shifted a backpack over her shoulder and ran toward his truck. She laughed when both beagles stuck their heads out the window, begging for pats. She obliged them. "You brought your dogs."

"There are some nice walking trails in the Pigeon River Forest."

"I've got my hiking boots on, so I'm ready." She also wore khaki shorts and an expensive brand-name black pullover with a white T-shirt underneath. Her hair hung in two long braids, making her look like a Girl Scout who knew her way around. The red lipstick was a dead give-away that she didn't.

"What's with the pack?"

She climbed into his truck. "Just some recording stuff."

He spotted Joan at the window and gave her a wave.

She waved back but had a pinched look on her face. He didn't need Bree's mom getting weird about him going out with her daughter. Maybe Joan always looked like that, but Darren knew better. He'd seen that kind of look many times in his life. She gave him the perfect Bay Willows cold stare.

"Is your mom okay with you doing this?"

Bree set her pack on the floor at her feet and waved off his question. "It's not like I need her permission—"

"Right." Stupid question to ask. Darren looked at her backpack. "What's the recording stuff for?"

"To record what I hear out there. Why aren't you working today?"

His turn to explain. "I worked last night."

Worry flashed quick across her face. "What'd you do?"

"Had to check out a complaint of ORVs tearing around after dark."

"ORVs?"

"Off-road vehicles. A couple of guys were riding four-wheelers on the walking trails where they shouldn't have."

Bree's eyes grew round as golden marbles. "What happened?"

"I issued them tickets."

"Were they mad?"

Darren chuckled. "They weren't happy."

"Are you ever afraid? I mean, you're out there by yourself, right?"

"Yeah, but most folks are just out to have fun. On occasion they get out of hand. Or don't have the proper registration or licensing. Usually it all goes fine."

"What if it doesn't?"

Darren turned and headed south. "I call for backup if needed."

"Oh." She bit her lip. "Have you ever had to do that?"

"Sure, yeah." Darren didn't want to get into the dangers he faced. For the most part, people didn't do much more than mouth off. But there'd been moments when Darren wasn't sure what might happen. Moments when he'd had to confront men with weapons hunting illegally.

The key was never letting his guard down and preparing for the worst. He had over ten years of experience under his belt. Teri had over fifteen when she'd transferred in as his immediate supervisor. She was seasoned, knowledgeable and used to working more populated areas than Darren. Another Teri could be vying for the same position he wanted.

"How often do you have to do that?"

He shrugged. "If we're investigating a big poaching ring or something, we'll work in pairs. Call in the supervisor or sometimes team up with the county sheriff's department. I stay safe."

Bree looked scared. For him.

He didn't want that. At least with her, he already knew the worst case scenario. She'd leave for a long time. Too long to make something more with her. No matter how much he liked hanging out with her, he needed to keep his guard up. The guard she kept climbing over.

He changed the subject. "So tell me, what do you want to record?"

She brightened. "Things like the breeze through the trees, maybe even the sound of elk. Do they make much noise?"

Darren chuckled. "Not now. But during mating season in the fall, the males make a big show, bellowing and shaking trees with their antlers in order to impress the females."

"Wow. That must be something. Funny how God instills that competitive drive in animals."

"People, too." Darren wanted that promotion.

He'd do everything he could to make sure this time, he got it.

"Yeah, but maybe we compete for the wrong reasons."

He looked at her. "What makes you say that?"

"Oh, I don't know. Have you ever second-guessed why you wanted something?" Bree clicked on the radio, and a soft country song about unrequited love spilled out.

"Not until she took off."

Bree chuckled. "That sounds bitter."

He shrugged. "It is what it is. Are you having doubts about going to Seattle?"

"No. I don't know. Maybe. What if I'm not good enough?"

Darren glanced her way. He knew all about those kinds of thoughts. Driving across the country by herself to start a new life took guts. Her desire to conquer what lay off the beaten path suddenly made a lot of sense. This woman was scared. For all the right and wrong reasons. "You wouldn't have been chosen unless you were good enough."

Bree smiled, making those dimples tease him. "The same can be said of you. Raleigh's the one who made the mistake by walking away."

"Hmm." Darren focused on the road ahead.

It was a compliment he didn't want to hear, especially from a woman who'd do the same thing.

Chapter Eight

Bree looked out the window, in awe of the various shades of green displayed from new leaves to rich grass and dark evergreens. Darren drove slowly along an unpaved road through a stretch of open fields. His dogs hung their heads out the back windows, sniffing the fresh air.

"What do they smell, do you think?"

"All kinds of game. Squirrel, deer, elk."

Bree inhaled a hint of pine and decayed leaves as they drove over a small branch.

"It might have been a bad idea to bring the dogs. If we see elk, they're bound to bark."

Bree looked in the back and smiled. "I'm glad you brought them. They look happy."

He chuckled. "Wait till we're walking."

Bree could relate. This felt a whole lot like unworried freedom. "Thanks for bringing me out here."

"No problem." He concentrated on turning

onto another trail through a thicket of scrubby pine. Then he reached into the glove box and pulled out a couple of dog chew bones that he gave to Mickey and Clara before raising the back windows. He slowed to a stop and pointed. "See there, through those trees?"

Bree matched his near whisper. "Where?" An elk stepped from behind a cluster of bushes, followed by another one and another. "Oh. Wow."

"Yeah."

They watched in silence as the small group of elk lingered, grazing on the new grass poking up through the old. The dogs were busy with their bones and stayed quiet.

Bree glanced at Darren's strong profile. She was tempted to run her fingertip down the straight line of his nose. He hadn't shaved, and the light stubble along his jawline made her want to find out if those whiskers might be soft or scratchy. She folded her hands in her lap to keep from touching him to find out. Then she said the first thing that popped into her mind. "Where are the babies?"

"Calving starts the end of this month." He pointed. "There's a pregnant cow."

Bree spotted the elk that looked a little fatter than the others, but she'd have never guessed it carried a calf. "Look at that."

"Yeah."

She sensed Darren's gaze and turned.

He looked right at her.

She stared back.

The interior of the truck grew tight. Time had stopped and held its breath, like her. She leaned toward Darren and then hesitated. She didn't dare make that first move. Didn't dare act on the overwhelming desire to kiss this man. Would he push her away? What if he didn't?

One of the dogs barked, a bellowing sound that shattered the moment and made the elk trot off. The other beagle chorused in with a deeper bugling sound.

Bree laughed, even as Darren scolded his dogs to stop. She patted Clara's head, grateful the dog had kept her from making a big mistake. Bree scratched behind the dog's velvet-soft floppy ear. "They're gone, silly."

Darren hushed the dogs again before backing up his truck. "We might as well hit the trailhead and walk."

"That'd be great." Bree couldn't shake the disappointment of not acting on impulse. It would not have been smart to kiss Darren, but it sure felt like she'd missed out yet again.

When they finally parked, Darren quickly hooked up the dogs' leashes and got out. He pulled a couple of water bottles from a small cooler in the open truck bed and handed one to Bree.

"Thanks." She slipped it into an outside pocket of the backpack and then hoisted the whole thing over her shoulders.

"I can carry that."

"It's not heavy." Bree reached toward one of the dogs. "Can I walk one?"

He handed over Mickey. "He likes to stop and sniff, so you'll have to tug him along. No dogs at your house?"

Bree slipped her hand through the handle. "We had a cocker spaniel growing up, but my parents didn't replace her after she died. There was no point with my sister headed for college and me busy with music lessons."

"When did you start playing the cello?" Darren led the way toward the trail.

Bree thought a minute. "I switched from the piano to the cello in fifth grade."

"Why the cello?"

She shrugged. "I liked its sound, but I think it had more to do with hiding behind it. The piano was out there front stage, and as a kid, that was pretty scary."

He gave her a long look.

Bree grinned. "You know, I'm working on that whole bravery thing."

He chuckled. "You're doing a good job."

"Thanks to you."

"Me?" Darren looked appalled, as if he didn't want the responsibility of bringing her out of her shell.

It wasn't all his doing, but he'd certainly helped the process she'd started when she'd mustered the courage to apply for the music residency. She patted his shoulder and felt the muscles tense beneath the fabric of his T-shirt. "You've given me opportunities to stretch. I'm in the middle of the woods and it's all good. I appreciate it."

"You're welcome."

They walked in awkward silence, stopping every so often to let the dogs sniff the ground more thoroughly. Bree kicked herself again for being too afraid to kiss him when the opportunity had presented itself. But then, she had a hunch that kissing Darren might shoot her straight to the moon when she needed to keep her feet firmly planted on the ground.

She glanced at the trees marked with blue paint that guided their steps along a barely discernible trail. The sun's golden rays danced through the spring-green canopy of leaves. Birdsong echoed louder than the breeze gently swishing through the trees. It was beautiful. A perfect composition of beats and chords.

"Can we stop for a bit?"

Darren nodded. "You okay?"

She nodded. "I'd love to record this."

He looked at her as if she were crazy. "Record what?"

"The birdsong, for one. It's so loud."

"Okay, sure." He took Mickey from her.

She slipped off her backpack and opened it. Out came a throw blanket and a recording device hooked to her notebook. While she set everything up, she spotted Darren taking a long swig from his water bottle before offering the rest to his dogs. The beagles lapped at the spout.

"I've never seen a dog drink directly from a water bottle before." Bree knelt on the blanket.

Darren shrugged. "They're used to it. So, what do you have to do here?"

"Just hook up the mic to my notepad and record. Do you mind?"

"Not at all." But he looked hesitant to sit on the blanket.

Bree shifted to sit cross-legged and patted the empty spot next to her. Mickey took that as an invitation to curl onto her lap. She spread her arms wide and smiled. "See? There's plenty of room."

Okay, this is different.

Darren lay on a small stadium blanket, staring at the sky above. His hands were behind his head, and his jeans-clad legs stretched off the blanket onto the ground. Bree's legs did, too. She wore shorts and the grass had to itch, but she hadn't moved.

His dogs made a good barrier, curled between them, sleeping. Darren had never considered the beagles as chaperones, but that's exactly the role they played today, keeping him from taking Bree into his arms. Keeping him out of trouble.

Bree had been serious about recording nature sounds he gave only a passing thought. She'd stayed quiet, listening while recording. If he'd interpreted the half smile on her face correctly, she savored the dee-dee-hum of chickadees, chattering of red squirrels and squawking calls of crows. Nothing exotic. Simple sounds from basic wildlife were considered music to her ears. Surely she could be happy here.

He heard it, too. The music of nature. For once, instead of listening for movement, for voices or law breakers, he lay still and simply listened. Darren shouldn't have felt this comfortable next to a woman like her.

Yawning, he rolled onto his side and looked at her. Really looked at her. Bree's eyes were closed while she stroked Mickey's ears. The beagle rested his head on her midsection, claiming her as his own.

Darren envied his dog. "So, what are you going to do with the recording?"

She didn't open her eyes. "Listen to it and be inspired."

"Inspired?"

Bree sat up and clicked off the recording. She

laughed when Mickey readjusted and crawled onto her lap with a contented sigh. "I love this dog."

"I think the feeling is mutual." Darren gave Mickey a scratch behind his ears. "So, back to being inspired—how's that work?"

"I record lots of sounds. I've got traffic recorded from outside my apartment. I've recorded the waves crashing against the shore at my parents' cottage and even crickets chirping from the garage. Anything that might spur ideas for notes, or give me a feeling that I can translate into music on paper or my computer."

"Huh. How much time do you spend between practicing your cello and writing music?"

"Hours and hours."

"You spend a lot of time alone." Not unlike his day of patrolling an area alone and then completing reports from the solitude of his dining room table. Alone.

She shrugged. "Well, yeah, but it's not like I go to a nine-to-five job. Even playing professionally in an orchestra, I worked on my own. We came together to rehearse, but practice is still pretty much a solitary thing, unless I get together with the string section."

Her world was different than his, but similar in some ways. "Right."

Her cell phone buzzed, but she ignored it.

"Aren't you going to check that?"

Bree picked up her phone, glanced at the text and rolled her eyes. "There, checked."

He chuckled. "Telemarketer?"

"No. A family friend." She scrunched up her face. "That's not quite right, either. Philip is a guy I'd been dating until we broke up before I came up north. He wasn't right for me."

"What was wrong with him?" Darren didn't like the idea that she'd had a boyfriend. Up until now he'd thought… He didn't know what he'd thought.

"According to my parents, he's perfect, but he didn't support my decision to accept the music residency, for one thing."

"So you kicked him to the curb."

She chuckled. "That's one way of saying it. Too bad he won't stay on the curb."

"What do you mean?" Darren's voice grew sharp.

"He keeps texting me. He wants to know how I'm doing, as if I'm heartbroken or something." She shrugged. "I don't know. Maybe because I've known him a long time. His parents and mine are friends."

He shouldn't have dug, but something didn't feel right. "How long were you two dating?"

She looked away. "A couple of years, maybe."

Darren's stomach turned. Two years was a

long time. Long enough to be considered serious. That guy's frequent texts meant he wanted her back. Plain and simple. Would Bree take him back? She'd said that her parents wanted them together. That usually pulled weight. A lot of weight.

"We better go." Darren stood.

Bree looked surprised, then disappointed, but she nodded. "Right. Sure."

Darren gathered the leashes of both dogs and pulled them off the blanket so Bree could fold it.

She stashed everything in her pack and shifted it onto her back. She reached out her hand. "Want me to take one?"

He wrestled with an odd notion of protecting Mickey from her heartless abandonment and realized that was crazy. Bree didn't want to go into details about her failed love life any more than he did his. It should have been enough to say that neither of them had worked out.

It wasn't, though. Darren battled a twisted feeling of déjà vu. He didn't like another guy vying for Bree's attention or chasing after her heart.

He handed over the beagle's leash. "Thanks." They walked back in silence.

At the truck, Bree asked, "Everything okay?"

"Yeah, why?"

"You seem quiet."

He needed to get a grip and grabbed the quickest excuse handy. "Thinking about next week's class. It needs to be good."

"Why wouldn't it be?"

"The morels might be plentiful in the woods at my folks' place, but I want everyone to get enough. Although, there will be a tour of the maple sugar shack. Probably a small jug of syrup, too."

Bree's eyes lit up. "Will we see how the sap is made into syrup?"

Darren shook his head. "Just an explanation. The sap is collected at the end of March through the first week of April or so. It doesn't keep long and has to be boiled down right away."

"Oh." She looked disappointed again.

Was she really into all this nature stuff? Or was this a way of reeling him in only to cut him loose when it was time for her to leave? Like she'd cut loose a guy she'd been dating for two years. Darren tried to shake off those thoughts. Bree wasn't like that. But then, how'd he know? He'd met her only a week and a half ago.

He loaded up his dogs in the backseat and then climbed in behind the wheel. Glancing at Bree sitting pretty in the passenger seat, he needed a swift kick upside his head. Maybe he hadn't learned his lesson, if he thought he could trust Bree with his heart. He wouldn't be enough for a girl like her.

* * *

Thanks again for showing me the elk. It was very inspiring.

Bree sent the text to Darren and waited.

He didn't respond.

She waited a few seconds more. Maybe he was busy. She prayed he was safe, not tracking down some troublemaker that might turn violent.

She set aside her phone and finished drafting a piece she'd started months ago, at a time when she'd felt stuck. Trapped between Philip's promises and pressure from her parents to get engaged.

God had given her courage then. Courage to see how she'd let everyone else call the shots in her life. Too afraid to step out, she'd settled. Not anymore. Applying for that residency had shifted her thinking and her feelings, too. She wanted more out of life. She wanted fire. Whatever that fire proved to be.

She could easily get burned if she let Darren shift her thinking that they had a future. What would it be like if they had more time to explore the attraction between them? Would they always do these kinds of things, or was he simply showing her a good time as promised before she left?

She felt alive around him. Both comfortable and uncomfortable.

He'd been distant when he drove her home.

And she didn't quite buy his excuse about the up-coming class preoccupying his thoughts. Something had changed in him, and she wished she knew what it was.

Her phone whistled with an incoming text.

She reached for it, hesitated a second or two and then clicked open the message.

You're welcome.

Darren had replied with the same sort of to-the-point message she'd come to expect. No smiley faces or anything added on like the texts she sent. Maybe she'd imagined something that wasn't even there. And maybe Tuesday's class couldn't come quickly enough. Unless she saw him sooner, like at the Mother's Day brunch. Closing her eyes, she felt crazy for hoping. Even so, Bree sent a prayer heavenward asking God to guide not only her steps to the future but also her heart. That organ beat to its own tune. One inspired by Darren.

Sunday morning dawned with warmth and sunshine. Darren had driven to his parents' house so he could ride into town with them for church. He'd been roped into attending Mother's Day brunch afterward at the Maple Springs Inn. The place Bree would play. Darren couldn't believe he was here willingly, walking the streets

of his hometown as if it didn't matter anymore. Maybe it didn't.

"Thank you for coming. It means a lot to me." His mom looped her arm through his.

"Couldn't let the ticket go to waste." Monica had purchased enough tickets through the chamber of commerce for the whole family to go. As many as were home, anyway. There was no way he could have backed out. Funny thing was, he didn't want to.

"It's a good thing you're not staying away from Maple Springs anymore." His mom patted his arm. "I'm glad you're moving on."

He covered his mom's hand with his own. He wasn't sure about that but gave her the peace she sought. He knew his mom had worried about him. "About time, I suppose."

"To everything there is a season." His mom gripped his hand and squeezed.

"You're right. Seasons come and go." Change was inevitable, but he didn't have to like those changes.

Darren thought more about his mom's reference to the book of Ecclesiastes. *There is a time for everything, and a season for every activity under the heavens.*

He'd been lax in reading his bible for too long, but knew the third chapter of that book pretty well. The simplicity of King Solomon's wise words had always appealed to him.

One verse that came to mind was *a time to weep and a time to laugh.* Bree had helped him with that. Showing her around dispelled a lot of the gloom he'd been under. If today brought him face-to-face with his ex-fiancée, he'd have to deal with it.

A time to keep and a time to throw away.

His time with Bree was limited, only a couple more weeks. Instead of fearing it, maybe he should simply enjoy it. Laugh more and worry less.

Entering the Maple Springs Inn, Darren inhaled the smells of good food and rich coffee. He scanned the fancy lobby with its huge fresh floral displays while they waited in line to enter the dining room. A couple of hours spent here wouldn't kill him. Seeing Raleigh wouldn't, either. Time to let it go. It was time to throw away the bitterness.

"Whoa, Darren, you're here." His brother Matthew carried his wife's tank of a six-month-old baby.

"So are you. When'd you get in?" His brother worked on a Great Lakes freighter and was typically gone this time of year. He leaned toward his sister-in-law for a quick hug. "Morning, Annie. Happy Mother's Day."

"Thanks. Good to see you." She moved on and gave his parents hugs, too.

"I traded shifts so I could be home for this."

He nodded toward Annie. "Didn't want to miss her first Mother's Day."

The baby reached toward him, so Darren took the kid from his brother and gave him a friendly bounce. He hadn't seen much of Matthew or Annie since they'd married in February. "Hey, little Jack. What are they feeding you? You're a load."

"He eats everything in sight." Matthew stepped closer. "She's not here, in case you're wondering."

"You've been inside?"

"To ask for a couple of tables put together. Zach and Ginger are coming, Cam, Monica, Marcus, Ben and Erin. Mom would want us sitting together."

"Then I'm glad I came." It wouldn't have been good if he'd missed this. Darren would have been the only local sibling to do so had he not agreed to come. His sister Cat was on assignment somewhere, and his little brother Luke was finishing up his college classes downstate. Both good excuses. Darren's fear of running into his ex-fiancée paled in comparison.

He spotted Bree and openly stared. Dressed in a pretty yellow-print dress with her hair swept up into a swirl at the back of her head, she reminded him of the small yellow trout lilies scattered on the floor of the woods. Sturdy enough to withstand a late snow but too delicate to thrive after being picked. Just like she wouldn't thrive here without a large orchestra to keep her engaged.

Bree saw him and rushed toward him. Her lips were stained the color of ripe berries and more tempting than ever. "You're here!"

"I'm here," he repeated. Holding on to Jack kept Darren from sweeping Bree into his arms.

"And who's this?" She took the baby's hand and laughed when he gurgled at her.

"My nephew, Jack."

Her golden eyes softened into an oddly sappy expression. Even for her.

"What?" he teased.

"Nothing, I—" She looked away. "You're good with him."

"And that surprises you?" Just because he growled about summer residents didn't mean he'd do that to kids. She should see him in action with the area schools. He'd been told his classroom presentations were some of the best.

"Bree." His mom reached for her hands. "I'm looking forward to hearing you play. This is a perfect Mother's Day gift, having most of my kids with me."

Bree's eyes widened, but she smiled. "Darren said he had a big family."

Darren watched, helpless, as his mom introduced her. Every one of his brothers and sisters present looked pointedly at him after hearing her described as *Darren's friend*.

The doors to the dining room finally opened, cutting short the conversation.

"Gotta run. See you inside." Bree gave Jack's chubby hand another playful shake before taking off to disappear down a hallway.

"Who's she?" Matthew asked.

"A friend." Darren shifted the baby to his other arm.

"You sure about that?" Matthew took Jack back as they headed into the dining room.

"I'm not sure of anything anymore."

Matthew gave him a look of understanding. "Give it time."

Time was a luxury he didn't have with Bree.

Their long table had been set up near the windows overlooking the park and Maple Bay. Looking at the public beach with its long stretch of sand and lifeguard chair, Darren recalled the summer that he, his brothers and cousins had *owned* the raft at the edge of the swimming area.

They'd grappled with a group of cocky teens from Bay Willows who'd tried to take over their space. That tussle for turf dominion had resulted in a lifeguard posted on that raft from then on. Sure, a lifeguard might have been a good idea, but it was a sore reminder that what belonged to the locals didn't. Not really. He'd resented the influx of summer residents flooding his town ever since that incident.

He glanced at Bree seated in the corner. Sunshine shimmered in her hair. She didn't take the beauty here for granted. Bree acted more like a guest because, really, that's what she was. She had no permanent roots here.

Bree focused on her sheet music. The cello she played stood nearly as big as she and rested against her knee. Her movements were confident yet refined. Delicate and pretty. She was younger than the three other women playing smaller stringed instruments. The music dipped and swirled and Bree played with an intensity he could relate to. She loved what she did. Not unlike the passion he had for his job and the woods.

She glanced at him and then focused back on the sheets of paper scattered on the stand in front of her. Bree came from a different world than his, with summer homes and prestigious careers, but she seemed to understand him better than most. Certainly, better than Raleigh ever had.

He'd rushed that relationship when he'd had all the time in the world to make sure it was right. He didn't have that kind of time with Bree. Not enough time to trust these new feelings. He'd been wrong before, but could Bree be right—for him?

His youngest sister, Erin, sat next to him and leaned close to whisper, "She's good."

"Huh?" Darren's thoughts scattered.

"Your girlfriend."

"She's not my—"

Erin gave him a look. "Oh, come on. She just looked at you as if she's wandered the desert and you're fresh water."

Darren felt his face heat. "Yeah, well..."

Erin giggled. "And you looked back the same way."

"Would you stop?"

His little sister grinned. "It's all good. I get it."

Darren didn't like the idea of Erin "getting" anything. His sister might be an adult, but to him, she'd forever be that sweet twelve-year-old who'd begged to tag along.

"What a scowl," Erin teased.

He pinched his sister's knee. "I'm trying to listen."

Erin squirmed, bumping the table. And that earned them a fierce look from their mom.

Darren glanced at Bree.

A hint of a smile hovered around her lips, barely creasing those dimples. She'd seen them alright, but it hadn't thrown off her concentration. This gig was probably child's play for her.

The mini concert ended and the audience clapped. Darren watched as the quartet stood and bowed. Could Bree join them now? The restaurant staff lifted the chafing dish lids on the long buffet table, and folks lined up for brunch. The quartet resumed playing as background music.

He sighed. How long would he have to wait to talk to her?

If he wanted his family to believe he and Bree were merely friends, he'd give her a wave and go. If he was smart, he'd stop seeing her outside the wild edibles class as if they were dating. He'd simply wait until Tuesday to see her again.

If he was smart, he'd stop thinking there could be anything more than merely a brief connection, a temporary courtship with Bree.

Chapter Nine

Darren was early and remained in the van. He wasn't in the mood for today's class. Maybe because Bree's mom planned to go, and that put him under the microscope. Joan Anderson had a way of looking over her glasses at him, as if inspecting and then finding him lacking somehow. It put him on edge.

He'd entered field reports for the last couple of days into his laptop while waiting. The windows were down, but the breeze off the lake was much too warm for early May. Crazy weather. Cold then hot.

"Good, you're here." Stella didn't wait for an invitation. She climbed right up into the front passenger seat.

He hadn't heard her approach and chuckled. "So are you. What's up?"

"I had to drop some letters in the mail, so I left the cottage early. Plus, I'm nosy. What's going on with you and Bree? Joan says you've been spending a lot of time with her."

Darren saved his document and then closed the laptop lid. "Simply showing her the sights as offered at your house over dinner."

Stella gave him a satisfied grin. "Exactly. And?"

"And nothing." But that wasn't true. His attraction to her had started the minute they'd met. No matter how Darren looked at it, this relationship couldn't end well. "It's not like that, Stel. She's a nice girl and all, but—"

Stella narrowed her gaze. "She's no girl. She's a full-grown woman who's accomplished and professional."

All the more reason why she wouldn't stick around. "I realize that, but—"

"But what?"

Darren offered up the easiest excuse handy. "I'm not interested."

Not interested in getting hurt. Not interested in becoming the object of disapproval from yet another Bay Willows family.

"Joan's worried you'll sweep Bree off her feet."

Darren laughed. "Yeah, right."

Stella lowered her voice. "You're the kind of guy Bree needs."

Darren took the bait. "And what kind is that?"

"The kind who will support and cherish her. You're the keeper kind."

Darren snorted. He wouldn't keep well for two years while she chased after whatever it was she wanted. "What makes you think she'd keep me? She just got rid of her last boyfriend."

"Yeah, finally." Stella's expression didn't joke. She looked far too serious.

"What makes you say that?"

"He was very image-oriented. He treated Bree—" Stella suddenly stopped and waved out of the open window.

Bree and her mom pulled into the parking space next to them.

Darren nearly growled. Nice timing. It should have been enough to know that Stella didn't like the way this guy had treated Bree, but it wasn't. Bree had said that her parents had loved the guy.

He got out of the van and spotted crutches in the backseat of Bree's car. As much as he wanted to talk to Bree, he needed to schmooze her mom a little. That meant putting to rest any fears Joan had about him sweeping Bree off her feet. As if he could.

He needed Joan's stamp of approval when it came to job performance. He cleared his throat. "Hi, Joan. Do you need help getting in the van?"

"Thank you, but no, Bree will drive."

He looked at Bree.

"I'll follow you," she said.

Changing the location of today's morel hunt proved a good idea considering Joan's physical limitations. She could hang out on his parents' deck instead of trying to negotiate uneven ground in the woods.

Maybe that would earn him points. His folks were good people. "Let me see your phone."

Bree placed a gold rhinestone–encrusted case in his hand.

He looked at the gaudy thing, flipped it over and then looked at her. "Really?"

"What? Stella gave me that." Her voice challenged him to make something of it.

He chuckled. The case looked like something Stella might pick out. He pulled up Bree's GPS app, punched in his parents' address and then showed her the map. "It's about ten miles north of town, in case we get separated. Watch out for this curve right here." He pointed to the road that suddenly veered left after topping a hill. "It can be dangerous if you're going too fast."

"I'll be careful. Thanks." No irritated tone this time at his caution.

He tapped the roof of her car and looked around.

Across the street he spotted the rest of their class swarming toward them. They looked every bit the country club crowd, dressed in summery shorts and bright colors. Even Ed, who approached from a block away yet, wore a pair of multicolored shorts Darren wouldn't have been caught dead in. As a regional supervisor, Darren would need to lead by example. And that might mean treating the summer crowd a little more softly. Could he do it?

To everything there is a season...

Maybe this was his season of change.

He glanced at Bree still seated in her car, chatting with her mom. The sound of multiple conversations going at once flooded his senses, pushing out his thoughts. He'd been standing around deep in thought while everyone waited for directions. Waited for his leadership. About time he stepped up.

Darren clapped his hands together once. "Let's load up and head out."

In the van, he took a head count and then made his way north to his parents' home. Talk about worlds colliding. He was about to set loose a group of folks from Bay Willows in his family's woods. At least his parents had his back if anything went wrong.

He hoped Bree did, too.

Bree followed Darren as he pulled into a long circular gravel drive surrounded by a rich green lawn. A huge log-styled home that looked like it had been added on to more than once sat farther back. A walkway of flat slabs of stone connected the driveway to a front porch complete with rocking chairs. Talk about country charm.

"This is lovely." Bree's mother gawked out the window.

"Yeah." Bree parked next to the van and peered through the windshield.

This fine home surprised her. Not because of Darren's parents—the place suited them—but considering the chip on their son's shoulder, she would have expected Darren to have grown up somewhere much more modest. The other side of the railroad tracks made more sense than this rolling lakeside retreat.

The passenger side door opened, and Darren offered her mother his hand. "My mom has refreshments on the back deck, and then we'll decide whether to hunt morels or take the tour of the sugar shack first."

"That'd be good." Her mother nodded, clearly impressed.

"I'll get the crutches." Bree dashed around the car in time to see Helen and Andy Zelinsky coming toward them.

"Glad you could make it." Helen reached for Bree's hands. "And I hope you brought your cello."

Bree felt her cheeks warm at the questioning look her mother gave her. "Yes, I did."

"The quartet was fabulous, but I want to hear just you play." Helen looked up. "And ideally that storm will stay away long enough for today's morel hunt."

Bree took in the dark clouds gathering in the western sky. The weather forecast had said nothing about rain today. "Helen, this is my mother and the organizer of the class, Joan Anderson."

"Good to meet you, Joan." Helen glanced at the soft cast and crutches. "I'm sorry, but it's a bit of a hike to the backyard. Maybe we should relocate to the sugar shack."

"Oh, no. I'm fine. Really. The crutches are better support than my cane. At least for now." Her mother had been given the green light to use a cane. She could put weight on her foot, but with caution.

Helen, not looking fully convinced, moved on and greeted the others. She gave Stella a big hug.

"Maybe Darren should carry you," Bree teased.

Her mother glared at her. "I'm perfectly capable of walking."

But Darren had overheard and walked toward them. "Need help?"

Bree had to own that she wouldn't mind being carried by him. "Maybe stand by, in case."

He nodded.

Bree's mother proved them both unneeded as she negotiated the walkway around to the back of the house without incident. The backyard proved even nicer, with frontage on a small inland lake and even a small sandy beach. The deck was expansive, too, with part of it covered. Underneath that generous overhang stood a table laden with iced tea, lemonade and a tray of snacks. Their group surrounded said table without hesitation and gobbled up cheese dip and crackers and homemade cookies.

Darren asked Joan, "Can I get you something to drink?"

"Bree will do that. But thank you."

As Bree waited for an opening around the refreshment table, Stella stood next to her. "Helen's a great cook. I remember Darren once brought me a tray of her homemade pierogi."

"They're nice people." Bree meant it. Darren's parents were real, salt-of-the-earth kind of people. Nothing like Philip's parents, who were stuffy even by her standards.

Philip had been uptight, too, making critical comments about her hair and how she dressed. Even her attempts to help others. She'd given up a midweek gig with a group of struggling young musicians because they'd played in a grungy coffee house in an area Philip hadn't liked.

Bree had been weak then, letting him interfere with her goals. Seattle promised not only professional dreams but also an escape from the expected routine.

She glanced at Darren. He stood next to his father, and they laughed about something. The affection between the two men was clear. They spoke to each other with mutual respect and acceptance. Darren had found his path. It was no wonder he'd never moved away; he had everything right here.

Bree envied his sense of contentment. She'd feared getting stuck in the same place whereby Darren welcomed it. She wanted change. He didn't. They were two different people chasing completely different things. Not exactly a good foundation for a lasting relationship. They didn't stand a chance.

Thunder rumbled louder. Darren looked up at the sky and frowned. He'd kept his ear tuned into the approaching storm while the group scoured his parents' woods for morels. Whites were popping, and everyone went crazy finding *just one more*.

Lightning flashed. He'd waited too long, and that wasn't smart. Darren blew his whistle. "Let's go. Now."

"It'll blow over." Ed's greedy onion bag bulged with morels.

"I'm not taking any chances." Darren stared the old guy down while the women scurried out of the woods.

He heard Stella shriek when the first gigantic raindrops hit. The window of opportunity to stay dry had definitely closed.

"Fine." Ed moved forward.

"Let's head for the sugar shack. That's closer than the house." Darren brought up the rear with Bree.

"This is kind of fun." She gave him a smile that sliced through him.

Getting caught in the rain with her would have been interesting if they'd been alone. Fortunately, for both their sakes, they weren't. "Yeah, right."

Bree frowned at his sharp tone.

"Look—" The roar of the rain tore at his attempt to apologize. He watched Bree as she ran ahead of him, the rain soaking through her T-shirt and shorts. Let her think he was a grump. That was safer.

The deluge hit while the group was in the middle of his parents' mowed lawn. He'd never seen seventy-year-olds move so fast. When they made it into the sugar shack, his mom met them at the door with a stack of towels.

"Nice touch with these." Darren dried off as he looked around. His mom had brought the party inside the sugar shack. Cozy for sure.

"I heard the thunder, and your father helped me move everything out here. We can hang out comfortably until the weather passes." His mother handed Bree a towel. "I hope you don't mind, but I had Andy bring in your cello case. Your car was unlocked."

"Thank you. Might as well set up now." Bree wrapped the towel around her neck and shoulders, under the fat braid of her hair. Her wet bangs were plastered against her forehead, making her golden eyes seem huge and incredibly pretty.

"Need help?"

"I got it." She waved off his offer.

Darren quickly took a head count. Everyone accounted for. No one lost but him. Every time he looked at Bree.

His mom had everything in hand like always. She'd make this his best class yet with such a party atmosphere. Laughter rang through their gathering as his class attendees dried off. The stainless steel evaporator gleamed, reflecting their little group crammed into this small space. Folding chairs had been set up for seating in addition to the benches against the wall.

Funny, but Darren didn't feel crowded.

Stella and Ed and the rest helped themselves to the snacks his mom had set out on the huge oak desk. He and Matthew had moved that desk out of Annie's house last year. When he'd been afraid to walk around in his own hometown. That time seemed far away.

He watched Bree push a folding chair into a corner near the light of a window. Carefully she opened her case, pulled out the gleaming wooden cello and settled it against her leg while she grabbed her bow. Even in a damp T-shirt and shorts, Bree looked refined.

"She's good for you," his mom whispered as she wrapped her arm around his waist. "She brings you back to life."

"She's leaving for two years." It came out a low growl.

His mom rubbed his back, slow and comforting like when he was little. "I'm sorry, honey."

He shrugged off her touch. "It's no big deal."

Rain clanged against the tin roof above. Lightning flashed, followed by a clap of thunder so loud that it rattled the windows. A couple of the women squealed, then laughed.

Darren hoped that wasn't an answer to his fib. Bree was turning into a very big deal. He watched her as those first mellow notes she played seeped into space, quieting the chatter. He didn't recognize the tune; he wouldn't. He didn't listen to this kind of stuff. Maybe he should. The silky sound of whatever it was she played captivated him. Her cello coupled with the rhythmic beats of rain hitting the roof mesmerized all of them into silence.

Bree gave him a soft smile, making her dimples a whisper.

He smiled back. His mom said she was good for him. Maybe that was true. She'd drawn him out of the gloom he'd been under for a long while.

Bree focused on playing.

Darren didn't look away. He watched her fingers slide up and down the neck of the instrument with confidence. She tilted the bow with such grace, nodding her head in time with the music.

"She's good," his mom whispered.

He nodded. "Too good for here."

Bree played piece after piece as the storm rumbled away into the distance, leaving behind a soft rain. Occasionally she'd look into Darren's intense gaze. His bright blue eyes burned through her, shooting sparks to her fingers and toes. She played to him.

It had quieted down enough to hear about the maple operation and had been for a few minutes now. She finished the piece and leaned back, feeling oddly drained.

"Aww." One of the women said. "Don't stop."

"It's close to end time." Bree looked at Darren for help, but he didn't seem in any hurry to leave.

"One more." Darren's voice coaxed, impossible to refuse.

"Yes, encore. Encore," some of the others chanted.

"Okay. Here's one that I composed, but it's not finished yet." Bree launched into the restless piece she'd been working on since applying for the music residency.

She'd added to it after coming up north. She'd added more after meeting Darren, but the remainder of the piece eluded her. Like the future path she'd committed to taking, the music twisted and turned only to stop, waiting for the next chord. The next step in her life.

She held her bow still and took a deep breath to calm her racing pulse. "That's it."

Stella clapped first. Followed by the rest of the class.

Bree glanced at Darren.

He gave her a quick nod.

What was he thinking? Any thoughts about her? Lately, he'd taken center stage in her mind.

Bree blew out her breath, stood and bowed. "Thanks. I'll turn it over to our hosts."

Helen Zelinsky spoke up. "Thank you so much for playing, Bree. It was beautiful. If everyone will gather round, Andy will explain how we turn sap into syrup, and then we have a little something for you to take home."

Bree quietly returned her cello to its case while listening to Darren's father. The process of collecting sap, boiling it down to syrup and then bottling it sounded like hard work. It had to be. Creating something so sweet didn't just happen.

She glanced at Darren again. Something sweet boiled between them, too, but it wouldn't keep. How could it from such a distance away? Literally across the country.

She heard Ed peppering Andy Zelinsky with questions.

Darren made his way toward her and pointed

his thumb at the group. "I guess I'm not the only one he challenges."

Bree whispered back, "Maybe it's a compliment, him giving you a hard time."

"Maybe." He reached for her cello case. "I'll load this in your car."

"I've got it." Bree stalled him. She didn't let people carry her case. His parents had grabbed it earlier without any damage, but she hadn't known about it.

He lifted his hands in surrender, smiling. "Okay."

She tried to listen to the presentation, but her focus was shot with Darren standing so close.

"That was amazing, by the way," he whispered near her ear.

"Yeah?" Bree reeled, feeling the warmth of his breath brush her skin. Darren's father still spoke in the background, wrapping up his speech. Class was over but Bree wished it wasn't. She wished—

"So, what inspired you to write that last song?"

"A lot of things." Bree lifted her cello case, putting space between them.

"Anything from up here?"

Should she tell him that he'd been part of what she'd composed? Her feelings for Darren had translated well into notes on a page. Really well. "Some."

He gave her a languid smile. "Tell me."

The pull between them tightened.

Andy Zelinsky walked past them with a box. The entire class swelled around him as he handed out small bottles of maple syrup.

Bree stepped back to get out of the way and bumped into Darren. She froze when his hand slipped to her waist in an attempt to guide her forward. She closed her eyes. Only for a second to savor the rush of his touch before moving away. "Thanks."

"No problem." His voice sounded rough.

Bree focused on making it out the door, bulky cello case in hand. At the door, she set down her instrument and reached for Helen's hands. "Thank you for making this class special."

Helen pulled her into a hug instead. "You made the day. God's got plans for you, my dear. Stay tuned into that."

Bree returned the embrace, careful not to hang on too tightly. How'd this woman know she searched for her place in the world? How much more could she see?

Bree pulled back but didn't meet Helen's gaze. "Thank you."

Darren's mom smiled. "You're welcome."

Bree quickly made her escape. Outside the rain had stopped, leaving behind clear skies and sweet-smelling air. The Zelinskys' lawn glittered like diamonds where sunshine hit water droplets clinging for life. Another half hour or so and the grass would be dry. The sparkle faded like a memory.

Bree glanced at her left hand, which was bare of any rings. She wore no jewelry but a watch around her wrist that showed they'd gone over their class time yet again.

She glanced at her mother hobbling ahead on crutches. Would she mind that they'd gone long? Bree's heart pinched at the thought of leaving, of moving so far away.

"Beautiful playing, Bree." Stella grinned at her as they approached the driveway. "It sounded different than when you practice."

Bree tipped her head. "What do you mean?"

"More passionate." Stella winked.

Bree's stomach flipped. "Oh, well, I, uh—"

"It's okay, honey. That's a good thing. Don't ever be afraid to feel."

Surely Stella didn't see into her heart, too. "Thanks. I'll remember that."

"See that you do."

Bree lifted the hatchback of her car, settled her cello inside and closed the trunk with a soft clunk. She spotted Darren on his cell phone, his brow knitted together and his face ashen.

Bree's stomach tightened. She was feeling—feeling like something was terribly wrong. She strained to listen, but the chatter of Stella and Ed and the others as they loaded into the van kept her from hearing anything clearly.

When she overheard Darren mention the hospital, she moved toward him and touched his arm. After he pocketed his phone, she asked, "What is it?"

Darren's parents stood close enough to hear, too, and both looked worried.

"That was Kate. Neil's been in a motorcycle accident. They're at the hospital and it doesn't look good."

Bree squeezed his forearm. "I'll take you there."

Darren looked like he'd been whipped. "But the van."

Andy Zelinsky stepped in. "Give me the keys. I'll drive them back."

"But— "

Helen backed him up. "I'll drive Joan and then bring your dad home. Darren, go with Bree."

Bree felt thrown into a bad dream. She'd spent enough time with Kate and Neil over the weekend to care. They'd been nice to her. And now? She closed her eyes.

Dear Lord, please touch Neil and be with Kate.

Darren handed over the keys to his father and then reached toward her for hers. "Let's go."

"I'll drive. Get in." Bree turned to her mother. "I'm not sure when I'll be home. Will you be okay?"

"Of course. Go." Her mother glanced at Darren, then back to her. "And be careful."

Bree didn't waste more time. Darren had slid into the passenger seat. He looked like he expected to lose his friend.

Please, God. Not more loss for him. Not this way.

Bree slid behind the wheel and clicked her seat belt. She noticed that Darren hadn't. "Buckle up."

He complied but didn't say a word.

Pulling out of the Zelinskys' driveway, she drove back the way they'd come. She needed to get him there fast but in one piece; she let up some from the gas pedal. "What happened?"

He shrugged. "Kate said he'd hit a deer."

"Oh." Bad news.

"It was raining."

Worse news. "I'm so sorry."

"Just drive." Darren's voice was low and craggy-sounding. The man was scared.

Bree covered his hand and squeezed. Her breath caught when Darren threaded his fingers through hers and tightened his hold. She prayed again. The same prayer as before.

This wasn't good. Not good at all.

Chapter Ten

No one liked hospitals, with the antiseptic smells and winding hallways that required instructions to find a room. Darren was no exception. He wiped the palms of his hands on his pants before entering the emergency room.

The TV blared in the main waiting area, where several people sat. He didn't see Kate. Had they moved Neil to a room already? Maybe everything was okay. He stepped up to the nurses' station and gave his friend's name.

"Oh. The family are gathered in the small waiting room around the corner." Her face looked grave. Much too grave.

That look hit him in the midsection, stealing away his breath. Neil was hurt badly and there was nothing Darren could do to change that. One more thing he couldn't control.

He felt Bree's hand slip into his own.

For a moment, he'd forgotten she'd come with

him. His throat closed up tight as he squeezed her hand, grateful for her calming presence.

They turned a corner and entered the smaller waiting room. Kate looked up, her eyes puffy and red. Neil's parents were there, too. Darren opened his mouth to speak, but nothing came out.

"Any news?" Bree rushed toward Kate, hands outstretched.

Darren watched his friend's wife hold on to Bree as if she were a lifeline. *What if Neil—* He didn't finish his thought. He couldn't. Darren had known Neil most of his life. He was a nice guy who didn't deserve this freak accident.

"We're waiting to hear." Kate reached toward him.

He grabbed her hand and squeezed. He still couldn't seem to form the right words, but Kate understood. She gave him a watery smile.

More people entered the waiting room—the minister who'd married Kate and Neil, followed by Kate's parents. Kate leaned against her mom while the minister offered to pray. More hand-holding.

Bree stood beside him and grabbed his hand.

Darren couldn't focus on the minister's words. All he could think of was what Neil faced. Would he come out of this the same? What if he didn't? What then?

"Amen," Bree whispered, but didn't let go.

They sat down and waited. Darren listened to Kate explain what had happened in a soft, broken voice.

Her mother cried.

After fifteen minutes, Darren couldn't take the hushed voices, the tears. He stood and stared a moment at the coffee dispenser on a counter near a small sink, along with cups, sugar and powdered creamer. Bad coffee was not what he needed.

"I'm going for something to drink. Can I get anyone anything?"

Folks shook their heads.

"I'll go with you." Bree followed him out.

Darren walked the hallway, took a couple of turns and stopped where it dead-ended at an open area with a couch. A wall of windows showcased a spectacular view of Maple Bay. He glanced at the small table beside the couch. It held an open Bible and a lamp that had been left on.

The urge to clear off that table with one swipe overwhelmed him, so he stepped closer to the window and bumped his forehead against the cool glass, helpless.

Bree didn't say a word, but stood close. Right next to him, offering her support if he needed it.

He needed far more.

Darren touched her fat braid. Feeling its weight,

he lifted it and pulled off the elastic band at the end. Then he unraveled the strands, threading his fingers through the mink-colored mass of hair. It felt silky-soft and pretty. Like her. He let her hair drop against her shoulder.

Bree searched his eyes. "What can I do?"

Make things stay the same.

He'd almost said it aloud. Bree couldn't turn back the clock any more than she could change her plans to leave. Her future promised a different path than his. A path far away. He handed back the elastic band.

Bree took it without a word and then wrapped her arms around his waist. She rested her head against his shoulder.

Darren didn't dare move. He kept his arms at his sides, draped over hers, and closed his eyes fighting his desire to touch her. Whatever was between them couldn't end well, and holding her was only going to make things worse.

When Bree drew away, he reacted and pulled her back, only closer. He buried his face in her neck, into all that hair he'd let loose. She smelled good, like flowers and sunshine and rain.

She trembled.

Maybe that shudder had come from him.

"Darren?" Her whisper should have warned him to back away, but it sounded more like a question. Or a plea.

Darren answered the only way he knew how. Crushing his lips against hers, he kissed her.

A few minutes later, Bree stared at Darren's broad shoulders. She'd pulled her hair back, anchoring it at the base of her neck with the elastic band Darren had pulled out of her hair.

Now was not the time to fall in love.

Certainly not in such a short time, but then, feelings this strong and reckless were new to her. Scary, too. She followed him back to the waiting room with an unopened soft drink can in her hand that made her fingers cold.

They'd shared only a couple of kisses. Kisses of comfort that she'd hoped to ease his worry. Her hopes had backfired the moment she deepened the kiss. Backfired, big-time. Who'd she think she was kidding? She'd wanted to kiss him. Wanted him to kiss her back and keep kissing her. But Darren had soon skittered away from her like a spooked rabbit. He wouldn't look her in the eyes when he'd mumbled that they should return.

Bree walked behind him, boring holes into his back with no success of seeing into his heart. They entered the small waiting room filled with new tension. Everyone looked ready to burst into tears, and guilt immediately smote her for worrying over a kiss.

She watched as a doctor talked to Kate. He

spoke too low for Bree to hear, but from the look on Kate's face, the news wasn't good. Bree glanced at Darren.

He ran a hand through his hair. He must have been able to hear the news, because his eyes grew shiny wet as whatever the doctor shared with Kate sunk in.

Bree wanted to go to him but stayed put. Now wasn't the time for embraces, nor could she share her feelings. Bree needed to leave him alone.

The doctor left and people swarmed Kate.

Darren leaned close and whispered near Bree's ear. "You might as well go home. I'll catch a ride back to Bay Willows later for the van. It looks like a rough night ahead."

Staying wouldn't be good for either of them; she might do something else she'd regret. "How bad?"

"Neil's in surgery. They're hoping to save his leg, but there's a lot of damage."

Bree cupped her mouth.

Darren awkwardly patted her back. "Go on. Go home."

She nodded and slipped out of the room unnoticed. Heart heavy, Bree made her way out to her car. Climbing behind the wheel, she placed the can of pop into the cup holder and rested her forehead on the steering wheel. Tears ran down her face, so Bree gave in and cried.

Her phone rang.

"Hello?"

"Bree? Baby, what's wrong?"

Philip!

Her stomach turned and she sniffed. Why hadn't she checked who it was? Or let it go to voice mail? "It's nothing."

"Sounds like something."

She cleared her throat, hating the edge in Philip's voice that wasn't concern. "A friend's in the hospital."

"What friend?"

"You don't know him." Bree sniffed again.

Silence.

"Was there a reason you called?"

"Yes, actually there was." Philip chuckled. An irritating sound. "I was thinking about coming up. Take in some golf and give you a good send-off."

Bree closed her eyes. "Please don't."

"There's no reason we can't be friendly, Bree. Our parents are friends."

There was every reason. "Philip, please."

"Think about it." He paused and then added, "Sorry about your friend."

"Thanks."

He disconnected.

Bree stared at her phone. Why wouldn't he leave her alone?

She drove toward Bay Willows, but instead of pulling into her parents' driveway, she headed for

Stella's cottage. She passed by the community building where Darren's work van sat parked. Seeing that green vehicle brought new tears to her eyes.

At Stella's, Bree got out, bounded up the porch stairs and knocked.

Stella opened the door wide. "Bree, come in. You okay?"

"I don't think so." She walked into her friend's open arms.

Stella gathered her close and led her toward the kitchen. "Tell me what happened. Is his friend going to be okay?"

"They're not sure." Bree explained the situation while Stella made tea.

"That's not what's really bothering you, though, is it?" Her elderly friend set a cup of herbal tea on the table along with the honeypot.

Bree shook her head. "I have feelings for Darren."

Stella brushed aside Bree's bangs like she was a child with a skinned knee. "Is that such a bad thing?"

"It's the last thing either of us wants."

"Why?"

"Because I'm leaving in two weeks. I'm not passing up my chance to do something special, and I'm not getting stuck here."

Stella frowned. "How do you know there's nothing here for you?"

"I just know." After talking to Jan Nelson, the Bay Willows music school looked unlikely to get off the ground anytime soon. The board couldn't agree on who they wanted to reach or what venue they'd provide. There were few opportunities here for her.

Bree sipped her tea, but it didn't quell her concerns, her fear.

"Has Darren asked you to stay?"

"No." He might not return her feelings. Even after that earth-shaking kiss. She grabbed the little ceramic pot decorated with bees and drizzled more honey into her tea.

"Then there's nothing to worry about. Right?" Stella's expression betrayed that sentiment. She looked concerned too.

"You're probably right." Bree joined Stella in putting up a good front, but it didn't make her feel any better.

She wanted more with Darren, but it'd be a huge mistake to give up this opportunity. One she'd regret the rest of her days. That kind of resentment wouldn't be fair to him. She'd resent staying behind to see where this went, and then what if they ended up nowhere?

Her plans had been so clear before. Why so much muddiness after a kiss? Didn't seem fair having to choose between following her dreams and her heart.

"I think I should leave early for Seattle." Bree

could run, away from her feelings and the man who owned them.

"When?"

Her mother wasn't quite ready to take over the class, but she would be after next week. Bree would simply steer clear of Darren until then. No more off-the-beaten-path outings. And no more kisses. Vacation was officially over. She'd miss Memorial Day with her family if she left early, but the Anderson barbecue and the Maple Springs parade were small sacrifices in the scheme of things. Her heart twisted. Some things couldn't be helped.

"After the next class."

Stella gave her a sad-eyed look of disappointment. "Falling in love is not the end of the world."

"For me, it is." Bree ran her finger around the rim of the tea cup. "For me, it sure is."

Darren's phone whistled with an incoming text. He waited until he stopped his truck at a red light before checking who it came from.

Bree.

How's Neil?

Guilt ripped through him. He should have called her or texted. He should have let her know last night when things had improved, but he'd been spent. He called her.

"Hey, Darren." Her voice sounded incredibly soft.

Remembering the feel of her hair and the texture of her lips, he gritted his teeth. "Neil is stable. Are you home?"

"Yes, but—"

"Can I swing by?"

"Umm. Sure."

"See you in about ten minutes."

He'd planned on seeing Bree today anyway. He would have called her from the hospital, maybe to meet up for dinner or something. They needed to have a talk. He blew out his breath. He couldn't use Neil's accident as an excuse for the way he'd kissed her. It'd be convenient—understandable, even—but false. He'd kissed her because he'd wanted to. Plain and simple.

Only it didn't feel simple. That couple of kisses hadn't been enough. He wanted more than she could give him. More than he should ask for.

When he pulled up in front of the Anderson cottage, Bree was there, waiting for him on the porch. Her hair hung loose, draping her shoulders, but worry marred her pretty brow.

She hurried toward him, scanning his faded jeans and cotton shirt. "No work today?"

"I took the day off."

"Can we walk?" Bree scrunched her nose. That meant she needed to talk, too. More scary stuff.

He surveyed the neighboring cottages. More of them were opening up now, getting ready for summer. Gardeners worked on lawns or planted flower beds and boxes. Raleigh's family usually arrived after Memorial Day, so she wouldn't be around Bay Willows when the hired help was opening up the cottage. He'd always had a better chance of running into her in town anyway.

No matter how he sliced it, he was a baby. Scared of the woman he used to love and scared of the woman he could love if she stuck around.

"How about down by the water?" he suggested.

"I know a shortcut. Come on." Bree waved him out of the truck. "You said Neil is stable. What's that mean?"

Darren ran a hand through his hair and got out of his truck. "I'm sorry I didn't text you or call last night. The surgeon saved his leg. They pumped him full of antibiotics and he responded well. The doctors expect a good recovery in time. He woke up after surgery, and Kate was able to talk to him."

"Thank You, God." Bree closed her eyes. Her concern was real. She truly cared.

Guilt smacked him again. He hadn't given her enough credit. He'd lumped her in with what he'd thought were pretentious summer folk. People he'd resented since he was a kid. He'd even kept the comparison of her to his ex-fiancée alive after it was obvious that Bree wasn't anything like Raleigh. Bree was different. Special.

"I was on my way to see him when you texted."

Her brow furrowed again, and she stopped walking. "Oh, I'm sorry. Did you need to go?"

He shook his head. "I'll go later. I needed to see you today. To talk."

"Yes. Me, too." Bree slipped through a hedge of bushes on a worn downhill path to the lake. "Watch your step."

The incline was indeed steep, but short. Lazy waves lapped against the sand mixed with rocks and pebbles. Many docks had been installed for the season and reached out like fingers into Maple Bay.

They crossed the road onto a narrow sidewalk that followed the shoreline. The warm sun caressed his back and shoulders until the lakeside breeze blew in crisp over the still chilly waters.

Bree shivered and crossed her arms.

Darren wrapped his arm around her, drawing her close. "Cold?"

She tensed but didn't pull away. "Thanks."

He might as well start the conversation they needed to have. "I'm not sorry I kissed you."

"I am."

He stopped and faced her. "Why?"

She wouldn't look at him. Her gaze hit him somewhere in the middle of his chest.

He lifted her chin and ran his fingertip where her dimples showed when she smiled. Bree wasn't smiling now. "Why are you sorry?"

She glared at him. "Because I have feelings for you. Because I'm leaving soon and I don't want to—"

He leaned down and kissed her. Quick and hard.

She pushed him away. "That's not helping."

Hearing her admit that she cared did something to him. Something he didn't expect. Something he didn't want to lose. "Why Seattle? Do you really have to go way out there?"

"Seriously? Don't even think of asking me to stay." Now she looked angry.

He didn't want to let this die, but then, what kind of chance did they have after only a few dates? "I suppose we can keep in touch."

That sounded lame even to his ears. They'd known each other only a couple of weeks, but that was long enough to have *feelings* for each other. Very real feelings he should have known better than to pursue. Hadn't he learned his lesson? Whirlwind romances didn't last.

Even if they kept in touch, he knew how it'd go. They'd do fine for the first few months, until the novelty wore off. They couldn't maintain a long-distance relationship for two years. When

Bree left, they'd be done. He'd known that all along and yet he'd let her in. He'd let himself care.

"I suppose we could." She bit her bottom lip. She wasn't convinced, either.

He wanted to kiss her again but started walking instead. "It is what it is."

"Right," she agreed, skipping to catch up. "What happened last night is reason enough not to get involved, considering the circumstances. We can remain friends."

Darren let loose a sarcastic chuckle. There was no going back to that, not after that kiss. They might have something to build on if distance wasn't an issue, but— He looked up and froze.

Heart pounding in his ears, Darren stared at his ex-fiancée, hand in hand with Tony, walking the shoreline. The couple was headed straight for them.

Bree saw them, too.

He stared at Raleigh's cool gaze and didn't look away. The woman seemed perfectly at ease, as if it was no big deal what she'd done to him.

He curled his hands into fists but forced them back open when he felt Bree's touch to his arm. He took a deep breath. He'd been running from this moment for over a year and a half. Today he faced his past. Ironic, considering he discussed his future with Bree.

He didn't move or speak. He simply stood

there and stared at the two of them. At least Tony looked uncomfortable, and that gave Darren some satisfaction.

"Hi, Darren." Raleigh stopped in front of him. Her blond hair glimmered in the sunshine, but she didn't look as good as he remembered. She looked thinner. More hollow. Her heavily made up eyes narrowed. "And Bree. I didn't know you two knew each other."

"Yeah." Darren didn't offer any explanations.

"How are you?" Bree's voice lacked its usual warmth. If he hadn't known her, he wouldn't have been able to tell she was being short. Almost rude—for her.

"Can't complain." Raleigh flicked her hair over her shoulder.

That was a new one. He seemed to remember that Raleigh typically had something to complain about. Darren looked at his friend, the guy he'd grown up with. They'd ridden the bus together, played sports and pretty much shared everything. He could add girlfriends to that list now.

Darren curled his fists again. "Tony."

Tony finally met his gaze. He looked sheepish, as if thinking the same thing as Darren. "How've you been?"

That was the question of the century. Being chased out of his own hometown for fear of this face-to-face pretty much summed up how he'd been. No matter how much he wanted to vent,

Darren didn't bother. The effort didn't seem worth it anymore. "I've had my moments."

That got to Raleigh. She kicked at an imaginary pebble on the sidewalk. "We're moving to St. Louis at the end of the month. Tony accepted a position there. Good future and all."

Darren clenched his jaw. They both chased a lifestyle instead of a life. He expected to feel angry, but the sadness that shot through his veins surprised him. There was no going back for them. Things had changed forever.

Darren was suddenly okay with that. Finally. "I hope you guys find what you're looking for."

Raleigh's eyes widened at the resignation in his voice. She looked unsettled as if his forgiveness wasn't something she expected. He might have misread her. He'd been good at misreading her. "Yeah, you too."

Darren stepped off the sidewalk to let them pass. He didn't look back. He felt Bree's hand slip into his own and gave her fingers a squeeze. "Want to grab lunch?"

Bree looked back at the man and woman who'd once torn his world apart. "Are you okay?"

Darren considered the question. Was he? "Doesn't matter."

"Do you want to talk about it?"

"No. I'm done with all that. With them." Glancing at Bree's hand wrapped firmly in his own made him wonder if maybe he'd found what he truly wanted.

Bree was real and she cared. Problem was, he didn't want her to leave. But by asking her to stay, he might lose her forever.

Chapter Eleven

Darren's stony expression made Bree nervous. He was either angry or hurting or both and she didn't know how to help. So she remained silent as they cut through the line of willow trees that marked the main entrance of Bay Willows.

The sidewalk ended but they continued walking, through the public boat launch toward the public beach. The sun shone high in the sky, making the blue waters of Maple Bay glimmer. A couple of sailboats skimmed the horizon.

She should say something.

"Want to sit down?" Darren broke their silence and headed for one of several park benches. "I don't really want lunch, do you?"

Bree scrunched her nose. She'd eaten breakfast a couple of hours before Darren had picked her up. She slipped next to him but not too close. "No. Not really. I'm sorry about running into them."

Darren shrugged. "Bound to happen. I don't know what I was so worried about."

"Maybe you weren't ready before." Bree took in the view and sighed. "Beautiful, isn't it?"

"I think so." Darren gazed out at the lake a moment and then turned toward her. "Why isn't this enough for you people?"

You people? Bree didn't react to the harsh tone of his voice. "What do you mean?"

He leaned his elbows on his knees. The blue polo shirt he wore stretched taut across his back, begging for her touch. She kept her hands to herself. He didn't look like he'd welcome her comfort.

He sat back and blew out his breath. "All my life I've heard summer residents say they could never live up here year-round. It's too small, there isn't a mall, there isn't this or that. They complain about all the things that make Maple Springs special, yet every summer, here you all come."

Bree shifted. "For many, it's an escape up north. A good vacation place that's just not reality."

He gave her a hard look. "What about you?"

She stared straight back. Bree didn't like where this was going. "I love a good vacation like everyone else, and thanks to you, that's exactly what I had."

"So that's it. That's all this has been. Just forget about your feelings?"

Feelings she'd admitted to not wanting. "I have to."

"Why?"

Her defenses rose. "If I wasn't satisfied playing with the symphony in Detroit, a small regional chamber orchestra up here won't fill the gap. It can't provide the opportunities I need."

He leaned back, making the park bench squeak. "Be careful chasing ideals and bright lights. Sometimes the simple things are what matter most in life. And sometimes, the most fulfilling."

She didn't want to hear it, especially from him. Who was he angry with? Raleigh or her? Maybe both. "Why the big chip on your shoulder when it comes to the resort crowd? And why on earth would you fall for someone like Raleigh?"

His blue eyes glittered with anger.

Bree might have pushed him too far, but instead of trying to smooth it over or backtrack, she remained quiet. Waiting. She wanted to know.

Finally, he said, "See that raft over there in the swimming area?"

Bree nodded.

"Growing up, winter was tough for me as a kid. We lived far out and there was little to do after school before we got into high school sports. Come spring, my brothers and I stayed in town after school. We'd hang out and we owned this beach. At least until the summer crowd showed up and we had to share. I didn't like sharing."

Bree could easily picture Darren as the kid he'd painted. Roaming around this small town with an arrogance of his own. "And?"

He shrugged. "As far as I was concerned, that raft belonged to me and mine as soon as the water warmed enough to get in it. We'd earned it after the boredom of a long winter. And no one tested us, no one tried to take it from us, until summer break and the Bay Willows crowd came. You guys have your own private beach barred to locals, but every year your kids had to have our beach and raft. One summer, I'd had enough and took a stand. My brothers and cousins had my back."

"How old were you?"

He shrugged. "Maybe thirteen."

"What happened?"

"A fight ensued, and Parks and Recreation posted two lifeguards at the public beach from then on. One on the raft and one near the bathhouse. It might sound silly now, but I got the message loud and clear. The summer crowd comes first. As a kid I didn't understand how much this town relied on the dollars tourists bring to the area. I felt diminished, as if locals get the scraps. I was sick of coming in second place."

"You've been protecting your town ever since, trying to hang on to what's yours."

"Something like that." He stared out over the bay.

It made sense. And must have made Raleigh's betrayal slice even deeper. Darren was stuck in old resentments, and she didn't want to get stuck.

He looked at her, and something shifted between them. A new level of understanding. "I've got to head back. Are you walking with me?"

"Yes, I'll walk with you." She stood.

He hadn't invited her to visit Neil, but then, she didn't expect him to. She had her cello practice yet to do. Still, she didn't like things left between them like this. An uncomfortable impasse. She held out her hand. "Friends?"

He took her hand and squeezed before letting go. "Always."

Did he mean it? She hoped so. She didn't have much time for close friends but knew Darren could be one of them. He could be more if she wasn't leaving. Much more.

As they walked back the way they'd come, Bree prayed this music residency would finally answer her own needs to be more. Chasing shadows of something she couldn't even name was getting old, but she couldn't give up on her dreams of composing yet. Not without hearing her music played. Not without making some kind of impact.

Bree glanced at Darren. Hands in pockets, he looked pretty gloomy. "Tell me about foraging for asparagus in the next class," she said. "It's one of my favorite vegetables."

He chuckled. "You're in for a treat. I've been out to a couple of spots and cut the ferns so we'll have lots of good shoots to pick for class."

"How will you remember where they are? The ones you cut." They rounded the corner, and her parents' cottage came into view. Too soon, their walk was over, but at least it ended on a lighter note, talking about class. She walked him to his truck.

"I'll remember."

She had no doubt that would be true. Stella had once said that Darren knew the woods and countryside like the back of his hand. Like he owned it. In a way, he did. This area was his home, a place he loved the way she loved music. That'd never change.

She smiled up at him. "Thank you for stopping by. And for our talk."

He looked like he wanted to say more.

Bree was glad he didn't. Her mind was set on leaving, but it wasn't as if she didn't have her doubts.

"See you Tuesday." He slid into the driver's seat.

Her heart broke at the finality in his voice. No more off-the-beaten-path trips or spending time alone. Not if she wanted to stay committed to leaving.

"See you Tuesday." She waved as he pulled out.

She'd say goodbye after class and hope Darren made good on keeping in touch. For now, that's about all she could do.

When Tuesday's class came, Bree was a bundle of conflicting emotions. She could hardly wait to get settled in and explore the artsy neighborhood of her residency in Seattle. She'd checked the area out online. It looked so different from where she'd lived and worked in Midtown Detroit. Half the country away, but she looked forward to scouring the eclectic shops and downtown center.

Darren hadn't texted her, but then, she'd always been the one to text first. She didn't have much to say, and that didn't bode well for staying in touch after she left. After saying goodbye tonight.

She finished lacing up her trail boots and glanced at her phone again. No texts. Not one. Not even from Philip, which was a welcome relief. She slipped the phone in the back pocket of her jeans and found a restaurant receipt from her lunch with Kate a couple of days ago. Staring at it, Bree sighed. She crumpled it up and threw it in the trash before heading downstairs.

Bree had sent a plant to Neil and Kate at the hospital. She'd made sure to include a get-well card with her cell phone number in case they needed anything. Kate had called right away to thank her, and they'd met for lunch. Neil was doing well, and Bree had admitted to caring for Darren.

Kate hadn't been surprised. She'd encouraged her to go through with her plans, though, stating that if what they'd started was real, they'd make it last. Easy for her to say. Kate spoke from a different place, though. Her husband could have been killed in that motorcycle accident. Time could be cut short when least expected. All the more reason not to leave anything undone or unsaid.

Bree met her mom in the kitchen. "Are you ready?"

"You go ahead. I think I'll drive so I don't have to climb into that van with a cane."

"I can take you." Her mother drove a sporty little crossover SUV that would do fine on the dirt roads they'd likely take, but Bree didn't want her mom getting lost.

Her mother looked away. "You go on ahead to the community building. I'll be there shortly and then we'll see."

Bree hesitated. "You're sure? I can wait."

Her mother waved her away, agitated. "Go. I'll see you in a bit."

"Okay." Bree grabbed her edibles basket and headed out the door.

Another glorious day greeted her, along with newly arrived neighbors waving their hellos. Bay Willows had sprung to life with Memorial Day weekend only a few days away. Traffic had picked up, too, as the summer crowd descended. The image of Darren as a boy defending that raft at the beach flashed through her mind. His place would always be here.

She quickly walked the couple of blocks to the community building. Sure enough, Darren's van sat parked in front. Her pulse raced even as her pace slowed. Five days. She hadn't seen or heard from him in five days. She'd better get used to missing him. Plain and simple.

Darren stepped out of the building and spotted her. "Hello."

"Hi." She fought the urge to throw herself into his arms. "Need help with anything?"

"Nothing to do, really, but wait. Did you bring a knife?"

Bree tipped her head back and groaned. "No. I forgot."

He smiled. "I've got extras for those of you who don't check your calendar list."

"Good." She couldn't think of anything else to say, so she stood next to him, waiting quietly for everyone else to arrive.

Darren was quiet, too.

They'd been reduced to inane small talk—as if nothing had happened between them. No kisses, no baring of their souls. Bree had thanked Darren for a good vacation. They'd had many moments that she'd cherish as memories, but like all vacations, they came to an end. Their relationship would too.

"Great day today." Ed walked toward them and patted his side. He wore a leather sheath attached to his belt. "Got my knife."

"Nice." That was no knife. More like a small machete. Bree giggled and glanced at Darren.

He smiled, as well.

Bree was going to miss this class and the comradery she'd had with the group.

Be careful chasing ideals and bright lights. Sometimes the simple things are what matter most in life.

Darren's words echoed through her mind, taunting her.

She'd miss him. Maybe more than she expected.

"Beautiful day, isn't it?" Stella walked toward their little group and gave Bree's back a comforting touch. "How are you?"

Bree's eyes burned. Clearing her throat, she forced a bright smile. "Ready to find wild asparagus."

"Me, too." Stella's concerned gaze didn't miss a thing. "I'm here if you need me."

Bree looked away. "I know. Thanks."

"Let's load up." Darren opened the van doors. Once everyone had climbed inside, he took a quick head count like always.

"Can we wait a couple more minutes for my mother?" Bree pulled out her phone, ready to call her, when a bright blue Cadillac coupe pulled in next to them and honked.

Bree knew that car.

Her mother sat in the passenger seat and opened the window. "We'll follow the van."

Bree stared, her stomach turning.

"Hi, Bree." Philip's voice sounded smooth as satin and equally slippery.

She glared at her mother. Her mother's bit about driving separately was a ruse. She'd known Philip was coming up north. After she'd asked him not to, Philip had persuaded her mother to give him an invitation.

"He wanted to surprise you." Her mother gave her a sheepish smile as if that made everything okay.

Philip smiled. "Surprised?"

"Not really." Bree climbed into the van and stared straight ahead.

She heard her mother's gasp. "Bree…"

Darren approached the Cadillac. "It's a ways out where we are headed." He jotted something down on a piece of paper in his tidy little notebook and handed it to her mother. "If we get separated, we'll meet up at this general store. That's the address and my cell number."

"Okay." Her mother nodded.

Bree peeked into the Cadillac, catching Philip giving Darren a once-over. Something about the hard line of Philip's mouth made her want to spit nails. He had no right to be jealous. No right to be here.

Darren climbed into the driver's seat. "Everyone buckled in and ready?"

Their group chorused agreement.

He looked at her. "Bree?"

"Yes?"

"Your seat belt."

She fumbled with her phone and dropped it. She started to pick it up, but Darren got there first.

He handed it back and touched her hand. "I take it that's *your* ex."

She nodded.

"You okay?"

She grabbed her seat belt and buckled up. "Yes. I'm fine."

Darren watched her closely.

She looked away. "Let's just go."

So that was the guy. Philip. Bree's ex-boyfriend. Darren glanced in the van's rearview mirror. The flashy blue coupe followed close behind. He'd gotten a good look at him before they'd left

Bay Willows and Darren didn't like what he saw. Philip dripped success with his styled blond hair and straight white teeth. There wasn't the air of wannabe successful ambition that Tony had. This guy was already there.

If Bree had broken up with a guy like Philip to pursue her dreams of composing, what chance did Darren have?

None.

He pulled onto a dirt road that led to the first foraging spot. Dust flew and Darren couldn't deny the pleasure in knowing that Philip's expensive car was getting dirty. Nice and dirty.

Cresting a small hill, Darren pulled over. This was a desolate spot save for the large farm in the distance. All along the roadside and up against old barbed wire fencing grew the wild asparagus.

Last week, Darren had cut down most of the old fern stalks, but he'd left a few to mark where he'd been. He could see from here where new sprouts had grown up tall. These would be easy pickings for everyone.

He turned in his seat. "You guys know the drill. Meet me at the back of the van for instructions and whistles. Anyone who forgot a knife, I have extras."

He glanced at Bree. She'd been quiet the whole way. Now wasn't the time to dig about Philip and why he was here. Bree hadn't looked surprised or too pleased. She'd once said that Philip had tried to talk Bree out of going to Seattle. Honestly, Darren couldn't blame him. Darren had wanted to do the same thing, but holding a person back never worked.

Stepping toward the rear of the van, he watched as Philip made a show of turning his Cadillac around before parking it a car length behind them, but faced the way they'd come in. He got out and then helped Joan. The guy leaned against the driver's side door when Bree went over there.

Darren could barely hear them, but he thought he heard Philip say something about relocating. To be near Bree. And Darren's gut twisted. He couldn't hear Bree's response or see her expression with her back to him, but those pretty shoulders of hers looked tense.

The urge to knock the arrogant smirk off that guy's face burned hot. Darren blew out his breath and opened the dual doors at the back of the van. He grabbed the box containing the red whistles and extra paring knives, then turned to the proper page in their wild edibles pamphlet and held it up. Instruction time.

"This is going to be pretty easy. Wild asparagus looks pretty much the same as domestic. There will be stalks growing along that fence line. There are pictures of what the mature ferns look like in your booklet, so you can look for them later in the year. To get new sprouts, the old stalks have to be cut down this time of year. I did this about a week ago. Anyone is welcome to come back in a few days and check for more. But do not cross the fence line, as that's private property. Please be considerate and make sure everyone has cut a few stalks before going back for more. I have another field prepped after this one."

Everyone scattered.

Philip walked toward him. The guy was dressed in khakis and a patterned button-down shirt. Not nearly as tall but slender, Philip approached with a slink to his step and held out a hand. "Joan tells me you're quite the outdoorsman."

Not a compliment. Darren shook the guy's soft hand anyway. "Yeah."

"Can you really eat this stuff?" Philip's lips curled into a half smile.

Bree had dated this pompous idiot? Darren caught her gaze.

She rolled her eyes as if he'd spoken the thought aloud. Then she turned to her mom. "Do you want me to pick for you?"

Joan limped forward, leaning on her cane. "No. I want to see what it looks like."

Darren could easily envision mother and daughter taking a tumble on the incline of the ditch and offered Joan his arm. "The next spot might be better for you since the ground is more level. We won't be here long."

"Oh." Joan hooked her elbow around his and waved off her daughter as they crossed the uneven dirt road. "You go ahead."

Bree hesitated a moment, watching Philip.

"I'll hang here and check my messages." Philip strolled back to his car and climbed in.

Darren watched Bree. She nearly slid down the ditch, intent on catching up with Stella. The two women spoke softly as they cut stalks side by side and moved on. He could only imagine what Stella said. She'd cast a couple of disgusted looks toward the blue coupe.

On the other side of the road, Joan let go of his arm. "Philip comes up every year, usually around the Fourth of July, with his folks. Our families have been friends for years. He's decided to move out west, too. I sure hope they get back together."

Not what Darren wanted to hear, but not surprising that Joan would prefer the golden boy over him. Darren wouldn't ever be on Joan's list of eligible bachelors for her daughter. His salary, even with the field supervisor promotion to sergeant, wouldn't come close to what Philip pulled in.

"Does Bree want that?"

"They've broken up before, so we'll see. He's got a good future. Security and all."

"Right." What else could he say? Bree hadn't mentioned that they'd called it quits only to get back together. She hadn't been real talkative about this guy or the issues they'd had. But then he hadn't been a fountain of information about Raleigh either.

He stopped at the edge of the ditch with Bree's mom so they could watch everyone cutting spears of wild asparagus. He glanced at the Cadillac and Philip. Darren drove an old pickup truck.

"Would you look at that?" Joan exclaimed. "That looks just like real asparagus."

"It is real, just not cultivated." His defenses rose.

Joan looked through him, catching the hidden meaning he hadn't meant to make. "You mean planted."

Darren glanced at Bree. She was cultivated, groomed for success and with her focus and talent, she'd succeed. He had no doubt about that. Whether fishing for smelt, cleaning them, scouring the woods for morels or playing her cello, Bree gave her all. But not her heart. She didn't want to make room in there for him. Was that because the golden boy still cornered the market there?

"I think that's it." Stella climbed up from the ditch, her little basket loaded with green spears and even some that trailed wispy branches.

"How's it look, Ed?" Darren had gotten used to checking with Ed before wrapping things up. The guy loved it.

"I think she's right. We got most all of it." Ed sheathed the machete knife.

Several of the other women were climbing up onto the road as well, comparing their finds. A few picked some spindly-looking daisies and pink clusters that grew along the road in clumps. Nothing on the protected list. Common wildflowers.

Bree came up last after holding on to everyone else's baskets. At the top, she stumbled. Her basket teetered and a few spears fell out.

Darren picked them up and offered them back.

"Thanks." Bree dragged her fingers across his palm, scooping up the stalks.

His gaze lingered on her apple-colored lips. He knew the softness there, the sweet taste. How long would it take to forget the feel of her kiss? The warmth of her embrace. "You're welcome."

She stared back, her golden eyes dark and stormy. Was she thinking the same thing?

"Ready to go?"

"Yes." Soft as a whisper, Bree walked past him and climbed into the passenger seat of the van.

She looked like a woman in turmoil, alright.

She wasn't the only one. He might have shown her what lay off the beaten path, but she'd walked right into his heart and made a mess there.

Chapter Twelve

The next field wasn't far away. Bree took in the beauty of a vast meadow dotted with daisies and Lake Michigan shining as a sparkling blue ribbon in the distance. She sighed. The view didn't matter, not when Philip's relocation announcement stole away her peace. What was he thinking, doing something like that?

She couldn't tell Philip where to live and work, but she could draw the line when it came to her. She'd let him edge his way back into her life before because they'd known each other a long time. Because their families were friends and wanted them together. But this time, they were through. She was done.

Bree glanced at her mother. With Darren's steadying hand, her mom sliced an asparagus spear and then plunked it in her basket. Bree should have been honest with her parents when it came to Philip, especially her mother.

"When do you leave?" Philip followed her.

She swallowed irritation and focused on the ground. "Soon."

"I can help you drive out and then fly back. Use it as an office space scouting trip."

"I'm good. I don't need your help." Bree cut a thick, short stalk of asparagus.

Philip stepped in front of her. "You can do your thing and I can expand my business. It'll be perfect."

Bree straightened to face him. "Breaking up wasn't only about the music residency."

His brown eyes narrowed. "Sure it was."

"I'm not interested in getting back together." She forced herself not to look away.

"Is this about him?" Philip gave a nod toward Darren.

"No." Bree was firm in her answer. It was none of Philip's business anyway. "This is about me and what I want for my future. We don't want the same things."

"Playing in that grungy coffee house wasn't safe—"

"Yes, it was. But it wasn't really the location, was it? You were—" Bree stopped.

He stepped closer. "Suppose you tell me what I was?"

He was a host of things she shouldn't put up with. He'd tried to dictate what she did or didn't do. She'd been perfectly safe in that coffee house, but Philip didn't like that she went somewhere he didn't want to go. Nor did he like the young composer she'd tried to help develop.

She shook her head. He'd never listened before. Why would he now? "I'm not going there. What matters is that I don't want you in my life."

There. She'd finally said it without flinching.

The steely look in Philip's eyes showed he struggled with hearing her, struggled to rein in his temper. One more reason she regretted a relationship with him. His fuse was much too short.

She made a move to step past him, but Philip blocked her path. Bree swallowed hard. "We're done."

"I don't think we are." His voice was softer than usual. He sounded perfectly calm, almost as if he joked with her, but there was an edge she'd never heard before.

One look in his eyes and Bree shivered. She stepped back.

Philip laughed, spreading his arms wide in surrender. "You're so touchy."

Bree searched his face, but the odd fury was gone. She didn't wait for it to come back and slipped past him. Her fingers shook when she bent to cut the spear of asparagus she'd nearly stepped on. Settling the wild veggie in her basket, she moved closer to her mother.

"Here, you take these." She dumped her basket into her mother's. "I'll go get more."

"There's enough for dinner tonight. I invited Philip to stay with us." Her mom stepped forward to pick another green spear.

"Not a good idea, Mom."

"Why not?"

Bree briefly closed her eyes. They needed to have a talk, but not here. No way could she let Philip stay for dinner or anything else. She'd planned to leave early in the morning and didn't want Philip following her. Didn't want Philip staying behind when her father wasn't up north yet, either. "Trust me on this."

"It'll be fine." Her mother limped away to slice another spear. Her mom did pretty well with her cane. She'd be even stronger by next week's class.

"You okay?" Darren whispered.

Bree jumped. "Fine."

She watched Philip hold the basket for her mother while she bent and sliced the tender stalks of green. Bree needed to make him leave. She'd ride back to town with him. With her mom there, she'd spell it all out if she had to. Whatever it took.

"You sure?" Darren's voice sounded harsh. He looked like a bull ready to charge if she said the word.

The last thing Bree wanted was a scene. She laid her hand on his arm. "Please. It's fine."

But it wasn't. Bree had never felt this rattled

before. Maybe she'd imagined that dark look in Philip's eyes. But what if she hadn't?

Something didn't feel right. Darren wasn't sure if it was his jealousy kicking in or if Philip might be a wolf in sheep's clothing. Very expensive clothing. He'd be all over the guy if needed, but Bree had said she was fine. Philip stayed near Joan, away from Bree.

"Aren't you going to do something about that?" Stella poked him with her elbow.

"About what?" Darren sliced an asparagus stalk.

"Philip," Stella whispered through her teeth. "He's moving out there."

Darren couldn't keep a guy from relocating. "I heard."

Stella stared him down.

"What?"

"You're better for Bree."

"Thanks for your vote, but that's up to her, now, isn't it?"

Stella poked him again. "So? Go out there and see her."

"Seattle's not exactly across the pond."

Stella shook her head. "Youth is wasted on the young."

"What's that supposed to mean, anyway?"

"It means you're seeing only obstacles and not

possibilities. Don't lose her to distance, Darren. She cares for you."

"Hmm." There was no right reply to such a comment.

He knew that Bree didn't want to care. She didn't want a relationship between them to get in the way of her plans. If she got back with Philip because he was willing to move near her, there wasn't much he could do about it. He wasn't getting into that position again. Losing out to golden boy success.

There wasn't much he could do to gain Joan's approval, either. Not when the woman wanted Bree and Philip back together. A family's opinion carried a lot of weight when it came to relationships. Mothers knew if a guy wasn't good enough for their daughters. Unless that mother didn't really know her own daughter.

He turned to Stella. "How well do you know this guy?"

Stella shrugged. "Well enough to know that I don't like him. Bree broke up with him once before but took him back."

"What happened?"

Stella shrugged. "I'm not sure. She never talked much about it."

He should stop digging and talk to Bree. Relationships were an odd place of discovery. Sometimes it took a while to realize why things didn't work. He checked his watch. Their class time was spent. "Okay, everyone, let's load up."

"'Bout time. My bag is near bursting." Ed made his usual grumbles. His plastic grocery bag was indeed packed full. Ed's thinning dark hair had been blown out of place by the wind, and holding that long field knife made him look like an old pirate. All Ed was missing was the black patch over one eye.

Darren laughed.

"What's so funny?" Ed didn't look amused.

"That's some knife." Darren slapped Ed on the back.

"My daughter gave it to me for Christmas." The old man sheathed it with a scowl.

"Good gift." He nodded and counted heads as they loaded into the van. Six, seven, eight, nine—Bree made ten, but she hesitated before climbing in.

"Joan's riding back with me in case I get turned around." Philip thumbed toward his Cadillac. He'd already started the slick coupe, no doubt to kick in the air conditioning.

"Hang on and I'll go with you." Bree handed Darren her basket. It overflowed with green spears and leggy stalks. "Can you take this for me? I'll see you back at the community room."

"No problem." He took the small basket, covered her hands and searched her face. "Everything okay?"

She wouldn't meet his eyes but gave his hand a quick squeeze. "See you in a few."

He watched her dart toward Philip's coupe.

Philip held the driver's seat forward for her to climb into the back while Joan tried opening the passenger door without success.

"It's locked." Joan tried it again. "Philip?"

"I'll get it in a minute." Philip's smooth voice sounded more like a shrill growl.

He'd only met the guy today, but that voice didn't sound right. Philip sounded nervous.

The hairs on his arms itched with a tingling sensation Darren knew all too well. He set Bree's basket down and walked toward the idling car. He was used to acting on hunches, but his mind raced for an excuse to get the women back in the van.

Before Darren took more than five steps, Philip had slipped behind the wheel and driven off without Joan.

Fast.

Dust kicked up from behind the car, which tore down the road, its back end fishtailing on the packed dirt.

"Philip!" Joan nearly fell as she quickly backed up.

Darren steadied her shoulders. "Get to the van."

She coughed but didn't move. "Why—"

"Now, Joan." Darren's instincts took over. He

could barely make out the license plate through the cloud of dust, but managed to memorize some of it and quickly jotted it down.

Joan stood gaping after the speeding car. "Why would he do that?"

Darren called Bree's cell and got voice mail. "Call me."

Something was definitely wrong. He wrapped his arm around Joan's shoulders and quickly led her back to the van. "What's Philip's last name?"

"Ah…let me think." She shook her head as if trying to clear it before climbing in. "I've known them for years, why can't I think… Johnson!" Joan's face paled. "Do you think he *took* her?"

"Maybe." Seemed pretty obvious after the way he'd left Joan. The woman could have been hurt.

Joan gasped, and her shoulders quivered with a sob ready to roll out. She looked like she was about to crumple into a heap but blathered on. "It's my fault for letting him come up. I thought if Bree saw him again, they could work things out."

He touched her arm. "Hang with me, Joan, okay? We'll figure this out." He sounded more confident than he felt. His instincts screamed that Philip had kidnapped Bree. His hand tightened around his cell. If he was wrong—

Deep down, he knew he wasn't.

Philip Johnson. Could the name be more common? Searching for such a common name to match what little he had of a plate number would be slow. He quickly texted Bree and waited a couple of seconds. Nothing. Not even a smiley face or question marks.

Nothing.

Darren's blood ran cold.

Stella popped down from inside the van and helped Joan into the passenger seat. "Buckle up, now. That's it."

He gave her a grateful nod with his phone to his ear.

"Let's go after him, Darren." Stella stood with hands on hips.

As if he could. He had no idea what direction Philip had gone. He'd waste time driving aimlessly and couldn't do that with a van full of civilians. If Philip had truly taken Bree against her will—and that fact hadn't firmly been established yet—Darren needed to tread with care. Philip struck him as the kind of guy who'd sue at the drop of a hat. He'd been awfully jumpy right before taking off. Was that when he planned this...

"What are we waiting for?"

"Yeah, let's go." Echoes of agreement came from the rest of them. Ed had even pulled out that knife.

"Put that thing away before someone gets hurt," Stella yelled as she climbed back into the van.

An argument ensued, and Darren raised his hand to quiet them as he made another phone call. "Stan? It's Darren. A situation might be developing, and I need to trade vehicles. Meet me in front of the Bayside General Store. I'm less than ten minutes away. Good."

Darren climbed behind the wheel and started the engine. "Buckle up and hang on. This is going to be a rough ride."

"Let's go get Bree," Connie called out.

More bluster from his elderly avengers.

In other circumstances, he might have laughed. Ideally, when this was over, he could have a good laugh with Bree. His gut twisted. He didn't have a good feeling about this, though, and his hunches were usually right.

Turning the van around on the narrow dirt road, Darren glanced at Bree's mom. She gripped her cane tight. So tight, her fingers looked white. "It's going to be okay."

Joan's eyes were wet, but she'd calmed down. Her face remained pale. "He won't hurt her. He's crazy about her."

Or plain crazy.

The occupants in the van quieted as reality hit. Bree was in danger. How serious the danger was yet to be determined. As he tore down the dirt road with the windows open, dust sifted in and choked off conversation.

He glanced at his phone lying in the console

next to him. *Come on, Bree. Give me something here. Are you okay?*

A few minutes later, Darren's phone buzzed to life with a text, and his heart stopped when he read it.

M ID V Rd. HEL

He grabbed his phone and called for backup. "Looking for a newish bright blue Cadillac coupe registered to a Philip Johnson last on Middle Village Road. Looks like an abduction."

He heard the sharp intake of Joan's breath.

That sound tore through him as he pulled into the parking lot of a little old general store in the middle of nowhere.

Darren was out of the van and heading for his fellow CO's truck in seconds. "Take these people back to Bay Willows. I'm going after Johnson."

Stan nodded and tossed him the keys.

Darren caught them and turned back to Joan. She looked so small and sick with worry in the passenger seat. "I'll find her. I'll bring Bree back."

Joan nodded, trying to be brave. It was then that he saw the resemblance Bree had to her mom. That willingness to stretch and conquer fear.

Fear for Bree's safety cut through him. He prayed that he'd find her quickly. And he prayed he'd find her safe.

* * *

"Philip! Slow down." Bree tried to climb into the front seat, but Philip pushed her back. She slammed hard against the leather seat. "What's wrong with you? Stop this car right now!"

He didn't say a word.

She looked out the back window. Already they were far away, speeding down the road. Through the cloud of dust, she spotted Darren with her mother leaning against him. She could have been hurt by Philip tearing away like he had. Tears stung the corners of her eyes.

Mom.

She heard her cell phone's muffled ringtone. It had to be Darren. She reached for her phone but came up empty. She searched the floor, the seat. Nothing. It must have fallen out of her pocket.

"Don't answer that," Philip growled.

Her phone kept ringing, making her frantic. "I can't even find it. Will you please stop the car?"

"Shut up!" His shrill voice slapped her ears.

She looked at his reflection in the rearview mirror. Philip had a wild look in his eyes that she didn't like. Didn't trust, either. She quickly scanned the floor, felt under the front seats. Nothing. "Where are we going?"

"Someplace to talk."

"There's nothing more to say—" Her phone buzzed with an incoming text. Where was it?

"You wouldn't return my calls or my texts. I had to come up here so you'd see."

"See what?" Bree felt along the crease in the backseat. Her fingers connected with the plastic rhinestone-encrusted case. Slowly she pulled it out, keeping it low so Philip wouldn't see.

Darren had texted her.

"That we belong together. We always have."

No, they didn't. Bree knew the moment he'd freaked over her application to the music residency that she needed to get out of their relationship once and for all. Philip had gone on a rant, saying he wouldn't allow it.

At the time, she'd nearly laughed because he'd acted like her nephew during one of his temper tantrums. She'd thought Philip couldn't have been serious. Like an idiot, Bree had believed his excuse of stress for the bizarre behavior. Right now he was acting the same way. Oh, why hadn't she told her parents then?

Quieting her voice, she tried again. "Stop the car, let me get in the front seat and then we can talk."

"No."

Bree searched the vast fields and wooded hills beyond. Where were they? They'd driven onto pavement, and Philip floored it. There were no street signs that she could see. She hit Reply, focusing on where they might be so she could tell

Darren as soon as she knew something. Anything.

"I'll do the thinking for both us. You just stay quiet back there," Philip barked.

Bree racked her brain. Glancing around the car's interior, she knew she had to find a way to escape and fast. They came to an intersection, and Bree peered out the side window. She spotted a green road sign. Elated, she typed the street name into her phone while keeping it low, out of Philip's sight. She hit Send, hoping it made sense.

"Give me that." Philip reached for her phone.

She wrestled away from him. "Stop it."

The car jerked sideways, nearly going off the road as Philip grabbed her hair and pulled hard.

"Ow!" She dropped her phone to grab his hand.

He pushed her back again. Harder this time. "Don't make me hurt you."

The tone of his voice stopped her cold. Would he really *hurt* her? Up until this point, she hadn't thought him capable. She'd known him for years. Surely he wouldn't…

She glanced at him again in the rearview mirror.

Philip stared back. He didn't look right. "Don't think I won't."

"Why?" It came out a raw whisper. "Why are you doing this?"

His feverish gaze shifted to the road ahead of them. "I saw how that guy looked at you."

Darren.

"We're friends, Philip. That's all." Bree appealed to his common sense, but this wasn't a jealous fit. Philip had been jealous of the young composer. Philip had been many things, but never crazy.

This was crazy.

Bree closed her eyes and prayed. *Dear Lord, please get me out of this. Please help Darren find me.*

Philip took a turn. According to the dashboard, they headed north. "I won't let him have you."

"Where are we going?" she croaked.

"You'll see."

She searched the floor for her phone. It lay under the passenger seat. Reaching for it, she dialed 911.

Philip's hand swooped down and grabbed it. She pulled at his arm, but he jerked away, pressed the button to open his window and threw it out.

"No!" Bree turned and watched it bounce once, twice, three times before it lay along the narrow, sandy shoulder of the road. Her only connection to Darren now gone.

Her stomach twisted. She mopped the sweat that beaded along her hairline with shaky fingers. *Find me, Darren. Please find me.*

The window remained open and the warm air whipped in, beating up her now throbbing head and tossing her hair in all directions. She had to think.

Think!

They were miles from town but no longer in the desolate area they'd come from. Though sparse, there were houses on this road. Even a couple of farms. The surroundings looked familiar, too. She'd been on this road before. Last week on the way to the Zelinsky home, she'd followed the van.

Her pulse picked up speed.

She had to do something fast before Philip pulled off somewhere. Before he made good on his threat to hurt her. Somehow she had to get out of this car.

Bree stared at the road ahead. There was a sharp turn somewhere on this road that Darren had warned her about. She remembered slowing down... Had they already passed it? No. She spotted a big old farmhouse up ahead, and her memory sharpened into focused clarity. That curve was coming up soon.

She buckled into the backseat belt and loosened it. She'd need some give in order to make this work. Biting her lip till it bled, she leaned forward enough to see how fast Philip drove. She couldn't see over his shoulder, but she could reach down to the button that controlled the position of his seat.

"You have to slow down," she yelled.

"Not till we're there."

"But there's a curve up ahead, and you won't make it if you keep driving this fast."

He let up a little, but not much, and slightly turned his head. "Don't mess with me."

"I'm not." She clicked the lever to move the seat forward.

Philip swore and slammed on the brakes. "What are you doing?"

She kept pushing that seat forward even as Philip tried to bat her hand away. The car swerved and he overcompensated, sending the car out of control.

They flew off the road, and it felt like they went airborne, floating for a second or two. But it was enough time to let go.

Bree grasped her knees, tucking herself into an airline crash position she'd seen in movies.

They hit hard. Her head slammed into the back of Philip's seat before she was thrown hard against her own.

Through the haze of Philip's curses, she heard grass and clumps of dirt whipping against the bottom of the car as they continued too fast through the field. The deafening sound made her head spin.

Then they stopped with a jarring crunch of

metal, a shuddering thud that made her teeth chatter as she flew forward once again. The seat belt bit into her belly, making her heave. Her forehead hit the corner of the driver's seat and she saw stars.

In that flash of sparkling darkness, the last thing Bree heard was the poof of a deployed airbag and Philip's pained groan.

Chapter Thirteen

Darren drove east on Middle Village Road. No sign of Philip's Cadillac. Not that he expected to see it. Darren was a good fifteen minutes behind them. Too much could happen in fifteen minutes.

What if he hurts her?

Darren pulled over. Scanning the open fields and tree line beyond, he pushed those what-ifs out of his head before he lost it. He focused on entering Bree's cell phone number into the laptop and waited for the tracking program to locate it. He'd find them. No matter what, he'd find them.

State Road. He called in that they'd headed north and he was in pursuit.

He prayed again for Bree's safety.

As for Philip's…he wanted to rip that guy apart.

Taking off fast, Darren heard his tires squeal on pavement. He glanced at the screen, but Bree's cell still showed the same location. He made the turn onto State and drove a mile or so, but no vehicles were in sight. He caught a flash of something shiny on the side of the road and pulled over once again.

It was Bree's phone on the ground. He picked up the sparkly case and bounced it against the palm of his hand. He had nothing to go on now. He kicked the truck's tire before climbing back in.

Chatter over the wire confirmed two units were heading north as well. The state police and the county sheriff's department were involved. His gut clenched when he heard the announcement that Philip's Cadillac had been reported in a crash with airbags deployed by the vehicle's security system.

Cold fear clamped down hard as he heard the location. He knew exactly where they'd gone off the road. He got on the wire and announced he was only minutes south and on his way.

His hands gripped the steering wheel until they hurt. He knew the sharp curve on that road. His thoughts raced faster than his driving. What would he find?

God, please keep her safe.

When he finally pulled off the road before that deadly curve, what he saw made him believe God had answered his prayer. The Cadillac was upright and slammed head-on into a small tree. The front end was crumpled in, but the windshield remained intact. It was amazing that the coupe hadn't flipped and rolled.

He heard sirens in the distance as he ran toward the vehicle, still idling with a chug, chug and clanging sound. Steam poured out from under the hood. He reached into the open driver's side window and pushed Philip back against the seat. He looked dazed, mumbling.

"Where is she?" Darren scanned the interior of the coupe. No Bree.

"Can't have her." Philip's nose was swollen and red. Darren hoped it was broken.

He grabbed the guy's shirt collar. "Where's Bree?"

"I don't know."

Darren let go and Philip slumped over. He turned off the engine and reached for the trunk release. Hearing it pop, he went behind the car and searched. The only thing in there was a fancy duffel bag. Darren didn't bother opening it.

Slamming the trunk, he turned around and scanned the horizon, finally spotting her in a field.

Bree ran, tripped and fell. She got up again and ran some more toward a house set way back from the road. Smart girl. She was going for help. And too far away to hear him if he yelled.

Darren ran back to his truck, jumped in and drove off the road into the field with teeth-rattling speed, beeping the horn as he went. The truck bounced over ruts, but he didn't let up on the gas.

Bree stopped running. She looked straight at him and crumpled to the ground.

Darren slammed the truck into Park and got out at a run. His throat closed up tight, making it difficult to speak. He knelt down and gathered Bree into his arms, whispering, "It's over."

Bree hung on tight, sobbing.

He stroked her hair, pulling out bits of dried grass, and kissed her forehead. A lump had formed there. She needed medical attention; they were no doubt on the way, signaled by the deployed airbags. He cradled her close, breathing in her scent. She smelled like the outdoors, like spring air and sunshine. His Bree. "I've got you. I've got you..."

"I knew you'd find me," she choked out. "I prayed that you would."

He held her tighter, trying to ease the trembling that wracked her delicate frame. Hoping to cease his own shaking. He'd never felt so helpless before. He could have lost her. She could have been killed if that car—

Darren refused to think about that now. He pulled back and searched her face and body. Other than the goose-egg on her forehead, scratches on her arms and legs and a puffy dark mark on her shin that had the makings of an ugly bruise, she looked whole.

He brushed hair away from her lips. "Where else are you hurt?"

She shook her head. "Just sore, nothing serious."

"What happened?"

"I couldn't talk sense into Philip. He was crazy and wouldn't stop the car. I remembered this road from when we went to your parents' house, so I waited for the curve. Then I messed with his seat trying to distract him enough to slow down, get him to stop—" Her bottom lip trembled.

He brushed his lips over hers, featherlight in case even that hurt. Kissing her was killing him right along with thoughts of how badly that crash could have ended.

When she deepened the kiss with the same desperation, he pulled her even closer. Grateful for this brave girl, his heart broke with every breath and every murmur.

The sirens sounded closer. He opened his eyes and spotted the flashing lights from the police and emergency responders drawing near, pulling off the road.

He cupped her face. "We've got to go."

"No." Bree didn't move. Her brow furrowed and she gripped his forearms.

He gently pulled her up with him. "I'm right here. I won't leave you."

She clung to his hand until she climbed into the truck.

He offered her phone. "The police will want to see this, but you should call your mom. Let her know you're okay."

She nodded. Her face streaked with dried tears, she hit a couple of buttons and connected. "Mom?" Her voice wavered. "No. I'm okay. Darren found me. I'm with him now. The police are here, too."

He reached for her hand and felt her tremble again.

Her eyes filled with new tears that ran down her cheeks. "No. No. Philip didn't hurt me."

He could have.

Darren felt sick with relief. This could have been worse. Much worse. The urge to rip that guy apart washed over him anew. He grasped the steering wheel with both hands, squeezing tight. Would Bree press charges? Maybe she wouldn't have to.

He could arrest the guy, but knew he shouldn't. He couldn't be objective and didn't want his feelings for Bree to come back and bite him. He'd give the police a statement and let them handle it. They'd have enough to haul Philip to jail.

Bree sat on a gurney in the back of the ambulance while a paramedic examined her. Through the open doors, she watched as Philip was questioned by police and then taken into custody.

She clutched the edge of that gurney hard, fighting wooziness.

She'd gotten him arrested.

Bree blew out her breath. No, that wasn't right. Philip had made his own choices by coming here. He'd taken hers away by not letting her go. Her heart pounded hard, like when she woke from a bad dream. Her head hurt and her muscles were sore. She wanted to go, get away from all of this. Now.

Darren spoke with another state trooper and gave her a hint of a smile. The same smile he'd given her when they'd eaten s'mores in front of a crackling fire in his home. The image beckoned her to return there, safe and sound. But that wasn't home. It couldn't be.

The paramedics quit prodding and poking, satisfied that she had nothing worse than a mild concussion. Nothing a good amount of rest wouldn't cure. They'd nixed her idea of leaving for Seattle in the morning, stating she was in no condition to drive cross-country.

"Can I please go now?"

"In a minute." The state trooper who'd been talking to Darren stood before her. "I need to ask you a few questions."

Her gaze flew to Darren's.

He slipped next to her, grabbed her hand and squeezed. "Just tell him what happened."

Bree swallowed hard against nausea and re-told the story.

The whole time, she thought about Philip's parents and how they'd react when they heard the news that their son had been arrested. Because of her. Would their business suffer? Would anyone back home find out? Would they care?

Would their parents remain friends? Doubtful. Her stomach pitched. It'd be easier on everyone if she let this incident go, but she'd let too much go unnoticed for too long.

"He didn't hurt me." The memory of Philip pulling her hair flashed through her mind. If they hadn't crashed, would he have really hurt her?

She closed her eyes, searching for direction. What was the right thing to do here?

"You gave your consent to go with him. Is that right?" the trooper clarified.

She opened her eyes. "Yes. I didn't want my mother to ride alone with him."

"And why was that?" He jotted down notes.

Bree looked at Darren.

He gave her an encouraging nod, but his expression was closed. He was leaving it up to her how much to tell or not tell. He gave her the power instead of taking over and talking for her.

Time to be heard. She took a deep breath. "He's been harassing me ever since we broke up with constant texts and calls…"

Bree explained everything she knew. Philip

showing up to tell her about his plans to relocate, the creepy feeling she got when he wouldn't let her pass by him earlier and even how Philip had been jealous of Darren. She also gave permission to check her cell phone records.

The state trooper didn't look a bit shocked.

It all felt foreign to Bree as she explained how Philip had tried to mold her into what *he* wanted while they'd dated. Subtly at first, until he wouldn't let her be who she was. He fought against her dreams and ambitions, but he'd never been crazy like this.

She'd tried breaking things off with him once before, but his pleas to get back together had been persuasive. Their families had been, too. Feeling trapped, the music residency had come at a perfect time, when she'd needed a clean break with distance.

"Anything else you can add?"

Bree gripped Darren's hand tighter. "That's pretty much everything."

The trooper snapped shut his notebook. "We'll contact you if we need anything else."

"I'm still leaving for Seattle in a couple of days." Bree could hardly wait to get away and put this far behind her.

"Noted. We have your number."

"Thank you." Bree followed Darren to the big black DNR truck.

He held the door open for her. "Isn't that a little early to leave?"

She climbed into the passenger seat. "Nope. I want out of here."

The ride back to Maple Springs was a quiet one. She glanced at Darren and the hard set of his jaw and wanted to cry. The truck's console equipped with a laptop and radio stood between them, but soon they'd have half a country separating them. She'd miss him. Surely, he'd miss her too. Wouldn't he?

Almost to Maple Springs, Darren pulled off into an elementary school parking lot on the edge of town, cut the engine and turned in his seat.

Her stomach dipped and rolled.

He searched her face. "Thank you for helping out with the wild edibles class."

Bree's eyes burned. "You're welcome."

He looped her hair behind her ear. "I mean it, Bree. You've helped me face a few things about myself. The way I view people. The way I view you."

She swallowed hard as tears ran down her cheeks. This sounded a lot like a goodbye speech.

"You'll be surrounded by your family, and that's good. You need them now. Give yourself some time to get through this before leaving. You did the right thing today by telling the police what's been going on. You're a brave woman, Bree."

"It didn't feel right or good," she whispered. It was all she could manage around the tightness of her throat.

"I know. I'm proud of how you handled yourself. Using your head may have saved your life."

Her chin shook and then her shoulders.

"Aww, Bree, please don't cry."

She covered her face with her hands. "I'm sorry."

Darren got out of the truck, walked around and opened her door. "Come on, sweet. Don't do this."

She sobbed harder when he lifted her into his arms and shifted into the passenger seat. He settled her onto his lap, cradling her close. "It's going to be okay."

It didn't feel okay.

What if she had to testify? Philip would make bail, and then what if he came after her again? She leaned into Darren's broad chest, spent. "I want to go."

Darren kissed her temple. "I don't want you to. Stay here. Stay with me."

Her heart pinched with temptation to accept. He was safe and strong. But she couldn't spend every day glued to his side. She pulled back and searched his face. "I can't."

"Yes, you can."

She closed her eyes. "Please don't."

"We have something here. Why let that go?"

Kate had said that if their feelings were real, they'd keep. But could they really keep for two years? Everything had an expiration date if left unattended for too long. Visiting only a couple of times in between might spoil an otherwise decent friendship. Unless…

Bree threw down the gauntlet. "Come with me. They must have conservation officers out there, too."

Darren's face fell.

In that one look, Bree knew he wouldn't. He couldn't. Neither of them wanted to risk their dreams on an untried relationship. Darren loved this area too much to leave it. He wanted the supervisor position that would only entrench him further in this county. His home. She'd known that from the start. She didn't blame him. In fact, she understood. Perfectly.

"Now you know how I feel," she whispered.

He nodded, looking exhausted. "Yeah. I do, and I'm sorry."

"Me, too."

The thing about vacations was knowing when they were over.

Darren pulled into the drive in front of the Anderson cottage. He wouldn't linger. Bree needed to be with her family right now. With Joan. A place he didn't belong.

Bree opened the door but didn't get out. "Come in with me?"

"I'd better not."

"Please."

She'd been through a lot today, and yet he'd pressed her to stay in Michigan. As much as it hurt to hear her refuse him, he was proud of her resolve. Proud of her commitment. It was something he understood.

He spotted Joan standing under the porch light with her cane in hand. "But your mom—"

"Will want to thank you. I'm not getting out until you do." Bree lifted her chin.

He blew out his breath and rubbed the back of his neck before climbing out of the truck. He met Bree on the sidewalk. "Only for a minute."

She grabbed his hand.

He threaded his fingers through hers and squeezed. When they stepped up on the porch, he could tell that Joan had been crying. Her eyes looked puffy and her face was red. Despite her uppity ways, she didn't deserve the frantic worry she'd been put through. He couldn't imagine the guilt she must feel knowing she'd been so wrong about the golden boy.

Bree ran into her mother's arms.

"Your father's on his way." Mother clung to daughter. "Your sister, too. She wants to drive with you to Seattle, and I won't let you refuse."

Bree nodded.

Darren shifted his stance. He was glad Bree wouldn't be alone on that long trek. Very glad. But it was time to go. Time to let her go, too. He stepped back.

Joan glanced at him as if she'd forgotten he was there. She extended her hand. "Thank you, Darren. Thank you for bringing her home safe and sound."

Darren cleared his throat as he gripped her hand, shocked when she pulled him toward their embrace. He gave both women a brief hug. "Your daughter never lost her cool, and that made a huge difference."

"I knew you'd find me," Bree added.

"Darren, please come in." Joan kept her arm around Bree's shoulders.

"I've got to go. This truck belongs to another CO." He didn't belong here. He couldn't rehash this afternoon with two women in tears. Besides, he and Bree had said everything that needed saying. The longer he hung around, the harder it would be not to beg. He wanted Bree to stay but understood why she couldn't.

Joan nodded. "Come this weekend, then. The whole family will be here to give Bree a proper send-off."

Bree looked at him but didn't press.

"I'll think about it." Darren's skin itched thinking about it. This was Bree's world, not his.

"We'd be honored." Joan gave him an encouraging smile that softened her face, erasing the pinched look he'd often seen before. That disapproving look was gone, too.

"Mom, go on inside. I'll be there in a minute." Bree practically pushed her mother into the house before turning back to him.

He backed up, taking a step down off the porch. It brought him eye to eye with Bree. He wanted to touch her but kept his hands at his sides.

"Thank you," Bree whispered. Her pretty eyes were puffy and red-rimmed. "For everything."

His throat felt tight. "You're welcome."

She cupped his face and kissed him hard.

He kissed her back, clenching his hands into fists to keep from drawing her too close. Too close to ever let go. Darren had to let her go. This was goodbye.

Bree pulled back and rested her hands on his shoulders. "Text me? I want to know how you do with that promotion."

"Okay, sure." He backed down another step.

Bree gave him a watery smile and then went inside.

Through the windows, he saw Joan wrap her into another hug. Darren walked away with a heavy heart.

Two years was a long time. Too long.

Memorial Day, Darren found himself paired with his father in a game of horseshoes. A family tradition, but Darren's head wasn't in the game. Neither was his heart. He'd received a text from Bree that morning. She and her sister had made it to Seattle. She was settling into the dorm-like studio apartment that came with her residency and already loved the area.

She might as well have tied him to a block of cement and thrown him overboard. The tone of that text made it pretty clear that Bree wasn't coming back. He'd known from the start that she'd leave. So why'd he allow his feelings to grow into something that felt a lot like love? It sure stung like love.

Love beareth all things, believeth all things, hopeth all things, endureth all things.

He'd heard that as part of the message the previous morning. He'd attended the church where his brothers Zach and Matthew went. A community church with little of the traditional pomp he was used to. He'd listened, though. Listened hard.

God, what are You trying to tell me?

His father slapped him on the back. "Your turn."

"Huh? Oh. Yeah." Darren took the shoe and threw. It clanged against the cast-iron pin and then took a roll off to the side, landing in deep grass outside the lane of play.

"That's a horrible throw," Monica jeered.

Darren shrugged.

"Okay, who died?" Monica asked.

Cam pushed at her shoulder. "Give it a rest."

Monica pushed him back. "Give what a rest? I'm just asking."

Darren held the other shoe. "You two done?"

"If you don't land a ringer, you and Dad lose," Monica said. "And that'll make me and Erin the winners."

"Under duress. Darren's not in usual form," Cam said.

Monica grinned. "Still counts."

"Yeah, still counts." Erin looked at him with concern in her eyes. Big brown puppy eyes, he used to tease her. "You okay?"

Darren paused from throwing. "I'll live."

Erin shrugged. "I don't know. You seem really sad."

He chuckled. "I'll get over it."

"But will you get over her?" Cam asked.

That was the question. One he'd asked himself about a hundred times since dropping Bree off at her parents' cottage less than a week ago. His whole family knew Bree had left. They knew about her scare with Philip, too. The abduction had hit the local news. It was no wonder Bree had skipped out early, missing her family picnic.

Maybe they hadn't had one. He'd talked to Stella, and she hadn't said anything about the Andersons having a get-together. Maybe he'd swing by and check on her later in the week.

Darren prepared to throw but his sister's voice intruded, knocking off his concentration once again.

"How's that poem go?" Erin mumbled a few lines. "Wait, I got it. If you love something, let it go. If it comes back to you, it's yours forever. If it doesn't, then it was never meant to be."

Cam groaned.

Darren did, too. "That's corny."

Erin smiled. "Don't you think she'll come back, even for a visit?"

Bree's family summered here. That didn't mean she'd want to come back for him. She'd texted him, though, and he hadn't yet replied.

"Your turn, son," his father reminded him.

Darren stalled as that simple command echoed through his soul. Maybe it was his turn to prove he was worthy to be loved. He needed to let go of past hurts and failures and be the man he needed to be. Supporting Bree, instead of trying to change her mind. Her dreams. He needed to text her back. Go visit her, even.

Their father shook his head. "Will you throw that shoe so we can go eat?"

Darren launched the cast-iron horseshoe. It arced high and landed with a metal-whirling-around-metal sound. Everyone hooted and hollered, but not Monica or Erin. They both groaned when he scored the win with a ringer.

Darren turned to his baby sister. "Looks like the win was never yours to keep."

"Ha, ha." Erin rolled her eyes.

As they made their way to the house, Darren turned that hokey little poem over in his head. He'd let Bree go, alright. But then, she needed to fly on her own before she'd ever be happy being his.

His grandmother had called dating "courtship." He'd had only a temporary courtship with Bree. Neither were ready for anything permanent. At least not yet. Both of them had work to do.

The scripture he'd heard rolled through his thoughts once again. Maybe it was time to trust that God would bring them together when the timing was right.

Chapter Fourteen

A month later

Darren entered the courtroom for Philip's preliminary examination. The idiot had stuck with his not guilty plea, so here they were, wasting time figuring out if this would go to trial. Darren hoped to spare Bree and her mom from that. He was an eyewitness for the prosecution. Surely his testimony would be enough for probable cause and seal the false imprisonment charges. If the defense was smart, they'd settle for a plea bargain.

Stepping toward the front, Darren spotted long mink-colored hair and froze. Bree was here. He hadn't expected to see her at this stage of the game. She hadn't said anything about it, but then they hadn't spoken or even texted in the last couple of weeks. Finally losing touch after only a month apart.

Darren had been promoted into the supervisor position he'd applied for. His boss had said that he'd received several recommendations from folks in Bay Willows. Darren finally had everything he'd wanted, but one thing remained out of touch. Across country.

He slipped quietly into the bench seat behind her and her family. The wood creaked when he sat down, announcing his presence.

Joan turned and gave him a warm smile.

He nodded.

His cell phone vibrated with an incoming text. It came from Bree.

Talk later?

His heart lodged somewhere in his throat. He texted back.

Sure.

The hearing started, and sure enough, Bree was called to testify right after the arresting officer. Taking the stand, she didn't look at him. Darren wished that she would, for moral support at the very least, but not once did her gaze connect with his.

He couldn't look away. She seemed more confident than he remembered. She answered the questions with poise but not indifference. Recalling the events affected her, but she didn't cry. She didn't waver, either, staring Philip down until he looked away. That sent a message of its own. One Darren hoped hadn't escaped the eyes of the judge.

When the defense attorney cross-examined Bree, Darren gripped the edge of his seat until he thought his fingers might break. The urge to rip Philip and his fancy attorney apart surged hot through his veins, but Darren stayed quiet.

When Bree finally stepped down, she held her head high but still didn't look his way. Incredible since he sat right behind her. She avoided him but wanted to talk later. What did that mean?

His gut clenched. Had she found someone else?

He ran a hand through his hair. Feeling fidgety, Darren wiped his palms against his thighs, waiting for Philip to take the stand, but both attorneys approached the judge instead.

The three spoke too softly to hear, but Darren knew Philip was doomed. That guy couldn't defend himself, not against what Bree had told the court. The golden boy was guilty and rightfully tarnished.

Silence settled over the too warm courtroom, and Darren shifted. His empty gun holster tapped against the back of the bench with a resounding thwack that seemed to echo through the chamber.

Philip turned and glared at him.

Darren stared back.

The guy didn't look sorry. If anything, Philip seemed even more arrogant, finally looking away when his attorney returned to his side.

And then it was over. The defense accepted a misdemeanor plea. The judge sentenced Philip to twelve months of probation, anger management classes, a fine and orders to stay away from Bree. No contact whatsoever. No jail time, either, but considering this was Philip's first offense, Darren hadn't expected more.

While Bree and her family shook the prosecutor's hand, Darren made for the doors. He'd wait for them in the hallway.

He didn't have to wait long.

"Darren, how are you?" Bree's mom was the first to greet him with a warm hug. "This is my husband, Ron. Bree's father."

"I'm fine, Mrs. Anderson. Mr. Anderson." Darren offered his hand to Bree's father. "And how are you both?"

"Glad this is over. Why don't you come by the cottage later for dinner?"

Darren glanced at Bree.

"Please say you'll come?" Her smile flashed those dimples he'd missed.

He missed her, and without even thinking, he agreed. "Okay, sure."

"We'll see you at home," Joan said with a wave.

Bree's parents left, and she looked a little nervous. "There goes my ride."

Darren chuckled. They were the next town over. A little far for Bree to walk home. "Seriously?"

"Yes, seriously." Her dimples flashed deeper as she took in his sergeant badge. "How's your new job?"

"Good. I got several recommendations after that day. One from your mom. Did you know that?"

"Yes. She thinks you're very sharp." She looked up into his eyes. "Can we walk?"

Darren hesitated. Would this be good or bad?

Bree looked worried. "I mean, if you have time. You're on duty."

"I have time." He'd make time. All the time he could with her.

He held open the door for her, and they walked outside into the warm sunshine of late June. The sidewalks swarmed with tourists. With the Fourth of July falling on the upcoming weekend, this week and next would be the busiest of the season with the arrival of so many vacationers. He'd already had an active few days working with his COs on the bay, making sure boaters stayed sober and safe.

"You look impressive in that tie, by the way. Do you have to wear one now?"

"No. It's my dress uniform. I'm supposed to

wear it every time I go to court. I'm surprised I wasn't asked to testify."

Bree glanced at him, and her golden eyes reflected the sun. "I didn't want you to. Not if it wasn't needed. That's why I'm here instead of a written statement. I didn't want this to go to trial."

He stopped walking and faced her. "Why didn't you call me?"

Bree groaned. "I wanted to. But I was asked not to talk about the case. I knew if I called—texted, even—you might call back, and then I'd tell you everything. I was so scared that our relationship might get dragged into all this and hurt your new position. I didn't want your reputation questioned because you got involved with me while on duty."

He looped the ends of her hair around his fingers. "You didn't have to protect me. We've got nothing to hide or be sorry for. As my grandmother used to say, we were only courting."

"Is that so?" Bree laughed and ran her finger down the length of his tie. "And now what are we doing?"

He stilled her hand by covering it with his own. "That's up to you."

She looked up. "I miss you."

"I miss you, more than I thought possible." He pulled her to him.

"Oh, Darren, what are we going to do?"

Holding her close, he buried his face in her hair. She smelled like wildflowers and sunshine. A scent he couldn't seem to forget. He brushed his lips against her neck and smiled when he felt her tremble. "We'll figure it out."

"I'm here for the week."

He kissed her hard and quick. One week. Enough time and not nearly enough time to work toward making that temporary courtship more permanent.

Chapter Fifteen

A year later

Are you at home?

Bree texted Darren and waited. He knew she was flying in for the Fourth of July. It was her vacation, and she'd planned to come home.

Home.

Ever since she'd left for Seattle, Bree had considered Maple Springs home. It's where Darren was, and he'd become her safe place—the place where she felt the most like herself. He'd helped her become the person she longed to be. Confident and maybe even a little fearless.

Darren's presence in court had given her courage. She hadn't looked at him for fear he'd see right through her brave facade. Despite her attempt to protect both families from a trial, the Johnsons had severed their relationship with her parents that day, right before Philip's preliminary exam had started. They blamed her for everything. In the past, such an incident would have made her crumble, but she stood firm and faced them all. And justice was served.

Darren was what she wanted, and now—

She grinned and texted again.

Where are you?

Her phone whistled with an incoming message. Finally.

Give a guy a chance to respond. I'm home. Where are you?

On my way.

Bree pocketed her phone and pulled out of her parents' driveway in her mom's car. She could hardly wait to share her news. Big news, too. She hadn't seen Darren since he visited her in March. He'd come out to see her at Christmastime, too, since the symphony schedule over the holidays was crammed with concerts and she couldn't get away.

She'd had the best Christmas ever. Spent with Darren. They'd picked out a tree together and decorated it with strung cranberries and popcorn. During the in-betweens, they'd video-chatted and burned up each other's cell phone batteries. She hadn't been home since last summer. And it felt like coming home to the place she belonged. For good.

Once out of town, Bree pressed the gas pedal, eager to tell Darren so many things.

Darren looked at his two beagles sharing a big dog bed. They'd watched him buzz around his house, making sure everything was picked up and clean.

Mickey thumped his tail.

"You'll be happy to know that Bree is coming over." He'd expected her to call from the airport so he could pick her up. Evidently her parents had done that. And that was okay, he supposed.

He looked forward to telling her his news. It was big news, especially for him. He heard a knock on his door and his dogs ran toward it, barking. Pulse pounding, he followed.

Bree stood on the porch. She'd cut her rich brown hair; it hung loose and tempting at her shoulders. She'd let her bangs grow out, too, and with them pushed to the side, she looked prettier than ever. Especially wearing a sundress that hugged her slender form.

Mickey and Clara yipped with excitement.

He stared. "Wow, you look great."

"You, too." She smiled, flashing those dimples he loved. "Can I come in?"

"Of course." He laughed and backed up. "Sorry."

His dogs whined and begged for attention at her sandal-clad feet. They'd missed her, too.

Bree gave them each pats.

Darren shooed them away and pulled Bree into a hug. "I missed you."

"You have no idea how much I missed you." Bree clung to him. "And I have something to tell you."

"I have news for you, too." He kissed her, quick and hard.

Bree laughed when they broke apart. The dogs circled them both, tails wagging and yipping for attention. Their turn. She knelt down and gave each dog a hug. "Is this what you want?"

Darren ordered the dogs to their bed. They scampered to obey his master tone. He got first dibs on Bree's attention. "Come in and tell me."

She followed him to the kitchen. "Maybe you should go first."

"Want something to drink?" Darren opened the fridge and pulled out a can of pop.

Bree leaned against the counter, glowing with excitement. She waved away the can. "Later. Tell me your news."

Darren took a deep breath. He'd waited till now to tell her. "I've been interviewing with the Washington Department of Fish and Wildlife. I have a job out there."

Bree openly stared at him, and then her eyes filled with tears. "When did you interview?"

"Christmastime. I met with their captain when I was out there. I've video-conferenced a few times since."

She blinked. "But you said you'd never move."

"Things change." He smiled. *He'd* changed.

Bree still looked like she couldn't believe what he'd done. He didn't know if that was good or bad. "But what about your supervisor position here? The one you'd wanted for so long."

"I talked to my boss. I may be able to return. They can't guarantee my same position or location, but I have good internal references. I figured we'd know after a year or so where we want to be. When you finish your residency."

"Oh, Darren." Bree launched herself into him and hung on. "I don't know what to say. You'd move for me?"

He hugged her close. He'd learned that he'd move around the world and back if it meant they could be together. Forever. As much as he loved Northern Michigan, he loved her more. She'd become his home. His real home, and that's what mattered most. "Yes, Bree, I'd do that, because I love you."

"Oh, I love you, too." She pulled back and laughed. Tears streamed down her cheeks. "But you don't have to—"

Sure he did. It was time to take that next step

in their relationship. "I can't do this distance anymore. Nothing matters if I can't share it with you."

She put a finger against his lips. "I'm moving here."

He grabbed her hand. "But you haven't finished the residency." He couldn't let her give that up.

She only smiled broader, and her eyes shone with excitement. "I have finished. I went as far as I wanted to go. I learned a lot. More than I ever expected. I worked hard, but the longer I stayed, the more I knew I wanted to leave. I wanted to come home."

"What about your dream to hear the music you've created played?"

"Maybe the whole reason God gave me this opportunity was to prove that my desire for fame was misplaced and not the best use of my gifts. Hearing my piece—you know, the one I played in the sugar shack—hearing it played by the strings section in Seattle wasn't what I thought it would be. Nice, sure, but empty. There was no deep, lasting impact on anyone but me. I realized that instead of trying to prove my music worthy, I need to show others why theirs is worthy. Does that make any sense?"

Maybe. He rubbed the back of his neck. "So, you quit?"

She laughed. "Not right away, but after I got a call from Jan Nelson, I sure did."

"Who's she?"

"A Bay Willows board member who is behind the Bay Willows School of Music. It's not a music camp catering to the residents' kids like I'd originally thought. Jan has some great connections, and the board decided to give her free rein. The program will be geared toward college students who want intensive training in professional development with sessions ranging from a couple of weeks to three months of study. Right up my alley. You're looking at the first faculty artist hired."

Before Darren could join in her excitement, he had to know that he wasn't the reason she'd abandoned her dreams and left Seattle. He didn't want that forever between them. "What if I had moved out there before you got this call? Would you still have taken it?"

Bree bit her lip. "I would have wanted to, but knowing you'd given up everything you loved… I don't know. I would have talked to you first, you know, and found out what you wanted to do."

Good enough. Darren opened his arms wide. "Well, then, congratulations."

She jumped into his embrace. "I'm so excited. I mean, this is a ground-floor opportunity. It's something I can grow with and help mold. I'll travel some, work with planning and admissions, but the best part is that I get to live here with something really special to do."

"Instead of just vacationing."

She pulled back and looked him straight in the eyes. She glowed from the inside out. "You're my vacation, Darren. But I need to make it permanent, if you're willing to make it so."

He knew where this was going and grinned. "Yeah? What did you have in mind?"

"I should probably wait and let you get used to having me around all the time, but...well, sometimes a woman has to brave up and ask..."

He threaded his fingers through her hair. "Ask what?"

Bree tipped her head back. "Will you marry me?"

"Funny you should ask that. Wait here." He let go of her and headed down the hall, into his bedroom, for yet another surprise.

Bree paced the kitchen floor, waiting. What was taking him so long? They'd shared so much at Christmas, and yet Darren hadn't let on that he'd been working on a way for them to be together. He'd never once asked her to give up the residency, even when she'd complained about how hard it had been.

She heard his footsteps and whipped around. She knew what he'd gone to get, but seeing that small black velvet box in his hands caused her to tear up all over again.

"I'm not giving you this if you're going to cry," his deep voice teased. Gently, ever so gently.

"I'm just happy. Darren, I never dreamed I'd be this happy. I nearly settled—"

He hushed her with his fingers against her lips, like she'd done to him earlier. "We've both made mistakes, but God had better things in mind for us. He knew we'd be *us*."

Bree sniffed. "Yes, He knew. And I love *us*."

"Me, too." Darren opened the box to reveal a beautiful solitaire diamond engagement ring. "And so, to answer your question, yes, Bree. I will marry you."

She gasped at the ring's unique setting. Two white gold swirls cradled the diamond amid folds of more white gold. "Where did you find this?"

"A new jeweler in Maple Springs designs them. I took one look at it and thought of you."

"It's gorgeous." She held out her left hand for him to slip the ring on her third finger. It fit perfectly. "How'd you know my size?"

"Your mom told me."

Bree gave him a sharp look. "She knew about this before me?"

"Hey, you're the one who proposed. I was getting ready to, clearing it with your folks and all."

"Yeah, and you've gotten pretty chummy with

them from what I hear. Mom says you're over there a lot."

He shrugged. "Just making the rounds while checking on Stella."

No doubt fixing things too. Her mom had said that Darren had helped her father with a host of little projects. "Well, thank you."

"You're welcome."

Bree stared at the ring, a pledge of their love and commitment. He'd been planning this all along. Taking his time and getting it right. Getting to know her parents, too.

She recalled Darren's poetic descriptions of the area when they'd first met. This ring reminded her of that, only warm summer moonlight instead of winter blue. He had a way of not only seeing the beauty surrounding him but also protecting it. He was music in the making, filling her with emotion that translated well into notes and chords. Inspiring her. He'd always inspired her.

God had brought them together under the guise of a wild edibles class. Little had Bree known that she was in for the experience of a lifetime. Life with Darren promised love and acceptance and her innermost dreams come true.

Epilogue

The last Saturday of the summer and it was a hot one. Standing along the shoreline of Lake Michigan's Maple Bay, Darren waited for Bree, his bride.

It was a small wedding ceremony with only their closest friends and family. Neil stood next to him, cane in hand, as Darren's best man. Bree's sister had accepted the role of matron of honor and she stood on the other side of him. Waiting, too.

Despite the stifling temperatures, a cool breeze blew in from the lake. He felt his phone vibrate with an incoming text from the depths of his pocket. He'd turned the volume off for the ceremony. Who texted him at this moment, of all moments?

It dawned on him who it might be and he grabbed the phone for a quick peek.

"What are you doing?" Neil hissed.

"It'll only take a second to check." Yup, the text came from Bree, making him smile.

For a split second, Darren's stomach flipped. What if— No. Not a chance. He read her message.

Are you ready?

Her question was followed by several hearts.

Darren chuckled. No worries about his bride showing up today. He texted her back.

Hurry up.

The music started. A gentle sound of a string quartet played something soft and sweet. He'd get to know this kind of music pretty well in the coming years. He looked forward to attending the concerts Bree would take part in and help plan.

Bree loved her new job. Loved the process of interviewing musicians for the following year when the school officially opened for their first sessions. Already they had a good roster of college and post-college students registered to attend. Darren had no doubt that this was where she was meant to be. Here in Northern Michigan, impacting the lives of others. Making a difference in his.

Finally he spotted her walking toward him on the arm of her father, and his breath caught.

She was beautiful in a simple white gown with a top of delicate lace. Pretty, like her. She didn't wear a veil. Her hair had been swirled up into a loose knot. Within the mink-colored mass, she'd tucked tiny white baby's breath that grew wild around here. She carried a bouquet of sunflowers bundled with more of the airy white wildflower.

He cleared his throat, trying to loosen the emotion that tightened it. He felt Neil's hand grip his shoulder. Darren needed to get it together. He'd have to talk if they were to exchange their vows.

But right now, all he could do was watch Bree walk toward him, her golden eyes shiny and wet. If she starting crying, he'd be hard-pressed not to join her.

So Darren scanned the guests present to get a handle on his composure. Stella dabbed at her eyes with a tissue, as did his mom and even Bree's mom. This joy was certainly contagious.

He'd waited a long time for this moment. God had given him the right woman not only to share his life but also to open his eyes. None of them were good enough but for the grace of God. They were all God's people, whether they knew it or not.

Darren needed to serve with that in mind. Always. *To everything there is a season, and a time to every purpose under heaven.*

* * * * *

Dear Reader,

Thank you for picking up a copy of my latest book in the Maple Springs series and the continuing tale of loss and love within the Zelinsky family. I hope you've enjoyed Darren and Bree's journey to real love.

This might have been the most difficult book I've ever written. I had quite the time getting a handle on what these two people not only wanted but also needed. In the end, it all boiled down to how they viewed themselves—incorrectly and certainly not as God saw them.

None of us are good enough outside God's grace. Only through Him and His gift of salvation are we perfected and made whole. No matter what comes our way, what hurts we've experienced in or out of our control, God can heal them if we keep our hearts tuned toward Him.

May your innermost dreams come true, and happy reading.

God bless,
Jenna Mindel